MUSIC:

Adventures in Listening

MUSIC:

Adventures in Listening

JOSEPH MACHLIS

*Professor of Music,
Queens College of the City University of New York*

W · W · NORTON & COMPANY · INC · New York

For Marsha, Jeanne, and Joseph

Contents

Final Scene • Anton Webern • Pieces for Orchestra, Opus 6, Nos. 1, 2 • Piece for Orchestra, Opus 10, No. 3

UNIT VIII · MUSIC IN AMERICA

UNIT I

WHAT MUSIC
IS MADE OF

1

Music in the Life
of Man

Music is one of the great arts of our civilization. How shall we define art? The great Russian writer Tolstoi said that art "is a human activity whose purpose is to transmit to us the highest and best feelings to which man has risen." Art expresses certain thoughts and emotions of the artist—his vision of beauty, his feeling about life, his hopes and dreams. All this he puts into his work. Each work of art, whether it is a poem, a painting, a piece of sculpture, or a piece of music, has a secret at the heart of it, a personal message from the artist to you. When you understand this secret you receive the artist's message: you feel some of the emotions he felt when he created the work of art.

Art brings us its message in various ways: through the words of the poet, the colors of the painter, the marble of the sculptor, the movements of the dance. Music speaks to us through sound. By means of the sounds that travel so lightly through the air, music arouses our emotions and sends forth patterns of beauty that bring joy to millions of people all over the world.

What Is Art?

Music is not an art that is separate from life. On the contrary, it reflects every side of man's existence.

Among savage tribes, music has a part in all important events. Love, courtship, marriage, sowing and reaping, hunting and war, religious ceremonies, mourning for the dead—each of these has its own songs or dances.

So too the folk music of Europe and America has produced songs that re-

*Music Springs
Out of Human
Experience*

3

flect all phases of life—work songs, love songs, play songs, cradle songs, drinking songs, patriotic songs, marching songs, children's songs, dance songs, songs of sorrow and joy. Thus music springs out of life itself and expresses the deepest feelings of man. Because of this it has been called "the language of the emotions." For music speaks directly to the heart. It says things that could never be said in words. It is a universal language that is understood by men in all lands.

How to Listen to Music

A generation ago it was not easy to hear a symphony. You had to go to the concert hall and buy a ticket. When you finally got to the concert, you were likely to *listen* when the orchestra began to play. Today all you have to do is to flick a knob, and music comes pouring into the room. On Sunday morning millions of people flick that knob, and for the next ten hours they are surrounded by music. They talk to each other, they eat, they read the funnies and do crossword puzzles, and all the time the sounds are flowing past their ears.

But the great composers did not write their music to serve as a background

A NEW YORK PHILHARMONIC CONCERT IN CENTRAL PARK.
Music is one of the great arts of our civilization.

THE UNIVERSITY OF WASHINGTON ROTC BAND.
Music arouses our emotions.

for other activities. There is only one way to listen to their works, and that is—to listen! When you listen to an important musical work, make sure that you are not doing anything else, such as talking or reading. The sounds are forming patterns, and you cannot understand them unless you hear how the patterns are related. This you will do only if you give your full attention to what is going on.

In addition, try to hear a piece of music again and again. Hearing a musical work for the first time is like traveling on a train through unknown territory. Although you get a general impression, you are barely able to notice the details. The best way to become a music lover is to own a record player and buy the recordings of the works you like, or to listen to those works again and again in your school library. You will be surprised at how much more the music will mean to you once you become familiar with it.

For our first listening experience we turn to six selections that show how composers, in their music, reflect various emotions of man's everyday life. We will hear a dance, a march, a love song, a wedding march, a lullaby, and a piece inspired by religious feeling.

Music that Expresses Emotion

1. Polka from *The Bartered Bride* by Bedřich Smetana. A *polka* is a lively dance of Bohemia (now Czechoslovakia) that became popular all over Europe. In his opera *The Bartered Bride,* the Czech composer Bedřich Smetana captured the spirit of the folk songs and dances of his homeland. The music of this polka suggests activity—bodies leaping about, twisting and turning—while the melody moves about gaily.

5

2.   Triumphal March from *Aïda* (ah-eé-da), by the Italian composer Giuseppe Verdi (ju-séh-peh véhr-dee). The conquering hero Radamès (rad-dah-méss) is welcomed at the gates of Thebes by the King of Egypt, his court, and the people. The full orchestral sound creates a mood of victory. The main melody of the march is carried by the trumpet, an instrument associated with the outdoors and with military events. This music brings us all the pomp of a triumphal march.

3.   *Serenade* by Franz Schubert is one of the world's favorite love songs. A *serenade* is an evening song, such as a lover would sing beneath the balcony of his beloved. Schubert has suggested this in the piano part that is the background for the melody. The chords are played *staccato* (stah-káh-toh)—that is, short and detached—as if they were being plucked on a guitar. The melody is sung in a mood of tenderness. The poem consists of three stanzas.

Let my songs implore you gently through the silent night;
In the stillness, oh my darling, bring me love's delight.
Hear the willows murmur softly in the silv'ry light, in the silv'ry light;
Safe at last where none may harm you, have no fear, my love . . .
  Have no fear, my love.

Hear the birds who call you gently. Ah, they plead for me!
Sweet their song, so full of sorrow; now they speak for me.
They must know a lover's longing, know the pain of love—
  Know the pain of love . . .

Let their tender voices reach you, let them touch your heart.
Oh my darling, I await you! We will never part!

4.   Wedding March from *A Midsummer Night's Dream* by the German composer Felix Mendelssohn. In his music for Shakespeare's immortal comedy, Mendelssohn caught the spirit of wonder that surrounds the play. The famous Wedding March suggests the happy ending when the Duke of Athens marries Hippolyta. It is longer than most people think, because only the first part is now played at weddings. A trumpet call introduces the main melody in a holiday mood. After a quiet section we hear the main melody again. Then comes another quiet section, after which the main melody returns. A flourish of trumpets brings the piece to a brilliant end.

5.   Berceuse (behr-súz) from the ballet *The Firebird* by the Russian composer Igor Stravinsky. (The French word *berceuse* means a lullaby or cradle song. By a *ballet* we mean a dance piece or the music that accompanies it.) *The Firebird* is based on a Russian fairy tale concerning a magic creature, half woman, half bird, who is captured by Prince Ivan. In return for her freedom she gives him one of her golden feathers. When Ivan enters the ogre's castle he waves the magic feather, whereupon the Firebird appears. She drives the monster and his courtiers into a frenzy; then she lulls them to sleep with a lullaby. At this point is heard the lovely Berceuse. The melody is *legato* (le-gáh-toh, smooth and connected, the opposite of staccato). The music flows quietly, as a lullaby should.

6. The Hallelujah Chorus from *Messiah*, by the German composer George Frideric Handel, is a wonderful example of music inspired by religious feeling. After Handel completed it, his servant found the composer with tears streaming from his eyes. "I did think," Handel exclaimed, "that I did see all Heaven before me, and the great God Himself!" The music moves forward with a steady beat as the key word, "Hallelujah," is sung over and over. The first line of the text—"For the Lord God omnipotent reigneth!"—takes on great majesty. Notice the exciting effect when sopranos and altos sing the words "King of Kings and Lord of Lords" while the tenors and basses repeat "Hallelujah!" The drums beat, trumpets resound; this is music of grandeur and power.

2

Melody and Harmony

Everybody loves a good tune. For melody is that element of music which is most appealing. It is what we remember and whistle and hum. Melody has been called "the soul of music." We know a good melody the instant we hear one; it moves us even if we may not be able to explain why. Because of this mysterious power, the world has always loved those composers who had the gift of creating beautiful melodies.

A *melody* is a series of tones that we hear as a single musical thought. When we hear a melody we feel that the tones were not thrown together in any old way. On the contrary, we realize that they have been arranged in a definite order, with a beginning, a middle, and an end.

Just as every face we see is different from all other faces, so every melody we hear has its own personality. This depends on the way it moves:

1. The melody may move up or down (since we think of one tone as being higher or lower than another).
2. It may move forward in longer or shorter notes.
3. The distance from the lowest to the highest tone of the melody—that is, its *range*—may be narrow or wide.
4. The melody may move by step or by skip.
5. The skips may be narrow or wide.
6. The melody may move slowly, or moderately, or at a lively speed.

7. The melody tones may be smooth and flowing (legato) or short and detached (staccato).
8. They may be loud or soft.

A melody like *America* moves within a narrow range, either by step or with narrow skips, at a fairly slow pace. *The Star-Spangled Banner,* on the other hand, is marked by bold leaps and a wide range, and moves more quickly. It is quite clear which of the two is the more active tune. So, too, if we compare two melodies such as *Silent Night* and *Columbia the Gem of the Ocean,* we would not find it hard to decide which is the patriotic song and which is the hymn.

Melodies create moods and express feelings. We hear them as being sad or gay, gentle or vigorous. They speak directly to our hearts. In this lies their magic and their power.

How a Melody Is Built

When we write or speak, we think not in complete sentences but in shorter groups of words such as phrases and clauses. So too, a melody—that is, a musical thought—unfolds in units known as phrases. By a *phrase* we mean a small unit of meaning within a larger structure. If we had to hear the whole melody at one stretch we might lose our bearings. Instead we absorb one phrase at a time.

The phrase is rounded off by a *cadence,* by which we mean a kind of resting place in music. The cadence serves to mark off one phrase from the next. It is the point where we have a chance to draw our breath and to prepare for the next phrase. In the middle of the melody we will hear an *incomplete cadence,* which is like a comma in punctuation, showing that more is to come. At the end we hear a *complete cadence,* which is like the period at the end of a sentence.

You can see for yourself how phrase and cadence work if you sing the simplest kind of tune, such as a nursery rhyme. The melody of *London Bridge,* for example, divides into two equal phrases: *London Bridge is falling down, falling down, falling down . . . London Bridge is falling down, my fair lady.* The cadence at the end of the first phrase is incomplete: the melody moves upward, like a question. The second phrase ends in a complete cadence on the word "lady." We find here a question and answer; the second phrase grows out of the first and completes its meaning.

The same thing can be observed in another famous tune: *The farmer in the dell, the farmer in the dell . . . Heigh-ho, the merry-o, the farmer in the dell.* The first phrase moves in an upward direction, like a question, ending in an incomplete cadence. The second phrase—the answer—moves downward and ends in a vigorous full cadence.

An important feature of the melody is the climax, where the emotion reaches its highest point. Our national anthem reaches a fine climax in the last phrase, on the words, "O'er the land of the free . . ." There can be no doubt in anybody's mind that this song is about freedom. It is clear, too, that freedom is not won easily, to judge from the effort we have to make to get up to the highest tone.

We usually hear melody against a background of harmony. We have *har-mony* when two or more tones sound at the same time: harmony re-lates to chords and their movements. A *chord* consists of several tones that are played at the same time and form a unit.

Harmony is to melody what perspective is to painting: it lends depth to the melody, supplies background and support. This is apparent when we lis-ten to a singer accompany his melody with chords on the guitar. Melody and harmony are closely connected. If a wrong chord is struck, our ears tell us at once that there has been a mistake.

In Schubert's *Serenade,* which we discussed in Chapter 1, the melody was presented by the singer, while the accompanist supplied the harmony—that is, the chords—on the piano.

How Harmony Supports Melody

Consonance and Dissonance

When we combine certain colors, the effect is soft and restful. Other colors clash and make an exciting effect. So too, certain combinations of tones give us a feeling of rest, while others strike us as being restless and incomplete. *Dissonant* chords create tension; *consonant* chords relax the tension. The dis-sonant chord needs a consonant chord to complete it. The dissonant chord therefore moves to a consonant chord.

Just as a drama has to have suspense, so music has to have dissonance. Without it, a piece would be unbearably dull. Dissonance is the spice of mu-sic. It creates the tension we need, just as consonance brings us the relaxation

MEINDERT HOBBEMA, *THE AVENUE, MIDDELHARNIS.*
Harmony is to melody what perspective is to painting.

we need. Like light and shade in a painting, both are necessary in a musical work.

Chords that sound very dissonant to us the first time we hear them seem less so after we grow used to them. This has been true all through history. Composers have always created new harmonies that shocked their listeners; yet a generation later, those harmonies were accepted by all. In this way composers led their fellow men to accept new combinations of sounds. It stands to reason that the music of the nineteenth century is more dissonant than that of the eighteenth, and the music of the twentieth century is more dissonant than that of the nineteenth.

REMBRANDT VAN RIJN,
A GIRL WITH A BROOM.
Like light and shade in a painting,
both consonance and dissonance
are necessary in a musical work.

*Six Great
Melodies*

1. *Turkish March* from *The Ruins of Athens* by Ludwig van Beethoven (báy-toh-ven). This catchy march is one of a series of pieces that the great German composer wrote for a play describing how Athens was almost destroyed by the Turks. For his *Turkish March* Beethoven created a gay staccato melody in high register. (By *register* we mean the general area where the music lies, whether low, middle, or high. The upper register is brighter, the lower register is darker. Going from low to high register increases tension, just as going from high to low decreases it.)

The melody of the *Turkish March* has phrases of equal length, each rounded off with a cadence. It moves mostly by step or with narrow skips. The March begins softly, grows louder, and in the end dies away. It is as if a far-off procession came closer, passed us by, then moved off in the distance.

2. *I Love You* by Edvard Grieg. This famous song is a musical love-letter written by the Norwegian composer when he was twenty-one, the year he be-

came engaged to his cousin Nina Hagerup. Theirs was a happy marriage. In later years Grieg declared, "My best songs were composed for her." The poem is by Hans Christian Andersen, the Danish writer who won international fame with his fairy tales.

You are my life, my soul, my very being;
You bring my heart its hope of blessedness.
I love you more than all things under heaven;
I love you, dear—I love you, dear,
I love you, dear, now and forevermore—
I love you, dear, now and forevermore!

I think of you with all my heart's devotion;
To you alone I turn for happiness.
In time to come, wherever fate may lead me,
I love you, dear—I love you, dear,
I love you, dear, now and forevermore—
I love you, dear, now and forevermore!

A short introduction on the piano sets the mood. Each line of the poem is set to a phrase, with a cadence at the end of the line (except lines 4—5, which make up one phrase). The piano supplies the harmony. Notice how the song grows louder and moves higher up to the climax on the last line —"I love you, dear, now and forevermore!" The high point of the melody comes, of course, on the word "love."

3. Galop from *The Comedians*, by the modern Russian composer Dmitri Kabalevsky. A *galop* is a lively dance performed with light hopping movements. The melody of this piece is gay and vigorous. After a brief introduction we hear a hopping tune in high register, very fast and loud, that moves downward over a wide range. The piece is spiced with dissonant harmonies of the twentieth century. The middle part is introduced by the bright sound of the xylophone. (For a description of this instruument, see p. 35.) Then the opening melody returns.

4. *E lucevan le stelle* (And the stars shone brightly) from *Tosca*, by the Italian composer Giacomo Puccini (jáh-co-mo poo-chée-nee). For an example of melody in a sad mood we turn to the lament from the last act of Puccini's opera *Tosca*. The action takes place in Rome in the year 1800, while the Italians are plotting a revolution against their Austrian masters. The painter Mario Cavaradossi has been sentenced to death. He bribes the jailer to allow him to write a last letter to his beloved Tosca. Remembering their happiness together, he bids farewell to love and life in a moving aria. (An *aria* is a solo song in a larger work such as an opera.)

E lucevan le stelle
e olezzava la terra—
stridea l'uscio dell' orto—
e un passo sfiorava la rena.
Entrava ella, fragrante,
mi cadea fra le braccia . . .

And the stars shone brightly,
And the air was mild and fragrant—
The garden gate was opened
And footsteps approached so lightly.
She stood before me, radiant;
In my arms I held her . . .

11

Oh! dolci baci, o languide carezze,
mentr'io fremente
le belle forme disciogliea dai veli!

Svanì per sempre il sogno mio
d'amore . . .

L'ora è fuggita
e muoio disperato!
e muoio disperato!

E non ho amato
mai tanto la vita,
tanto la vita!

O fond embrace, o languorous caresses.
My heart was trembling,
Enraptured by the wonder of her glorious
beauty!

My dream of love is now destroyed forever . . .

My hour is fleeting,
And I must die, despairing!
And I must die, despairing!

How cruel is Death!
Ah, life was never sweeter—
Never sweeter!

The melody is introduced in the orchestra, while Mario interrupts with short phrases on a single note, as if he were thinking aloud. Then he takes over the melody, a slow gentle song that works up to a passionate cry as he realizes the cruelty of his fate. The music grows louder and higher in register until the climax, when the melody rises to its highest note. This beautiful aria is in the great tradition of Italian opera.

5. Polka from *Schwanda the Bagpiper* by the modern Czech composer Jaromir Weinberger. Like Smetana before him, Weinberger found inspiration in the songs and legends of his native land. His opera *Schwanda the Bagpiper* is based on the adventures of a jolly peasant who tries to cure the sad Queen Iceheart by playing his bagpipes. He succeeds so well that the Queen joins him in a rollicking polka. (The only one who is unhappy about this is Schwanda's wife.) The opening measures suggest the sound of Schwanda's bagpipes. Then is heard the lively melody of the Polka. It is a sturdy tune that moves forward briskly, with much staccato. The melody of the middle section is quieter, more legato. Then the first tune is heard again, growing louder and jollier as it brings the piece to a happy ending.

6. *Johnny Comes Marching Home* from *Folksong Symphony* by the American composer Roy Harris. "This," wrote Harris, "is the famous song that came out of the Civil War. In it I hoped to capture the spirit of joy which our people would feel when the men came home from war." Trumpets and drums remind us of men marching, flags flying, crowds cheering. The melody consists of four phrases, one for each line of the poem. The first two phrases push upward; this is balanced by the downward curve of the last two.

When Johnny comes marching home again, Hurrah! Hurrah!
We'll give him a hearty welcome then, Hurrah! Hurrah!
The men will cheer, the boys will shout, the ladies they will all turn out
And we'll all feel gay when Johnny comes marching home!

Harris has added dissonant harmonies that give the Civil War melody a twentieth-century ring. The mood changes for the second stanza; the marching song is changed into a quiet legato melody.

The old church bell will peal with joy, Hurrah! Hurrah!
To welcome home our darling boy, Hurrah! Hurrah!
The village lads and lassies gay with roses strew the way.
We'll all feel gay when Johnny comes marching home!

The mood of the opening section returns with the final stanza:

Get ready for the jubilee, Hurrah! Hurrah!
We'll give the hero three times three, Hurrah! Hurrah!
The laurel wreath is ready now to place upon his loyal brow,
And we'll all feel gay when Johnny comes marching home!

LEONTYNE PRICE AND
WILLIAM WARFIELD
AS PORGY AND BESS.

7.   Love Duet from *Porgy and Bess*. George Gershwin's "folk opera" has
become a classic. The action revolves around the Negro inhabitants of Cat-
fish Row in Charleston, South Carolina. In this work Gershwin went far beyond the limits of the ordinary Broadway musical. As a result, New York
was not ready to receive *Porgy and Bess;* it ran for only four months. *Porgy
and Bess* came into its own only after Gershwin's death. It was revived
throughout the 1940s with growing success. In 1952 our State Department
sent the opera, with an all-Negro cast, on a tour of Europe and the
Soviet Union. It played everywhere to enthusiastic audiences. Since then
the work has been acclaimed all over the world as *the* American opera.

The duet between Porgy and Bess is one of the highlights of the opera.
We know that, despite Porgy's nobility of character, his love is doomed to
fail, since Bess cannot resist the temptations that surround her. Which
only makes more moving the one moment when she is able to respond to
Porgy's love. The melody, with its dramatic wide leaps, is typical of Gershwin.
Notice how naturally he molds this melody to the sound of everyday American speech.

$$\text{❧}\ |\ 3\ |\ \text{❧}$$

Rhythm and Meter

The Nature of Rhythm

Melody and harmony, we saw, unfold together. They have to move forward together, in rhythm. By *rhythm* we mean the orderly movement of music in time.

Rhythm is closely related to body movement, to physical action, and to the dance. When rhythmic patterns are repeated over and over they have a strong hypnotic effect upon us. For this reason rhythm has been called "the heartbeat of music." When we say of a dance-band musician that "he's got rhythm," we mean not only that he plays in time so that we are able to dance, but that he has a certain something that makes us want to dance.

Rhythm springs from the need for order that is in every one of us. When

LINCOLN MEMORIAL, WASHINGTON, D.C.
Rhythm springs from the need for order that is in every one of us.

certain patterns are repeated over and over again, we come to expect them. There is rhythm in nature—the regular succession of night and day, high and low tide, summer and winter, sleep and waking. There is rhythm in the repeated patterns of painting, sculpture, and architecture. Rhythm plays an important part in poetry, where the syllables are arranged in such a way that the pattern of accented and unaccented syllables is repeated again and again:

> Oh líft me ás a wáve, a léaf, a clóud!
> I fáll upón the thórns of lífe—I bléed!
> —Shelley, *Ode to the West Wind*

But in music, which keeps rushing past our ears, rhythm is of the utmost importance. Indeed, the American composer Roger Sessions has stated that "an adequate definition of rhythm comes close to defining music itself."

*Metrical
Patterns*

For music to be able to flow through time, time must be organized. The organization of musical time is known as *meter*. Time in music is organized in units known as *measures*; each measure contains a fixed number of beats. The *accent* falls on the first or strong beat. Since the accent returns at regular intervals, we become aware of a metrical pattern.

The simplest pattern consists of two beats to the measure, a strong beat alternating with a weak one: ONE two ONE two . . .; or in marching, LEFT right LEFT right. This is known as *duple meter* (such as we find in *two-four time*). Examples of duple meter are simple nursery rhythms like *London Bridge* and *Twinkle Twinkle, Little Star;* quick march tunes such as *Yankee Doodle* and *The Stars and Stripes Forever;* songs like *Dixie* and *Oh Susannah.*

Another basic pattern is that of three beats to the measure, or *triple meter*, which is counted ONE two three ONE two three. This is the pattern of *three-four time* that has always been associated with the waltz and minuet. (A *waltz* is a popular dance in triple meter. A *minuet* is a stately dance that originated in the court of Louis XIV of France in the middle of the seventeenth century.) Two celebrated examples of triple meter are *America* and *The Star-Spangled Banner.*

The pattern of four beats to the measure is known as *quadruple meter.* This is the pattern of *four-four time,* which is counted ONE two three four ONE two three four. It is found in some of our most popular melodies: *Columbia the Gem of the Ocean, Battle Hymn of the Republic, Old Man River, Auld Lang Syne.*

The pattern of six beats to a measure, such as we find in *six-eight time,* is broader and more flowing than the ones just mentioned. It gives a kind of rocking effect, and is often used for boat songs and cradle songs. The main accent falls on the first beat, with a lighter accent on the fourth: ONE two three, Four five six. Well-known examples are *Sweet and Low, Silent Night, Believe Me if All Those Endearing Young Charms,* and *Drink to Me Only with Thine Eyes.* This pattern is known as *sextuple meter.*

There are also patterns of five, seven, eight, nine, or more beats to a measure. But the four meters just mentioned are the ones we hear most frequently.

1. *Marche militaire* by Franz Schubert is one of the most beautiful of all marches. It is bright and gay, and suggests a military procession. The piece is in two-four time: two beats to a measure, with the accent on the first. We hear an appealing tune by one of the greatest masters of melody that ever lived. The melody extends over a wide range, is active and full of movement. The middle part is quieter and is marked by a graceful lyricism. Then the opening section is repeated.

2. *Waltz of the Flowers* from *Nutcracker Suite* by the most popular Russian composer, Peter Ilyich Tchaikovsky (chy-kúv-skee). The word *suite*, as used by nineteenth-century composers, indicates an instrumental work consisting of a number of short movements united by a central idea. A suite may be either an independent work or a set of numbers drawn from a longer work such as an opera, a ballet, or music for a play. The *Nutcracker Suite* was drawn from a Christmas Eve ballet about a little girl who dreams that the homely nutcracker she received as a gift has turned into a handsome prince. (Russian nutcrackers often have the shape of a human head.) The fairy-tale atmosphere of the ballet inspired Tchaikovsky to write some enchanting music.

The *Waltz of the Flowers* is the finale of the ballet. (A *finale*—pronounced fee-náh-lee—is the final number or section of a musical work.) This piece is in three-four time. The introduction presents a series of broken chords on the harp. When the tones of a chord are played in succession instead of together the chord is said to be "broken." This is the natural way of

WALTZ OF THE FLOWERS FROM *THE NUTCRACKER.*

playing chords on the harp. The Italian word for harp being *arpa,* a broken chord is called an *arpeggio* (ahr-péh-jo).

The waltz itself Tchaikovsky marked "sweetly, in a most singing manner." It opens with an upward-leaping melody that is most attractive. A contrasting melody consists of a series of downward leaps. Both melodies are repeated. Together they make up the opening section of the waltz.

The middle section, too, consists of two melodies. The first is bright, in high register, and moves by skips. The second, by contrast, is in low register, and moves mostly by step. After the second melody has been played, the first is repeated.

Now the opening section is heard again. The music works up to a climax by growing louder, faster, and higher in register. The ending is most brilliant. With its suggestion of ballerinas in white, this graceful waltz has all the charm of nineteenth-century ballet.

3. March from *The Love for Three Oranges,* by the modern Russian composer Serge Prokofiev (sayrj pro-kúf-yev). Here is an exciting example of four-four time. It comes from a fairy-tale opera about a melancholy prince who suffers from an imaginary sickness from which he can be cured only if he is made to laugh. There is an amusing contrast between his timid personality and this bold march.

The piece opens with a call by trumpets and drums. Then we hear a staccato melody with heavy accents. The dissonant harmony has a twentieth-century sound. The melody is heard three times, the first time soft, the second loud, the third very loud. In between these we hear new material, for contrast. Notice the steady beat that never wavers, and the dissonant chords at the end.

4. Barcarolle from *The Tales of Hoffmann,* by Jacques Offenbach (zhak óff-en-bakh), who was born in Germany but won great success in Paris. The third act of the opera is set in Venice. It is night; the sky is studded with stars. In this lovely setting is heard the Barcarolle. This word comes from the Italian *barca,* a boat. A *barcarolle,* therefore, is a boat song, generally in six-eight time. The pattern of six beats to a measure suggests a gentle gliding over the water.

The legato melody flows gently, accompanied by rippling arpeggios on the harp. As is to be expected, this is not an active tune; it moves by step, with an occasional narrow skip, within a narrow range. The melody pauses for a cadence after each phrase. Toward the end of the piece it rises to its highest point—the climax of the Barcarolle. Then it subsides to a quiet ending.

5. *Saber Dance* from the ballet *Gayane* (Happiness) by the modern Russian composer Aram Khatchaturian (kah-cha-tóo-ryan). This popular music, in four-four time, shows the power of rhythm; it has a rapid beat that never changes. The melody is heard in high register, with quick repeated notes that create a mood of excitement. The music suggests tribesmen leaping through the air, brandishing their sabers. Dissonant harmonies tell us that

this piece belongs to the twentieth century. Through syncopation, the composer achieves an effect of energy and power. (*Syncopation* involves a shifting of the accent from the strong beat of the measure—the first beat—to a weak beat or off-beat. It is the basis of American jazz, and has been widely used by European composers as well.)

The middle section of the piece presents a legato melody based on an oriental tune. Then the first melody returns, in high register as before. The persistent rhythm builds up tension. At the very end, the music quiets down.

HOE-DOWN FROM THE BALLET *RODEO.*

6. *Hoe-Down* from *Rodeo* is by the modern American composer Aaron Copland, who has been remarkably successful with ballets based on American themes. The heroine of *Rodeo* is an awkward cowgirl. When she transforms herself into a charming young lady, she finally gets her man. *Hoe-Down* is a vigorous piece in two-four time that makes us think of a Saturday night far from the big city—the world of the village fiddler and the square dance. The melody is lively; the rhythm rushes along, carrying the listener with it. The dissonant harmony is of the twentieth century. The middle section is quieter and introduces some syncopated rhythms. Then the square-dance tune returns and brings the piece to a boisterous end.

꧁ 4 ꧂

Tempo and Dynamics

The meter tells us how m[...] not
tell us whether these beat[...] by the
tempo, which is the rate o[...]

The rate at which we m[...] our emotions. We walk briskly when
we are light-hearted; we drag our feet when we are weighed down by grief.
The same is true of musical tempo. Vigor and gaiety go with a brisk tempo,
sorrow and despair demand a slow one. A funeral march moves at a slow
pace, a love song or lullaby at a moderate pace, a drinking song at a vigorous
tempo, a peasant dance at a lively one.

The tempo terms are usually given in Italian. This custom stems from the
seventeenth and eighteenth centuries, when Italian opera and Italian musicians were popular throughout Europe. The most important terms are:

largo—very slow and broad
adagio (ah-dáh-jo)—slow, leisurely
andante (ahn-dáhn-teh) —fairly slow, at a walking pace
andantino (ahn-dahn-tée-no)—a little andante, somewhat faster than andante
moderato—moderate
allegretto—fairly fast, not as lively as allegro
allegro—fast, cheerful, happy
vivace (vee-váh-cheh)—vivacious, lively
allegro molto—very fast
presto—very very fast

Of great importance are the terms that indicate a change in tempo. The
main ones are *accelerando* (ah-cheh-leh-ráhn-do)—getting faster; and *ritardando*—holding back, getting slower.

Dynamics means the degree of loudness or softness at which the music is
played. This too, like the tempo, is related to our emotions. Mystery and fear
call for a whisper, even as joy or excitement goes with a loud cry. A lullaby
or love song will be soft and tender. A war dance or triumphal march is
loud and vigorous. The principal dynamic indications are:

pianissimo (abbreviated *pp*)—very soft
piano (*p*)—soft
mezzo piano (méh-tso pyáh-no, *mp*)—moderately soft
mezzo forte (méh-tso fór-teh, *mf*)—moderately loud
forte (*f*)—loud
fortissimo (*ff*)—very loud

Among the directions for changing the dynamics, the most important are:

crescendo (kreh-shén-do)—growing louder
decrescendo (dáy-kreh-shen-do)—growing softer
diminuendo (dee-min-yoo-én-do)—growing softer

Crescendo and decrescendo are among the most important effects available to composers. By increasing the volume of tone or decreasing it, the composer may increase or decrease the tension. He may also make it seem as if the music is drawing closer to us and then moving away. We heard a fine example of this crescendo-decrescendo pattern in the *Turkish March* of Beethoven.

The Expressive Power of Tempo and Dynamics

1. *In the Hall of the Mountain King* from *Peer Gynt Suite No. 1,* by Edvard Grieg. The widely loved Norwegian composer wrote his *Peer Gynt* music as a set of short pieces for a play by his countryman, the dramatist Henrik Ibsen. He afterward selected the most popular numbers and combined them into two concert suites.

Ibsen's play centers around a peasant lad called Peer Gynt, whose restless spirit is forever getting him into trouble. At one point he wanders into the dark realm of the Mountain King. Elves and gnomes surround him, and lead him about in a dance that grows faster and wilder. Peer feels he will never escape alive. Fortunately the Mountain King's daughter has taken a liking to him, and saves him.

The melody starts out in the dark lower register, pianissimo, in four-four time. It is a staccato tune that is repeated over and over again, growing faster and louder as it gradually rises to the upper register. Excitement is increased, in the second half of the piece, through syncopated rhythm; we hear heavy chords in the orchestra on the off-beat. Through a steady crescendo, accelerando, and rise in pitch, Grieg increases the tension until the shattering fortissimo at the end, marked *fff* (very very loud).

2. *The Pines of the Appian Way* from *The Pines of Rome,* by Ottorino Respighi (res-pée-gee). In four-four time. In this piece the Italian composer looks back to the ancient days of glory when the Roman Empire ruled the world. The tempo is that of a march. The opening measures evoke a misty dawn on the Appian Way, where Caesar's legions once advanced. A steady drumbeat, very soft, suggests soldiers in the distance. We hear a gradual crescendo; nearer and nearer comes the tread of marching feet. The music builds to a powerful fortissimo; the trumpets blare. As Respighi described his vision: "The army of the Consul advances in the brilliance of the newly-risen sun towards the Sacred Way, mounting in triumph to the Capitol."

3. Slavonic Dance No. 10 by Antonín Dvořák (dvór-zhok). Like his countryman Smetana, Dvořák captured in his music the spirit of the folk songs of
his native Bohemia. His Slavonic Dance shows the simple beauty of Czech
national melodies. It is an Allegretto in triple meter. In this piece tempo and
dynamics change much less than in the two pieces we just heard. The opening section presents a legato melody, very expressive, that moves by step
within a narrow range. It contrasts with a second melody that is staccato and
moves by skip; this tune goes at a livelier pace. The middle section presents
a new melody in which an ascending phrase is answered by one that descends.
The composer contrasts soft and loud passages. Then the opening part is
repeated.

4. *Russian Sailors' Dance* from the ballet *The Red Poppy,* by the modern
Russian composer Reinhold Glière (glee-áir). In two-four time. This piece
consists of a melody that is played twelve times; each time something is
changed: the melody itself, the harmony, rhythm, tempo, dynamics, instruments, register. It is as if a character in a play appeared in each scene in a
different costume. He remains the same, but his appearance changes again
and again.

After a brief introduction marked Allegro, we hear the tune in low register, forte. It is an active melody with syncopated accents, suitable for a
sailors' dance. Now it is played Moderato, in the upper register, with a few
notes added to the tune; then in a still higher register. We next hear it loud
and lively; after that at a slower pace in a more lyrical mood; then very
quietly, with new harmonies. From here on the music grows steadily faster
and louder, higher in register and brighter in color, until the dazzling
climax at the end.

5. *Infernal Dance of King Kastchei* from *The Firebird,* by Igor Stravinsky.
In Chapter 1 we studied the Berceuse from Stravinsky's famous ballet. The
action, you will recall, centers about the magic bird who helps Prince Ivan
overcome the evil King Kastchei. The ogre has cast a spell over thirteen
young princesses, whom he keeps captive in his castle. Prince Ivan succeeds
in freeing them, and marries the most beautiful among them.

Kastchei's *Infernal Dance* suggests the evil atmosphere that surrounds the
monster and his court. It is performed when the Firebird, having come to
Prince Ivan's help, puts Kastchei and his courtiers into a frenzy; they dance
until they are exhausted. This is a feverish dance in syncopated rhythm,
with sudden accents. Dissonant harmonies heighten the tension. Fragments
of melody emerge now and again, only to be swallowed up in the seething
sounds. A steady crescendo and accelerando (louder and faster) builds to
the frenzied climax. At the end the music is *fff.*

6. The Final Scene of *The Firebird* accompanies the betrothal of Prince
Ivan and his princess. The music opens at a majestic pace, in triple meter.
A tender melody is repeated over and over, first softly but gradually growing
louder. The orchestra builds up to a climax, whereupon the opening melody

FINAL SCENE OF *THE FIREBIRD*.

is repeated at a faster tempo. The meter changes to an unusual pattern—seven beats to a measure. In the final measures the music returns to the original tempo. The full orchestra sings the melody in a triumphal mood as the prince leads his bride before the assembled guests. At this point both the stage and the music are bathed in a golden light.

 5

How Music Is Put Together

The artist shapes his material in such a way that we will be able to grasp its outlines easily and clearly. He tries to create a beautiful design that will give us pleasure. By *form* in a work of art we mean the arrangement of the material so as to achieve the best effect.

THE CAPITOL AT WASHINGTON.
By form in a work of art we mean the arrangement of the material so as to achieve the best effect.

Form is important in painting, sculpture, architecture, poetry, drama, and the novel. In all of these, the work of art is clearly before us. We can look again and again at a painting, a piece of sculpture, or a building. If we have missed a detail of a poem or novel, we can turn back a page and re-read the passage. But music, like a film, is always in motion. A piece is never before us as a whole. Its sounds die away as soon as they reach our ears, giving way to other sounds. For this reason form is doubly important in music. It helps to make clear the design of a composition, so that we may relate the beginning to the middle and the middle to the end.

The composer repeats his material in order to help us grasp his meaning. But if he only repeated, he would soon grow boring. He introduces new material for the sake of contrast; but if he kept introducing new material all the time, he would bewilder us. He strikes a balance between the two. He repeats enough to achieve a feeling of unity, but brings in enough new material to obtain variety. The basic law of musical form is *unity and variety*. This is achieved through *repetition and contrast*.

Three-Part Form (A-B-A)

This principle shows itself in a popular pattern in music known as *three-part form* or A-B-A. The first section presents a musical idea; the middle section introduces a new idea, supplying variety; then the first part is repeated, which establishes a feeling of unity. We also find A-B-A form in architecture, when the two outer sections of a building give us a sense of unity while the middle part supplies variety. We have heard several examples of A-B-A form, among them *Marche militaire, Saber Dance,* and *Hoe-Down*.

In order to introduce the necessary variety, the middle part of the piece (B) should present a contrast to the first and last sections (A). The composer may accomplish this in a number of ways. A vigorous rhythm in the first section may be contrasted with a flowing melody in the middle part, or the other way around. The first section may be agitated, the middle part

23

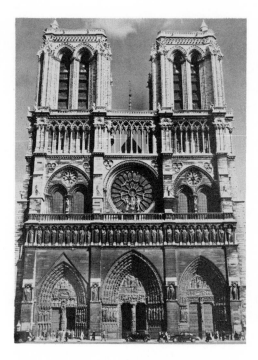

CATHEDRAL OF NOTRE
DAME, PARIS.
A-B-A form in architecture.

calm. The first part may lie in the dark lower register while the second is in the middle or upper register. The first part may be loud, the middle part soft; the first staccato, the middle part legato. The first part may be played by one group of instruments while the middle part is played by another. In these and similar ways the composer achieves the necessary contrast between the A and B sections.

From the simplest folk song to the greatest symphony, music shows the striving for unity and variety through repetition and contrast. Because of this striving, the masters created the great forms of music that bind the individual tones into a phrase, the phrases into a movement, and the movements into a complete work just as logically as, in a novel, the individual words are bound together in phrases, sentences, paragraphs, sections, and chapters.

Rondo Form

By extending the A-B-A principle we obtain the pattern A-B-A-B-A. This is the pattern of the *rondo,* a lively movement in which a theme returns again and again, alternating with another theme. (When a musical idea is used in the construction of a large musical work, it is known as a *theme.*) If the main theme alternates with two other themes we have a pattern such as A-B-A-C-A. The basic feature of the rondo is the repetition of the main theme, which has to be an appealing melody since it is going to be heard again and again.

Theme and Variations

In a *theme and variations* the composer announces his basic idea at the outset. In each succeeding variation, he brings back the theme in a new guise. (We studied a theme and variations in the last chapter—the *Russian Sailors' Dance* from *The Red Poppy.*) He may add notes to the melody; he may

24

change the harmony, or the meter and rhythm. He may shift the melody from soft to loud, from slow to fast, from low to high register; he may combine it with another melody, or give it to other instruments. As a result of all these changes the original melody takes on a different character, so that what first appeared as a serenade may return as a funeral march, a folk dance, a boat song, or a military march. The composer achieves unity through the return of the theme; he achieves variety by changing the basic idea in each variation.

1.   Minuet from Symphony No. 39 by Wolfgang Amadeus Mozart (móh-tsart). The minuets of the eighteenth-century masters were not intended to be danced to. Instead they captured the grace of the stately court dance within a work of art. The Minuet from Mozart's Symphony No. 39 does just that. It is marked Allegretto and, like all minuets, is in three-four time.

This Minuet is a perfect example of A-B-A form. The opening section (A) is marked forte; it has a certain pomp and graciousness of movement. The melody extends over a wide range. The middle part (B) is quieter, gentler in mood. Then the opening section is repeated.

2.   *Pomp and Circumstance,* March No. 1 by Edward Elgar. This celebrated march was written for the coronation of King Edward VII in 1901. Although it is played all over the world, it is most popular in England; its chief melody, sung to the words *Land of Hope and Glory,* is a kind of national anthem second only to *God Save the King.* The piece consists of two sections, each of which is repeated; the result is an A-B-A-B pattern. This is an extension of A-B-A form.

The opening section is a restless Allegro in two-four time, in a very active rhythm. The theme is staccato; it is heavily accented and extends over a wide range. Then the excitement simmers down. We hear a stately legato melody that moves mostly by step within a narrow range. Soft at first, it is repeated in a loud and majestic manner, like music for a great ceremony. The opening section is repeated. Finally the legato tune returns, sung by the full orchestra in triumph, fortissimo. A brief coda, based on the opening theme, brings the piece to an end. (A *coda*—the Italian word for *tail*—is a section at the end of a piece that gives us a sense of conclusion.)

3.   Rondo from *Eine kleine Nachtmusik* (A Little Night Music) by Wolfgang Amadeus Mozart. (The German title is pronounced éye-neh klí-neh nákht-moo-zeek.) This Allegro in four-four time consists of a principal theme that is heard three times, alternating with a contrasting theme. We are dealing here with a rondo in A-B-A-B-A form. The main theme is an upward-skipping melody in high register, active and staccato. The other theme lies a little lower in register. It starts out with a downward skip. Notice that the harmony of the eighteenth century is much less dissonant than is the harmony of more recent times. The main theme, after its final appearance, is expanded into a coda that brings the piece to a happy ending. This music has all the grace and charm of Mozart's lighter works.

SPANISH DANCE FROM *LA VIDA BREVE*.

4. Spanish Dance No. 1 from *La Vida breve* (lah veé-da bráy-veh) by Manuel de Falla (fá-ya). Just as Smetana and Dvořák based their music on the
folk songs and dances of Bohemia, so the modern Spanish composer Manuel
de Falla found inspiration in the music of his homeland. His opera *La Vida
breve* (Life is Short) evokes the passionate melodies of the Spanish Gypsies.
The Spanish Dance opens with a lively tune in triple meter, piano, in the
upper register. This melody (A) suggests the rhythm of a graceful dance.
It is followed by a section based on Spanish dance rhythms in low register
(B). When the principal melody is heard again (A), it is varied and
woven into new patterns. Now a contrasting melody appears (C), in low
register, with heavy accents. Then the original melody (A) leads into a brief
coda that brings the dance to a brilliant close. The form of this piece, then,
is A-B-A-C-A.

5. Theme and Variations from *Appalachian Spring* by Aaron Copland.
Like *Rodeo,* Copland's ballet *Appalachian Spring* is thoroughly American in
its setting. The action centers about a wedding ceremony among simple farm
folk. The Theme and Variations comes from a section of the ballet that
shows, as Copland explained it, "scenes of daily activity for the bride and her
farmer-husband. There are five variations on a Shaker theme. The melody I
borrowed and used almost literally is called *Simple Gifts."* (The Shakers
were a religious sect that flourished mainly in New York State.)

The theme, in two-four time, is played softly in a simple manner. It is a
lyrical melody in folk style that moves mostly by step. The first variation,
marked "A trifle faster," presents the tune a little louder and in higher
register, with a change of instruments. In the second variation we hear the

theme in low register, against syncopated chords. Next is a vigorous variation marked forte. The tune is presented by trumpets twice as fast. Notice that the harmony of this twentieth-century piece is spiced with dissonance. The final variation is marked "Broadly." The melody is presented by the whole orchestra in a heavy legato, *fff,* which brings this section of the ballet to a triumphal end.

6.   Prelude and Farandole from *L'Arlésienne* (lar-lay-zyén), by Georges Bizet (bee-záy). This music was written to accompany a drama called *L'Arlésienne* (The Woman of Arles) by the French writer Alphonse Daudet (doh-dáy). The play dealt with the life of the peasants in and around Arles, which is in Provence (pro-váhns). Not far from the Mediterranean Sea, Provence is famous for the beauty of its landscape, its cloudless blue sky and dazzling sun. The painters Vincent Van Gogh (van gókh) and Paul Gauguin (go-gán) lived in Arles for a time and captured on their canvases something of the sun-drenched atmosphere of Provence. So did Bizet in his music.

Daudet's play failed. But the concert suite that Bizet arranged from his music soon became extremely popular. After his death, a friend of his fashioned a second suite. Through these two works Bizet's music for *L'Arlésienne* lives on long after the play has been forgotten.

The Prelude is the first number of Suite No. 1. A *prelude* (préh-lyood) is

VINCENT VAN GOGH, *A VIEW OF ARLES: THE ORCHARD.*
Arles, in Provence, is famous for the beauty of its landscape.

a piece that is played as an introduction to a play, an opera, or another piece. This Prelude, an Allegro in four-four time, presents a theme and four variations. The theme, an old Christmas carol of Provence called *The March of the Three Kings,* is a sturdy melody consisting of four phrases, each four measures long. The theme is announced by the orchestra very loud and staccato, in middle register. In the first variation the theme is heard in a higher register, very soft and legato, with changed harmonies. Second is a lively variation that begins pianissimo but works up to an exciting fortissimo. The third variation is slower, and changes the melody as well as the accompaniment. The last variation returns to the tempo of the opening. Played fortissimo by the full orchestra, the theme is transformed into an energetic march. There is a brief coda based on the opening notes of the theme, and the Prelude dies away.

Four measures of tapping on the tambourine, very very soft (*pppp*), introduce the Farandole. (A *farandole* is a popular street dance of Provence in which couples hold hands in a procession, winding in and out as they follow the leader.) The Farandole from *L'Arlésienne* is based on a lively staccato theme that is first heard very softly and gradually works up to a fortissimo. There follows a conversation between the theme of the Prelude and the melody of the Farandole; we hear a phrase of one answered by a phrase of the other. At the climax of the piece both themes are combined, the theme of the Prelude serving as an accompaniment to the Farandole. The music becomes faster, louder, gayer, wilder. A brilliant coda marked *ffff* brings the piece to an exciting close.

Getting to Know the Instruments

STRINGS AND WOODWINDS

Music is carried through the air by vibrations. These vibrations are launched by a musical instrument or a voice. When they reach our ears we hear them as musical sounds.

A musical *instrument* is designed to set up musical vibrations and launch them into the air. Instruments enable us to control the pitch. This is determined by the rate of vibration, which depends mainly on the length of the vibrating body. For example, a string or column of air of a certain length will vibrate at a certain speed and produce a certain pitch. A shorter string or column of air will vibrate more rapidly and produce a higher pitch; a longer string or column of air will vibrate more slowly and produce a lower. *Pitch* therefore is that quality of a tone which enables us to call it "high" or "low." Other factors also influence the pitch, such as the width, thickness, density, and tension of the vibrating body.

Instruments also enable us to control the *duration* of the tones (short or long); the *volume* (loud or soft); and the *timbre*. Timbre refers to the tone color of the sound, according to the instrument that produces it. (The word has been taken over from French and is pronounced tám-br.) Each instrument shapes the sound wave in its own way. As a result, the same pitch will sound different on the piano, the violin, or the trumpet.

Instruments figure in our music singly; in small groups (chamber music); and as part of the orchestra or band. In the orchestra they are divided into four sections or choirs: string, woodwind, brass, and percussion.

The Nature of Musical Instruments

Instruments of the Orchestra: The String Section

The string choir of the orchestra includes four instruments—violin, viola, violoncello (known as cello), and double bass. These have four strings that are set vibrating by drawing a *bow* across them. The hair of the bow is rubbed with rosin so that it will grip the strings. The player holds the bow in his right hand. He moves his left hand along the fingerboard, pressing down a finger now at one point, now at another. By doing so he leaves part of the string free to vibrate. When he moves his hand from one point to another he changes the length of this part, which changes the rate of vibration—and the pitch.

VIOLIN

VIOLA

CELLO

DOUBLE BASS

29

The *violin* is universally admired for its singing tone; this brings it, of all instruments, closest to the human voice. It is also capable of brilliance and dramatic effect.

The *viola* is somewhat larger than the violin. Its strings are longer, thicker, heavier; its range is lower, its tone is huskier.

The *cello* (common name for *violoncello*) is lower in range than the viola. This instrument is notable for its lyric quality, which takes on a dark color in the low register.

The *double bass,* known also as *contrabass,* is the lowest in range of the string group. Therefore it plays the bass part—that is, the foundation of the harmony. It also is used to accentuate the rhythm.

The string instruments are capable of a variety of effects:

1. *Vibrato* (vee-bráh-toe) is the throbbing tone achieved when the player, while pressing down on the string, keeps moving his finger away from and back to the required spot.

2. The *mute* is a small attachment that muffles and changes the quality of sound.

3. *Double-stopping* involves playing two or more strings of an instrument at the same time.

4. *Pizzicato* (pit-sih-cáh-toh) is executed by plucking the string with the forefinger instead of using the bow.

5. In *glissando* the player moves a finger of his left hand rapidly along the string. This sounds all the pitches of the scale.

6. *Harmonics* are flutelike tones in the very high register. They are produced by lightly touching the strings at certain points while the bow is drawn across the string.

7. In a *trill* we rapidly alternate the tone with its upper neighbor. This often gives a birdlike effect.

8. *Tremolo* involves repeating a tone rapidly through a quick up-and-down movement of the bow. It is often used for moods of suspense and excitement.

9. The string instruments are able to produce both a beautiful singing legato and a light staccato.

The string section has come to be known as "the heart of the orchestra," which shows how important this choir is. The strings also figure prominently as solo instruments and in chamber music—duos, trios, quartets, quintets, and the like.

The Woodwind Section

The woodwind choir of the orchestra consists of four principal instruments and an instrument related to each: flute and piccolo, oboe and English horn, clarinet and bass clarinet, bassoon and contrabassoon. Saxophones too are included in this group. Besides being prominent in the orchestra, the woodwinds are used as solo instruments and in chamber music.

The tone is produced by a column of air vibrating within a pipe that has little holes in its side. When one or another of these holes is opened or

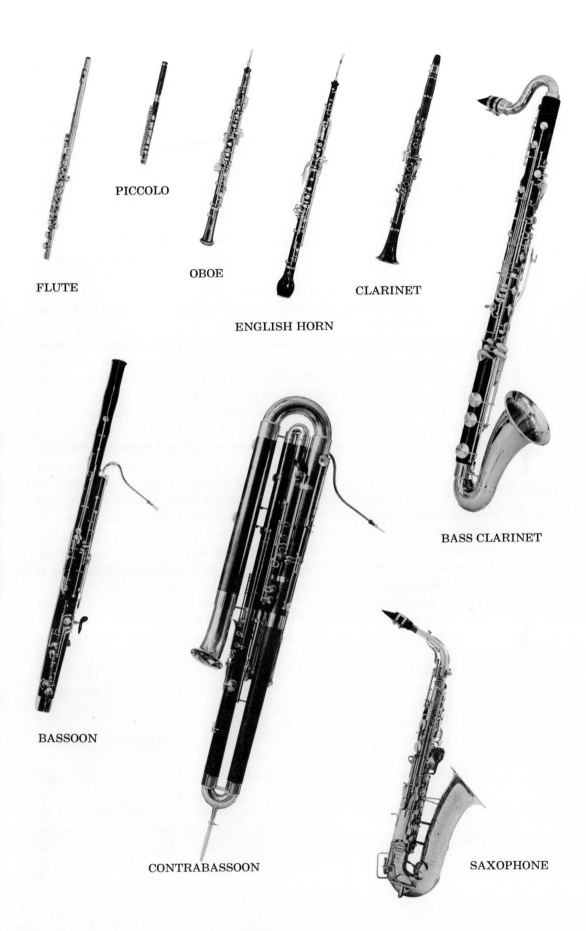

FLUTE

PICCOLO

OBOE

ENGLISH HORN

CLARINET

BASS CLARINET

BASSOON

CONTRABASSOON

SAXOPHONE

31

closed, the length of the vibrating column of air within the pipe is changed. This changes the rate of vibration—and the pitch. The little holes are opened and closed by a mechanism of keys that fits the player's fingers. The woodwinds are extremely agile instruments.

The *flute* is the soprano of the woodwind choir; its timbre is bright and birdlike. The present-day flute is made of metal; originally the instrument was made of wood. The player holds the flute horizontally and blows across a little mouth hole cut in the side of the pipe.

The *piccolo* has a piercing sound that produces the highest tones in the orchestra. In its upper register it takes on a shrillness that can be heard even when the whole orchestra is playing. It is half the size of the flute and plays an octave higher. (An *octave* is the distance between any tone and the tone of the same name above or below it, as from C to C in the series C, D, E, F, G, A, B, C.)

The *oboe* has a double reed in its mouthpiece, consisting of two slips of cane shaped in such a way as to leave between them a narrow passage for air. Its tone is intense and reedy. Because it sounds somewhat like a shepherd's pipe, the oboe lends itself to pastoral effects. The *English horn* is neither English nor a horn (since horns are brass instruments); it is an alto oboe. Its wooden tube is wider and longer than that of the oboe, and ends in a pear-shaped bell that largely accounts for its gentle tone.

The *clarinet* has a single reed, a small elastic piece of cane fastened against its chisel-shaped mouthpiece. The instrument has a beautiful liquid tone as well as a remarkably wide range from low to high and from soft to loud. The *bass clarinet* has a rich singing tone, and a range one octave lower than the clarinet.

The *bassoon,* a double-reed instrument, has a reedy, intense tone that is very expressive. It supplies a foundation for the harmony in the wood-wind choir, just as the double bass does among the strings. The *contrabassoon,* also known as *double bassoon,* produces the lowest tone in the orchestra. Its tube, over sixteen feet in length, is folded four times around to make it less unwieldy.

The *saxophone* combines the features of the woodwinds with a body made of brass. It has a single reed. The saxophone blends well with either woodwinds or brass, and is used both in the jazz band and the symphony orchestra.

The woodwinds are not as unified a group as the strings. Nowadays they are not all made of wood, and they represent several methods of setting up vibration:

1. By blowing across a mouth hole (flute and piccolo).

2. By blowing into a mouthpiece that has a single reed (clarinet and saxophone).

3. By blowing into a mouthpiece fitted with a double reed (oboe and bassoon).

Woodwinds do, however, have two features in common. First, the holes in the side of the pipe. Second, their timbres are such that composers usually write for them as a group.

Listen carefully to the record illustrating the string and woodwind instruments of the orchestra. Try to hear the recording several times, so that you will become familiar with the timbres of the different instruments and their capacities.

Getting to Know the Instruments

BRASS AND PERCUSSION

*The Brass
Section*

The brass section consists of the trumpet, horn, trombone, and tuba. These instruments have cup-shaped mouthpieces (except for the horn, whose mouthpiece is shaped like a funnel). The column of air within the tube is set vibrating by the tightly stretched lips of the player; these act as a kind of double reed. In order to go from one pitch to another the player uses a slide or valves; he also changes the pressure of the lips and breath.

The *trumpet* has a bold, resonant tone that lends brilliance to the orchestral sound. This tone goes with martial pomp and vigor (as in the famous melody for trumpets in the Triumphal March from *Aïda*). Played softly, the instrument commands a lovely round tone. The muted trumpet is much used. A pear-shaped mute, of metal or cardboard, is placed in the open end of the instrument, the bell. When the muted tone is forced, we hear a harsh snarling sound that is not soon forgotten.

The *horn,* generally called the French horn, is descended from the hunting horn. Its golden tone can be mysterious in soft passages and majestic in loud. The muted horn has a poetic faraway tone. However, if the muted tone is forced, we hear a rasping, frightening sound.

The *trombone*—the Italian word means "large trumpet"—has a sonorous tone that combines the brilliance of the trumpet with the majesty of the horn. In place of valves it has a movable U-shaped slide that changes the length of the air column in the tube. Composers use the trombone to achieve effects of nobility and grandeur.

The *tuba* is the bass of the brass choir. Like the double bass and the contrabassoon, it supplies the foundation for the harmony. Its dark tone ranges from velvety softness to a growl.

TRUMPET

TROMBONE

TUBA

CORNET

EUPHONIUM

FRENCH HORN

A number of brass instruments are used in military and outdoor bands. Most important of these is the *cornet,* which has a shorter body than the trumpet. It is more agile but less brilliant than the trumpet. Among the brass-band instruments are the *flügelhorn,* which is similar in shape to the cornet but wider; the *baritone* and *euphonium,* which are tenor tubas; and the *helicon,* which is a double-bass tuba in circular form, so that the player is able to carry it over his shoulder. An American type of helicon is the *sousaphone,* named after the famous bandmaster John Philip Sousa, who helped design its bell.

The *bugle,* originally a hunter's horn, has a powerful tone that carries well in the open air. Since it is not equipped with valves, it is able to play only certain tones of the scale, such as are heard in the duty calls of the army.

The Percussion Instruments

The percussion section includes a variety of instruments that are made to sound by striking or shaking. They fall into two groups: those of definite pitch, which are tuned to exact musical tones, and those of indefinite pitch, which are not. Among the instruments of definite pitch are the *kettledrums* or *timpani,* which are used in sets of two or three. The kettledrum is a copper shell across which is stretched a "head" of calfskin held in place by a metal ring. The player is able to change the tension of this calfskin head with the aid of screws or a pedal; thereby he changes the pitch. The instrument is played with two padded sticks, which may be either soft or hard. Its dynamic range extends from a mysterious rumble to a thunderous roll.

The *glockenspiel* (German for a set of bells) consists of a series of horizontal tuned plates of various sizes, made of steel. The player strikes these with mallets, producing a bright tinkling sound.

The *celesta* looks like a small upright piano. It is played, like a piano, by means of a keyboard. Its steel plates are struck by small hammers and produce a silvery sound.

The *xylophone* (zý-lo-fone) consists of tuned blocks of wood that, when struck, produce a dry, crisp timbre. Expert xylophone players attain dazzling speed and accuracy.

The *marimba* is a xylophone of African and South American origin that produces a gentle reedy sound. It is much used in Latin-American dance music.

The *vibraphone* combines the principle of the xylophone with propellers, one to each note, which are driven by an electric motor. Its unusual tone is marked by a slow vibrato that can be controlled by changing the speed of the motor. The instrument (popularly known as "vibes") plays a prominent part in jazz.

Chimes consist of a set of tuned metal tubes of various lengths suspended from a frame and struck with a hammer. They are frequently used to imitate church bells.

Among the percussion instruments of indefinite pitch are the *bass drum,* which produces a low heavy sound, and the *side drum* or *snare drum,* whose rhythmic rat-tat-tat is associated with military parades.

TAMBOURINE

CELESTA

CHIMES

CASTANETS

TRIANGLE

XYLOPHONE

SNARE DRUM

GONG

BASS DRUM

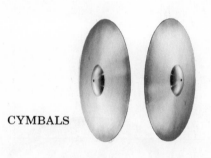

CYMBALS

KETTLEDRUM

GLOCKENSPIEL

37

ORGAN

HARP

PIANO

The *tambourine* is a small round drum with "jingles"—little metal plates —inserted in its rim. It is played by striking the drum with the fingers or elbow, by shaking, or by passing the hand over the jingles. The tambourine is much used in the folk dances of Italy.

Castanets are widely used in Spain. They consist of little wooden clappers moved by the thumb and forefinger of the player.

The *triangle* is a small round bar of steel bent in the shape of a triangle. It is open at the upper end and, when struck with a steel beater, gives off a bright tinkling sound.

Cymbals are two large circular brass plates of equal size. When struck sidewise against each other, they produce a shattering sound. A single cymbal, when struck lightly with a drumstick, produces a mysterious sound.

The *gong* is a broad circular disk of metal, suspended in a frame so as to hang freely. When struck with a heavy drumstick, it produces a deep roar.

Other Instruments

The *harp* is one of the oldest of musical instruments. Its strings are played by plucking and produce a silvery tone that blends well with the orchestra. The pedals shorten the strings, thereby raising the pitch.

The *piano,* a most popular instrument, is widely used in the home as well as on the concert stage. Whereas the violinist or clarinetist needs someone to accompany him, the pianist is able to play both melody and harmony. This makes the piano an extremely useful instrument. Its strings are struck with little hammers controlled by a keyboard. The full name of the instrument is *pianoforte,* the Italian for "soft-loud," which shows its ability to play both soft and loud, with many shadings in between.

The *organ,* once regarded as "the king of instruments," is a wind instrument. Air is fed to its pipes by mechanical means. The pipes are controlled by two or more keyboards and a set of pedals that is really a keyboard played by the feet. The organ produces a majestic sound that is able to fill a huge space, hence its usefulness in church. There are also organs in which the sounds are produced by electronic means.

The instruments described in these chapters form a large and vivid group. To composers, performers, and listeners alike they offer a rich variety of colors that make possible every shade of musical expression.

The Sound of Brass and Percussion

Listen to the examples of brass and percussion sound. As with the examples of the strings and woodwinds, try to hear the recording a number of times until you are familiar with the timbres of the various instruments and their capacities.

❧ 7A ❧

Getting to Know the Orchestra

The modern orchestra has grown into an ensemble of over a hundred players. (*Ensemble*—pronounced ahn-sáhm-bul—is the French word for "together" and denotes a number of musicians who play as a group.) The players are divided into the four sections or choirs that we have described. In large orchestras, about two thirds are string players, one third are wind players. From three to five men take care of the percussion. A modern symphony orchestra is made up in the following way:

Strings, about 65:	18 first violins 16 second violins 12 violas 10 violoncellos 10 double basses
Woodwinds, about 15:	3 flutes, 1 piccolo 3 oboes, 1 English horn 3 clarinets, 1 bass clarinet 3 bassoons, 1 contrabassoon
Brass, 11:	4 horns (or 5) 3 trumpets 3 trombones 1 tuba

The violins are divided into two groups—first and second violins. Each group plays its own line of music. In the woodwind section, one of the players of the principal instrument doubles on the related one. The third flutist also plays piccolo; one of the oboists doubles on the English horn, and so on. Saxophones are added for certain works. When necessary a larger brass section is used, with additional horns and one or more extra trumpets. Included in these ensembles are two harps and, for certain modern works, a piano.

Orchestras differ widely from one another in regard to their seating plan, but they all follow the same principle: the softer instruments—that is, the strings—are up front, the louder ones, such as the brass and percussion, are in the back. Below is a characteristic seating plan of a large modern orchestra.

The ensemble is directed by the conductor. He beats time (meter); he indicates the entrance of the various instruments, the shadings in the volume of tone (dynamics), and many other details. He makes the orchestra play according to his understanding of the music. Standing on the podium with his baton raised, the conductor may be compared to a general at the head of his troops. It is his task to bring the ensemble to life and to mold the musicians into a unified group.

THE BOSTON SYMPHONY ORCHESTRA
with its conductor, Erich Leinsdorf.

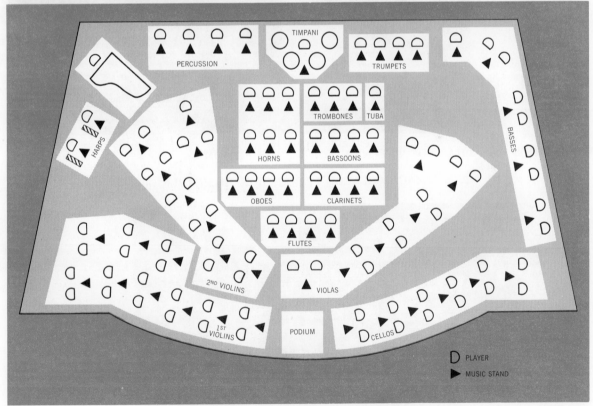

THE SEATING PLAN OF THE BOSTON SYMPHONY ORCHESTRA.

THE FIRST-VIOLIN SECTION OF THE NEW YORK PHILHARMONIC.

WOODWINDS AND BRASS OF THE NEW YORK PHILHARMONIC.

THE ITHACA COLLEGE PERCUSSION ENSEMBLE.

LEONARD BERNSTEIN WITH THE VIOLAS, CELLOS, AND DOUBLE BASSES OF THE NEW YORK PHILHARMONIC.

The conductor has before him the *score* of the work. This consists of from a few to as many as twenty-five or more lines, each of which represents one or more instrumental parts. You can see from the illustration of an orchestral score on the next page that the instruments are grouped together in families, the woodwinds on top, then the brass, percussion, and strings. All the lines together make up a single line of sound. What is going on in the orchestra is indicated at any given point straight down the page.

The Art of Orchestration

The composer bent over a page of score paper may be compared to a weaver combining threads of different colors or a painter mixing his colors. He imagines the sound in his mind as he blends the different tone colors. He fashions the score so that the melody will stand out clearly against the background; he distributes the music among the various instruments and groups. The art of writing for orchestra or of arranging a piece for orchestra is known as *orchestration*. Some people have the mistaken notion that one man writes the music while another orchestrates it. This is true of popular dance music, the scores of Broadway musical shows, and in Hollywood. But in art music the composer is also the orchestrator. What he says and how he says it are part of his way of imagining sound. This is so personal that we can often recognize who wrote a piece just from the way the horns or strings are handled.

Listening to the orchestra is a favorite pastime of the musical public today. Most of this listening is done via phonograph, radio, and television, so that many listeners never come in contact with the living orchestral sound.

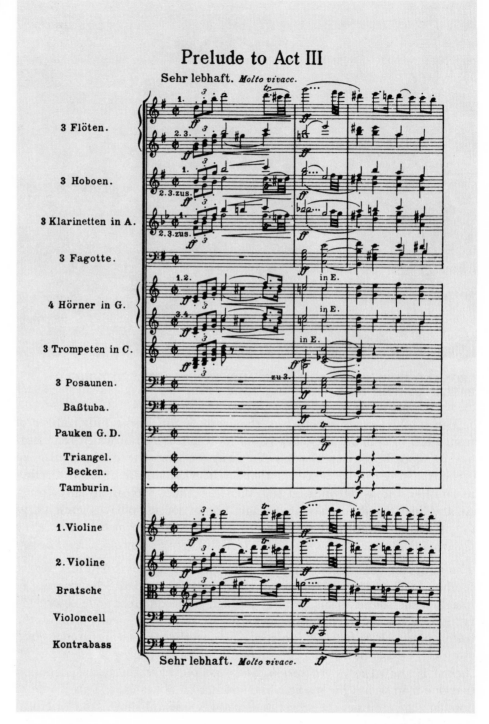

A PAGE OF SCORE: WAGNER, PRELUDE TO ACT III OF *LOHENGRIN*.

This is a great pity, for no mechanical transmission can ever do justice to the marvelous sound of a great orchestra. By all means listen to recordings, since you will learn very much from them. But consider those as a preparation for the live performance, not as a substitute!

1. Hungarian March from *The Damnation of Faust* by Hector Berlioz (béhr-lee-ohz). This outstanding French composer was a master of the art of orchestration. His vivid imagination is shown at its best in the celebrated march that he based on an old Hungarian war song. A martial Allegro in duple meter, it opens with a fanfare on the horns and trumpets, forte. (A *fanfare* is a short tune for trumpets, used as a signal in battle, hunting, or various ceremonies. In the plays of Shakespeare, for example, the arrival of a prince is frequently announced by a fanfare.) The principal melody is a vigorous tune, played mainly by the woodwinds.

The middle section introduces a melody played by woodwinds and strings. Berlioz obtains a bright orchestral sound by keeping the music in higher register. A transition leads back to the opening theme, which is introduced in the low register, in a mysterious pianissimo, by cellos and double basses. The piece, therefore, is in three-part or A-B-A form. The music grows steadily louder, faster, higher in register. A brilliant coda rounds off the march in a surge of sound from the full orchestra.

2. Prelude to Act III of *Lohengrin* by the German composer Richard Wagner (vóg-ner). This exciting composition sets the mood for the wedding of the knight Lohengrin to Elsa, the princess whom he has successfully defended against the false accusations of her enemies. The Prelude, in duple meter, is taken at a very lively tempo. The fortissimo opening captures the attention immediately. A robust theme is presented by woodwinds, brass, and strings, giving an impression of boundless energy. Excitement is heightened when a powerful theme appears in the horns and trombones, fortissimo, in a very active rhythm. The effect is nothing short of dazzling.

The middle section of the Prelude, by contrast, is quiet and lyrical. Woodwinds and strings set the mood; the melody is legato, the rhythm flowing and relaxed. Then the music returns to the mood and tempo of the opening (A-B-A).

3. *Dance of the Tumblers* from *The Snow Maiden* by the Russian composer Nicholas Rimsky-Korsakov. The fairy-tale operas of Rimsky-Korsakov show his love of bright orchestral colors. The *Dance of the Tumblers* shows off his brilliant style. Marked Vivace, this piece suggests physical movement; one can almost see the agile tumblers as they whirl around and around. After a brief introduction, the woodwind instruments announce a melody in the style of a Russian folk song (A). This melody alternates with another tune, also in Russian folk style (B), which makes its first appearance in the strings, forte. In form this piece is an A-B-A-B with coda. The music never relents in its forward drive, sweeping us along on its powerful rhythm to the very end.

4. *The Great Gate of Kiev* from *Pictures at an Exhibition* by the Russian composer Modest Musorgsky (moo-sórg-skee). An exhibition of paintings by a friend of his inspired Musorgsky to write a suite of piano pieces, each evoking the mood and atmosphere of a particular picture. Many years after his death the French composer Maurice Ravel, who was a great admirer of

Musorgsky, arranged the piano suite for orchestra. This work consequently unites the genius of the Russian master and the orchestral magic of the Frenchman.

The final "picture" in Musorgsky's suite was inspired by the painter's design for a gate in the ancient city of Kiev. The piece suggests a religious procession through the gate accompanied by the ringing of bells. It is an Allegro in four-four time. Beginning forte, the orchestra sings a Russian melody that seems to have come out of a time long past. This tune is repeated over and over throughout the piece. Massive harmonies, played fortissimo, alternate with a series of gentle chords in the style of a chorale. (A *chorale* is a hymn or a melody in the style of a hymn.) Now the brass instruments shatter the air, against a background of scales; now the chorale returns like a prayer. And always the music moves in a stately rhythm towards the grand climax at the end.

5. *The Incredible Flutist* is a ballet by the modern American composer Walter Piston, from which he arranged a concert suite that has become popular. The action takes place in a Spanish village where a circus arrives during carnival time. The star of the show is the Incredible Flutist, whose playing charms even the circus animals. He charms also the pretty daughter of one of the merchants of the village. But there is time for only a brief flirtation, since the circus must be on its way. And so the Incredible Flutist is off to new adventures—but not before everyone has joined him in a gay polka.

Tango of the Merchant's Daughters. A *tango* is a dance of South American origin. Marked Moderato, Piston's Tango is in five-eight time, that is, five beats to a measure. This alternation of three and two creates a most graceful effect. A legato melody, extremely lyrical, is introduced by the strings. It is heard four times: piano, mezzo piano, mezzo forte, and forte; first in middle register, the next two times an octave higher, finally an octave higher still, with ever more glowing orchestration. This is a fine example of how a composer may build up tension, a little at a time, with each repetition of a theme.

The middle section presents a tense rhythm that suggests the stamping feet, abrupt movements, and flashing eyes we associate with Spanish dancing. A staccato melody is played in high register by the woodwinds. The percussion instruments add to the excitement. Then the suave melody of the first section returns, to round out the A-B-A form.

Entry of the Circus—Circus March. The village square fills. There is great excitement among the crowd as the circus troupe arrives. This is suggested by a staccato melody, dissonant harmonies, strongly marked rhythms, and the clatter of the drum. The grand parade files past to the accompaniment of a march played by woodwinds and brass without strings—a twentieth-century sound. The music is loud and brash, as it should be. The enthusiasm is catching: even a little dog is heard barking his welcome.

The *Spanish Waltz* is played at a rapid tempo, forte. Woodwinds and strings join in presenting a graceful melody whose accent falls on the offbeat. The use of the upper register and the bright orchestration contribute to the lively effect. Notice the ending on a soft pizzicato.

Polka—Finale. The woodwind instruments introduce the staccato tune of the Polka. In this gay finale of his ballet Piston uses a device that never fails to build a rousing climax. A short melody is repeated over and over, each time a little faster, louder, higher in pitch and with more brilliant orchestration, so that there is a steady rise in tension from the soft beginning to the exciting end.

How Music Is Written Down

Musical notation shows the movement of the tones by indicating their pitch (high or low) and duration (long or short). The notes are written on the *staff*, a series of five horizontal lines with four spaces between, each representing another degree of pitch. (The *tone* is what you hear, the *note* is what you see on the printed page.) The lines and spaces are named after the first seven letters of the alphabet.

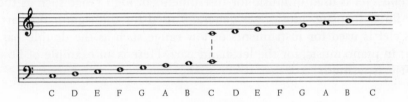

If we look at the keyboard of the piano we notice that the octave from C to C includes seven white keys and five black.

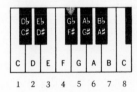

The black keys are named in relation to the white keys. The upper neighbor of C is C-sharp. The lower neighbor of B is B-flat. You can see that C-sharp is the same as D-flat, D-sharp as E-flat, F-sharp as G-flat, G-sharp as A-flat, A-sharp as B-flat.

47

From one key to the next is a distance of half a tone or a *semitone,* as from C to C-sharp or from B to B-flat. Where the white keys have a black key between them they are two semitones or a whole tone apart, as from C to D, D to E, F to G, G to A, A to B. Where the white keys have no black key between them they are a semitone apart, as from E to F and B to C. Similarly, where black keys have one white key between them they are a whole tone apart, as from C-sharp to D-sharp.

The pitch may be altered by five signs known as *accidentals.* A *sharp* (♯) raises the pitch by a half tone (semitone). A *flat* (♭) lowers the pitch by a half tone. A *natural* (♮) cancels these, restoring the original pitch. A *double sharp* (✖) raises the pitch by two semitones or a whole tone. A *double flat* (♭♭) lowers the pitch by two semitones.

The *clef* is a letter sign placed on the staff in order to indicate the pitch of the notes. It is written on a certain line from which the other lines are reckoned. The G or *treble clef* establishes the second line of the staff as G above middle C. (The bottom line of the staff is counted as the first.) The F or *bass clef* establishes the fourth line as F below middle C. Other clefs are used too, but these two are the most common.

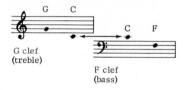

G clef
(treble)

F clef
(bass)

The treble clef is used in music for instruments of high range such as the violin or flute. In piano music it is generally used for the right-hand part. The bass clef is used for instruments of low range such as the double bass and tuba; in piano music, for the left-hand part. Here is an example of how piano music is written:

etc.

Time Values

The duration of the notes is indicated by a simple system. When the *whole note* receives four beats, a *half note* receives two, and a *quarter note* one beat. A quarter note is equivalent to two *eighth notes;* an eighth note equals two *sixteenths.* Smaller subdivisions such as thirty-second and sixty-fourth notes are also used.

whole   half   quarter   eighth   sixteenth   thirty-second   sixty-fourth

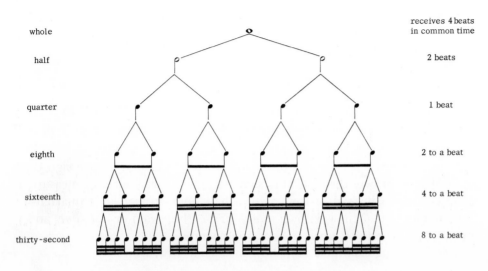

whole — receives 4 beats in common time
half — 2 beats
quarter — 1 beat
eighth — 2 to a beat
sixteenth — 4 to a beat
thirty-second — 8 to a beat

A note may be divided into three equal notes of the next lower value, in which case we have a *triplet*.

A *tie* connects two successive notes of the same pitch, lengthening the first by the value of the second. A *dot* after a note lengthens its time value by half.

$4+2=6$ $2+1=3$ $2+2=4$ $1+\frac{1}{2}=1\frac{1}{2}$ $1+1=2$

$4+2=6$ $2+1=3$ $1+\frac{1}{2}=1\frac{1}{2}$

Time never stops in music, even when there is no sound. Silence is indicated by *rests,* which correspond in time value to the notes.

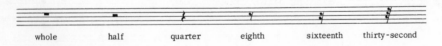

whole   half   quarter   eighth   sixteenth   thirty-second

The *time signature* indicates the meter. The upper numeral shows the number of beats in the measure; the lower shows the kind of note that receives one beat. The time signature $\frac{2}{4}$ means that there are two beats to a measure, with a quarter note receiving one beat. In $\frac{3}{4}$ time there are three beats to a measure; a quarter note receives one beat. In $\frac{4}{4}$ time there are four beats to a measure. In $\frac{6}{8}$ time there are six beats to a measure, with an eighth note receiving one beat.

49

Following are the most frequently encountered time signatures:

Duple meter	$\frac{2}{2}$	$\frac{2}{4}$	$\frac{2}{8}$
Triple meter	$\frac{3}{4}$	$\frac{3}{8}$	$\frac{3}{16}$
Quadruple meter	$\frac{4}{4}$	$\frac{4}{8}$	
Sextuple meter	$\frac{6}{4}$	$\frac{6}{8}$	

Also in use are $\frac{9}{8}$ (3 groups of 3) and $\frac{12}{8}$ (4 groups of 3). Twentieth-century music shows a wide use of odd-numbered patterns such as $\frac{5}{4}$ or $\frac{5}{8}$ (2 plus 3) and $\frac{7}{4}$ or $\frac{7}{8}$ (4 plus 3).

$\frac{4}{4}$ time is known as *common time* and is often indicated by the sign **C**. A vertical line drawn through this sign (**¢**) indicates that the measure is counted in two instead of four, with a half note—instead of a quarter—receiving one beat. This is known as *alla breve* (bráy-vay) or *cut time,* and is mostly used when the music goes at a fast tempo.

The following examples show how the system works:

A fine example of triplet rhythm is contained in the chief melody of the
Triumphal March from *Aïda*. This, you will recall, is the theme played by
the trumpets:

UNIT II

SONG
AND
PIANO PIECE

8

The Art Song

An *art song* is a composition for voice and an instrument, generally the piano. Songs may also be accompanied by a group of instruments or an orchestra. The term *art song* is used to distinguish this type of song from the folk song and the popular song (although a number of art songs have been written in folk or popular style). Song makes use of the most personal of all instruments—the human voice. The instrumental *accompaniment* presents the harmonies that support the melody. It also creates the necessary mood and atmosphere for the vocal line.

There are two principal types of song structure. In *strophic form* the composer writes a melody for the first stanza (or strophe) of the poem, which he then repeats for each additional stanza. Thus, although one stanza may tell how the lovers met, a second how they fell in love, and a third how they were cruelly separated, all three stanzas are sung to the same melody. Folk songs are generally in strophic form.

The other type is known as *through-composed* or "composed throughout" —that is, the music follows the story and changes with each stanza according to the text. As a result, the music reflects what is taking place at any particular point in the poem.

The strophic form is best for songs set to simple lyric poems. On the other hand, a dramatic or story-telling poem calls for the through-composed form. In this chapter we shall study examples of both types.

Other types of song stand between the two categories we have just described. These combine the strophic method with the through-composed. For example, in Schubert's *Serenade,* which we studied in Chapter 1, the same music is used for the first and second stanzas of the poem; but the third stanza, which brings the climax of the song, is set to new material.

*The Life of
Franz Schubert*

Franz Schubert, the greatest song writer that ever lived, was born in a suburb of Vienna on January 31, 1797. His father was a schoolmaster who loved music and taught Franz the violin; an older brother taught him to play the piano. Franz's beautiful soprano voice gained him a place in the church choir, and when he was eleven years old he entered the Imperial choir school. He was the most gifted pupil there. One of the teachers said, "Whenever I try to show him something new, he already knows it. It's as if he learned straight from heaven!"

Schoolmaster Schubert was a practical man. Although he enjoyed music as a hobby, he was opposed to it as a profession. Musicians, he insisted, had a hard time earning a living. He wanted his sons to follow in his footsteps. When Franz was sixteen he gave in to his father's wishes. He left the Imperial choir school and began to teach the younger children in his father's school.

But he was not meant to be a teacher. He was of a dreamy nature and could not keep order in a room full of mischievous youngsters. The moment school was over, he withdrew to his little room in the attic. There he found refuge in reading the verses of the new German poets, especially Johann Wolfgang von Goethe (gér-teh). As soon as he read a poem he thought of a melody to go with it. Some of his most beautiful songs took him only a few hours to write down. He was seventeen when he composed his song *Gretchen at the Spinning Wheel*, to Goethe's poem. A year later—in a single afternoon—he wrote down his setting of Goethe's *The Erlking*, one of his greatest songs.

Franz's lovable nature won him the loyalty of a little band of followers—poets, painters, musicians. They appreciated him even if the world did not. They kept telling him that if he continued to teach he would end by stifling his genius. Franz knew that they were right. Finally he left his father's school and went to live with one of his friends. Neither of the young men had much money, but they managed somehow. Now Franz could give himself to the music that welled up in him.

During the remainder of his short life Franz Schubert held no fixed position. He lived with one or another of his loyal friends, most of whom were just as poor as he. When they got hold of some money they shared it and had wonderful times. But there were also lean days when they barely kept body and soul together. And all the time the music came pouring out of him. As one of his friends said, "Everything he touched turned into music." A visitor once asked him, "How do you compose?" "I finish one piece," he replied, "and begin the next."

Schubert had very little talent for the practical side of life. Publishers soon discovered that, by refusing his manuscripts, they could beat down his price. He gave away—for the price of a meal—songs which after his death sold in the hundreds of thousands and made fortunes for the publishers. He gradually realized that the gift to create was not enough for an artist. "The state should support me," he remarked sadly, "so that I may be untroubled and free to compose."

As the years passed, he grew more and more discouraged. There were still moments when he thought he might find success. More often he was in the grip of despair. "Every night when I go to bed," he wrote, "I hope that I may never wake again, and every morning renews my grief." Yet he understood that his sorrow nourished his music and gave it a deep tenderness. "My music is the product of my talent and my misery, and that which I have written in my greatest distress is what the world seems to like best."

Somewhere in this dark period he realized that fate had decided against him. "It seems to me," he wrote, "that I no longer belong to this world." It was in this mood that he made his final effort. In the last year of his life he produced a series of masterpieces, among them the great Symphony in C major, the Quintet for Strings, three piano sonatas, and thirteen of his finest songs, among them the celebrated *Serenade*.

With these works behind him he told his brother Ferdinand, "Now I see how much I still have to learn." But his time had run out. His health ruined by years of poverty and improper care, he fell ill with typhus. His last wish was to be buried near Beethoven, whom he worshipped above all other composers. Schubert died in Vienna on November 19, 1828. He was thirty-one years old, an age when other artists have barely reached their maturity; yet he stands among the masters. He left no possessions except "a pile of old music valued at ten florins"—about eight dollars. Yet this old pile contained his unpublished manuscripts, symphonies, chamber music, piano pieces, songs—a treasure beyond price. For in them he bequeathed to the world the gift of immortal melody.

1. *The Erlking (Der Erlkönig)*. Allegro, $\frac{4}{4}$. This masterpiece of Schubert's *Six Great* youth was written in 1815. It captured the spirit of Goethe's famous poem, *Songs* which was based on the legend that whoever is touched by the King of the Elves must die.

> Who rides in the night through storm so wild?
> A loving father who holds his child.
> He clasps the feverish boy in his arm,
> He holds him firmly and keeps him warm.

Father:	"My son, my dearest, you tremble with fear."
Son:	"Oh father, see, the Erlking is near!
	He stands before me with crown so fair."
Father:	"My son, you see a shadow there."
Erlking:	"My lovely child, oh come with me,
	We'll play and laugh without a care.
	I'll show you flowers beyond compare,
	And my palace of silver and gold."
Son:	"O father, dear father, now surely you hear
	The Erlking whispering soft in my ear!"
Father:	"Fear nothing, oh fear nothing, my son,
	You hear the leaves that move in the wind."
Erlking:	"You'll come with me, oh my darling child,
	And my lovely daughters will welcome you
	With their dancing and singing in endless delight.
	They'll rock you to sleep in the stillness of night,
	They'll rock you to sleep in the stillness of night."

Son: "Oh father, dear father, you surely can see
The Erlking's daughters beyond that tree?"
Father: "My son, my son, I see nothing there;
The willows are standing silent and bare."

Erlking: "My sweetest child, I love your adorable face,
And if you're not willing, I'll take you by force!"
Son: "Oh father, dear father, he seizes my arm—
Help me—the Erlking has done me harm!"

The father shudders, he hastens ahead,
He comforts the child who sobs in despair.
At last—at last he reaches home.
But in his arms the child . . . lay dead.

The ghostly atmosphere of the poem is reflected in the piano part. Galloping triplets (three notes to a beat) are heard against a rumbling in the bass, conjuring up the desperate father as he rides with his sick child

through the night. As befits a dramatic ballad, the song is through-composed; the music follows the action with a steady building up of tension. The three characters of the tale are vividly portrayed. The feverish child sings short urgent phrases. The father, comforting his son, sings a more rounded line. As for the Erlking, his music is gently pleading.

This is a song of which a master would be proud. That it was written by a boy of eighteen is little short of a miracle.

2. *Rose Upon the Heather (Heidenröslein)*. Allegretto, $\frac{2}{4}$. The strophic song is well illustrated by this little Schubertian gem. The melody is repeated for each stanza. Here is a song marked by simplicity, love of nature, and enchanting melody.

Once there was a lovely rose,
    Growing in the heather . . .
Came a boy and saw her there,
He approached and found her fair,
Watched with joy and pleasure.
    Little rose so young and fair,
    Rose upon the heather!

Said the boy, "You'll come with me,
    Rose upon the heather!"
Said the rose, "My thorns you see?
You will long remember me
When I show my anger!"
    Little rose so young and fair,
    Rose upon the heather!

Savagely he plucked the rose,
    Rose upon the heather!
Bravely she attacked the foe,
Fought to save herself from woe,
Yet the boy was stronger . . .
    Little rose so young and fair,
    Rose upon the heather.

The mood is indicated by the marking *lieblich* (with charm). The melody moves lightly, mostly by step, within a narrow range, against an accompaniment of simple chords. The two lines at the end of each stanza form a *refrain*—that is, a thought or a phrase that is repeated again and again in the course of a poem or a song. Each refrain is followed by a little postlude on the piano. (A *postlude* is the opposite of a prelude: it comes after the action is completed, like an afterthought.)

SCHUBERT'S MANUSCRIPT FOR *HEIDENRÖSLEIN.*

Notice the beautiful climax when the melody line rises to its high point on the first line of the refrain—"Little rose so young and fair"—only to descend gracefully on the second line: "Rose upon the heather!"

Lit - tle rose so young and— fair, Rose up - on the heath - er.

3. *Who Is Sylvia?* Moderato, $\frac{4}{4}$. Schubert's settings of Shakespeare are, naturally, of special interest to the English-speaking world. The lines in praise of Sylvia from *The Two Gentlemen of Verona* inspired one of his most beautiful songs.

> Who is Sylvia, what is she,
>> That all our swains commend her?
> Holy, fair and wise is she;
>> The heav'ns such grace did lend her
> That adored she might be.
>
> Then to Sylvia let us sing,
>> That Sylvia is excelling,
> She excels each mortal thing,
>> Upon the dull earth dwelling;
> To her garlands let us bring.

The introduction on the piano consists of a succession of chords in eighth-note rhythm. This pattern persists throughout the song. Over it we hear a broad legato melody that proceeds mostly by step and narrow leap, yet covers a wide range:

Who is Syl - via, what is she,— That all our swains com - mend her?

The climax of the melody comes in the last phrase, on the words, "That adored she might be," with an upward leap of an octave followed by a downward leap of an octave. Two wide skips in such close succession give this melody its tension.

That a - dor - ed she might be.

The same melody is heard in each stanza; hence this is an example of strophic form. A little postlude on the piano at the end of the first stanza prepares us for the second. The same postlude brings this lovely song to a close.

4. *The Two Grenadiers* by Robert Schumann. Moderato, $\frac{2}{4}$. Schumann's most famous song is based on a heroic ballad by Heinrich Heine (hý-neh). Just as Goethe was the favorite poet of Schubert, Heine was the favorite of Schumann. The poem tells of two of Napoleon's soldiers who return from captivity in Russia and learn that their Emperor has been defeated.

Two soldiers returning at last to France,
  Set free from their prison in Russia;
And when they came to the German frontier
  They lowered their heads in anguish.
For there they discovered the sorrowful news
  That France in disgrace had retreated,
Her army in ruins, her power destroyed,
  And the Emperor, the Emperor defeated!

Then tears filled the eyes of the grenadiers,
  Oppressed with grief at these tidings.
The older said, "All hope is gone!
  My wounds ache and burn in torment!"
The other said, "The end has come!
  My life has lost its meaning.
But I've a wife and child at home
  Who need me to protect them!"

"Who cares for wife, who cares for child?
  My heart feels a grander emotion!
Let them go and beg if they wish to eat—
  My Emperor, my Emperor's defeated!
Oh brother, grant me one request;
  I feel my end approaching;
Oh promise you'll carry my body to France,
  And lay me to rest in my homeland.

The cross of honor that I won—
  Lay it upon my bosom;
You'll place my musket in my hand,
  And set my sword beside me.
And so I'll lie in my grave at rest,
  Like a sentry waiting and watchful,
Until I wake to the clangor of guns,
  The thunder of hoofbeats in battle.

Oh, see how my Emperor rides over my grave,
  While swords shine bright in the sunlight,
  While swords shine bright in the sunlight!
Then armed like a warrior I'll rise from the grave
  To serve my dear Emperor forever!"

Like *The Erlking*, this dramatic ballad is through-composed. The brief prelude on the piano creates a martial mood, as does the opening phrase of the melody:

Two sol-diers re-turn-ing at last from France, Set free from their pris-on in Rus-sia;

When the soldiers learn the sorrowful news, the music is dark in color. Their agitation is reflected in an accelerando. The request of the second grenadier to be buried in France builds up tension. The climax is very grand. As the soldier pictures himself lying in his grave "like a sentry," the vocal line rises in a great crescendo to the sound of the French national anthem, the *Marseillaise* (mar-say-áyz):

And so I'll lie in my grave at rest, Like a sen-try wait-ing and watch-ful, Un -

til I a-wake to the clang-or of guns, The thun-der of hoof-beats in bat-tle.

It is a most exciting effect. The final phrase reaches a fortissimo and quickly subsides. A little postlude of gentle chords brings the song to its pianissimo ending.

5. The *Lullaby* of Johannes Brahms is one of the world's best-loved songs. It is in ¾ time. The piano accompaniment sets up a gentle rhythm with a rocking effect, over which there unfolds a legato melody. The music reflects the spirit of the words. The melody consists of four phrases, each four measures long. There are two stanzas, with the same music for each (strophic form).

> Dearest child, go to sleep . . . May the angels protect you
>   And guard you from harm through the shadows of night.
> When the sun will rise to awaken the earth,
>   God will open your eyes and fill them with light.
>
> Dearest child, go to sleep . . . May the angels protect you
>   And send you sweet dreams from heaven above.
> When the sun will rise to awaken the earth,
>   God will open your eyes and surround you with love.

Go to sleep, and good night, May the an - gels pro - tect you, And___

guard you from___ harm through the shad - ows of night.

6. *None But the Lonely Heart,* by Peter Ilyich Tchaikovsky. The Russian master's emotional music lent itself to sad moods. His most famous song is a setting of a poem by Goethe that is like a cry of despair:

> None but the lonely heart can know my sadness,
> Alone and far away from joy and gladness.
> I search the sky above, I seek in anguish;
> Ah, but in vain I wait for my beloved!
>
> None but the lonely heart can know my sadness,
> Alone and far away from joy and gladness;
> Alone and far away from joy and gladness.
> My senses fail, I am consumed with anguish!
> None but the lonely heart can know my sadness . . .

The song is an Andante in common time. The melody is announced at the outset by the piano. It opens with a wide downward leap that gives the music its melancholy quality.

None but the lone - ly heart can know my sad - ness,_____

The second stanza duplicates the melody of the first for two phrases. Then the piano introduces a melody that moves upward to a great climax. From this emotional high point tne music descends, in a pianissimo, to the despairing mood of the closing lines.

The songs we have just discussed are but a few examples of a rich literature that ranges from the comic to the tragic. But all, no matter what their mood, base their power upon the appeal of melody and the power of the human voice to express emotion.

9

The Piano Piece

The Popularity of the Piano Piece

As the piano became popular, a wide variety of composers created pieces suitable for both the concert hall and the home. The piano piece was cultivated by composers of many nations. But the central figure in its development was Frédéric Chopin (fray-day-réek shoh-pán), who is known in the history of music as the "Poet of the Piano."

The Life of Frédéric Chopin

The national composer of Poland was half French. His father emigrated to Warsaw, where he married a lady-in-waiting to a countess. Frédéric was born in Warsaw on March 1, 1810. Like a number of great composers, he was a child prodigy. He began to compose at the age of seven, and played in public when he was ten.

At the Warsaw Conservatory Frédéric received a thorough musical education. When he had finished his studies he appeared at a concert before the musical world of Warsaw. He had now learned all he could in Warsaw; it was time for him to make his gifts known to the world. There was a banquet in his honor on the eve of his departure from his native city. Together with his best friend, a young man named Titus, Frédéric set out on his journey.

He had a strange feeling that he would never see Poland again. He was right.

When the two young men arrived in Vienna they received disturbing news. Warsaw had risen in rebellion against the soldiers of the Czar; the Polish patriots were determined to throw off the yoke of their Russian masters. Titus decided to return at once and fight for his country. Frédéric wanted to go too, but Titus dissuaded him. "You were not meant to be a soldier," Titus said. "You will serve our country in a better way—by making the name of Poland famous throughout the world." With a heavy heart Frédéric took leave of his friend.

His playing impressed the Viennese public, but he felt restless and sad. He worried about his family and friends. Finally a letter arrived from his parents telling him to continue his journey. He set out for Paris, which at that time was the musical center of the world. On his way he learned that the Polish capital had been captured by the Russians and the rebellion was crushed. He poured his grief into the flaming defiance of the *Revolutionary Etude*.

At last he reached Paris. He was alone, far from his family and friends; he thought of continuing to London, even to America. One night, as he was wandering along the boulevards in a sad frame of mind, he met a Polish prince who knew his family in Warsaw. Prince Radziwill introduced his young countryman into the aristocratic circles of Paris, where Frédéric's playing caused a sensation. He decided to remain in Paris, and spent the rest of his life in his adopted city.

Paris in the 1830s was the artistic center of the world. Frédéric Chopin became friendly with the leading artists of the city—the composer Franz Liszt, the painter Eugène Delacroix (de-lah-crwáh), the novelists Victor Hugo and Balzac. These men were creating a new spirit in art, and Chopin soon took his place among them. Unlike his friend Liszt, he did not like to play in public. His music was too personal, he felt, to conquer a large audience. "The crowd embarrasses me," he told Liszt. "I feel paralyzed by their curious glances." This sensitive musician felt more at home in the drawing rooms of countesses. There he relaxed, coaxing from the piano harmonies and rhythms whose like had never been heard before.

One evening Liszt introduced him to the most famous Frenchwoman of her time, Baroness Dudevant, who wrote novels under the name of George Sand. A deep friendship developed between them. George Sand realized that Chopin was not strong and needed someone to look after him. When she took her two children to the island of Majorca for the winter she invited Chopin to accompany them. They settled in a deserted monastery that had a garden full of oranges and lemons. Here Chopin completed his book of twenty-four preludes.

Mme. Sand left a fascinating description of this great artist at work. "His creative power was spontaneous and wonderful; it came to him without effort or warning. But then began the most heart-rending labor I have ever seen. He would shut himself in his room for days, pacing up and down, breaking his pens, repeating and modifying one bar a hundred times. He would spend six weeks over a page, only to end by writing it out finally just as he had sketched it in the original draft."

During the next eight years Chopin spent his summers at Mme. Sand's chateau in the country. Safe from the noise and distractions of Paris, he wrote some of his greatest works there, although his health steadily grew worse. The doctors realized that he was suffering from tuberculosis, but there was little they could do for him. George Sand nursed him tenderly. Sustained by her affection, he continued to compose.

Yet, despite their love for each other, disagreements came between them. Mme. Sand, although born an aristocrat, held radical views in politics and joined those who were plotting a revolution against the Bourbon king, Louis Philippe. Chopin, on the other hand, was strongly conservative. In addition, he was drawn into quarrels between Mme. Sand and her children. Finally the friendship ended in bitterness. According to Liszt, "Chopin felt and often repeated that in breaking this long affection, this powerful bond, he had broken his life."

He spent some months in England and Scotland, but his strength was ebbing; he composed no more. He returned to Paris mortally ill and died there on October 17, 1849, at the age of thirty-nine. The leading artists of Paris came to his funeral; George Sand stayed away. And on his grave a friendly hand scattered a goblet of Polish earth, so that he might lie in the soil of his native land.

*Seven Famous
Piano Pieces*

1. *Revolutionary Etude.* A fiery Allegro in $\frac{4}{4}$. This, we saw, was the composition into which Chopin poured his feelings when he received word that the Warsaw rebellion had been crushed. An *etude* (áy-tyood) is a study piece that concentrates on problems of technique. In the hands of Chopin the etude became a work of art. The *Revolutionary Etude* opens with a fortissimo outcry. A melody in octaves and chords unfolds against rumbling arpeggios in the bass. This melody is like a defiant summons to action.

There is a slight lessening of tension in the middle section, so that the return of the theme is all the more dramatic. The piece ends with an exciting coda.

2. Nocturne in E-flat. The *nocturne* derives its name from the Latin *nox,* night—in other words, a night piece, in the style of a song that a lover might

sing underneath his lady's balcony. The mood is tender, as is apparent from this most famous of Chopin's nocturnes, an Andante in $\frac{12}{8}$ time. The opening melody is repeated, but with the trills and ornaments so characteristic of Chopin. Toward the end of the work the music rises to a passionate climax in the upper register. Chopin was hardly out of his teens when he wrote this widely loved piece.

ARTUR RUBINSTEIN.
One of the great Chopin
interpreters of our time at
the keyboard.

3. *Polonaise militaire.* The *polonaise* was the dance performed by Poland's nobles and their wives as they passed in procession before their king. It was in $\frac{3}{4}$ time, at a moderate tempo, with the accent on the second beat of the measure. By reviving this stately court dance, Chopin became the national poet looking back to the days of Poland's glory, as though to promise his countrymen that their freedom would soon return. The *Polonaise militaire,* marked Allegro con brio (fast, with energy), is in A-B-A form. The opening melody is staccato and brusque; it has a military character. The middle

part, in contrast, is a flowing legato melody that moves with wide leaps across a wide range. Then the A section is repeated.

The *Polonaise militaire* is a bright piece that reveals the heroic side of Chopin's genius. What this music means to his countrymen is indicated by the fact that in 1939, when the Nazis invaded Poland, the Warsaw radio broadcast the opening measures of this melody on the hour to inform the world that the city was still holding out.

4. *La Campanella,* by Franz Liszt. Allegretto in ⁶⁄₈. *La Campanella* means "the little bell." In this piece the composer showed off the upper register of the piano. He used a melody by the Italian violinist Niccolò Paganini, which he ornamented with trills, rapid runs, repeated notes, and wide leaps that require great accuracy. The effect is one of sheer lightness and grace. This piece has to be played by a true virtuoso. (A *virtuoso* is a performer who is a master of his instrument. Hence *virtuosity* represents the highest degree of technical perfection in an artist.)

La Campanella is really a set of variations. The theme is a graceful staccato melody that moves by step and by skip over a fairly wide range. It is

presented in high register, softly. The right-hand thumb plays the tune, which is ornamented with high notes; this involves wide leaps. From here on we hear the melody in various rhythms, now in the left hand, now in the right, combined with trills and other ornaments. Finally the theme is presented in a dazzling display of octaves. The coda is marked Animato (animated), and brings the piece to its brilliant conclusion.

5. *Moment musical* in F minor, by Franz Schubert. Allegro moderato in ²⁄₄. This "musical moment" has all the wistful charm that we associate with Franz Schubert. *Moment musical* (mo-máhn mu-zi-cáhl) implies a piece that comes to the composer as a sudden inspiration and lasts only a little while. Over a staccato accompaniment in the left hand, the right hand traces a charming little tune. This melody is embellished with grace notes. A *grace note* is a very short note that has no time value of its own but is attached to the longer note that follows, as an ornament. You can always tell a grace note on the page because it is printed in smaller type than the other notes:

6. *Träumerei* (*tróy-meh-rye,* Dreaming), by Robert Schumann. Inspired by his love for his children, Schumann wrote a number of piano pieces that recall the moods and adventures of childhood. Many of them are easy enough for youngsters to play. The most famous is this reverie, an Andante in ⁴⁄₄ which presents one of the world's beloved melodies. Like many of Schumann's melodies, this one moves by skip rather than by step, and covers a wide range. It has the quality of a lovely daydream.

67

7. Waltz in A-flat, by Johannes Brahms. Moderato, $\frac{3}{4}$. When Brahms went to live in Vienna, he was fascinated by the waltz rhythm associated with the Austrian capital. Especially he admired the music of the "Waltz King," Johann Strauss. His own waltzes are not as lively as those of Strauss, but they have a quiet charm all their own.

The Waltz in A-flat has always been a favorite with the public. It presents a melody that moves by narrow skip and by step in four-measure phrases. The chief tune alternates with a subordinate phrase in the pattern A-B-A-B-A. Marked "tender and graceful," this Waltz shows Brahms' gift for flowing melody.

UNIT III

OPERA
AND
BALLET

❧|10A|❧

Getting to Know Opera

An *opera* is a play that is sung. Opera therefore is related to the theater, and operatic music is dramatic music. Opera combines vocal and orchestral music with ballet, poetry and drama, acting, scenery and costumes. The singers perform as soloists and in small groups; there may also be a chorus. The gifted opera composer is one who knows how to combine all these elements into an exciting musical drama.

The characters in an opera sing to each other instead of speaking. This of course goes against what happens in real life. Yet every art is based on certain conventions that go against real life. The characters in Shakespeare's dramas speak in blank verse, which they would hardly do in everyday speech. The people in a play are seated in a room from which one wall is missing so that the audience may look in. A poem may say simple things, but its lines are carefully arranged in patterns of meter and rhyme. A painting gives us an impression of depth, yet it is painted on a flat canvas. All these conventions are accepted by the spectator because, through them, the art work is able to arouse his emotions and his imagination. It is perfectly true that the characters in opera do not behave as people usually do. However, by violating the law of reality they create a reality of their own, which moves us in a very special way.

In many operas the dialogue that carries the plot and explains the action is presented in a kind of "talky" music known as *recitative* (reh-sih-tah-téev). This kind of musical recitation imitates the rhythms of speech. At the lyrical moments recitative gives way to an *aria* or sustained song. The aria is pure melody shaped to the curve of the human voice. It is what audiences wait for, what they wildly applaud, and what they remember.

71

THE METROPOLITAN OPERA HOUSE AT LINCOLN CENTER, NEW YORK

The emotional conflicts in opera are underlined by the contrast between different types of voice. The *soprano* is the highest female voice. The *coloratura soprano* is a brilliant type of voice that is able to execute rapid scales, trills, and leaps in the very highest register. The lyric soprano is a warmer, more expressive type of voice, as is the dramatic soprano. *Mezzo-soprano* and *contralto* are lower in range than the soprano. The hero of an opera is generally a *tenor*. Sometimes he is a *baritone,* a type of voice that has a lower range and fuller quality than the tenor. The *bass,* the lowest male voice, is generally assigned to roles associated with age and dignity.

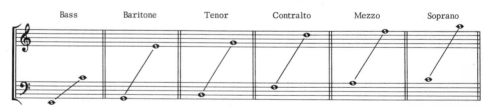

Shown above is the comfortable range for each type of voice; but singers are sometimes required to go beyond these limits.

Of great importance are the ensemble numbers—duets, trios, quartets, quintets, and so on—in which several characters pour out their feelings at the same time. The chorus is used together with the solo voices or it may function independently in the mass scenes. The orchestra provides the accompaniment, sets the mood, and creates the proper atmosphere for the various scenes. It may also play a piece before the opera or between the acts. A ballet may be included to provide a dance spectacle in the course of the action.

The text of an opera is called the *libretto,* and must be planned in such a way as to give the composer full opportunity for the various numbers—arias, duets, ensembles, choruses, marches, ballets, and finales—that make up an opera. At the same time the librettist has to create characters that reveal themselves through the drama. Above all he must fashion a story that lends itself to music.

The Life of Georges Bizet

Georges Bizet, composer of the greatest French opera of the nineteenth century, was born in Paris on October 25, 1838. He came of a musical family: his father taught singing, his mother was a talented pianist. Georges, as a small boy, was in the habit of listening to his father's lessons through the door, and would then repeat what the pupils had sung without ever having seen the music. He entered the Paris Conservatory when he was ten, and in the following years won all the prizes—for sight singing, piano-playing, organ, and composition. Finally he won the most important prize offered by the Conservatory, the Prix de Rome (pree duh rome), which gave him a three-year stay in the Italian capital at the government's expense.

His visit to Italy stimulated his imagination; he fell in love with the sun-drenched landscape of the south. When his scholarship was over he returned to Paris and became active in the musical life of the city. His early operas showed his interest in far-off lands. *The Pearl Fishers* was set in Ceylon; the action of *Djamileh* took place in Cairo. And in his incidental music to Alphonse Daudet's drama *L'Arlésienne* (The Woman of Arles), he conjured up the sunny fields of Provence. Thus he was well prepared for the great task of his life—the writing of *Carmen.*

Bizet's masterpiece was based on a celebrated tale about the loves of a fascinating Gypsy girl. *Carmen* showed the new interest of the nineteenth century in the common people; it was about Gypsies and soldiers, about smugglers and outlaws. Bizet expressed their emotions with passionate intensity. The audience that attended the opening night of *Carmen* at the popular opera house of Paris, the Opéra-Comique (o-pay-ráh coh-méek), was not accustomed to such realism on the stage. Some were shocked, others bored, but all failed to see the genius behind this great work. And the music critics were the blindest of all.

Still, the opera was not a total failure. The rumor spread that it was not quite respectable, and this attracted a number of people to the Opéra-Comique. *Carmen* was presented thirty-seven times in the next three months, an average of three times a week. In addition, the manager offered Bizet a contract for his next work. The failure of *Carmen* was mainly in Bizet's mind. He had put every ounce of his genius into the score, and he was bitterly disappointed when Paris failed to take his opera to its heart. His delicate constitution, worn out by months of overwork, was unable to bear the blow. He went to the country, near Paris, to recover his strength; but a throat infection brought on a fatal attack. He died in his thirty-seventh year, on June 3, 1875, just as the curtain had fallen on another performance of *Carmen*—and just when he had found his mature style.

Carmen was immediately dropped by the Opéra-Comique. However, within three years the opera made its way to Vienna and Brussels, London, and New York. Five years later it returned to Paris, was hailed as a masterpiece and became the most popular French opera ever written. Today, almost a century later, it remains one of the world's best-loved operas.

The Story of Carmen

The curtain rises on a square in Seville. Soldiers loiter before the guard house. Micaela (soprano) appears, inquiring for Don José. The young men try to flirt with her but she withdraws. A trumpet in the distance announces the changing of the guard. A crowd of street boys march with the soldiers, who are led by Lieutenant Zuniga (bass) and Corporal Don José (tenor). The clock strikes twelve. Girls come out of the cigarette factory and chat with the young men who are waiting for them. The girls are smoking—a daring detail in 1875! The young men throng around the fiery young Gypsy, Carmen (mezzo-soprano).

Don José, waiting for Micaela to return, is deep in thought. Carmen, annoyed by his indifference, takes a flower from her dress and throws it to him. José, bewildered, picks it up. Meanwhile the clock strikes in the factory and the girls withdraw. Micaela enters, bringing José a letter from his mother. The duet between them establishes José and Micaela as the "good people" in the play.

Micaela's departure is followed by a quarrel in the factory between Carmen and another girl. At once the stage is filled with chattering women. Carmen is led in, insolent, self-assured, and tries to strike one of the women who demands that she be sent to jail. Lieutenant Zuniga and his men go off to obtain an order for her arrest. Carmen, hands tied behind her back, is left in the care of José.

At once she tries to win him over. Near the ramparts of Seville, she tells him, is an inn where she will soon be dancing the gay seguidilla. What is more, she will dance it with him—if he will only set her free and join her there. José tries to resist temptation, but he doesn't have a chance. By the time the lieutenant returns, the rope around Carmen's wrists has been loosened. She is marched off to jail guarded by José. Their plan works perfectly; when they reach the bridge she knocks him down and escapes.

The second act takes place in the inn on the outskirts of Seville. Carmen sings a song celebrating the joys of Gypsy life. Lieutenant Zuniga flirts with Carmen, but her thoughts are on Don José. He had received two months in jail for helping her escape, and has just been set free. The bullfighter Escamillo (baritone) arrives and finds himself attracted to Carmen—which does not please Lieutenant Zuniga in the least. Both men leave, the lieutenant promising to return.

Two of the Gypsy smugglers invite Carmen and her two friends, Mercedes and Frasquita, to join them in a little business deal that evening: the girls will distract the guards while the smugglers bring their cargo across the border. Mercedes and Frasquita accept with delight, but Carmen remains behind to wait for Don José. The Gypsies leave, suggesting that Carmen recruit her new lover into the smugglers' band.

The scene between Carmen and José covers a variety of moods. She begins by dancing for him, accompanying herself on the castanets. José is enchanted. However, when the bugle sounds from the distant barracks, he prepares to leave. Carmen becomes furious at a sweetheart who puts duty above her; she mocks him and tells him to go. Don José assures her that he loves her. When Carmen realizes her power over him, she decides to lure him into the smugglers' band. Why, she asks, doesn't he join the Gypsies and follow her into the mountains, where they could live in utter freedom. To desert the army? José is horrified. He begs her not to tempt him, and begins to realize that he must give her up.

At this point there is a knock on the door. Lieutenant Zuniga breaks in. He cannot understand why Carmen would waste her time on a common soldier when she can have an officer. He orders José to leave. José, mad with jealousy, draws his sword. The two men fight and are separated by the Gypsies, who disarm Zuniga and lead him out. José no longer has a choice: he has attacked an officer and can return no more to the life he knew. The smugglers welcome the deserter with a rousing finale that hails the freedom of their lawless life.

The third act is laid in a lonely mountain pass that is the hideout of the smugglers. Don José gloomily reflects on his situation. His mother still thinks him an honest man. If she only knew! Carmen, who has already tired of him, suggests that he ought to return to his mother. They quarrel.

There follows the Card Trio that is one of the highlights of the opera. Frasquita and Mercedes tell their fortunes. The cards promise each what her heart desires—to Frasquita a handsome young lover who will take her away on his horse, to Mercedes a rich old husband who will die and leave her all his money. Carmen cuts the cards and draws the ace of spades—death! "I've read it well—first I, then he." But she is resigned, for she knows that fate cannot be cheated. The smugglers go off with their cargo, leaving Don José to guard the pass.

Micaela arrives, hoping still to save José from destruction. Then comes Escamillo, eager to join Carmen. An argument develops between the bullfighter and the jealous José. They draw their knives but are separated by the Gypsies. Escamillo invites them to his forthcoming bullfight in Seville. José learns from Micaela that his mother is dying and is persuaded to leave with her. "We will meet again!" he warns Carmen.

In the fourth act we see the square outside the bull ring in Seville. The crowd hails the toreadors, especially Escamillo, who is accompanied by Carmen. She is radiant. She notices Don José hiding among the crowd, and decides to settle things between them once and for all. Escamillo goes into the arena, followed by his admirers. Carmen remains to face the man whose life she has ruined.

The final scene between them is tense, violent. Each is driven by the basic law of his nature. José cannot give up his love; she cannot surrender her freedom. He begs her to go with him, saying that they will make a fresh start; but she refuses. Driven to the breaking point, he draws his knife and kills her as she tries to escape into the arena. The crowd hails the victorious Escamillo and pours out of the bull ring as Don José, dazed, kneels beside Carmen and admits his guilt.

75

Carmen, Acts I and II

1. The Overture foreshadows the contrasting moods of the opera. (An *overture* is a piece that serves to introduce an opera, drama, ballet, or similar long work.) The opening theme is one that will return in the last act outside the bull ring at Seville—a melody charged with excitement. Its gaiety is underlined by the pounding rhythm and bright orchestration:

There follows the suave melody of the Toreador Song:

The opening theme returns. Suddenly, beneath a tremolo on the strings, is heard the ominous theme of Fate that runs like a dark thread through the drama:

Notice the chord at the end of the Overture. It gives an effect of incompleteness. At this point the curtain goes up and the drama begins.

2. Habanera. Carmen's first aria is a *habanera*. This is a graceful dance rhythm in $\frac{2}{4}$, similar to the modern tango; it originated in Havana and became popular in Spain. Both the words and the music suggest Carmen's fickle character.

L'amour est un oiseau rebelle
  Que nul ne peut apprivoiser,
Et c'est bien en vain qu'on
    l'appelle
  S'il lui convient de refuser.
	Love is fickle and wild and free,
	  A bird that none may hope to tame,
	You will summon him quite in vain
	
	  If he decides to ignore your plea.

Rien n'y fait, menace ou prière,
  L'un parle bien, l'autre se tait;
	Nothing helps—neither threat nor prayer;
	  One may speak sweetly while the other
	    is quiet

Et c'est l'autre que je préfère:
  Il n'a rien dit; mais il me plait.
	Yet it's the other I prefer:
	  He said nothing, but I like him.

[Repeated by chorus]

L'amour est enfant de Bohème,   For love's a Gypsy child at heart,
  Il n'a jamais, jamais connu de   Who'll not be satisfied unless he's free;
    loi;
Si tu ne m'aimes pas, je t'aime;   If you don't love me, I love you,
  Si je t'aime, prends garde à toi!   And if I love you—beware!

[Repeated by chorus]

The second stanza of Carmen's song repeats and expands the idea presented in the first.

CARMEN, ACT I. A square in Seville.

3. Seguidilla and Duet. Carmen is seated outside the guard house, hands tied behind her back, and she begins singing to the seductive rhythm of the Spanish dance known as the *seguidilla* (se-ge-deé-ya).

Près des remparts de Séville,
  Chez mon ami Lillas Pastia,
J'irai danser la Séguedille
  Et boire du Manzanilla.
J'irai chez mon ami Lillas Pastia.
Oui, mais toute seule on s'ennuie,
  Et les vrais plaisirs sont à deux;
Donc, pour me tenir compagnie,
  J'emmènerai mon amoureux!
	Close to the walls of Seville,
	  With my good friend Lillas Pastia,
	I will dance the Sequidilla
	  And drink Manzanilla.
	I'll go to my friend Lillas Pastia.
	But it's very boring to go alone,
	  For true pleasures are shared by two;
	So, to keep me company,
	  I'll bring my sweetheart!

Mon amoureux, il est au diable,
  Je l'ai mis à la porte hier!
Mon pauvre cœur très consolable,
  Mon cœur est libre comme l'air!
	I sent my sweetheart to the devil,
	  I showed him the door yesterday!
	But my poor heart is very easily consoled,
	  My heart is as free as air!

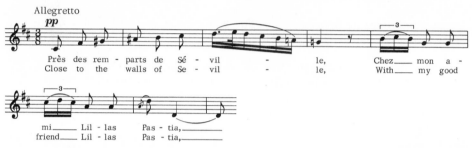

"Be quiet," Don José says sternly. "I told you not to speak to me." "But I'm not speaking to you," Carmen retorts. "I'm singing to myself. I'm thinking aloud—and there's no harm in that!" When she sees that Don José is weakening, she strikes home: "My soldier isn't a captain, not even a lieutenant. He's only a brigadier, but that's good enough for a Gypsy, and I'm quite content!" Don José is powerless against her. When she promises to meet him at the inn on the outskirts of Seville, he is ready to do anything for her—and lets her escape.

4. *Gypsy Song.* Carmen sings this number at the beginning of Act II, at the inn of Lillas Pastia. With each of the three stanzas the music becomes faster and wilder, building up steadily to the climax at the end.

Les tringles des sistres tintaient
  Avec un éclat métallique,
Et sur cette étrange musique
  Les Zingarellas se levaient.
	The Gypsy drums were beating loud,
	  And tambourines resounded brightly,
	And when they heard this music surging,
	  The Gypsy girls began to dance.

Tambours de Basque allaient leur
  train,
  Et les guitares forcenées
Grinçaient sous des mains
  obstinées,
  Même chanson, même refrain
  Tra la la la, tra la la la!
	The tambourines moved swiftly,
	
	  And the guitars, played
	By obstinate hands, pounded out
	
	  Ever the same song, the same refrain!
	  Tra la la la, tra la la la!

"The Gypsy men played with all their might. Their music bewitched the girls, who let themselves be carried away as in a fever, as by a whirl-wind . . ."

5. *Toreador Song.* Escamillo arrives at the inn and is hailed by his admirers. His celebrated aria describes the high point in a Toreador's life:

Votre toast, je peux vous le rendre,
  Señors, señors, car avec les
    soldats—
Oui, les Toréros peuvent s'entendre,
  Pour plaisirs ils ont les combats!

Le cirque est plein, c'est jour de
  fête!
  Le cirque est plein du haut en
    bas;
Les spectateurs, perdant la tête,
  S'interpellent à grand fracas!

Apostrophes, cris et tapage
  Poussés jusques à la fureur!
Car c'est la fête du courage!
C'est la fête des gens de cœur!
  Allons! en garde!

Here's a toast, a toast I drink gladly,
  Señors, señors, for we are brothers all!

Bullfighters and soldiers are brothers,
  For they both take delight in a good fight!

The arena is full on a holiday!—

  Full from top to bottom;

The crowd loses its head
  As it follows the exciting fight!

Shouts and cries and arguments
  Mount in fury!
For it's a test of courage—
This is a day for men of stout heart!
  Come! On guard!

Toréador, en garde! Toréador!
  Et songe bien, oui, songe en
    combatant
Qu'un œil noir te regarde
  Et que l'amour t'attend!

Toreador, on guard! Toreador!
  And remember, while you fight,

That a pair of dark eyes is watching you
  And that love awaits you!

To - ré - a - dor, en gar - de!____ To - ré - a-dor!__ To - ré - a-dor!__
To - re - a - dor, on guard!_____ To - re - a-dor!__ To - re - a-dor!__

The second stanza describes the encounter with the bull, the excitement of the spectators, the moment of victory—and the refrain: "And remember, while you fight . . . that love awaits you!" Thus, the change in the music from the stormy opening to the legato melody of the Toreador is caused by the change in his mood as his mind turns from thoughts of combat to the thought of love.

6. *Flower Song.* When Carmen scornfully tells him to go, since he does not love her, José sadly draws from his pocket the flower he has treasured these many weeks and sings the *Flower Song.*

La fleur que tu m'avais jetée,	Here is the flower that you threw me,
Dans ma prison m'était restée,	I kept it still in my dark cell.
Flétrie et sèche, cette fleur	Although faded and dry, this flower
Gardait toujours sa douce odeur;	Retained its sweet perfume;
Et pendant des heures entières,	And through many silent hours
Sur mes yeux fermant mes paupières,	It rested on my closed eyelids,
De cette odeur je m'enivrais	I delighted in its rare perfume,
Et dans la nuit je te voyais!	And in the night I saw you!

"I began to curse your name, I tried to hate you and to regret the fate that had sent you across my path. But then I felt only one desire within me, only one hope—to see you once again . . . Carmen, I love you!"

Andantino

La fleur que tu m'a-vais je - té - e, Dans ma pri - son___ m'é- tait res - té - e,
Here is the flow- er that you threw me, I kept it still___ in my dark cell.___

11

Carmen, Acts III and IV

1. Prelude to Act III. This orchestral introduction affords a breathing spell in the unfolding tragedy. A quiet solo on the flute, over harp accompaniment, prepares the listener for the scene in the mountain pass where the smugglers hide out. (The term *prelude* is used for a piece that introduces a single act of an opera. It is also sometimes used, like *overture,* for the piece that introduces the entire opera.)

2. *Card Song.* Carmen cuts the cards and draws the ace of spades. In an aria of enormous dignity she accepts her fate.

En vain pour éviter les réponses amères,
  En vain tu mêleras,
Cela ne sert à rien, les cartes sont sincères
  Et ne mentiront pas!
	In vain you shun the answer that you dread to hear,
	  In vain you cut the cards;
	To no avail! The cards are sincere
	
	  And will not lie!

Dans le livre d'en haut si ta page est heureuse,
  Mêle et coupe sans peur:
La carte sous tes doigts se tournera joyeuse,
  T'annonçant le bonheur!
	If in the book of heaven your page is bright,
	
	  Cut and deal without fear:
	The card in your hands will be a joyous one,
	  Announcing your good fortune!

Mais si tu dois mourir, si le mot redoubtable
  Est écrit par le sort,
Recommence vingt fois, la carte impitoyable
  Répétera: la mort!
	But if you are to die, if that dreadful word
	
	  Is written by Fate,
	Though you try twenty times, the pitiless card
	  Will repeat: Death!

CARMEN, ACT III.
A mountain pass, the hideout of the smugglers.

En vain pour é - vi - ter les ré-pon-ses a - mèr- es, En vain tu mê - le - ras,——
In vain you shun the an-swer that you dread to hear, In vain you cut the cards;——

3. *Micaela's Aria.* Making her way to the mountain pass, Micaela is overcome by fear.

Je dis, que rien ne m'épouvante,
    Je dis, hélas! que je réponds de
        moi;
Mais j'ai beau faire la vaillante,
    Au fond du cœur je meurs
        d'effroi!
	I say that I'll not be afraid,
	    I say, alas, I can depend on myself;
	
	But I pretend this courage in vain—
	    Deep in my heart I'm frightened to
	        death!

Seule en ce lieu sauvage,
    Toute seule j'ai peur,
    Mais j'ai tort d'avoir peur;
Vous me donnerez du courage,
    Vous me protègerez, Seigneur!
	Alone in this wild place,
	    Quite alone, I'm afraid,
	    Yet I'm wrong to be afraid;
	You will give me courage,
	    You will protect me, Lord!

    She is finally going to see the beautiful, dangerous woman who has taken
Don José from her. "But I shall not be afraid, I will speak firmly in her
presence. God, you will protect me!"

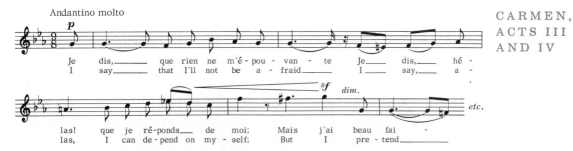

Andantino molto

Je dis,____ que rien ne m'é - pou - van - te Je dis,____ hé -
I say____ that I'll not be a - fraid____ I ____ say,____ a -

las! que je ré-ponds____ de moi; Mais j'ai beau fai -
las, I can de - pend on my - self; But I pre - tend____

4. Prelude to Act IV. A melody on the oboe is heard above an accompaniment of strings and drum, in the rhythm of an *aragonaise* (a dance from the province of Aragon, in a lively $\frac{3}{4}$ time). Despite its dance character, the music has a quality of foreboding.

Allegro vivo

5. Final Scene. "It's you?" Carmen asks. "It's me," Don José replies. People had warned her that he was back, she tells him, and that she ought to fear for her life. "But I am brave, I did not wish to run away." He comes not to threaten, he answers, but to implore. He asks her to go away with him so that they may begin a new life together. That, Carmen replies, is impossible. "Between you and me, everything is finished." "Then you do not love me any more?" "No, I do not love you."

CARMEN, ACT IV.
A square outside the bull ring in Seville.

Mais moi, Car-men, je t'aime en - co - re, Car - men, hé - las! moi, je t'a - do - re!
But   I, Car-men, I love you mad - ly! Car - men, a - las! I still a - dore___ you!

"But I, Carmen, I still love you. Alas, I adore you!" He promises to do anything she asks, he will even remain an outlaw for her sake, only she must not leave him. Carmen remains true to herself. She was born free, she insists, and she will die free.

The crowd in the arena is heard cheering the Toreador. Carmen runs toward the bullring, but José bars her way. "You love him?" he asks. "Yes, I love him!" Beside himself with rage, José insists that she come away with him. She pulls from her finger the ring he gave her and hurls it at him. He rushes at her, catches up with her at the entrance to the arena, and stabs her. The crowd hails the victorious Toreador and pours out of the arena as an agonized cry breaks from Don José: "You can arrest me. I killed her! Ah, my Carmen, my adored one!"

Thus ends this drama of love and death. Once you have heard it you will never forget it. And whenever you re-hear it, you will experience afresh the genius of Bizet and the passionate truth of his vision.

12

Italian Opera

Italy has always been the home of beautiful singing. So it is not to be wondered at that her composers developed an operatic art based on the expressive power of the human voice.

The Life of Giuseppe Verdi

Giuseppe Verdi, one of the most widely loved of all composers of opera, was born at Le Roncole, a village in central Italy, on October 10, 1813. His father kept a small tavern, and Giuseppe was raised in poverty. His first teacher was the parish priest. When he was ten he was sent to school in the neighboring town of Busseto. He learned to play the organ and soon became organist at the little church of his native village. He lived in Busseto with a shoemaker, a friend of his father, and on Sundays and feast days he would walk to Le Roncole barefoot, carrying his shoes so as not to wear them out.

His talent attracted the attention of a prosperous merchant of Busseto who loved music. He gave the youth a home and made it possible for him to continue his studies. When the penniless young musician fell in love with his benefactor's daughter, the merchant gladly accepted him as a son-in-law. Giuseppe and Margherita were married, and found great happiness together.

For the next three years Verdi was active in Busseto, but his thoughts turned more and more to Milan and its opera house, the famous La Scala. He finally decided to try his luck in Milan and arrived there with the manuscript of his first opera, which was accepted and produced at La Scala. As a result, the manager of La Scala gave him a contract to write three more operas.

At this point Verdi faced the first crisis of his career. He had lost his first child, a daughter, before coming to Milan. The second, a baby boy, was carried off by a fever. Then, several weeks later, his young wife died. "My family had been destroyed, and in the midst of these trials I had to fulfill my contract and write a comic opera!" This opera, called *King for a Day*, failed miserably. "In a sudden moment of depression I despaired of finding any comfort in my art and decided to give up composing."

The months passed, and the broken-hearted young composer kept to his decision. Although he had agreed to write two more operas, the director of La Scala did not press him. One night Verdi happened to meet this man, who showed him a libretto that had just been completed on the subject of Nebuchadnezzar, the King of Babylon who drove the Jews into capitivity. Verdi did not want to look at the script, but the director made him take it with him. "I came into my room and, throwing the manuscript angrily on the writing table, I stood for a moment motionless before it. The book opened as I threw it down. My eyes fell on the page and I read the line, *Go, my thought, on golden wings*." This was the first line of the chorus of captive Jews who, by the waters of Babylon, mourned their unhappy land. "Resolved as I was never to write again, I stifled my emotion, shut the book, and went to bed. I tried to sleep, but the music was running a mad course through my brain." In this fashion the musician was restored to his art. *Nabucco* (the Italian name for Nebuchadnezzar) was presented at La Scala the following season, won a triumph for the twenty-nine-year-old composer, and started him on a spectacular career.

Italy at this time was being born as a nation. The country was split into little states, most of them controlled by Austria. The Italian patriot Garibaldi was trying to free his homeland from the Habsburg yoke and to unite it under the House of Savoy. Verdi from the first identified himself with the national cause. "I am first of all an Italian!" he declared. In this tense atmosphere his works took on a special meaning for his countrymen. No matter in what time or place the opera was laid, they saw it as a symbol of their own sad plight. The chorus of exiled Jews from *Nabucco* became a patriotic song. As the revolutionary year 1848 approached, Verdi's operas furnished more and more material for the patriots. In the opera *Attila* the ambassador of the Romans says to the leader of the Huns, "You can take the world, but leave me Italy!" The line touched off wild demonstrations wherever the opera was given. In another opera a chorus of Italian knights vowed to drive the German invaders beyond the Alps. This chorus aroused frenzied enthusiasm throughout Italy.

Verdi became world famous with *Rigoletto, Il Trovatore* (The Troubadour), and *La Traviata* (The Lost One). Yet he remained a simple man at heart. He went back to his roots; he bought an estate at Busseto where he settled with his second wife Giuseppina, a famous soprano who had created the leading parts in his early operas. After Italy won independence Verdi was urged to stand for election to the first parliament. Although he was not interested in politics, he felt it was his duty to do whatever he could for the new Italy, and he served in parliament for several years.

With unflagging energy he moved from one masterpiece to the next. At the age of fifty-seven he wrote *Aïda*. At seventy-three he completed his greatest lyric tragedy, *Otello*. And at eighty he astonished the world with the comic opera *Falstaff*. He died in Milan on January 27, 1901, at the age of eighty-eight. His death was mourned throughout the world. He bequeathed the bulk of his fortune to a home for aged musicians that he had founded in Milan. Italy gave him the funeral of a national hero. Thousands followed his bier, and as they did they began to sing a melody—*Go, my thought, on golden wings.* It was the chorus from *Nabucco* that he had given his countrymen as a song of hope sixty years before.

*Giacomo
Puccini*

After Verdi, the most widely loved composer of Italian opera was Giacomo Puccini (jáh-co-mo poo-chée-nee). He was born in Lucca on December 22, 1858, and died in Brussels on November 29, 1924, at the age of sixty-six. Puccini produced the three most successful operas of the early twentieth century—*La Bohème, Tosca,* and *Madame Butterfly.* He was a romantic whose chief desire was to cast enchantment over the situations of everyday life—in other words, to make real life poetic. He was quite clear as to the scope of his gifts. "I am not made for heroic gestures. I love small things, and the only music I can or will make is the music of small things, so long as they are true and full of passion and humanity, and touch the heart." But when small things are true and full of passion and humanity, they become big things. For this reason Puccini's operas have delighted opera-goers the world over for more than half a century, and continue to do so.

*Three
Selections
by Verdi*

1. *Caro nome* (káh-ro nó-meh) from *Rigoletto.* Verdi's opera centers around the pleasure-loving Duke of Mantua (tenor), his court jester Rigoletto (baritone), and Rigoletto's young trusting daughter Gilda (jéel-dah, soprano). The Duke manages to win Gilda's love. But he soon tires of her and turns to other flirtations. She, however, remains faithful to the end, and when he is in danger she sacrifices her life to save him.

Her famous aria *Caro nome* occurs in the second act, when the Duke reveals to her that he loves her. He tells her that he is a poor student named Gualtier Maldè. After he leaves she repeats his name in ecstasy and pours out her feelings in a beautiful *coloratura aria*—that is, an aria in the highest, most brilliant register of the soprano voice, marked by a display of trills, arpeggios, rapid scales, and brilliant staccato notes. Notice how the flute, at the beginning of the aria, foreshadows the flute-like effect of the voice later on.

Caro nome che il mio cor	Dearest name, that taught my heart
festi primo palpitar,	All the joy of tender love . . .
le delizie dell'amor	How you waken sweet desire
mi dêi sempre rammentar!	For the one whom I adore!
Col pensier il mio desir	All my thoughts now turn to you,
a te sempre volerà,	All my hopes, my dreams, my life:
e fin l'ultimo sospir,	When I die, my very last breath
caro nome, tuo sarà . . .	Will repeat the name I love.

[*These lines are repeated for the rest of the aria.*]

2. *La Donna è mobile* (lah dóh-nah ay mó-bee-lay) from *Rigoletto,* Act III. This extremely popular aria is not only a delightful melody in itself but also reveals the character of the Duke, who lives only for his own pleasure. The music is bright, manly, assertive. Naturally, the Duke blames women for his own fickleness and selfishness.

The melody, an Allegretto in $\frac{3}{8}$, is repeated for a second stanza. Thus the aria is in strophic form. It is cast in the style of a gay waltz.

La donna è mobile qual piuma al	Women are frivolous, women are
vento,	changeable,
muta d'accento e di pensiero.	Now they adore you, now they ignore you!
Sempre un amabile leggiadro viso,	Women are lovable, women are dangerous,
in pianto o in riso, è menzognero.	One day they kiss you, then they dismiss you.

[*The first 2 lines are repeated.*]

È sempre misero chi a lei s'affida,	Smiling seductively, they bring us misery,
chi le confida mal cauto il core!	Yet we pursue them, tenderly woo them.
Pur mai non sentesi felice appieno	Pleasure and happiness lie at their mercy,
chi su quel seno non liba amore!	Though we may doubt them . . . can't do without them!

[*The first 2 lines of Stanza I are repeated.*]

87

3. Quartet from *Rigoletto,* Act III. Music drama is able to do something
that spoken drama can never do: it allows several characters to pour out their
conflicting emotions simultaneously. The ensemble—whether duet, trio,
quartet, quintet, or sextet—is one of the most exciting features of operatic
art. And the Quartet from *Rigoletto* is one of the most exciting among operatic ensembles.

RIGOLETTO, ACT III.   The Quartet.

The scene takes place in a deserted inn outside Mantua, where the Duke
has come to court the lively Maddalena (contralto). Rigoletto, wishing to
cure Gilda of her love, brings his daughter to see for herself how faithless her
sweetheart is. They peer into the inn through a crack in the wall, while the
Duke is flirting with Maddalena. He declares his love for her and promises to
marry her. She tells him that she doesn't believe a word he says; promises
are cheap.

Outside, the broken-hearted Gilda realizes that she has been betrayed,
while Rigoletto grimly swears to avenge his daughter. The Duke begins
alone with his romantic melody, an Andante in $\frac{4}{4}$; then the other voices join
in and blend with his.

DUKE

Bella figlia dell'amore,	Irresistible enchantress,
schiavo son de' vezzi tuoi;	I am dazzled by your beauty.
con un detto, un detto sol tu puoi	You could comfort all my pain and sorrow
le mie pene, le mie pene consolar.	With a single word, a single word of love.

Vieni e senti del mio core
  il frequente palpitar.
  Con un detto, un detto sol tu
    puoi
le mie pene, le mie pene consolar.

Oh my darling, could I tell you
  Of the anguish in my heart!
  You could comfort all my pain and
    sorrow
With a single word, a single word of love.

MADDALENA

Ah! ah! rido ben di core,
  che tai baje costan poco;
  quanto valga il vostro gioco,
mel credete, so apprezzar.

Oh you flatter most divinely
  And it really costs you nothing!
  Take my word, I know exactly
What your compliments are worth.

Son avvezza, bel signore,
  ad un simile scherzare,
    mio bel signor!

I must tell you very plainly
  You're exactly like the others.
    I know your kind!

GILDA

Ah, così parlar d'amore;
  a me pur l'infame ho udito!
  Infelice cor tradito,
per angoscia non scoppiar.

Ah, to speak of love so lightly!
  The very words he spoke to me!
  I cannot bear this dreadful torment;
My heart must break from sheer despair.

RIGOLETTO

Taci! il piangere non vale;
  ch'ei mentiva on sei sicura.
  Taci, e mia sarà la cura
la vendetta d'affrettar!

Quiet! There's no more time for weeping.
  Now you realize he was lying!
  Do not weep, my darling daughter,
I shall hasten our revenge!

An ensemble of this kind depends not so much on the individual lines as on the effect of the whole. The words can be understood only at the beginning, when each character in turn expresses his thoughts. Once the four voices are singing together, the text is no longer important; only the interplay of the melodies matters. For this reason the above lines are repeated over and over again throughout the Quartet.

4. *Un bel dì* (oon bel dee) from *Madame Butterfly*, Act II. The heroine of Puccini's moving opera is the fifteen-year-old Geisha girl Cio-Cio-San (cho-cho-sán, soprano), who is known as Madame Butterfly. When Lieutenant Pinkerton of the United States Navy is stationed in Japan, he goes through a Japanese wedding with her. For him this is a lark, but to her the marriage is as sacred as love itself. Pinkerton returns to the United States, promising to come back. Butterfly waits patiently for him, with their little boy and her faithful attendant Suzuki. Every one around her tells her that Pinkerton will never return, but Butterfly refuses to listen. When Suzuki voices her doubts, Butterfly replies with the great aria in which she imagines the moment of his return. The little Geisha takes on enormous dignity as she asserts her love and her faith.

*Three
Selections
by Puccini*

89

BUTTERFLY SINGING
UN BEL DÌ.

Un bel dì, vedremo	One day we'll be seeing
levarsi un fil di fumo sull' estremo	A thread of smoke arising from the sea,
confin del mare.	From the far horizon.
E poi la nave appare,	And then the ship appears,
poi la nave bianca	Then the white ship
entra nel porto, romba il suo saluto.	Enters the harbor, thunders its salute.
Vedi? È venuto!	You see? He has come!
Io non gli scendo incontro. Io no.	I don't go down to meet him. Oh, no!
Mi metto là sul ciglio del colle e aspetto,	I place myself at the top of the hill, and wait,
e aspetto gran tempo e non mi pesa,	And wait a long time, and do not mind
la lunga attesa.	The long waiting.
E . . . uscito dalla folla cittadina	Then . . . coming out of the crowded city
un uomo, un picciol punto	A man, a tiny speck
s'avvia per la collina.	That moves towards the hill.
Chi sarà? Chi sarà?	Who will it be? Who indeed?
E come sarà giunto,	And when he arrives,
che dirà? Che dirà?	What will he say? What?
Chiamerà Butterfly dalla lontana.	He'll call "Butterfly" from the distance.
Io senza dar riposta me ne starò nascosta	I shan't answer him—I'll hide,
un po' per celia, un po' per non morire	Partly to tease him, and partly not to die
al primo incontro, ed egli alquanto in pena	At our first meeting. And he, a little worried,
chiamerà, chiamerà:	Will call, will call,
"Piccina mogliettina,	"Little wife,
olezzo di verbena,"	Verbena blossom!"—
i nomi che mi dava al suo venire.	The names he gave me when he came here.
Tutto questo avverrà, te lo prometto.	All this will come to pass, I promise you.
Tienti la tua paura,	Keep your fears to yourself.
io con sicura fede l'aspetto.	I await him, secure in my faith.

Andante molto calmo

Un___ bel di, ve - dre - mo   le - var - si un fil di   fu - mo sull' e -
One___ day we'll be   see - ing   a thread___ of smoke a - ris - ing, From the

poco rall.

stre - mo con-fin del ma - re.   E   poi___ la na-ve ap - pa - re___
sea,___ from the far ho - ri - zon.   And   then___ the ship ap - pears.___

In Act III Butterfly's dream comes true: the ship does steam into the harbor. But Pinkerton is on it with the woman whom he regards as his real
wife—his American wife. Cio-Cio-San draws out the sword that was bequeathed to her by her father, and kills herself.

5. *Che gelida manina* (keh jéh-lee-dah mah-née-nah) from *La Bohème* (lah
bo-éhm) by Giacomo Puccini. Bohemia is the name given to any neighbor-
hood where artists live and work, or to the artistic life (as when we say,
"He's a bohemian"). The action of the opera takes place in the Latin
Quarter of Paris, on the left bank of the Seine, and concerns four young
men—a poet, a painter, a musician, and a philosopher—who live in an attic
and dream of the time when they will be successful and famous.

It is Christmas Eve, and Rodolfo, the poet (tenor), is trying to finish an
article he is supposed to write. But he is not in the mood. Suddenly there is
a knock on the door. Enter Mimi—and romance. She is a little seamstress
who lives at the head of the stairs. Her candle has gone out; will he please
light it? She leaves but soon returns, having missed her key. Their candles
are extinguished by a gust of wind; they search for the key on their knees, in
the dark. Rodolfo finds it and has the presence of mind to slip it into his

LA BOHÈME, ACT I.
Rodolfo and Mimi.

pocket. When their hands touch it is time for an aria—Rodolfo's—and it is in-
finitely tender and poetic.

Che gelida manina,	How cold your little fingers . . .
se la lasci riscaldar.	Let me warm them here in mine.
Cercar che giova? Al buio	Our search is hopeless . . .
non si trova. Ma per fortuna	Now all is veiled in darkness.
è una notte di luna,	See where the moon hides her pale silver beauty!
e qui la luna l'abbiamo vicina.	Her gentle glow soon will brighten the shadows.
Aspetti, signorina,	And now if you'll allow me,
le dirò con due parole chi son,	I should like so much to tell you
chi son, e che faccio, come vivo.	Just who I am, what my goal—my aims— my striving.
Vuole?	May I?
Chi son? Chi son? Son un poeta.	My life? My work? I am a poet.
Che cosa faccio? Scrivo.	A poet's pleasure? Rhyming!
E come vivo? Vivo.	A poet's pastime? Dreaming!
In povertà mia lieta	In poverty contented,
scialo da gran signore	Sonnets and songs I fashion
rime ed inni d'amore.	Out of love, out of passion!
Per sogni e per chimere	My castles in the air enfold
e per castelli in aria	Such fantasies and treasures,
l'anima ho milionaria.	I am indeed a millionaire!
Talor dal mio forziere	But now, as though by magic spell,
ruban tutti i gioielli	To my castle of dreams you come
due ladri: gli occhi belli.	And bring me strange enchantment.
V'entrar con voi pur ora	Your pale and haunting beauty
ed i miei sogni usati,	Wakens a poet's fancy:
ed i bei sogni miei	Rapture fills my heart!
tosto si dileguar!	Vision so bright and fair,
Ma il furto non m'accora	Alas, too soon may vanish . . .
poichè, poichè v'ha preso stanza	And yet I will banish all sorrow—
la speranza.	Hope enthralls my being!
Or che mi conoscete	Now you know my story . . .
parlate voi. Deh parlate.	Would you oblige me? Won't you
Chi siete? Vi piaccia dir?	Answer me freely and tell me yours?

The aria rises in a broad line of melody to the emotional high point
where we hear the love theme of the opera, on the words *Talor dal mio
forziere* ("But now, as though by magic spell, to my castle of dreams you
come"):

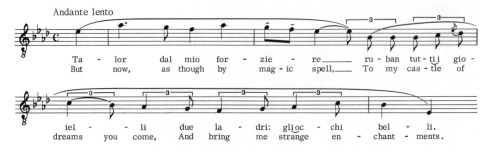

6. *Musetta's Waltz* from *La Bohème*. Musetta (soprano) is a pert young lady in love with Rodolfo's friend, the painter Marcello (baritone). They have quarreled and no longer see each other. She arrives at the Cafe Momus on Christmas Eve in the company of an elderly admirer (bass), whom she keeps addressing as though he were a pet dog. As soon as she sees Marcello and his friends, she does everything in her power to attract their attention.

LA BOHÈME, ACT II.   Musetta at the Cafe Momus.

She is especially annoyed that her former sweetheart pretends not to notice her. At this point she sings her famous Waltz, which is not only a lovely melody in its own right but also establishes her character as a pretty young girl who loves to flirt.

Quando me'n vo soletta per la via, la gente sosta e mira, e la bellezza mia— tutta ricerca in me, ricerca in me da capo a piè.	Smiling and gay, I stroll along the avenue alone, The gentlemen admire me so! Lured by my charm and beauty, They watch as I pass them by— I am the only one they adore!
Ed asaporo allor la bramosia	And when they smile I can sense their fierce desire
sottil che dagli occhi traspira e dai palesi vezzi intender sa	In their glance bright with passion, Their eyes revealing plainly how I tempt them . . .
alle occulte beltà.	Not a one can resist!
Così l'effluvio del desìo tutta m'aggira. Felice mi fa,	This endless game of gay flirtation I find delightful. What pleasure to charm them,

felice mi fa.

What pleasure to charm them!

E tu che sai,
che memorie ti struggi,
da me tanto rifuggi?

Lonely and grieving,
You wish you could ignore me,
And yet you still adore me!

So ben, le angoscie tue
non le vuoi dir—
non le vuoi dir, so ben—
ma ti senti morir!

In vain you still resist,
In vain you flee.
I know too well your heart is mine—
Darling, love only me!

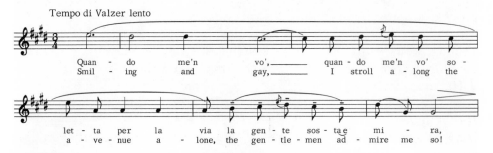

Tempo di Valzer lento

Quan - do me'n vo',_____ quan - do me'n vo' so -
Smil - ing and gay,_____ I stroll a - long the

let - ta per la via la gen - te sos - ta e mi - ra,
a - ve - nue a - lone, the gen - tle - men ad - mire me so!

Needless to say, Marcello cannot resist. Musetta finds an excuse to send the elderly gentleman away, and is soon happy in Marcello's arms.

The operas of Verdi, Puccini, and their countrymen represent Italy's major contribution to the art of music. They are emotional works that sing of love, sorrow, and joy. They are admired all over the world.

13

German Opera

German opera followed a different path from Italian and French opera. The Germans created a type of opera in which the orchestra played a crucial role. This development reached its highest point in the works of the greatest German operatic composer, Richard Wagner (vóg-ner).

He was born in Leipzig on May 22, 1813, the son of a minor official who died when Richard was still an infant. It was his stepfather, a talented actor, who encouraged Richard to take an interest in art.

The future composer had only about six months' instruction in music theory; the rest he learned by himself. When he was twenty he left the University of Leipzig, determined to make his way in the operatic world. He found a position as chorus master in a small opera house. In the next six years he gained experience as a conductor in small theaters in the provinces. He fell in love with the actress Minna Planer, whom he married when he was twenty-three. And he began to compose operas. From the beginning he wrote his librettos as well. In this way he was able to achieve the closest possible union between the drama and the music.

His first important opera, *Rienzi, Last of the Tribunes,* was based on a novel by the English writer Bulwer-Lytton. With the first two acts of *Rienzi* under his arm, Wagner set out to conquer the world. His destination was Paris. But the world was not easily conquered. Despite all his efforts, he was unable to persuade the directors of the Paris Opera to accept *Rienzi.* In order to earn a living he did odd jobs, such as arranging popular arias for the cornet, and wrote articles, essays, and reviews. Although he was poor and discouraged, he managed to complete *Rienzi* and worked on his next opera, *The Flying Dutchman.*

Just as he was beginning to lose heart, *Rienzi* was accepted by the opera house in Dresden. On his way to Dresden he saw the Rhine for the first time. With tears in his eyes, he later wrote, he "swore eternal fidelity to the German fatherland." *Rienzi* won a great success at Dresden. As a result, the thirty-year-old composer was appointed conductor to the King of Saxony.

After *Rienzi* Wagner moved away from grand opera, which was usually based on a complicated plot drawn from history. His next three operas—*The Flying Dutchman, Tannhäuser,* and *Lohengrin*—are highly poetic works based on German legends and folk tales. But the Dresden public was not prepared to accept Wagner's new style. They had come to see another *Rienzi,* and they were disappointed.

Many artists, eager for fame and wealth, have ended by producing what the public wanted. Wagner was not one of these. He wanted to create a serious theater that would serve his ideals. More and more he found himself opposed to the court, which regarded opera as an amusement. Wagner gradually realized that he could not reform the theater without trying to reform society itself. As the year 1848 approached, he found himself more and more in sympathy with those who dreamed of a revolution in Europe that would end the power of kings. Although it was dangerous for him to do so, he appeared as a speaker at a club of radical workingmen; and he published articles that expressed his views. "The present order," he wrote, "is hostile to the rights of man. The old world is crumbling to ruin. A new world will be born from it!"

The revolution broke out in Dresden in May 1849. The King and his court fled from the city. Within a few days the army of the King of Prussia arrived in Dresden and crushed the rebellion. The leaders of the uprising were captured. Wagner escaped, disguised as a coachman, and fled to Weimar (vý-mahr), where lived his friend, the composer Franz Liszt. There Wagner learned that a warrant had been issued for his arrest. With the aid of Liszt he made his way across the border and found refuge in Switzerland.

In the eyes of the world—and of his wife—Wagner was a ruined man. But he did not in the least share this opinion. "It is impossible," he wrote, "to describe my delight when I felt free at last—free from the world of ever unsatisfied desires, free from the distressing surroundings that had called forth such desires." He settled in Zurich and entered on the most productive period of his career. For four years he wrote no music at all. Instead he turned out a series of books in which he tried to explain his aims and ideals. Among these were *Art and Revolution, The Art Work of the Future,* and a work called *Opera and Drama,* in which he set forth his theory of the *music drama,* as he called his kind of opera. Then he began work on *The Ring of the Nibelung,* a cycle of four music dramas on the life and death of the German hero Siegfried. The cycle consisted of *Das Rheingold* (The Gold of the Rhine), *Die Walküre* (The Valkyrie), *Siegfried,* and *Götter-dämmerung* (The Twilight of the Gods).

In the middle of this task he grew tired, as he said, "of heaping one silent score upon the other." He wrote two music dramas that he thought might have a better chance of being performed: *Tristan and Isolde,* his master-piece, and *The Master Singers of Nuremberg,* one of the great comic operas of the world. These years were the darkest of Wagner's life. The mighty scores accumulated in his drawer without hope of performance, for there were neither theaters nor singers in Europe capable of presenting them. He was in bitter need of money. He had separated from Minna, who failed to understand him. He felt lonely and defeated, and thought in turn of com-mitting suicide, going to America, or escaping to the East.

At this point came a miraculous turn of events. An eighteen-year-old boy who loved Wagner's music ascended the throne of Bavaria as Ludwig II. One of the first things the young king did was to summon the composer to Mu-nich. Ludwig asked him to complete the *Ring,* and Wagner took up the task where he had left off a number of years before. A theater was planned espe-cially for his music dramas. And to crown his happiness he found a woman equal to him in will and courage—Cosima, the daughter of his old friend Liszt.

The victory of Prussia over France in 1870, which resulted in the founding of the German Empire, created an atmosphere of patriotism favorable to Wagner's music dramas. His theater was finally built at Bayreuth (bý-roit); his ideas and music spread across Europe. Wagner societies throughout the world gathered funds to support the theater. The *Ring* cycle was completed twenty-six years after he had begun it, and the four dramas were presented, in the presence of the German Emperor and the King of Ba-varia, at the first Bayreuth festival in 1876.

His last music drama, *Parsifal,* was based on the legend of the Holy Grail. Wagner finished it as he approached seventy. He died in Venice on February 13, 1883, truly a conqueror, and was buried in Bayreuth.

Wagner called his later works *music dramas* in order to stress the close connection he tried to achieve between music and drama. "Every bar of dramatic music," he believed, "is justified only by the fact that it explains something in the action or in the character of the actor."

To achieve this goal, he based his music dramas on a number of basic themes which—by their melody, harmony, and rhythm—suggest the various characters of the drama. These themes might also be associated with an emotion—love, hate, revenge; an object—the Gold of the Rhine, the Ring, the Sword; or a landscape—the Rhine River, Valhalla, the lonely shore of Tristan's home. The basic themes trace the course of the drama. They change as the characters change; they gather meaning from one scene to the next, until they themselves become characters in the orchestral drama that accompanies the drama on stage; they begin to represent the forces of good and evil, life and death, that rule the destinies of gods and heroes.

Richard Strauss, the most famous composer of the early twentieth century, was born in Munich on June 11, 1864. He won fame with a series of brilliant compositions for orchestra. Among them were *Don Juan, Death and Transfiguration, The Merry Pranks of Till Eulenspiegel,* and *A Hero's Life.* In the early years of this century Strauss conquered the operatic stage with three international successes: *Salome* (sá-lo-may), *Elektra,* and *Der Rosenkavalier* (The Knight of the Rose). After a long and active career Strauss died in his villa in the Bavarian Alps on September 8, 1949, at the age of eighty-five.

Strauss inherited the tradition of Wagner. But he introduced into German music something of the lovely melody of the Italians and the lively rhythm of the French. He transformed the orchestra into a huge ensemble in which all the instruments took part on an equal basis. His music is full of imaginative effects. The harmonies he used were in his day considered revolutionary. But he knew that in time they would be accepted, as indeed they were. It was Strauss's role to bring German music from the nineteenth century into the twentieth. This he did with such brilliance that he became one of the major figures of his generation.

1. *Song to the Evening Star,* from *Tannhäuser* (táhn-hoy-zer). During the Middle Ages the knightly poets of the courts engaged in tournaments of song. The action of this opera revolves around such a contest, Tannhäuser (tenor) being the chief knight-minstrel at the court of Thuringia. Both he and his friend Wolfram (baritone) love the Princess Elizabeth (soprano), although Tannhäuser has been unfaithful to her. In the last act, when Elizabeth is dying, Wolfram (vóol-frahm) sings a famous aria in which he invokes the blessings of the Evening Star upon her soul.

The *Song to the Evening Star* illustrates the difference in style between recitative, which imitates the patterns of speech, and the more melodious line of the aria. In the opening measures of the recitative, arpeggios in the orchestra suggest the broken chords of the minstrel's lyre. Notice the tremolos in the strings by means of which Wagner suggests darkness and fear. In the aria, simple chords in the orchestra accompany the melody. The recitative, in $\frac{4}{4}$, is marked Moderato. The aria is an Andante in $\frac{6}{8}$.

Wie Todesahnung, Dämm'rung deckt die Lande,	Twilight covers the land like the presence of Death,
umhüllt das Thal mit schwärzlichem Gewande;	And enfolds the valley in darkness.
der Seele, die nach jenen Höh'n verlangt,	Man's soul, longing for distant heights,
vor ihrem Flug durch Nacht und Grausen bangt.	Fears to pass through the shadow of night.
Da scheinest du, o lieblichster der Sterne,	Then you shine bright, O kindly star,
dein sanftes Licht entsendest du der Ferne;	And send your gentle light from afar;
die nächt'ge Dämm'rung teilt dein lieber Strahl,	Your lovely glow parts the twilight,
und freundlich zeigst du den Weg aus dem Tal.	To guide us, like a friend, out of the valley.
O du, mein holder Abendstern,	Oh, thou my lovely evening star,
wohl grüsst' ich immer dich so gern;	Gently I greet you from afar.
vom Herzen, das sie nie verriet,	Greet thou my heart's true love
grüsse sie, wenn sie vorbei dir zieht.	When her spirit soars aloft and passes thee by.
Wenn sie entschwebt dem Tal der Erden,	When she soars above earth's valley
ein sel'ger Engel dort zu werden,	To become an angel on high,
wenn sie entschwebt dem Tal der Erden,	When she soars above earth's valley
ein sel'ger Engel dort zu werden.	To become an angel on high.

2. *Magic Fire Scene,* from *Die Walküre* (dee vahl-kúrr-uh—The Valkyrie), Act III. The Valkyries, according to Norse mythology, were the nine daughters of Wotan (vó-tahn), father of the gods; his name survives in our *Wednesday*—that is, Wotan's day. It was the task of the Valkyries to circle above the battlefield on their steeds, pick up the warriors who had fallen in battle, and carry them off to Valhalla, the home of the gods, where they would sit feasting forevermore.

The action of *Die Walküre* revolves around the ill-fated love of Siegfried's

DIE WALKÜRE, ACT III. Wotan's farewell to Brünnhilde.

parents, Siegmund (séeg-moond) and Sieglinde (seeg-lín-duh). Siegmund, having incurred the displeasure of Wotan, must die. The father of the gods instructs the Valkyrie Brünnhilde (brun-híll-duh) to carry out the punishment. Moved to pity, she tries to save Siegmund. By disobeying Wotan she brings upon herself the full force of her father's anger. He decrees that she is to forfeit her position as a goddess and become a mortal, and know all the pain and sorrow of mortal women.

Brünnhilde, horrified, asks Wotan how he can possibly leave her to the mercy of any man who will overpower her. Wotan makes one concession: he will put her into a deep sleep and cause a magic fire to surround the rock on which she lies. Only the true hero—he who knows no fear—will be able to pass through the flames and claim her as his bride.

Sorrowfully Wotan bids farewell to her whom he loved so well. She lies down on the rock and sinks into a deep sleep as Wotan raises his spear to summon Loge, the god of fire.

Loge, hör'! Lausche hieher!	Loge, hear! Now appear!
Wie zuerst ich dich fand, als feurige Glut,	As I found you once, a flickering fire,
wie dann einst du mir schwandest,	As you vanished from me,
als schweifende Lohe;	An elusive flame;
wie ich dich band, bann ich dich heut!	As I bound you once, so I bind you now!
Herauf, wabernde Lohe,	Appear, flickering flame,
umlodre mir feurig den Fels!	Surround this rock with fire!
Loge! Loge! Hieher!	Loge! Loge! Appear!

(Wotan strikes the rock with his spear.)

| Wer meines Speeres Spitze fürchtet, | He who fears my spear |
| durchschreite das Feuer nie! | Shall never pass through the flames! |

The god of fire obeys; a curtain of flame surrounds the rock, gradually hiding Brünnhilde from view. Wagner's fantasy translates the soaring of the flames into music; the sounds crackle and leap into the air. Excitement is heightened by Wagner's use of chromatic scales. (The *chromatic scale* includes all the twelve semitones of the octave; on the piano, for example, the seven white and five black keys between C and C. Rapid chromatic scales are frequently used to suggest the sound of storm and wind; also emotions such as fear and suspense.) As the orchestra plays the serene theme of the Magic Fire, Wotan sings the last two lines of his farewell. We hear the theme of Siegfried; for he is the hero who, in the next drama of the *Ring* cycle, will fearlessly pass through the flames and awaken Brünnhilde with a kiss.

The final scene of *Die Walküre* evokes a mood of tender farewell. As the curtain slowly falls upon this German version of the "Sleeping Beauty" legend, the rock is enveloped in flames, against which is outlined the majestic figure of the father of the gods in his black cloak, spear uplifted. It makes an unforgettable picture, behind which we sense the mighty imagination of the magician of Bayreuth.

3. *Dance of the Apprentices* and *Entrance of the Master Singers* from *Die Meistersinger von Nürnberg* (The Master Singers of Nuremberg), Act III. Not only the knights of the medieval courts held tournaments of song; the citizens of the towns also had their music festivals, at which prizes were awarded for the best poems and songs. One such contest, held in the ancient town of Nuremberg, has been immortalized in Wagner's comic opera.

The *Dance of the Apprentices* takes place while the people of Nuremberg, in a holiday mood, await the arrival of the Master Singers. A group of journeymen (slightly older workmen) try to take the girls away from the apprentices. A staccato tune in $\frac{3}{4}$ time, a kind of rustic waltz, points up the clumsy movements of the merry lads as they perform a vigorous dance with the peasant girls. Notice the grace notes in the melody, which is repeated over and over.

There is mounting excitement at the arrival of the Master Singers. Attired in silks and satins, they advance with pompous dignity to the platform where the prizes are to be awarded. A steady crescendo suggests their ap-

DIE MEISTERSINGER VON NÜRNBURG, ACT III. The song contest.

proach. Now the theme of the Master Singers is heard in the brass, as the colorful procession reaches the scene:

A fanfare-like melody played by the brass choir brings the march to its majestic end. This music suggests a scene of brilliant pageantry. It is very grand, very Wagnerian, and very German.

4. *Der Rosenkavalier* (The Knight of the Rose), Closing Scene of Act II. In his enchanting comic opera, Richard Strauss conjured up the Vienna of Empress Maria Theresa in the middle of the eighteenth century. The action revolves around the eternal struggle between youth and its elders. The Princess Werdenberg—she is the wife of a Field Marshal, so she is known as the Marschallin—is in love with a youth of noble birth, Octavian. Through this love with someone much younger than herself she tries to hold on to her fading youth. Her cousin, Baron Ochs von Lerchenau, is an arrogant nobleman who has arranged to marry Sophie, the beautiful young daughter of an enormously wealthy merchant. He wants her dowry, and the merchant wants the prestige of having a nobleman for a son-in-law. It was the custom among the Viennese aristocrats for the bridegroom to send a silver rose to his bride. The Baron asks Octavian to deliver the rose. When Sophie and Octavian see each other, they fall in love immediately. And when Sophie later meets the Baron,

Two Scenes from Der Rosenkavalier

101

she decides she will never marry such a silly old boor. The rest of the plot centers around the efforts of the young lovers to outwit the schemes of their elders. Needless to say, love triumphs in the end.

In order to capture the spirit of Vienna, the original city of the waltz, Strauss composed some irresistible waltzes for his opera. These are scattered throughout the work. The principal waltz melody opens the final scene of Act II. The cowardly Baron has been lightly scratched in a duel with Octavian. He is lying down, his right arm bandaged. Restless, he wishes some romantic adventure would come along to distract him. Meanwhile, Octavian hits upon a plan to unmask the Baron for the scoundrel he is. He sends a faked letter to the Baron through Annina, who is helping him. The letter supposedly comes from a chambermaid who has caught the Baron's fancy, making a date for the following evening. The Baron falls into the trap.

BARON

(repeating what he had told the chambermaid)

"Ohne mich, ohne mich, jeder Tag Dir so bang,
mit mir, mit mir, keine Nacht Dir so lang."

"Without me your days will pass so slowly,
With me, time will never seem long."

(He catches sight of Annina, who holds out a letter.)

Für mich?

For me?

ANNINA

Von der Bewussten.

From someone you know.

BARON

Wer soll damit g'meint sein?

Whom do you mean?

ANNINA

Nur eigenhändig insgeheim zu übergeben.

I'm supposed to give it to you personally, in secret.

BARON

(to his servants)

Luft da!

Be off!

(They withdraw.)

Zeig' Sie den Wisch!

Give it to me!

(He tears the letter open with his left hand and tries to read it, holding it as far as possible from him.)

Such' Sie in meiner Tasch' meine Brillen.

Look in my pocket for my glasses.

(suspiciously, as she is looking)

Nein! Such' Sie nicht!
Kann Sie Geschriebnes lesen? Da!

No, don't look!
Can you read? Here . . .

"Herr Kavalier! Den morgigen
   Abend hätt' i frei.

Sie ham mir schon g'fall'n, nur
   g'schamt

hab' i mi von der fürstli'n Gnade,

weil i noch gar so jung bin.

Das bewusste Mariandel,
   Kammerzofel und Verliebte.

Wenn der Herr Kavalier den
   Namen

nit schon vergessen hat.

I wart' auf Antwort."

"Noble Sir, t'morrow night I'm off.

I like you fine, but I was bashful

While my mistress was there,

'Cause I'm so young.

Your devoted little Marianne,
   chambermaid, who loves you.

I hope, Noble Sir,

You have not forgotten me.

I wait for your reply."

BARON

(delighted)

Sie wart' auf Antwort!

Geht all's recht am Schnürl so wie
   z'Haus,

und hat noch einen andren Schick
   dazu.

Ich hab' halt schon einmal ein
   Lerchenauisch' Glück.

Komm' Sie nach Tisch, geb' Ihr die
   Antwort nachher schriftlich.

She waits for my reply!

It's going well, just like at home,

And so elegant besides!

I have all the luck of my ancestors!

Come back after I have dined, and I'll give
   you the answer in writing.

ANNINA

Ganz zu Befehl, Herr Kavalier.

Vergessen nicht die Botin?

At your service, my Lord!

You won't forget the messenger?

BARON

(ignoring her request for a tip, to himself)

"Ohne mich, ohne mich jeder Tag
   Dir so bang."

"Without me your days will pass so slowly."

ANNINA

(insistent)

Vergessen nicht der Botin, Euer
   Gnade!

Hasn't your Lordship forgotten the
   messenger?

BARON

Schon gut.

"Mit mir, mit mir keine Nacht Dir
   zu lang."

You may go.

"With me, time will never seem long."

*(Annina makes a gesture asking for her tip.
The Baron dismisses her with a promise:)*

Das später. All's auf einmal. Dann
   zum Schluss.

Sie wart' auf Antwort! Tret' Sie ab
   indessen.

Schaff' Sie ein Schreibzeug in mein
   Zimmer hin dort drüben,

dass ich die Antwort dann diktier'.

Later. All in one. When it's all finished.

She waits for my reply! In the meantime, go.

Bring pen and ink and paper to my room,

And I will dictate my answer.

*(Annina goes out, not without shaking her first at the Baron behind his back,
showing that she means to get even with him for his stinginess.)*

At this point the full orchestra takes over the theme of the waltz, as the Baron dances happily around the room. He takes a last sip of wine, and repeating again *Mit mir, mit mir keine Nacht Dir zu lang!* ("With me, time will never seem long!") he goes out.

5. Duet and Final Scene from *Der Rosenkavalier.* Octavian's plan works. In the final act, which takes place at an inn, the Baron is revealed as a thoroughly worthless character. Sophie's father realizes that he chose the wrong son-in-law; the Princess faces the fact that she cannot compete with youth. She surrenders Octavian to Sophie. The lovers give expression to their happiness in a beautiful duet.

In operas of the eighteenth century, the part of a boy or young man was sometimes sung by a soprano, mezzo-soprano, or contralto. Strauss revived this custom in *Der Rosenkavalier.* The part of young Octavian is performed by a mezzo-soprano. The final duet of the opera—between Octavian and Sophie—derives much of its charm from the intermingling of the two women's voices.

OCTAVIAN	SOPHIE
This alone—only this I know— That I love you and you love me!	Like a dream . . . Can it really be That I love you . . . and that you love me?

All else passes before me like
    a dream.
	We shall love one another
	    forevermore!

There you were, in a great house . . .
And they sent me there—to my
    happiness!
Oh, they were wise!
	You laugh? I am frightened,
	    as if
	I were standing at the gate of
	    Heaven.
	Hold me. I feel so weak . . . Hold
	    me tight!

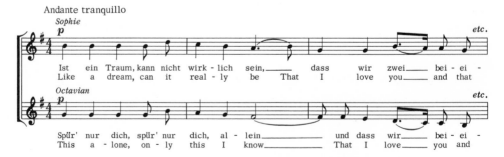

Footmen enter, carrying candlesticks. Sophie's father leads the Princess to her carriage. The merchant pats his daughter on the cheek and says good-humoredly to the Princess, "That's how youngsters are." They leave. Sophie sinks into Octavian's arms; he kisses her. They repeat the first stanza of their duet. Without noticing it, Sophie drops her handerchief. The lovers run off hand in hand. The stage remains empty for a moment. Then the center door opens. Through it, candle in hand, comes the Princess' little page boy. He looks for the handerchief, finds it, picks it up, and runs off. The curtain falls quickly.

Notice the soft staccato chords that descend from the upper register in a gentle curve. Celesta, flutes, violin harmonics. . .what an exquisite sound!

Der Rosenkavalier conjures up a world of beauty and elegance—a world that perhaps never existed save in the artist's dreams—yet for that very reason is all the more alluring.

Wagner and his disciples created a German opera based on the resources of the orchestra. Marked by expressive harmony, their art has exerted a powerful influence on the music of our time.

14

Getting to Know Ballet

A *ballet* is an extended dance piece that is either part of an opera or an independent work. Ballet has always been one of the most popular of the theater arts, for it is based on the appeal of the human body in motion. It is an imaginative art that unites dancing with acting, scenery and costumes, and —of course—music. The music is very important, since it not only enables the dancers to keep in step but also creates the proper mood and atmosphere for the ballet.

The Nature of Ballet

Ballet music must have a dynamic quality that will make both the dancers and their audience feel the basic rhythms of the dance. Even when we hear it in the concert hall, this music should still suggest the image of bodies in motion. In short, good ballet music is highly rhythmical, full of life and movement.

Ballets are written as part of operas, such as the ballets from Verdi's *Aïda* and Gounod's *Faust;* or they are independent works, such as Tchaikovsky's *The Nutcracker* or Stravinsky's *The Firebird.* Sometimes, instead of having music specially written for it, a ballet is danced to a piece of music that already exists.

1. *Dance of the Moorish Slave Boys* from *Aïda,* by Giuseppe Verdi. Allegro in $\frac{2}{4}$. This fine example of operatic ballet occurs near the beginning of Act II, while the Princess Amneris, daughter of the King of Egypt, is preparing for the triumphal return of Radamès, the general with whom she is in love. The Princess' attendants divert her with a graceful dance. The staccato

AÏDA, ACT II. Dance of the Moorish Slave Boys.

melody vividly suggests the slave boys who wear metal discs against their palms, which they tap together lightly as they perform this ballet. Notice how the music unfolds in symmetrical phrases, each rounded off with a cadence.

leggerissimo

2. *Polovtzian Dances* from *Prince Igor,* by the Russian composer Alexander Borodin. This opera is based on the adventures of a Russian warrior of the eleventh century. In the course of battle Prince Igor and his son are captured by warriors of the fierce Polovtzi tribe. The prisoners, being of royal blood, are received with great courtesy by the leader of the Polovtzi, who gives a

banquet in their honor. During this celebration the young warriors and maidens of the tribe perform the colorful Polovtzian Dances.

Polovtzian Dance No. 1. The mystery of the East is present in this lyrical number. The introduction presents a series of gentle harmonies, out of which comes an oriental-sounding tune that suggests swaying bodies. It is introduced by the oboe, "sweetly and expressively," against arpeggios on the harp:

In this dance, as in the two that follow it, we find that a rhythmic pattern is repeated over and over again. Such a pattern is known as an *ostinato* (obstinate) rhythm.

The *Polovtzian Dances Nos. 2 and 3* are as masculine in quality as the first is feminine. The second dance, marked Allegro vivo (fast and lively), is in $\frac{4}{4}$ time. It is based on an active melody that is repeated over and over again by various groups of instruments. The bass is syncopated. Its steady pulse shows how ostinato rhythm can take on an almost hypnotic quality.

The third dance is an Allegro in $\frac{3}{4}$, again based on a syncopated rhythm set off by the beat of the drum at the beginning of each measure. You can almost see the lithe warriors as they leap through the air clutching their bows and arrows. Most of the piece is played very loud, which makes all the more effective the unexpected pianissimo ending.

3.   Excerpts from *Cinderella,* by Serge Prokofiev. Throughout his career the modern Russian master was drawn to fairy tales, the world of children, and the ballet. In *Cinderella* he was able to unite these interests to produce one of the masterpieces of the modern dance theater.

Cinderella Goes to the Ball. Vivo (lively), $\frac{2}{4}$. This breathless number makes it clear that Cinderella is in a hurry to get there. Her excitement is underlined by an active staccato melody that covers a wide range, with plenty of twentieth-century dissonance in the background. The tension mounts to a climax when she arrives at the palace.

Cinderella's Waltz. Allegro espressivo (fast and expressive), $\frac{3}{4}$. Violins and violas introduce an appealing melody that suits the heroine of this romantic fairy tale. The music is designed to give a gifted ballerina every opportunity to show off her art. It also reveals Prokofiev as a master of mod-

CINDERELLA ENTERS THE BALLROOM.

ern melody. The coda builds to a climax in the three ways that so many composers have found useful for this purpose: it grows faster, louder, and higher in pitch until it reaches the brilliant upper register.

Midnight. Allegro moderato, $\frac{4}{4}$. The orchestra plays dissonant harmonies, fortissimo, as the palace clock prepares to sound the witching hour. The music mirrors Cinderella's panic as the moment arrives when she must tear herself away from her Prince Charming. The music is written from Cinderella's point of view; we hear eleven strokes but not the twelfth, as she has made her exit a moment before—with one slipper. The love-theme of the ballet is heard at this point, as the Prince searches in vain for the beautiful stranger. It is an Andante dolce (dóle-cheh—sweet).

Final Scene. Andante, $\frac{4}{4}$. The orchestral sound glows with tenderness and love. The music takes on immense sweep and power as Cinderella is reunited with her Prince. It is clear that they lived happily ever after.

4. Three Dances from *Estancia,* by Alberto Ginastera (hée-na-steh-ra), the leading composer of present-day Argentina. In this ballet Ginastera drew inspiration from the folk songs and dances of his native land. The work, he explained, "presents various aspects of the activities of an *estancia* (Argentine ranch). The plot of the ballet shows a country girl who at first despises the man of the city. She becomes attracted to him only when she sees him triumph over the most difficult tasks of the country."

Dance of the Farm Hands. Tempo giusto (jóos-to, strict time), ⁶⁄₈. This piece derives its power from rhythm rather than from melody. Chords are repeated in ostinato patterns, highly syncopated. They create tension; so does the dissonant harmony. In fact, this is the most dissonant music we have heard so far. Since a measure of six beats can be taken either as two groups of three or three groups of two, Ginastera achieves syncopation by shifting from one to the other. The piece begins forte and works up to a bright fortissimo climax.

The basic rhythm, showing the shift from duple meter (two groups of three) to triple meter (three quarter notes) in measure 3:

Wheat Dance. Tranquillo, ⁶⁄₈. A solo flute unfolds a dreamy melody against a pizzicato in the strings. The harmonies are mildly dissonant; a graceful ostinato rhythm casts its spell. The melody begins with phrases that move gently downward. In the middle part, by contrast, the movement is generally

upward. The first melody then returns in a simpler form (A-B-A), played by a solo violin. The music fades away to a *ppp* ending.

Final Dance (*Malambo*). (A *malambo* is a very fast Argentinian folk dance.) Allegro, ⁶⁄₈. This piece, like the preceding numbers, is based on a pattern of six beats that shifts continually from duple to triple meter. Ginastera's ostinato rhythms achieve great tension. Patterns based on syncopation add to the excitement. The piece begins *pp* and ends in a shattering *fff*.

Rhythm of the Malambo, *combining duple meter (two groups of three) in the first measure with triple meter (three quarter notes) in the second:*

The pieces studied in this chapter show how different composers have approached the problem of ballet music. All these compositions had one thing in common. The music was based on dynamic rhythm, and was clearly intended to accompany movement and gesture.

UNIT IV

MUSIC
WITH
A STORY

❧ |15A| ❧

Varieties of Program Music

In the songs and operatic selections that we heard, the words helped us understand what the music was trying to express. In orchestral music, on the other hand, there are no words to tell us what the music is about. All the same, many composers—especially during the nineteenth century—wanted their orchestral pieces to have a specific meaning. Thus came into being what is known as *program music*—music, that is, which suggests a definite story, scene, or mood. (The word *program* is used here in the same sense as when we say of a political candidate that he has a constructive program, meaning the things he stands for.) The composer may indicate the program either through the title of the piece or through an explanation added to the score.

Program Music

Program music, in other words, has a meaning that lies outside the realm of music. It is distinguished from *absolute music* (or "pure" music), which deals with abstract tone patterns that have no specific associations. For example, Symphony No. 39 by Mozart is an example of absolute music. On the other hand, *The Great Gate of Kiev* by Musorgsky and *The Pines of Rome* by Respighi are examples of program music.

The most important type of program music is the symphonic poem. A *symphonic poem*—also known as a *tone poem*—is a composition for orchestra in one movement, that suggests a specific story, scene, or mood. The symphonic poem is flexible in form, and follows the literary program on which it is based.

The Symphonic Poem

113

The Concert Overture

It often happened that an overture to an opera remained popular as a concert piece long after the opera itself was forgotten. Thus came into being a new kind of overture: a concert piece for orchestra in one movement, based on a literary or descriptive program. You can tell from the title whether an overture is meant to introduce an opera or stands as an independent concert piece. The presence of "to" in the title indicates a piece that is played before an opera, such as Mozart's Overture to *The Marriage of Figaro* or Rossini's Overture to *The Barber of Seville*. On the other hand, Tchaikovsky's *Overture 1812* is an independent concert piece.

Both the symphonic poem and the concert overture are orchestral pieces in one movement that suggest a specific story, scene, or mood. There is, however, an important difference between them. The symphonic poem, we saw, has no single musical form. Its form is determined largely by the literary program.

The concert overture, on the other hand, has a musical form independent of the program. It consists, as a rule, of three sections. In the first section the basic themes of the piece—two or three in number—are set forth or *exposed*. In the middle section these themes are developed; that is, the composer plays around with them, allows them to grow and to take on new shapes. In the final section the themes are *recapitulated* (restated) more or less in their original form. The three sections, accordingly, are known as Exposition, Development, and Recapitulation (or Restatement). The Exposition is rounded off by a little coda, or *codetta;* and the Recapitulation is followed generally by an extended coda that gives us a feeling of conclusion.

The concert overture, like the symphonic poem, attracted composers because of its ability to suggest a mood, an atmosphere, a scene, or a story. We will study two celebrated overtures: Mendelssohn's *A Midsummer Night's Dream* and Tchaikovsky's *Overture 1812*.

Incidental Music

Another attractive type of program music is music written as background for a play, to be performed between or during the scenes. Such music is known as *incidental music*.

Usually the composer selects the most popular numbers and arranges them in a concert suite. We studied two famous examples in Chapters 4 and 5: *In the Hall of the Mountain King,* from the music that Edvard Grieg wrote for Ibsen's drama *Peer Gynt;* and the Prelude and Farandole from the music that Georges Bizet wrote for Daudet's play *L'Arlésienne*.

Today incidental music (or background music) has moved from the theater to the motion picture. We have all experienced how greatly such music adds to a scene in a film.

Through the symphonic poem, the concert overture, and incidental music, composers developed three types of program music that enabled them to interpret a wide variety of poetic stories, scenes, and moods. Many of their works in these three areas are extremely popular today.

❧|15 B|❧

The Symphonic Poem, the Concert Overture, and Incidental Music

Paul Dukas (doo-káh) was born in Paris on October 1, 1865. He played a leading part in the musical life of France in the late nineteenth and early twentieth centuries. He died in Paris on May 17, 1935.

The Sorcerer's Apprentice *by Paul Dukas*

Dukas' symphonic poem *The Sorcerer's Apprentice* is based on a ballad by the German poet Goethe, about a sorcerer who has the power to bring various objects to life. The sorcerer's young apprentice has noticed that when his master wishes to fill the pots and pans, he puts a spell on a broom and commands it to fetch water from the well. The boy is fascinated by this trick and manages to learn the magic formula that breathes life into the broom. One day the sorcerer has an errand to do and leaves the house in charge of his assistant. The lad pronounces the magic words and commands the broom to fetch water. To his great delight the broom comes to life, marches to the well, and returns with two buckets of water. Back and forth goes the broom, bringing more and more water, while the apprentice enjoys his new-found sense of power. Suddenly he realizes that he has forgotten the magic phrase necessary to stop the broom. He pleads, he threatens, but to no avail. He watches with horror as the water rises about him. Finally, in desperation, he seizes an ax and chops the broom in two; whereupon two brooms begin to hop, skip, and jump, fetching twice as much water. The house is flooded, the apprentice is at his wit's end. Fortunately the sorcerer returns in the nick of time and pronounces the magic formula that restores everything to normalcy. He gives the boy a terrific box on the ear as a warning never again to play the magician. The apprentice, you may be sure, has learned his lesson.

The opening section establishes the atmosphere of the sorcerer's workshop. This music—slow, legato, and in high register—speaks of enchantment:

Assez lent

Presently the trumpet pronounces the magic formula. There is a silence, and the spell begins to work. Three bassoons introduce a staccato melody in a hippity-hop rhythm that suggests the angular movements of the broom:

This energetic little tune moves steadily forward, ever faster, higher, louder, as it is taken over now by the woodwinds, now by the brass, now by the strings. In the course of this development, the theme of enchantment that was heard in the introduction returns at a faster tempo in the violins:

A contrasting melody is introduced, in high register, by piccolo, flute, oboe, clarinet, and glockenspiel—a combination that makes a lovely sound. This theme is a new version of the melody that was first heard in the introduction.

The orchestra is full of movement and color as the music builds to the climax; brass instruments proclaim the apprentice's panic. He splits the broom. There is a breathless silence. Then the little theme of the bassoons begins again in the bass. Again there is a steady mounting of tension to a climax dominated by the brass. This is the point where the sorcerer returns and undoes the spell. A long pause, and we are back in the atmosphere of the opening measures; again there is magic in the air. At the very end we hear a gruff reminder of the broom theme.

The Sorcerer's Apprentice is extremely clear in form. The opening and end serve as a prelude and postlude that frame the work. The action itself divides into two parts, each of which begins softly in the low register and works up to a fortissimo climax in the high. When you hear this music, marked by dynamic rhythm and brilliant orchestration, you understand why Dukas's symphonic poem is popular all over the world.

*The Life of
Felix
Mendelssohn*

Felix Mendelssohn stands out among musicians for the fortunate circumstances that attended his career. He grew up in wealth; he found happiness in his personal life; and he was admired by a vast public. He was the grandson of Moses Mendelssohn, a celebrated Jewish philosopher of the eighteenth century. His father was a banker who loved art; his mother was highly cultured. He was born in Hamburg on February 3, 1809. His parents embraced the Protestant faith when he was still a child. They had a huge house on the outskirts of Berlin that became a meeting place for the most famous men in the city. The garden house, which seated several hundred guests, was a center of musical activity. Concerts were given weekly by Felix and his sister Fanny. Often an orchestra was engaged to present his compositions. One day, when he was only seventeen, the curly-haired lad led an orchestra in his *Midsummer Night's Dream* Overture. The audience compared him to the immortal Mozart.

The boy was given every opportunity to develop his talents. He received an excellent education at the hands of private tutors, and attended the University of Berlin. Then he spent three years traveling through Europe. This gave him an opportunity not only to broaden his education but also to make his music known in England, France, and Italy.

His first stop was London, which in a letter to his parents he described as "the grandest and most complicated monster on the face of the earth." From there he went to Scotland. In Edinburgh he visited the palace of Mary Stuart and sat in the little chapel where the unfortunate Queen was crowned. "Everything around is broken and moldering," he wrote home. "I believe I found, in the old chapel, the beginning of my *Scottish Symphony*." He journeyed to the Hebrides Islands and saw Fingal's Cave, a formation of rock jutting out of the sea. As Felix watched the waves roaring in the giant cave, he heard in his mind the opening measures of his *Fingal's Cave Overture*. His travels took him to Italy; he fell in love with its blue skies and warm-hearted people. In his *Italian Symphony* he captured the picturesque charm of that sunny land.

When his travels were over, Mendelssohn returned to his homeland. Before long he became the most famous musician in Germany. He was appointed conductor of the Leipzig orchestra, which he transformed into the finest in Europe. He also founded and directed the Leipzig Conservatory, which attracted students from all over the world. During the last fifteen years of his life, Mendelssohn's composing was carried on in the midst of a crowded career; this taxed his strength and caused his early death just as much as poverty and neglect might have done. He made ten visits to England, was honored by Queen Victoria, and was received with the greatest enthusiasm.

He returned from his last visit in a state of nervous exhaustion. The joy he found in the company of his wife and children was shattered by a severe blow —the death of his sister Fanny, to whom he was deeply attached. Six months later, on November 4, 1847, he succumbed to a stroke at the age of thirty-eight. Huge throngs followed his bier. Condolences came from all over Europe. A world figure had died.

The Overture based on Shakespeare's fairy play—an extraordinary achievement for a boy of seventeen—shows all the grace and lightness of Mendelssohn's style. Four chords on the woodwinds open the door to the enchanted realm of Oberon and Titania, the king and queen of the elves. Then comes

A Midsummer Night's Dream *Overture*

117

the fairy music—the first theme of the overture—which is introduced by the violins in high register, staccato, very fast and light:

Before long an energetic melody appears that serves as a bridge between the first and second theme. It is announced fortissimo by the first and second violins:

The second idea is a lyric theme that suggests the young lovers in the play. This is presented softly and expressively by the strings.

Third is the boisterous dance of the clowns, with its emphatic downward leaps, played by the flutes and violins:

As part of this tune, you will hear a sharp downward skip that imitates the braying of a donkey—that is, of Bottom the Weaver, on whom Oberon's magic spell has fastened the head of an ass. The melody at this point sounds like a "hee-haw." These three ideas are set forth in the Exposition, which is rounded off with a codetta based on the bridge theme.

The middle section of the Overture, the Development, is a fantasy on the first theme. The young composer explored all the possibilities of the idea and reworked it into ever fresh patterns. When this theme has been fully developed, the middle section comes to an end. The four mysterious chords of the opening are heard again, introducing the final section, the Recapitulation. Here the material is repeated more or less as we heard it before. An extended coda brings the Overture to a gentle conclusion. This coda is based on the rapid bridge theme that was heard earlier. Now the violins play it pianissimo, slowly:

A SCENE FROM
*A MIDSUMMER
NIGHT'S DREAM.*

As young Felix explained, "After everything has been satisfactorily settled and the principal players have joyfully left the stage, the elves follow them, bless the house, and disappear with the dawn. So ends the play, and my overture too."

In 1842, sixteen years after the Overture was written, King Frederick William IV of Prussia decided to have Shakespeare's comedy performed at the royal theater in Berlin, and asked Mendelssohn to write incidental music for the play. The composer added twelve numbers for this occasion, in which he recaptured the spirit of the concert overture he had written in his youth. Several of these pieces have become popular all over the world, among them the Wedding March we studied in Chapter 1.

The world remembers Felix Mendelssohn as a happy composer. He was endowed with great gifts, and he enriched his art with music full of grace and charm.

Valse triste (vahls treest), by the Finnish composer Jan Sibelius (sih-báy-lyoos), is a famous example of incidental music. It is one of the numbers that Sibelius wrote for the drama *Kuolema* (Death) by his brother-in-law, Arvid Järnefelt (yér-neh-felt). The *Valse triste* (Sad Waltz) accompanies the most important scene in the play. It is night. A son is watching by the bedside of his dying mother. He has fallen asleep from weariness. Gradually a reddish light fills the room. The sound of distant music is heard, taking shape as a melancholy waltz. The sick woman awakes and rises from her bed. She begins to move slowly in time with the music, and raises her hands as

Valse triste
*by Jan
Sibelius*

though to invite a host of invisible guests to join her. Now they appear, shadowy couples who glide about to the strains of an unearthly waltz. The dying woman mingles with the dancers. She tries to make them look into her eyes, but they avoid her glance. Then she sinks on her couch; the music falls silent. Gathering all her strength, she beckons to the guests to dance again. They return. Their dance grows ever faster and wilder. Suddenly there is a knock on the door, which flies open. The mother utters a despairing cry. The ghostly couples vanish, the music dies away. Death stands on the threshold.

The piece is a Lento (slow) in $\frac{3}{4}$ time. A mysterious pizzicato in the lower strings—double basses, second violins, and violas—serves to introduce the melody of the waltz, which is sung by the muted first violins and cellos. It is a haunting melody that moves by step within a narrow range:

The melody is repeated a tone higher, which heightens the tension. Then a ghostly sequence of chords in waltz rhythm is heard, out of which comes an expressive melody in the upper register.

Both themes are repeated. The music grows ever faster and louder, building to the climax. At the emotional high point the opening melody appears in longer notes against an agitated accompaniment. The music reaches a fortissimo, and subsides. The final chords are played in a ghostly whisper by four solo violins.

Incidental music should have the dramatic tension that belongs to the theater. Sibelius's *Valse triste,* like the examples of incidental music we studied in earlier chapters, possesses that quality in abundance.

16

How a Composer Expresses His Love for His Country

(NATIONALISM)

Nationalist feeling played an important part in nineteenth-century Europe, even as it still does today. When Napoleon conquered the different nations on the Continent, there developed a surge of patriotism in the occupied countries that helped to drive out the invader. Later, in 1830 and 1848, revolution spread throughout Europe as the nations who suffered under the yoke of the Austrian and Russian empires tried to regain their independence. The deep emotions aroused by these struggles found an outlet in music.

As a result, the nineteenth century saw the rise of a group of composers whose art expressed the spirit of their homeland. In the eyes of the world Frédéric Chopin is associated with Poland, Franz Liszt with Hungary, Giuseppe Verdi with Italy, Richard Wagner with Germany. Russia developed a national school headed by Tchaikovsky, Musorgsky, and Rimsky-Korsakov. Norway found her voice in the music of Grieg, Bohemia (now Czechoslovakia) in the works of Smetana and Dvořák, Finland in the art of Sibelius.

A composer can express his feeling for his country in several ways:

1. He can base his music on the folk songs and dances of his homeland, as Chopin did in his Mazurkas and Polonaises, Liszt in his *Hungarian Rhapsodies,* Dvořák in his *Slavonic Dances,* and Grieg in his *Norwegian Dances.*

2. He can base an opera on the life of the peasantry, as Smetana did in *The Bartered Bride.* Folklore elements are prominent too in the fairy-tale operas and ballets of Tchaikovsky and Rimsky-Korsakov.

3. He can build a work around a renowned king or hero of his country. The gods and heroes of the ancient Germanic legends live again in Richard Wagner's music dramas, especially in *The Ring of the Nibelung,* which revolves around the hero Siegfried. So too Musorgsky's opera *Boris Godunov* has as its central character a king famous in Russian history.

4. He can celebrate in his music a national victory, as Tchaikovsky did in

121

his *Overture 1812;* or he can express his people's hatred of foreign oppression, as Sibelius did in *Finlandia.*

5. He can write a work that exalts the beauty of his homeland. Examples are Smetana's *The Moldau* (a river) ; Musorgsky's *Night on Bald Mountain;* Johann Strauss's famous waltzes *The Blue Danube* and *Tales from the Vienna Woods;* and the music dramas of Wagner, which proclaim the beauty of the Rhine, of German forest and mountain.

6. A composer may associate his music with his nation's literature. Tchaikovsky, Musorgsky, and Rimsky-Korsakov wrote operas based on texts by the Russian national poet Alexander Pushkin. Schubert's settings of the poems of Goethe and Schumann's settings of the works of Heine enhanced the beauty of German poetry. So too, Grieg's incidental music for *Peer Gynt* and Bizet's music for Alphonse Daudet's *L'Arlésienne* show how a composer may enrich his nation's literature.

The Life of Peter Ilyich Tchaikovsky

"I am a Russian through and through," Tchaikovsky said of himself. "I grew up in a quiet spot and was saturated from earliest childhood with the wonderful beauty of Russian popular song. I am, therefore, passionately devoted to every expression of the Russian spirit."

Russia's most celebrated composer (his name is pronounced tchy-kóv-skee) was born in a distant province of Russia on May 7, 1840. His father was an inspector of government mines. Peter was a sensitive child who was morbidly attached to his mother. He was given piano lessons, as was common with children of the upper class, but it never occurred to his parents that he would become a musician. They intended him for a career in the government, and sent him to the aristocratic School of Law in St. Petersburg (now Leningrad) . He was graduated at the age of nineteen and became a clerk in the Ministry of Justice.

But his work bored him, and his thoughts turned more and more to music. Finally he informed his father that he had decided to resign from his position and devote himself to the art he loved. Peter's father pointed out to him that an honorable career awaited him in the service of the Tsar, and that a musician's life was beset with hardships. But Peter was not to be dissuaded. In the end his father gave his consent.

Peter entered the Conservatory of St. Petersburg. His was a modest goal: "To be a good musician and earn my daily bread." He worked so diligently that he completed the course in three years with a silver medal, and was recommended to teach at the new Conservatory of Moscow. In 1866 he arrived in Moscow to take up his post as professor of harmony.

During his years at the Conservatory Tchaikovsky composed the first works that bear the mark of his genius. At the same time he was very moody and given to attacks of depression. "Regretting the past and hoping for the future without ever being satisfied with the present—this is how my life is spent." More and more he was dissatisfied with his duties at the Conservatory. How could he compose when he had to devote most of his time to teaching? Yet how would he make a living if he didn't? At this time Tchaikovsky married a student of the Conservatory who had fallen hopelessly in love with him. His sympathy for his bride soon turned into an uncontrollable hatred. In a fit of despair he wandered into the icy waters of the Moscow River. Fortunately his good sense overcame his desire to do away with himself. Some days later he fled, on the verge of a serious breakdown, to his brothers in St. Petersburg.

In this desperate hour there entered his life, like a fairy godmother, one of the wealthiest women in Russia—Nadezhda von Meck, the widow of an industrialist. She lived in seclusion in her palace in Moscow, from which she ran her railroads, her estates, and the lives of her eleven children. Her passion was music—especially Tchaikovsky's. When she heard that he needed help, she decided to settle upon him an allowance that would enable him to devote himself to his art. The money she gave him made it possible for Tchaikovsky to go abroad until he had recovered his health. It freed him from the drudgery of teaching and launched him on the most productive period of his career.

Mme. von Meck wanted to be sure that her interest was only in the musician, not in the man; and so she laid down one condition—that they were never to meet. Thus began the famous friendship by letter which soon took on a tone of passionate devotion. For the next thirteen years Mme. von Meck made Tchaikovsky's career the central point of her life. She provided for all his needs; yet she held fast to her decision. Except for an accidental glimpse of each other—once at the opera, another time when she drove past his house in a carriage—they never met.

In gratitude for her assistance Tchaikovsky dedicated to Mme. von Meck his Fourth Symphony. Across the score he wrote: "To my best friend." His letters to her give us a fascinating glimpse of his methods of work. "You ask me how I manage the orchestration? I never compose in the abstract. I invent the musical idea and its orchestration simultaneously." Mme. von Meck inquired if the Fourth Symphony had a definite meaning. Tchaikovsky replied: "How can one express the indefinable sensations that one feels while writing an instrumental composition that has no definite subject? It is a musical confession of the soul, which unburdens itself through sounds just as a lyric poet expresses himself through poetry. The difference lies in the fact that music has far richer resources of expression. As Heine said, 'Where words leave off, music begins.' "

.The years covered by the correspondence saw the spread of Tchaikovsky's fame. He was the first Russian composer whose music caught on in the West. In 1891 he was invited to come to America to take part in the ceremonies that marked the opening of Carnegie Hall. From New York he wrote, "These Americans strike me as very remarkable. In this country the honesty, sincerity, generosity, and readiness to help you without a second thought are extremely pleasant. . . . The houses downtown are simply colossal. I cannot understand how anyone can live on the thirteenth floor. I went out on the roof of one such house. The view was splendid, but I felt quite giddy when I looked down on Broadway. . . . I am convinced that I am ten times more famous in America than in Europe."

The letters of his last years breathe the fear that he had nothing more left to say. "Is it possible that I have completely written myself out? I have neither ideas nor inclinations!" Yet ahead of him lay his two finest symphonies—the Fifth and the Sixth. Another source of sorrow was the end of his friendship with Mme. von Meck, which she broke off—without any explanation—as abruptly as she had begun it. One reason may have been the illness of her favorite son, and the thought that for years she had devoted all her care to a stranger instead of to her own family. Whatever the cause, Tchaikovsky was heartbroken at this sad ending of a beautiful friendship.

He came to St. Petersburg to conduct the first performance of his Sixth Symphony, the *Pathétique* (pah-tay-téek). The piece was not successful, mainly because Tchaikovsky was shy in public and did not conduct his music well. Some days later, although he had been warned that there was an epidemic of cholera in the capital, he carelessly drank a glass of unboiled water and caught the disease. He died within a week, on November 6, 1893, at the age of fifty-three. The suddenness of his death and the tragic tone of his last work led to rumors that he had committed suicide. Almost immediately the *Pathétique Symphony* became extremely popular and has remained so ever since.

Overture 1812

In his *Overture 1812,* which he wrote in 1880, Tchaikovsky gave expression to his feelings as a nationalist composer. This concert overture celebrates one of the most important dates in Russian history—the year of Napoleon's invasion and retreat. The French were defeated primarily by the Russian winter—that is, by the country itself. Tchaikovsky's piece, consequently, is a gesture of homage to his homeland.

The Overture opens with violas and four solo cellos in low register playing a chorale, like a prayer in time of need. (A *chorale,* you will recall, is a hymn or hymn-like tune.)

There is a steady mounting of tension, as if danger were approaching. Presently we hear a military theme symbolizing the Russian army. This is an active melody marked Andante, played mezzo forte by oboes, clarinets, and horns against the rat-tat-tat of the snare drum and a roll on the kettledrum:

An Allegro movement introduces a theme in strict time, in a tense rhythm. It consists of a rapid downward run followed by heavily accented chords on the off-beat (syncopation). It suggests strife between the opposing forces:

The enemy is represented by the opening phrase of the French national anthem, the *Marseillaise,* which is announced by horns and trumpets:

The orchestra manages to whip up intense excitement. When it calms down we hear a lyric theme, like a song of tenderness for the homeland, sung by violins and violas.

NAPOLEON'S RETREAT FROM MOSCOW, 1812.
Painting by Jan V. Chelminski.

There follows a tune in the style of a Russian folk dance, as though to symbolize the masses who will rise up in defense of their fatherland. It is a rhythmically active melody, played by flute and English horn against an ostinato rhythm on the snare drum:

When all these themes—the basic ideas of the Overture—have been set forth, the first section of the piece, the Exposition, is finished. The Development is based mainly on the Strife theme and the *Marseillaise*—that is, the theme representing the French army. In the Recapitulation the basic themes appear with the order slightly changed. The *Marseillaise* is heard in longer notes and builds up to a fortissimo climax; then it loses its power and disappears.

A transitional passage traces a broad descending curve, played by the woodwind and string sections in unison and octaves. (Instruments are said to be playing *in unison* when they play the same notes. They are said to be playing *in octaves* when they play the same notes in different octaves.) Now the opening chorale returns in triumph, *fff*, with the bells of Moscow pealing joyously. Most of the instruments join in playing the Russian army theme *ffff*, Allegro vivace. When this is repeated, we hear underneath it what was at that time the Russian national anthem, *God Save the Tsar,* blared out by the brass in the bass register. A brief coda, and the Overture ends in a blaze of glory.

Suite from
Háry János by
Zoltán Kodály

Zoltán Kodály (kóh-dye) was one of the leading composers of modern Hungary. He is known throughout the world for the suite from his operetta in folk style, *Háry János* (háh-ree yá-nosh). (An *operetta* differs from an opera in that it has spoken dialogue between the musical numbers.) The action of *Háry János* revolves around a retired old soldier with a lively imagination, who sits in the village inn day after day, telling his fellow peasants about the brave deeds of his youth. Most of his stories happen to be untrue, but they give great pleasure both to Háry and his listeners. The point is, of course, that Háry invents the things that all men wish had happened to them—moments of glory when the world was filled with admiration for their bravery.

Viennese Musical Clock. Háry fascinates his listeners with a description of the famous musical clock in the Emperor's palace. The piece is an Allegretto in $\frac{4}{4}$ time. Bells chime, setting up an ostinato rhythm. We hear a merry march, staccato, as the little soldiers on the clock prance by in their shiny uniforms, around and around:

There are no string instruments in this piece, only winds and percussion, which gives a twentieth-century sound. Each time the main theme returns, it is more colorfully orchestrated. Notice the effect of the piano, which is used as part of the orchestra only in modern works. The march ends bravely, fortissimo.

The Battle and Defeat of Napoleon. Háry, at the head of his brave hussars, attacks the French army. He brandishes his sword, and the French fall before him like tin soldiers—first two, then four, eight, ten. Finally Napoleon himself engages the invincible Háry in hand-to-hand combat but, as we might have known, is defeated. This march-like movement in $\frac{2}{4}$ begins with a lively melody in Hungarian style played by three trombones. It is first heard as from a distance, then louder, as though an army were approaching. Trumpets and trombones shout the call to battle. The orchestra is swept by dissonant harmonies as the conflict gets under way.

The French are represented by an unwieldy tune in $\frac{4}{4}$ played by trombones and tuba. When the battle is won the gay opening theme is transformed into a funeral march, sung mournfully by a saxophone. The movement trails off to a pianissimo ending as Napoleon, "shaking in every limb, kneels before his conqueror and pleads for mercy."

Entrance of the Emperor and His Court. Háry pictures the entrance of the Austrian Emperor and his nobles in the royal palace. Carried away by his imagination, the old soldier describes for his fellow villagers a scene that is much more Hungarian than Viennese. This is reflected in the wild flavor of the music. The movement is marked Alla Marcia (in march time), and is in $\frac{2}{4}$. The theme is carried by woodwinds and xylophone in unison and octaves. It is ornamented with grace notes in Hungarian folk style:

A contrasting tune that might have been a folk song is introduced by trumpets and cornets. Both melodies alternate; new material is introduced. Then we hear the two themes in more elaborate orchestration. The music grows faster and louder at the end, and ends *fff*. It is a grand procession, and Háry makes the most of it.

The works discussed in this chapter illustrate various aspects of nationalism in music. They prove eloquently how a composer may enrich his art if he shares in the hopes and dreams of his people.

17

Nationalism

(CONCLUDED)

The Moldau
by Bedřich Smetana

Bedřich Smetana was born in a village in Bohemia on March 2, 1824, and died in Prague on May 12, 1884. His career unfolded against a background of political agitation: Bohemia was restless under Austrian rule. Smetana sympathized with the patriotic cause and became the founder of the Czech national school. *The Bartered Bride,* an opera based on the life of the Bohemian peasantry, carried his fame all over the world. (We studied the Polka from this work in Chapter 1.) Equally successful was his cycle of six symphonic poems called *My Country,* in which he glorified Bohemia's heroes, her fields and mountains, and—in the best-known piece of the series—the beautiful river Vltava, better known in the West by its German name, Moldau.

In this symphonic poem the river becomes a poetic symbol for the country itself. Smetana explained what he had in mind in a program note that he added to the score. "Two springs pour forth in the shade of the Bohemian forest." These join in a brook that ultimately becomes the river Moldau. "Flowing through Bohemia's valleys, it grows into a mighty stream. Through thick woods it flows as the gay sounds of the hunter's horns are heard ever closer. It flows through grass-grown pastures where a wedding feast is being celebrated with song and dance. At night, nymphs from the forest play in its sparkling waves. Reflected on its surface are fortresses and castles—witnesses of bygone days of knightly splendor and the vanished glory of martial times." The stream races ahead through the Rapids of St. John, "finally flowing on in majestic peace toward Prague." The river passes the heights on which, long ago, stood the castle of Bohemia's kings. "Then it vanishes far beyond the poet's gaze."

The piece begins at a moderate Allegro. A light rippling figure is heard as a dialogue between two flutes. From this emerges the flowing theme of

THE MOLDAU (VLTAVA) AT PRAGUE.

the river—a legato melody in $\frac{6}{8}$ time, moving stepwise along the scale in a broad curve. Smetana derived this appealing tune from a Czech folk song.

Presently horn calls evoke a hunting scene. This is followed by a section called *Peasant Wedding*, in $\frac{2}{4}$ time, in the style of a folk dance. A jovial tune is presented by clarinets and first violins. As is to be expected, this theme is rhythmically more active than the opening melody.

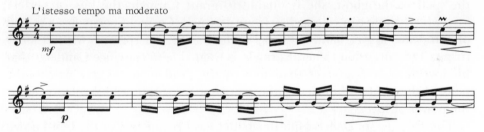

Then comes a passage in a mysterious mood, labeled in the score *Moonlight—Nymphs' Revels.* Wind instruments conjure up a romantic landscape; the arpeggios in the clarinet part are supposed to be played "in the manner of waves." Against this background muted violins and violas sing a melody "very gently and sweetly." (The figure "8" followed by a dotted line, in the example, means that the violins are to play the notes an octave higher than written.)

The theme of the river returns. Now the music grows louder and faster, suggesting the seething rapids near Prague. As the river approaches the ancient site of the royal castle, the principal theme returns in an exultant mood. (The third and sixth steps of the scale are raised half a tone. This, we will learn in a later chapter, means a shift from minor to major.) The brass instruments intone a triumphal chorale, as if the composer were promising his countrymen that their former glory will return. A gradual diminuendo is heard as the river "vanishes far beyond the poet's gaze."

The Czechs look upon Smetana's masterpiece as a national work that mirrors the very soul of their land. For the rest of the world it remains one of the loveliest examples of a symphonic poem inspired by patriotic feeling.

Ritual Fire Dance *from* El Amor brujo *by Manuel de Falla*

Manuel de Falla (fáh-ya), one of the greatest Spanish composers, was born in Cadiz on November 23, 1876. He left Spain in 1939 and spent the last seven years of his life in Argentina. There he died on November 14, 1946, at the age of seventy.

Falla was a nationalist. "Our music," he declared, "must be based on the natural music of our people. In our dance and our rhythm we possess the strongest of traditions that no one can wipe out." His fame rests on about half a dozen works, among them the one-act ballet *El Amor brujo* (el ahmór bróo-ho); the opera *La Vida breve,* from which we heard the Spanish Dance No. 1; and a ballet, *The Three-Cornered Hat.*

In *El Amor brujo* (Bewitched by Love) Falla conjured up the rapturous melody of the Andalusian Gypsies. The action revolves around a theme that is to be found in the fairy tales of all countries. The beautiful Candelas has been in love with a dissipated Gypsy. Now that he is dead, his ghost returns to haunt her. She is loved by the handsome Carmelo; but, under the spell of the ghost, she is unable to grant Carmelo the kiss of perfect love which alone can release her from the spell. Carmelo persuades a friend of Candelas, a girl named Lucia, to flirt with the specter, who at once turns all his attention to her. Carmelo is then able to convince Candelas that his love for her is greater than that of the dead man. As day dawns, the bells of the village chime, and the power of the ghost is broken forever by the power of love.

The *Ritual Fire Dance* from this ballet has become one of the best-known pieces of the twentieth century. It is marked Allegro ma non troppo e pesante (Fast but not too much so, and heavily). Trills played by violas and clarinets in low register create a ghostly atmosphere; this dance is intended, as the composer put it, "to drive away evil spirits." A striking ostinato is set up in the bass register, against which a solo oboe traces the famous melody:

Allegro ma non troppo e pesante

Being a dance, the music unfolds in regular four-measure phrases. The melody moves by step within a narrow range, with much repetition of single notes and groups of notes. This gives a primitive effect. Presently a contrasting theme is introduced by horns and first violins.

The two themes alternate in an A-B-A-B form with coda. Tension builds up steadily through a gradual crescendo and accelerando. At the very end the entire orchestra thunders out a chord over and over again in syncopated rhythm. This number makes its effect through the hypnotic power of ostinato rhythm and the excitement of twentieth-century dissonance.

Scene from The Devil and Daniel Webster *by Douglas Moore*

A delightful example of American nationalism is Douglas Moore's "folk opera," *The Devil and Daniel Webster*. This work is based on the celebrated story by Stephen Vincent Benét which tells how Daniel Webster matched his wits against the Devil's. The action takes place at the home of Jabez Stone in New Hampshire, during the 1840s. The inhabitants of Cross Corners are celebrating the wedding of Jabez and Mary. Everybody is in a holiday mood—until the arrival of an unexpected guest, a Boston lawyer named Scratch. "He is, of course, the Devil, a New England devil, dressed like a rather shabby attorney." The bridegroom is strangely upset when he catches sight of the unbidden guest. The village fiddler opens Mr. Scratch's box. Out flies a lost soul in the shape of a moth. Then the guests realize that Jabez Stone has sold his soul to the devil. They denounce Jabez and run away.

A SCENE FROM *THE DEVIL AND DANIEL WEBSTER*

Mary remains. She loves Jabez and will not abandon him. He confesses to her that, in his eagerness to become rich and win her love, he had indeed made a pact with the Devil. Daniel Webster—the great orator and the pride of New Hampshire—has remained too. He decides to help the young couple. When Scratch arrives to claim his due—Jabez's soul—Webster demands a trial for his client. Scratch summons from the depths of Hell a jury of famous American traitors. They are hardly likely to give Jabez a fair trial; yet the impossible happens: Webster is so eloquent an orator that he turns the tables on the Devil and persuades the jury to set Jabez free. "The neighbors rush in to drive the Devil out of New Hampshire, and the case ends with pie breakfast, as it should."

We hear the scene that follows Daniel Webster's decision to help Jabez and Mary. He sings a rousing tune, "I've got a ram, Goliath." This song reveals what kind of man Webster is: fearless, and against anyone who threatens the freedom of the people.

> I've got a ram, Goliath—
>   He was raised on Marshfield grain.
> He's got horns like a morning-glory vine
>   And he butts like a railroad train.
>
> I've got a ram, Goliath—
>   Named for the Philistine.
> And I wrestle him ev'ry Tuesday night
>   With these two hands of mine.
>
> I've got a bull, King Stephen—
>   A bull with a rolling eye.
> When he stamps his foot, the stars come out
>   And the lightning blinks in the sky.
>
> I've got a bull, King Stephen,
>   With a kick like a cannon ball.
> But he acts like a sucking turtle-dove
>   When I go into his stall.
>
> I'm not an idle boaster.
>   Let this be said of me:
> I was born in old New Hampshire
>   And always fought for the free.
>
> They know about Daniel Webster
>   Wherever the eagle flies.
> And they know he stands for the Union
>   And doesn't stand for lies.
>
> Ask at the workman's cottage,
>   Ask at the farmer's gate.
> They know about Daniel Webster,
>   The pride of the Granite State.
>
> They know about Daniel Webster
>   As only neighbors can.
> And he'll fight ten thousand devils
>   To save a New Hampshire man!

The melody of Moore's opera is molded to American speech and expresses

American feelings. Typical is Moore's use of syncopation. By putting a short note on the strong beat and a longer note on the off-beat he shifts the accent, as on the words "Goliath," "morning," and "railroad" in the following example:

The effect is completely American and completely charming.

After the song, there follows a short conversation between Mary, Jabez, and Webster. Mary wants to remain with her husband, so that they will face the Devil together. But Webster insists that she leave. "Frankly, madam, in a very few moments this is going to be no place for a lady." Mary asks how she can help, and Webster suggests that she can help them with her prayers. Notice how the musical background warms the dialogue and heightens its power.

Mary's Prayer is one of the highlights of the score. Here the melodic line rises to the almost Biblical simplicity of Benét's text.

> Now may there be a blessing and a light betwixt thee and me forever. For as Ruth unto Naomi, so do I cleave unto thee. Set me as a seal upon thy heart, as a seal upon thine arm, for love is strong as death. Many waters cannot quench love, neither can the floods drown it. As Ruth unto Naomi, so do I cleave unto thee. The Lord watch thee and me when we are absent from one another. Amen.

The Devil and Daniel Webster has established itself as an American classic. Its composer expresses American feelings in a sincere and convincing way.

The American composer Virgil Thomson is one of our leading nationalists. He has used American folk material with great imagination, especially in the scores he wrote for two films: *The River* and *Louisiana Story*.

The River was a documentary film showing what happened when industry invaded the peace and quiet of the Mississippi valley. From this score Thomson arranged a concert suite in four movements: *The Old South, Industrial Expansion in the Mississippi Valley, Soil Erosion and Floods,* and

Suite from The River by Virgil Thomson— Second Movement

133

Finale. We hear the second, which is based on popular melodies of the Old South.

Industrial Expansion in the Mississippi Valley opens with a flute solo. In the film, this accompanies a view of virgin forest. A tree is being cut. As it hits the river, we hear *A Hot Time in the Old Town Tonight,* played by a muted trumpet:

Then the trumpets introduce *Oh the Eagles They Fly High in Mobile:*

The industrial scenes in the film—glimpses of steel factories and steam whistles—are accompanied by dissonant harmonies played very loud. There follows an appealing melody that starts out in practically the same rhythm as *Oh the Eagles They Fly High*—but the notes are different. Then the two basic themes of the movement are repeated, fortissimo.

This music reveals Virgil Thomson as an American nationalist who treats our folk songs with imagination and affection.

How Composers Evoke
the Glamor of Far-off Lands

(EXOTICISM)

Exoticism in Music

One of the traits of nineteenth-century poetry was a longing for far-off lands. This interest in all that is foreign and strange is known in art and literature as *exoticism.* The composers of the nineteenth century took over this trend. They used the orchestra and the art of orchestration to create exotic color and atmosphere.

Exoticism in music revealed itself, in the first place, as a longing of the northern nations for the warmth and color of the South. French, Russian, and German composers found inspiration in Italy and Spain. There resulted such works as Bizet's *Carmen;* the Venetian act in Offenbach's *The Tales of Hoffmann,* from which we heard the Barcarolle; Mendelssohn's *Italian Symphony,* Tchaikovsky's *Italian Caprice,* and Rimsky-Korsakov's *Caprice on Spanish Themes.* This tradition lasted into the twentieth century, as is evident from the Spanish atmosphere of Walter Piston's *The Incredible Flutist.*

In the second place, exoticism found expression as a longing of the West for the fairy-tale splendor of the Orient. The glamor of the East especially attracted the composers of the Russian national school. A number of their works were inspired by the Orient. Several found favor throughout the world, among them Rimsky-Korsakov's *Scheherazade* and his opera *Sadko,* from which comes the famous *Song of India;* also Borodin's opera *Prince Igor,* which includes the *Polovtzian Dances* that we discussed in Chapter 14. Among the many works by French and Italian composers with an oriental setting two stand out: Verdi's *Aïda* and Puccini's *Madame Butterfly.*

The Life of Nicholas Rimsky-Korsakov

Rimsky-Korsakov (kór-sah-kov) was one of the most important representatives of nineteenth-century exoticism. His imagination was haunted by fairy-tale landscapes, by luminous seas and skies. His music has a picture-book quality that goes hand in hand with gorgeous coloring. He was one of the great orchestrators of the nineteenth century.

This happy artist was born in Russia, in the province of Novgorod, on March 18, 1844. At the age of six he began to study the piano, and composed his first pieces when he was nine. His parents realized that he had great musical talent, but at that time only two careers were open to the sons of the aristocracy—the army or the navy. Since Nicholas was the nephew of an admiral, he entered the Naval Academy in St. Petersburg when he was twelve and remained there until he was eighteen. The atmosphere in the Academy was not at all favorable for his artistic interests, but he managed to continue studying music.

Before long he joined a group of young composers who were trying to create a Russian national school. Along with Alexander Borodin (bóh-roh-deen) and Modest Musorgsky (moo-sórg-skee), Rimsky-Korsakov soon became one of the most important members of "The Five." The other two members of the group—Mily Balakirev (bah-láh-kee-rev) and César Cui (kwee) —are barely remembered outside their homeland. At this time the young naval officer was assigned to a training cruise around the world that lasted for three years. Separated from his comrades, Rimsky-Korsakov set to work on a symphony. He sent the score to Balakirev, movement by movement, for advice and correction. His duties as an officer interfered with his composing, but he pushed ahead in spite of all obstacles.

The squadron reached the United States in 1863. "Niagara Falls made the most marvelous impression on us," he records in his *Autobiography.*

"We rowed in a boat as near as possible to the falls." Since England was on the side of the South during the Civil War, her traditional enemy Russia sided with the North. "We followed the course of events with deep interest, though we kept exclusively within Northern territory. The expected war with England had not come to pass, and we did not have to threaten English merchantmen in the Atlantic."

The flotilla proceeded to South America. In the tropics the young composer was enchanted by the color and light that were later to vibrate through his music. "Wonderful is the tropical ocean," he wrote, "with its azure color and gleaming light, wonderful are tropical sun and clouds. But the tropical night sky over the ocean is the most wonderful thing in the world!" On his return to St. Petersburg, the symphony was performed and received an enthusiastic reception. The audience was surprised when a young man in naval uniform came out to acknowledge the applause.

Rimsky-Korsakov's compositions soon attracted the attention of the world. When he was twenty-seven he was appointed professor of composition and orchestration at the Conservatory of St. Petersburg. Two years later he resigned from the navy, and from then on devoted himself to his beloved art.

Rimsky-Korsakov had a great influence on the course of Russian music. His pupils included the leaders of the next generation of musicians, among them the most famous composer of our time, Igor Stravinsky. His operas delighted his countrymen. In these works Rimsky gave expression to his nationalism. Most of his operas were based on Russian folk tales or on tales from Russian history. After a productive and happy career, he died in St. Petersburg on June 21, 1908, at the age of sixty-four.

Scheherazade —First Movement

Rimsky-Korsakov is best known to the West through a work that evokes the picturesque atmosphere of the *Arabian Nights*. This popular piece shows all the exotic charm of his style as well as the brilliance of his orchestration.

The program note in the score tells us of the Sultan Schahriar who, "convinced of the faithlessness of women, had decided to put to death each of his wives after the wedding night. But the Sultana Scheherazade saved her life by diverting him with tales which she told him on a thousand and one nights." Among those were such classics as *Sinbad the Sailor, Ali Baba and the Forty Thieves,* and *Aladdin and his Wonderful Lamp.* "Conquered by curiosity, the Sultan postponed from one day to the next the execution of his wife." In the end, won over by the wit, the charm, and the beauty of the Sultana, he renounced completely his bloody vow.

Scheherazade consists of four movements, of which we shall hear the first. Actually, these are four symphonic poems on a single theme; hence the work is called a *symphonic suite.* The first movement, *The Sea and the Ship of Sinbad,* begins with an introduction marked Largo e maestoso (my-stó-so—majestic). We hear the two contrasting themes of the Sultan and his wife. The gruff theme of the Sultan is announced in low register by most of the orchestra, and makes him out to be a brusque man who is not to be trifled with:

Largo e maestoso

ff pesante

Scheherazade's melody—the theme of the Narrator—is presented by a violin solo in high register above arpeggios on the harp. It is an oriental melody and thoroughly feminine:

Lento

espressivo

etc.

There follows a vivid picture of the sea in $\frac{6}{4}$ time, marked Allegro non troppo (not too fast). This music is rich in color and atmosphere. Notice the use of $\frac{6}{4}$ time to suggest the rolling movement of the sea. The main theme is derived from the Sultan's theme, which makes sense: as he listens to the story, he follows in his mind the course of the ship.

Allegro non troppo

p

This theme is heard over and over again throughout the movement. The variety is supplied by the ever-changing colors in the orchestra. A contrasting melody, marked Tranquillo, consisting of a series of ascending chords, represents the calm of the sea:

Tranquillo

p

dim.

The theme of Scheherazade returns in the course of the movement in a new rhythm:

etc.

Exciting crescendos suggest the surge and thunder of the ocean. Throughout, Rimsky-Korsakov evokes the atmosphere of a fairy tale. There never was such a ship, there never was such a sea, save in that far-off land story-tellers dream of. The movement ends in a mood of gentle leave-taking.

Emmanuel Chabrier (shah-bree-áy) was born in Ambert, France, on January 18, 1841, and died in Paris at the age of fifty-three, on September 13, 1894. His masterpiece, *España*, was the result of a trip to Spain in 1882. He was fascinated by the passionate songs and dance tunes that he heard there, and wrote down a number of them. In *España*, as he explained later, he

España by Emmanuel Chabrier

137

contrasted two popular Spanish dances: the *Jota* (hó-ta), with its fierce dynamic rhythm, and the *Malagueña* (ma-la-gwén-ya), with its appealing melodies. The result was an exciting symphonic poem that made him famous throughout the musical world.

España is remarkable for its brilliant orchestration, especially the use of the brass choir; the surge of its rhythms, with an occasional use of syncopation; above all, for its irresistible melodies. A number of these are woven together in the colorful fabric of this Rhapsody for Orchestra. (A *rhapsody* is a fanciful composition that follows no set pattern. It presents a series of melodies that evoke a variety of moods. As a result the rhapsody sometimes sounds as if the composer, yielding to his inspiration, had made it up as he went along.)

After a brief introduction we hear the first theme, introduced by the bassoon, repeated by the horn, then taken over in a brilliant fortissimo by the entire orchestra:

The second tune equals the first in charm and gaiety. It is introduced by bassoons, horns, and cellos:

JOHN SINGER SARGENT, *EL JOLEO* (A SPANISH DANCE).

138

There follows a series of tunes that are just as appealing. In the second half of the piece these melodies are repeated with all kinds of changes in orchestration, register, dynamics, and other details. There is a build-up of tension throughout the coda, which brings the piece to a brilliant ending.

España is a dance rhapsody that sings of a sunny land. Spain—in this music—becomes a place of gaiety and charm, pictured with all the grace of a French imagination.

Ravel's *Mother Goose Suite* consists of a series of pieces based on French fairy tales. They were composed as piano duets (four hands) for the children of his closest friends. But it was only after he orchestrated the suite that this colorful work gained a worldwide audience.

We will hear the third movement, *Laideronette, Empress of the Pagodas*. What Ravel had in mind when he composed this music is indicated by the few lines he wrote on top of the score—a quotation from a famous French fairy tale. "She undressed and entered her bath. At once the pagodas and little pagodas began to sing and play their instruments. Some had lutes made of walnut shells, others had viols made of almond shells; for they had to have instruments suited to their size." (Lutes and viols were string instruments used in former times. A pagoda is a Chinese temple in the shape of a tower.)

The Empress of the Pagodas, it goes without saying, needs a Chinese atmosphere. Ravel gave it to her by using a scale of five notes: the *pentatonic scale* that is the basis of Chinese music. This scale can be played on the five black keys of the piano: C♯, D♯, F♯, G♯, A♯. All the melodies in this piece are based on these five notes. Through the use of xylophone, celesta, harp, and glockenspiel, Ravel achieves an enchanting sonority in the orchestra. It is as if the pagodas had little bells attached to them that tinkled in the breeze as the Empress took her bath.

The piece is marked Mouvement de marche (in march time). A brief introduction brings forth wisps of sound from the wind instruments against tremolos on the muted strings. The opening melody, played by a flute, is a pentatonic tune with a Chinese flavor:

Laideronette,
Empress of
the Pagodas
from Mother
Goose Suite
*by Maurice
Ravel*

The opening section presents two other tunes that are related to the first. The middle section begins with a melody in the woodwinds in the style of an ancient Chinese chant.

Here too we find a pentatonic melody with an exotic sound; it is played by the flute. Then the opening section is repeated, which gives an A-B-A form. The coda mounts in a steady crescendo to the final chord, which is repeated four times, very loud. It combines all the notes of the pentatonic scale:

With this sharp dissonance we are very much in the twentieth century.

Guaracha from Latin-American Symphonette by Morton Gould

Exoticism in music, like nationalism, has lasted into the twentieth century. Morton Gould is one of several American composers who have found inspiration for their music in Latin America.

The word *guaracha* (gwah-ráh-cha), widely used in Latin-American music, means a drinking song; also a dance. Its traits are ostinato rhythms, stop-and-go effects, and syncopation. Morton Gould's *Guaracha* is in cut time (alla breve), and is marked Moderately fast, lightly.

The bass clarinet traces a staccato rhythm that is repeated over and over in the accompaniment:

The first melody is played by the clarinets. Notice that in the fifth and sixth measures the syncopated accents upset the beat:

An unusual feature of the score is the use of four saxophones, a marimba, a guitar, and, for picturesque native color, a gourd. This is a dried round fruit whose seeds, when the gourd is shaken, make a rattling sound.

Muted trumpets introduce a jazz-like idea that is taken over by the clarinets. Then we hear the woodwind instruments play a broad curve of melody. For all its Latin-American atmosphere it has the quality of a Blues. It stops and starts again in the abrupt manner characteristic of the Guaracha:

The rest of the piece is woven out of these threads. As in most Latin-American dance music, the rhythm never stops. You would expect this kind of composition to work up to a brilliant climax. All the more effective, therefore, is the pianissimo ending.

It is evident, from the examples studied in this chapter, that a composer who wants to write exotic music must have a vivid sense of orchestral color. Beyond that he must be able to suggest the atmosphere of a particular place, in such a way that his music will take on the glamor we associate with far-off lands.

UNIT V

MUSIC
WITHOUT
A STORY

19

Getting to Know the Symphony

In the past few chapters we have discussed program music—music, that is, which suggests something outside the tones themselves, whether a poetic story, a scene, or a mood. We now come to a type of music which has no specific meaning that can be described in words. Here the "story" consists of the sounds themselves and the feeling that these sounds arouse in us. Such music is known as *absolute* or "pure" music.

*The Nature of
the Symphony*

Absolute music is presented in large compositions that consist of three or four parts or *movements*. These movements contrast in tempo, mood, and character. If the first is fast and dramatic, the second may be slow and lyrical, the third dance-like, and the fourth triumphal. (Other patterns are possible too.) If a work of this kind is intended for one or two instruments it is known as a *sonata*. If it is for a small group of instruments it is called according to the number of players: *trio, quartet, quintet, sextet, septet, octet.* If for solo instrument and orchestra, it is a *concerto;* if for full orchestra, a *symphony.*

Each movement is woven out of two or three basic ideas or themes. These themes no longer represent specific characters such as Scheherazade, the Sultan, or the Sorcerer's Apprentice. The "story" of the movement consists of what happens to the themes—how they are presented, how they grow and develop, and how they are restated at the end. Naturally, these themes may suggest gay or sad moods to you. But the composer makes no attempt to direct your imagination; he gives you no clues as to what he had in mind while he was writing the music. His main purpose is to organize musical ideas in such a way that they will make sense to you. He leaves you free to feel the music in your own way, and to attach to the piece whatever meaning you wish.

Since a movement of a concerto, symphony, sonata, or string quartet follows no story content, it has to be held together by purely musical means. Hence we will find that form and structure are very important in absolute music.

The Structure of the Symphony

A *symphony* is a large work for orchestra in several movements, usually four. These are usually arranged in the sequence fast, slow, moderately fast, fast. (There are, of course, many exceptions to this.) As we said, the movements contrast in character and mood. Taken together, they form a big architectural unit.

In any discussion of a symphonic movement you will find the words *theme* and *motive*. As we have learned, a *theme* is a musical idea that a composer uses in the construction of a larger work. A *motive* is a small unit within a theme, which may be taken out and treated in all sorts of ways in order to develop the theme. For example, if we think of *London Bridge* as a theme, its first four notes—on the words "London Bridge is"—would form one motive. The next three notes form a second motive, which is repeated a step lower and then returns to its original position—on the words "falling down, falling down, falling down." Finally the last four notes, on the words "My fair lady," make up a third motive. By breaking a theme into motives and playing with each of these as his fancy directs him, the composer develops his themes just as a novelist develops his characters.

The First and Second Movements

The first movement is woven out of two contrasting themes (or three), which are set forth or "exposed," developed, then restated. Hence its form is like the one we encountered in the concert overture, consisting of three sections—Exposition, Development, and Recapitulation (Restatement). If the Exposition sets forth two basic themes, the first is apt to be strongly rhythmic, the second lyric. A *bridge* or transition leads from the first theme to the second. The Exposition may be preceded by a slow introduction; or the movement may begin directly with Theme 1. A *codetta* (little coda) rounds off this section.

The Development is marked by a tremendous increase in tension. The composer explores the different ways in which his themes can grow; he varies them, he plays with them, he breaks them up into their motives, he reveals them in a new light. He may contract a theme or expand it. He may present it in longer or shorter note values. He may transform it by changing the melody and harmony, rhythm and meter, tempo and dynamics, register and type of accompaniment. He may assign it to various instruments, or combine it with a new melody. In the development section he is the master builder who fashions a dazzling structure such as we could never have foreseen. Conflict and drama are the very essence of the Development.

In the Restatement or Recapitulation we hear the themes of the Exposition more or less in their original guise; but they have taken on a wealth of new meaning for us because of the way the composer developed them. The

Recapitulation is followed by a coda, whose function it is to conclude the action and bring the movement to its appointed end.

The pattern we have just described is known as *sonata-allegro* or *first-movement form*. Its structure is made clear by the following diagram:

EXPOSITION	DEVELOPMENT	RECAPITULATION
First theme	Themes broken up into motives and fashioned into new patterns.	First theme
Bridge	Increase in tension.	Bridge
Second theme	Transition back to first theme.	Second theme
Codetta		Coda

The first movement is epic or dramatic in character. By contrast, the second is usually a slow lyrical movement. It may be an A-B-A form; sometimes it is a theme and variations. It is generally marked Largo, Adagio, or Andante.

A novel differs from a short story in that the characters of the novel grow and develop in the course of the action. The same distinction holds between simple A-B-A form and sonata-allegro form. In A-B-A form the themes do not change much. On the other hand, in the Exposition-Development-Recapitulation of sonata-allegro form the themes grow and create ever new patterns; in other words, they develop in the course of the movement.

The Life of Antonín Dvořák

Antonín Dvořák followed Bedřich Smetana as a leader of the Czech national school. He was born on September 8, 1841, in a village near Prague. His father kept an inn and a butcher shop; the boy grew up in poverty. At the age of sixteen he made his way to Prague, determined to become a musician. He studied diligently and acquired a mastery of his art, supporting himself by playing in an orchestra and giving lessons. Dvořák found his true style when he turned for inspiration to the songs and dances of his homeland. His music brought him fame both in Bohemia and abroad. In time he was able to give up his job in the orchestra and devote himself to composing, teaching, and conducting.

In 1892 Dvořák was invited to become director of the National Conservatory of Music in New York City. His stay in the United States was extremely fruitful. He produced his most successful symphony, "From the New World," and a number of other works, among them the *American Quartet* and the Cello Concerto. But he loved Bohemia so much that he could not be happy anywhere else. After three years he returned to his homeland and spent his remaining years in Prague, in the happy circle of his wife and children, students and friends. He died there in his sixty-third year, on May 1, 1904, revered as a national artist throughout his native land.

Dvořák came to the United States as one of the leading nationalists of Europe. He tried to lead his pupils towards a national art. At that time young American composers went to study in Germany and tried to write like the Germans. Dvořák was convinced that they would write original works only when they threw off the influence of Europe and learned to stand on their own feet. One of his pupils was the Negro baritone Henry T. Burleigh, who later won fame as an arranger of spirituals. The Negro spirituals he heard from Burleigh appealed to the folk poet in Dvořák. "These beautiful and varied melodies," he wrote, "are the product of the soil. They are American. They are the folk songs of America, and your composers must turn to them."

The time was not yet ripe for his advice to be heeded. But Dvořák's instinct did not mislead him. Years after he left this country American composers began to use folk material as the basis for their music. We have only to listen to such works as George Gershwin's *Porgy and Bess* or Aaron Copland's *Rodeo* to realize how accurately Dvořák foresaw the future.

Symphony No. 5 (From the New World)

In this celebrated work Dvořák put into practice what he preached and showed his pupils how they might construct a symphony using materials in the style of American folk tunes. Yet he was too much of a Czech to try to write an American work. The title *From the New World* indicates his aim, which was to record the impressions of a visitor, his response to the vastness and energy of a young country, and at the same time to express his longing for his own land. The work, consequently, is a mixture of Czech and American elements.

First Movement

The symphony opens with an introduction marked Adagio, in which the woodwind instruments create an atmosphere of mystery. Dvořák here was inspired by the songs of the Indians. The movement itself, a vigorous Allegro molto (very fast), is a clear-cut example of sonata-allegro form. It is based on three themes. The first is an energetic melody that opens with an upward-leaping arpeggio. Notice the syncopated rhythm in the second and fourth measures, where a short note falls on the beat, while the accented note falls on the off-beat:

The second theme is a wistful tune in the style of a Bohemian folk song, introduced by a flute and oboe. Like many melodies born of the soil, it moves within a narrow range and with much repetition of tones:

FIRST PAGE OF DVOŘÁK'S MANUSCRIPT FOR THE *NEW WORLD
SYMPHONY.*

Of the Negro spirituals that Dvořák heard from his pupil Henry Burleigh,
his favorite was *Swing Low, Sweet Chariot.* This melody suggested to him
the outlines of the third idea of the movement. Notice the syncopation in
the second and sixth measures:

The Development is a fantasy of the first and third themes, held together
by a persistent dotted rhythm. It is brief, clear-cut, and full of energy. The
Recapitulation repeats the thematic material. There is a grandiose coda
based on descending chromatic scales, and the movement ends with the
basic arpeggio of Theme 1.

*Second
Movement*

The slow movement is the famous Largo, in $\frac{4}{4}$ time. Mysterious chords, marked *ppp,* introduce a poignant melody in the style of a folk song. It is sung by the English horn:

Dvořák here caught the longing of the weary ones of the earth. The son of the peasants set down what he felt, and what he felt rings true.

The middle part begins with a touching melody in the style of a Bohemian lullaby:

This section includes another melody sung by the clarinet. Then a staccato melody on the oboe suggests an outdoor scene. The orchestra works up a fortissimo climax; and we hear a reminder of two themes from the first movement. When a composer brings back themes from an earlier movement the symphony is said to be in *cyclical form.* Such reminders help to bind together the different movements; they have the same effect as when, in a novel or a play, a character remembers something that has happened in an earlier part of the story.

The first section—that is, the melody of the English horn—is repeated, so that the movement is in A-B-A form. The mysterious chords that served as an introduction return as a postlude, and the movement ends pianissimo and Molto adagio (very very slow).

20

The Symphony

(CONCLUDED)

The third movement of the symphony is usually the dance movement. In the symphonies of the late eighteenth century the dance was a minuet. In the nineteenth century the minuet was supplanted by the *scherzo* (skér-tso; this Italian word means a jest or a joke). Both the minuet and the scherzo are generally in $\frac{3}{4}$ (or $\frac{3}{8}$) time. The scherzo goes faster; it is more rhythmic, more impetuous. In both the minuet and scherzo, the middle part is known as the *trio;* it is quieter and gentler than the first section. At the end of the trio the first section is repeated *da capo* (dah káh-po)—from the beginning. Hence both the minuet and the scherzo are in A-B-A form.

The Third and Fourth Movements

The fourth movement balances the first in size and importance. It may be in sonata-allegro form, like the first. Sometimes it is a gay rondo, or a theme and variations. The eighteenth-century symphony usually ended on a gay note, the nineteenth century symphony on a note of triumph.

The following outline gives a bird's-eye view of the four movements. However, do not forget that the laws of music are far more flexible than those of physics or biology. While many symphonies follow this pattern, quite a few do not.

MOVEMENT	CHARACTER	FORM
First	Epic-dramatic	Sonata-allegro form
Second	Slow and lyrical	A-B-A *or* Theme and variations
Third	Dance-like: Minuet (18th century) *or* Scherzo (19th century)	Minuet and trio (A-B-A) Scherzo and trio (A-B-A)
Fourth	Lively finale (18th century) *or* Triumphal ending (19th century)	Sonata-allegro, Rondo, *or* Theme and variations

151

New World
Symphony:
*Third
Movement*

The Scherzo of the *New World Symphony* is marked Molto vivace (very lively). It is a dance movement in $\frac{3}{4}$ time, and is Czech in atmosphere. This movement is a large A-B-A form (Scherzo and Trio) in which each section is itself a smaller a-b-a form. We could diagram such a movement as follows:

    A   B   A

a - b - a   c - d - c   a - b - a

The opening theme (a) is strongly rhythmic and impetuous. Staccato notes emphasize its liveliness:

Molto vivace

p

A contrasting legato melody (b) is introduced by the flutes and oboes. It is marked Poco sostenuto (rather sustained).

Poco sostenuto

p   3   *etc.*

The first theme (a) is repeated, and builds up to an *fff* climax.

The middle section—the Trio—opens with a kind of rustic waltz that is down-to-earth (c). It alternates with a melody that is very light and gay, in which every other measure contains a trill (d).

At the end of the Trio, Dvořák wrote "Scherzo D.C." (Da Capo—that is, from the beginning). The repetition of the Scherzo is followed by a coda that brings back the upward arpeggio of the first movement as well as the opening notes of the "Swing Low" theme. With this reminder of what came before—a reminder that establishes the cyclical form of this symphony—the Scherzo comes to an end.

*Fourth
Movement*

The fourth movement, a fiery Allegro, is a large sonata-allegro form in $\frac{4}{4}$ time. The composer may have wished to pay tribute to the energy of a young country; he opens this movement with a stormy introduction that leads into a vigorous tune in the style of a march. It is played by trumpets and horns:

Allegro

ff   3   *ff*

In contrast to this is the second theme, a legato melody sung by the clarinet, in the nature of a revery. We do not need to know what the composer is dreaming about in order to enjoy the flow of his inspiration.

The third theme is in the style of a popular song, as if Dvořák wished to pay homage to the masses who will build the New World. It ends with three descending notes that seem to be taken from the familiar round known as *Three Blind Mice.* Here is a vigorous melody that could have come only from an artist who loved life:

The three final notes of this theme are treated as a motive that is tossed around from one instrumental group to another.

In the Development and Recapitulation we hear themes from the earlier movements. They now appear as old friends whom we thoroughly enjoy meeting again. Motives from various themes are combined into new patterns—for example, a motive from the Largo and the opening notes of the Scherzo. A rousing coda brings this symphony in cyclical form to an exciting close.

The *New World Symphony* has always been a favorite with the American public. It is melodious, it is clear in structure, and it speaks directly to the heart.

❧ 21 ❧

Three Symphonists:
Schumann, Brahms, Tchaikovsky

The Life of
Robert
Schumann

Robert Schumann was born in Saxony, in the town of Zwickau, on June 8, 1810. He was the son of a bookseller. Robert spent happy hours browsing among the books in his father's shop. He wrote poetry, made up melodies at the piano, and held his comrades spellbound with the wonderful tales he invented. His father was proud of Robert's talent and encouraged him in his desire to become a musician. Unfortunately, the elder Schumann died when the boy was sixteen. Now his future lay in the hands of his mother, who was opposed to music as a profession. She insisted that Robert study law.

After a year at the University of Leipzig, Robert transferred to Heidelberg. He enjoyed the carefree student life but hardly ever attended the lectures on law. Instead he read poetry, took courses in philosophy and art, and spent hours daydreaming at the piano. He finally persuaded his mother that he would never be happy until she allowed him to become a musician. Reluctantly she gave her consent.

Determined to become a concert pianist, Robert went to study with the best teacher in Leipzig, Friedrich Wieck (veek). "I am so fresh in soul and spirit," he exulted, "that life gushes and bubbles around me in a thousand springs." He was eager to make up for lost time and worked hard at the piano. In order to improve his technique quickly, he invented a gadget that held his fourth finger fastened back while the others exercised. (The fourth finger is the weakest, and needs special exercise in order to gain independence.) Robert's gadget was so effective that he injured the muscles of his right hand and had to give up all hope of becoming a pianist.

The accident was a blessing in disguise, for it turned all his energies to composing. In a fever of inspiration he wrote the works that established his fame as one of the great composers for the piano. "Everything comes to me of itself," he declared. "Indeed, it sometimes seems to me that I could play

154

on forever and never come to an end." He felt truly inspired. "Often I feel such a need to compose that even if I were on a lonely island in the middle of the ocean I could not stop. It makes me altogether happy, this art!"

These years witnessed his courtship of Friedrich Wieck's daughter Clara. When he first came to study with her father, she was an eleven-year-old prodigy at the piano. Clara lost her heart to the young man. She was about sixteen when Robert realized that he loved her. Friedrich Wieck had no reason for objecting to Robert as a son-in-law. But he had taught his daughter for years and had developed her into one of the great pianists of her time. He was unable to surrender her to anyone else, and tried by every means in his power to destroy her love for Robert. For several years Clara was torn between the father she revered and the man she adored. At last, since she was not yet of age, the lovers were forced to appeal to the courts against Wieck. The marriage took place in 1840, when Clara was twenty-one and Robert thirty. His happiness overflowed into a type of music even more personal than the piano. This was his "year of song," when he produced over a hundred of the songs that reveal him as one of the foremost lyric composers of the nineteenth century.

The two artists settled in Leipzig, pursuing their careers side by side. Clara played Robert's music at her concerts and helped to spread his fame. Yet despite his happiness with her and with their children, he grew increasingly moody as the years passed; he suffered from nervous exhaustion that brought on a severe breakdown. The doctors advised a change of scene; the couple moved to Dresden, where Schumann seemed to recover. But the periods of depression returned ever more frequently. "In these years," he wrote, "I have been very industrious. One must work as long as day lasts. . . ."

In 1850 Schumann was appointed music director at Düsseldorf, on the Rhine. But he was not suited for public life. He could not organize music festivals, like Mendelssohn, or deal with masses of men; indeed, when he conducted he had difficulty in explaining his wishes to the orchestra. Before long he was forced to give up his position. During a tour of Holland, where Clara and he were received with great enthusiasm, he began to complain of "unnatural noises" in his head. In a letter to a friend, two weeks before the final breakdown, he bade farewell to his art. "The music is silent now. I will close. Already it grows dark."

Clara tried to nurse him back to health, but in vain. In a fit of depression, he threw himself into the Rhine. He was rescued and was put into a private asylum near Bonn. The darkness did not lift. He died two years later, on July 29, 1856, at the age of forty-six.

Schumann above all was a lyricist; his songs are among the finest of the century. His piano pieces are full of fantasy. Their titles strike a romantic note: *Papillons* (Butterflies), *Scenes from Childhood, Fantasy Pieces, In the Night, The Poet Speaks.* Romantic too are the four symphonies and the magnificent Piano Concerto in A minor. Schumann also wrote chamber music, incidental music, and a wide variety of choral and orchestral pieces.

Johannes (yo-háh-ness) Brahms was born in Hamburg on May 7, 1833. He was the son of a double-bass player who struggled to make a living. Johannes grew up in a tenement district near the waterfront. As a youngster he helped to increase the family income by playing the piano in dance halls and cafés. Despite all obstacles he forged ahead with his musical studies, and showed such talent that the leading teachers of Hamburg taught him for nothing. By the time he was twenty he had acquired a reputation as a pianist, and accompanied a well known Hungarian violinist, Eduard Reményi, on a concert tour. From Reményi he heard the Hungarian Gypsy melodies that he later made famous in his *Hungarian Dances*.

His first compositions made an impression on Joseph Joachim (jo-áh-kheem), the most famous violinist of the day, who made it possible for Johannes to visit Robert and Clara Schumann at Düsseldorf. The shy, golden-haired youth played for Schumann his first major work—the Sonata in C major. Schumann, then almost at the end of his own career, published an essay in which he hailed the twenty-year-old "young eagle" as a genius. Johannes became famous overnight.

Robert and Clara took the young man into their home and made him feel like one of the family. His friendship with these two great artists opened up a new world for Johannes. He returned to Hamburg; five months later came the tragedy of Schumann's mental breakdown. Johannes hurried to Clara's side. She embarked on a concert tour to raise the money needed for Schumann's illness; Brahms remained behind to look after her children, towards whom he felt like an older brother.

Schumann lingered on for two years, while Johannes was shaken by the great love of his life. Clara Schumann was then at the height of her fame. She was fourteen years older than Johannes and the mother of seven children; but to him she seemed the ideal of perfection. She for her part found a source of strength in the loyalty of the "young eagle," and watched his genius unfold as she had once watched Robert's.

For Johannes this was a period of storm and stress, as his letters to Clara reveal. "I regret every word I write you that does not speak of love, affection, and self-denial. I can do nothing but think of you." At the same time he was torn by feelings of guilt, for he loved and revered Schumann, his friend and benefactor, above all others. He thought of suicide and spoke of himself—at twenty-two!—as "a man for whom nothing is left."

The conflict was resolved the following year by Schumann's death. Another conflict took its place. Now that he was able to marry Clara, Brahms was faced with the choice between love and freedom. Time and again during his life he was torn between the two, and always decided in favor of freedom. His love for Clara subsided into a lifelong friendship. Twenty years later he was able to write to her, "I love you more than myself and more than anybody and anything on earth." Toward the end of his life, when a misunderstanding threatened to end their friendship, he wrote to Clara, "Today you must allow me to repeat to you that you and your husband represent the most beautiful experience of my life, that you stand for its greatest wealth and noblest meaning."

He began his professional career as a conductor at the court of the Prince of Detmold. After four years he returned to Hamburg, hoping to find a position in his native city. At this time the conductor of the Hamburg Symphony Orchestra retired; Brahms had every right to expect that he would be appointed as the new conductor. But the directors of the orchestra could not forget that he had grown up in the slums near the waterfront, and passed him by. Deeply hurt, Brahms decided to leave Hamburg. He settled in Vienna, and remained there for the rest of his life.

Brahms never married. Although he occasionally complained of loneliness and fell in love several times, he could not face the responsibility of being tied to anyone. "It would be as difficult for me to marry," he explained, "as to write an opera. But after the first experience I should probably try a second!" Thus he went his way through the musical circles of Vienna, a crusty bachelor whose rough exterior hid a tender heart. Clara Schumann's death in 1896 affected him deeply. He died ten months later, on April 3, 1897, at the age of sixty-four, and was buried not far from Beethoven and Schubert.

Brahms's genius turned naturally to the great forms inherited from the past—symphony and concerto, sonata and string quartet. His songs and piano pieces reveal him as a romantic lyricist, the heir of Schubert and Schumann. In them we find the blend of tenderness and strength so characteristic of his music. His four symphonies are among the most important of the century. Of his other large works, the best known are the *Variations on a Theme by Haydn,* the *Academic Festival Overture, the Tragic Overture,* the two Piano Concertos, the Violin Concerto, the Double Concerto for Violin and Cello, and his largest choral work, the *German Requiem,* written to texts from the Bible.

*Schumann:
Rhenish
Symphony—
First
Movement*

When Schumann moved to Düsseldorf he was warmly welcomed by the musical public of the Rhineland. The impressions that crowded in upon him at this time resulted in one of his happiest works, the Symphony No. 3, known as the *Rhenish.* In this work, he declared, he tried to make the popular elements stand out, "and in this I think I have succeeded."

The first movement has a wonderful vitality and freshness. It is marked *Lebhaft*—the German equivalent of Allegro—and opens with the great upward-leaping theme that dominates the movement. The wide leaps and extended range of this melody, as well as its forward drive, give an impression of vast energy. Notice the syncopated rhythm that results from ties across the barline:

This melody is repeated by various groups within the orchestra.

A bridge leads into the contrasting idea. This is a lyrical theme sung by oboes and clarinets, legato and piano. It moves mostly stepwise within a narrow range and shows Schumann's highly personal lyricism:

Exposition, Development, and Recapitulation flower out of the interplay between these two ideas; they represent the two sides of Schumann's nature—the one impetuous and bold, the other tender and poetic. When the fortissimo coda brings this sonata-allegro movement to its triumphal conclusion, we feel that Schumann has explored all the possibilities of his two themes, and has revealed them to us in a most imaginative fashion.

*Brahms:
Symphony
No. 3—
Third
Movement*

Brahms, like Schumann, carried his lyricism into the symphony. He substituted, for the impetuous scherzo, a melodious third movement in moderate tempo.

FIRST PAGE OF BRAHMS'S MANUSCRIPT FOR HIS THIRD SYMPHONY.

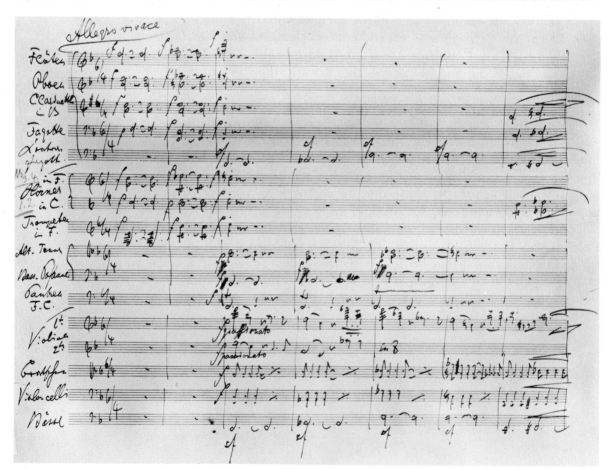

The third movement of his Symphony No. 3 is marked Poco Allegretto (a little allegretto) and is in $\frac{3}{8}$ time. The cellos introduce an impassioned melody that is played espressivo and mezza voce (méh-tsah vóh-tcheh, "half-voice,"—that is, softly and gently):

The middle section of this A-B-A movement is somewhat lighter in mood. Flutes and clarinets present a graceful melody:

The material of the first section returns with interesting changes in orchestration. For example, the heartfelt melody is now introduced by the horn instead of the cellos. A brief coda brings this beautiful song for orchestra to a close. The movement reflects Brahms's fondness for dark orchestral colors, his deep lyricism, and his manly emotion.

This exciting finale, an Allegro in $\frac{4}{4}$, begins fortissimo. The movement is in rondo form and alternates two contrasting ideas, in the pattern A-B-A-B-A-B-A. The two themes are not only repeated but are also developed; that is, they grow and change in the course of the movement.

The first is an impetuous idea based on passages rushing up and down the scale over a wide range.

Tchaikovsky: Symphony No. 4—Finale

The fact that this theme is played in unison and octaves by all the woodwinds and strings vastly increases its power. Tchaikovsky was extremely fond of this onrushing effect. He directed that the movement be played "with fire."

The second theme, based on a Russian folk song called *The Birch Tree,* serves as a perfect foil for the first. It is a plaintive little tune that moves gently along the scale and remains within a narrow range.

Tchaikovsky here demonstrates how a nationalist composer can use a popular melody as the basis for a symphonic movement. He handles this tune in the manner of a theme and variations, bringing it back again and again with changes in mood and instrumental color; rhythm and tempo (now faster, now slower, now in shorter notes, now in longer ones) ; dynamics (now soft, now loud); register (now high, now low); and type of accompaniment. At times he even combines his second theme with a motive extracted from the first. The movement rushes on with irresistible force until the moment when trumpets proclaim the dramatic "motto theme" with which the symphony opened. This motto theme, he wrote in a letter to Mme. von Meck, represented for him "the inescapable decree of Fate." Throughout the movement, and especially in the coda, Tchaikovsky moves from climax to climax, making the music go ever louder, faster, and higher in pitch. In this finale we find the brilliant orchestral writing and emotional style that have made Tchaikovsky's symphonies popular everywhere.

22

Getting to Know the Concerto

A *concerto* (con-tchéhr-to) is a large work in several movements for solo instruments and orchestra. When we listen to a concerto, our attention is focused on the soloist. For this reason, the piece has to give him every opportunity to display his technical powers. At the same time the concerto shows off the instrument and what it is able to do. In writing for soloist and orchestra, the composer is dealing with two different bodies of sound. The contrast between them creates dramatic tension, and this is the basis of the concerto's character and form.

In size the concerto may be compared to a symphony. Most concertos are in three movements: a dramatic allegro in first-movement form is followed by a songful slow movement and a brilliant finale. The finale is either a sonata-allegro form, a theme and variations, or a gay rondo. The basic themes of each movement may be announced by the *tutti* (tóo-tee; literally, "all"—that is, the orchestra as a whole) and then taken up by the solo part. Or the solo instrument may introduce the ideas, and the orchestra then comments on them.

An important feature of the concerto is the *cadenza*. This is a brilliant solo passage that is introduced into an orchestral work in order to show off the technique of the performer and the resources of the instrument. Originally the cadenza was improvised—that is, it was made up on the spur of the moment at the concert. Since not every performer was able to make up music as he went along, the custom was abandoned; the cadenza came to be written out beforehand, either by the composer himself or by a famous artist. The cadenza is one of the high points of a work, and frequently comes towards the end of the movement.

Edvard Grieg stands among the nationalist composers. As in the case of Smetana, his career unfolded during a patriotic struggle for freedom: Norway at that time was struggling for independence from Sweden. This cause, which Grieg supported with all his heart, was crowned with success towards the end of his life. "What has happened in our country this year," he wrote to a friend, "seems like a fairy tale. The hopes and longings of my youth have been fulfilled. I am deeply grateful that I was privileged to live to see this."

Grieg was born in Bergen on June 15, 1843, and died there on September 4, 1907, at the age of sixty-four. He was twenty-five years old when he wrote his Piano Concerto. It remained his masterpiece. The first movement is marked Allegro molto moderato (fast, but moderately so) and is in sonata-allegro form; it consists of an Exposition, Development, Recapitulation, and coda. The movement opens with a dramatic roll on the kettledrum. The first melody is quiet and suggests a northern landscape:

*Grieg: Piano
Concerto—
First
Movement*

If you examine this melody carefully you will notice that the pattern of the first two measures is repeated immediately on a higher degree of the scale. So too, the pattern of the fifth measure is repeated in the sixth, but higher. Such a repetition—on either a higher or lower scale step—is known as a *sequence*. Some of our most widely known melodies contain sequences. For example, in *London Bridge,* in the second, third, and fourth measures, on the words "falling down, falling down, falling down," we have a three-note pattern that is repeated a step lower and then returns to the original pitch. In *The Farmer in the Dell,* the melody pattern on the first six notes is immediately repeated at a higher degree on the scale. *America* contains an excellent example of sequence: the melody on the words "Land where my fathers died" is immediately repeated, a tone lower, on the words "Land of the Pilgrims' pride." You will find examples of sequence in many familiar tunes.

The main function of the bridge is to lead from the first theme to the second. Sometimes, however, this transition is made so attractive that it takes on the character of a theme. Such is the case with the bridge in the first movement of Grieg's concerto:

The second theme is marked Tranquillo e cantabile (can-táh-bee-lay)—that is, tranquil and songful. Introduced by the cellos and echoed by the piano, it too contains a sequence (under the brackets):

This melody contains a particularly fine example of a sequence:

The Development is based mainly on the first theme. The Recapitulation brings back the material more or less as we heard it in the Exposition. The climax of the movement comes with the cadenza, which presents the main theme in a dramatic form, with ascending runs, massive chords, and brilliant octaves. The movement ends with a coda marked Poco più allegro (a little faster).

It was given to Edvard Grieg to reveal the landscape of his homeland and the soul of his people. He fulfilled his role with such devotion that for the world at large he remains "the voice of Norway."

Mendelssohn: Violin Concerto— First Movement

Mendelssohn's is probably the most popular violin concerto ever written. He composed it with a definite soloist in mind—Ferdinand David, his concertmaster in the Leipzig orchestra. "I should like to write a violin concerto for you next winter," he informed David. "One in E minor is running through my head, and the beginning does not leave me in peace." Some time later he wrote David that "the whole of the first solo is to be for the E string." While he was writing the piece he frequently asked the concertmaster's advice as to what lay well for the hand.

In a piano concerto, the contrast between the solo sound and the orchestra is clearly defined, since piano tone stands out against all other instruments. In a violin concerto the problem is different; the solo instrument has to be kept distinct from the violins in the orchestra. Mendelssohn solved this through contrasts of register. The solo violin soars high above the orchestra so that the melody is distinct from the harmony. Or the solo line will descend to the middle register when the violins in the orchestra are playing in the upper range. In either case the listener has no difficulty in keeping the two bodies of sound apart.

The first movement is a sonata-allegro form marked Allegro molto appassionato (very fast and impassioned). It was customary at that time for the orchestra to play the opening section of a concerto before the soloist entered. But Mendelssohn brought in the violin solo at once, with an energetic melody that is the main theme of the movement:

Allegro molto appassionato

This idea is expanded and gives the soloist opportunity for brilliant display. Then the opening melody is proclaimed by the full orchestra.

As was the case in the Grieg concerto, the bridge that leads from the first to the second theme is made so attractive that it becomes a melody in its own right:

Then we hear the second theme, a lyric idea that serves as an area of relaxation in the forward drive of the movement. In contrast to the first theme, this melody remains within a narrow range and moves either by step or with narrow leaps:

Now that the two themes have been "exposed," they are developed with vigor and imagination. The cadenza is most exciting, and is in an unusual place. Instead of coming towards the end of the movement, as is customary, it is heard at the end of the Development and serves as a link between that section and the Recapitulation. Under a curtain of arpeggios on the violin, the opening theme is heard in the orchestra. From here to the coda the movement steadily builds up tension through a crescendo, accelerando, and rise to the brilliant upper register.

Mendelssohn's Concerto combines flowing melody with tender sentiment and brilliant technique. One can understand why it has remained a favorite with violinists and audiences alike.

UNIT VI

MUSIC IN HISTORY:
STYLES AND PERIODS

23A

Nineteenth-Century Romanticism

We have seen that the artist is part of the world about him. In expressing his own emotions, he also expresses the dreams and ideals of the time he lives in.

How Music Reflects History

For this reason art reflects the thoughts and feelings of different periods in history. An expert can tell at once to what era a painting or a piece of sculpture belongs. The same holds for architecture and music. Every work of art bears the stamp of the period and style from which it sprang.

Following is a table of the main style-periods in Europen history. The dates indicate approximately when each period began and ended.

850–1150 A.D.	Romanesque (Middle Ages)
1150–1450	Gothic (Late Middle Ages)
1450–1600	Renaissance
1600–1750	Baroque
1725–1775	Rococo
1775–1825	Classic
1820–1900	Romantic
1890–1915	Post-romantic (including Impressionism)
1910–	The New Music

We begin our study of music in history with the period that is still the most popular with the public—nineteenth-century romanticism.

The Romantic Movement

The history of art moves between two attitudes. In a certain period artists want their work to be orderly and serene. At another time they prefer that their art be full of strangeness and wonder. One generation accepts the traditions of the past, another rebels against tradition and seeks new paths. One generation tries to create beautiful designs and perfect forms. Another is more interested in expressing intense emotion. We call the one style classical, the other romantic.

Classic and romantic elements have existed throughout history. But in the years after the French Revolution the romantic point of view became so strong that the nineteenth century is known as the Romantic Era. At that time the middle class broke the power of kings and princes. A more democratic way of life came into being, and a new middle-class public for art. This public wanted a more emotional style than had the aristocrats of the old regime. Art began to emphasize the feelings of the individual. Nationalism came to the fore as a result of the Napoleonic Wars. Revolutions swept through a number of countries in 1830 and 1848. Europe was in turmoil in the first half of the nineteenth century. All this encouraged a more emotional style in literature, music, and art: a style that expressed personal feelings in the strongest possible way.

Thus, one of the most important traits of the new style was its emphasis on emotion. The romantic spirit expressed itself in the passionate style of such lyric poets as Byron, Shelley, and Keats. It was reflected in the novels of Walter Scott, Emily Brontë, and George Eliot; in the sympathy for the poor and the oppressed that we find in the novels of Charles Dickens and Victor Hugo; in the love of the strange and the fantastic that colors the writings of Coleridge, Hawthorne, and Edgar Allan Poe. Also in the dramatic painting of such artists as Eugène Delacroix (de-la-crwáh), Turner, and Corot (coh-róh). The romantic movement in music produced a brilliant line of composers who have remained enormously popular. Among them

EUGÈNE DELACROIX, *THE LION HUNT*.
Delacroix's painting mirrored the emotionalism and drama of the romantic movement.

are a number whose works we have studied: Schubert, Berlioz, Mendelssohn, Chopin, Schumann, Liszt, Wagner, Verdi, Gounod, Offenbach, Smetana, Brahms, Borodin, Bizet, Musorgsky, Tchaikovsky, Chabrier, Dvořák, Grieg, and Rimsky-Korsakov.

*Main
Characteristics
of Musical
Romanticism*

1. For centuries the artist had worked mainly for the aristocracy. He had been a commoner creating for princes who were interested in his art rather than in him. In the romantic period, for the first time, he addressed an audience of his social equals. His joys and sorrows could be expressed in his art. And so the romantic composers developed a style marked by *intense personal emotion,* such as we find in the music of Chopin and Tchaikovsky.

2. The romantic composers wanted to bring music closer to life. This desire led to an emphasis on program music, especially the *symphonic poem.* Through the symphonic poem and other types of program music, the art of music moved ever closer to its sister arts of poetry and painting.

3. The rise of national feeling in Europe after the Napoleonic Wars encouraged the rise of *musical nationalism.*

4. Romantic longing for far-off lands led to *musical exoticism,* which went hand in hand with the growing ability of the orchestra to evoke color and atmosphere.

5. The growth of the middle-class public had important results. Music moved from the palace to the public concert hall. A paying public made possible larger and better orchestras. As a result, composers could write

JOSEPH M. W. TURNER, *GRAND CANAL, VENICE.*
The romantic longing for far-off lands led to exoticism in music and painting.

more difficult pieces and experiment with new sound effects. This led to greater emphasis on the art of *orchestration.*

6. There now appeared the concert artist who went from city to city captivating the public. With this came a new emphasis on the personality of the performer, and a great interest in *virtuosity*—that is, the utmost mastery of technique.

7. The new middle-class public needed more and better-trained musicians than formerly. In addition, a more democratic society needed more and better schools. This led to the founding of important music schools in the principal cities of Europe, such as the Conservatory of Leipzig, founded by Mendelssohn; the Conservatory of St. Petersburg (now Leningrad), founded by Anton Rubinstein; and the Conservatory of Moscow, founded by Nicholas Rubinstein.

8. The composer played a more important part in organizing musical life and educating the public. Composers became active as teachers, critics, conductors, organizers of festivals, and directors of conservatories.

9. The desire for personal expression of an intimate kind led to a great interest in the *short lyric forms:* the romantic song and piano piece.

10. At the same time the romantic composers continued to cultivate the large forms of absolute music, especially the symphony and concerto. The romantic symphony was marked by vivid color, picturesque atmosphere, grand climaxes, and intense drama. We heard movements from several romantic symphonies and concertos.

Two Romantic Composers:
Franz Liszt and Hector Berlioz

*The Life of
Franz Liszt*

Franz Liszt, one of the most striking figures of the romantic period, was born in the village of Raiding, in Hungary, on October 22, 1811. His father, Adam Liszt, was a steward on the estate of Prince Esterházy, the wealthiest nobleman in the country. Franz showed great talent at an early age, but Adam did not have the means to give him a musical education. Whereupon Prince Esterházy and several other Hungarian noblemen saw to it that the boy was taught properly. Adam took his son to Vienna, where Franz astonished the public with his playing. The great Beethoven himself prophesied a brilliant future for him.

When Franz was eleven, his father and he set out for Paris. They hoped that he would be admitted to the Conservatory; but no foreigners were allowed to study at the famous school, and the director refused to make an exception for Franz's great talent. Adam and his son overcame this disappointment. Franz studied with other masters, worked diligently, and after several years became the most dazzling pianist of his time.

Franz was extremely handsome and had a magnetic personality; he enchanted his audiences. He was the first one to play a full piano recital in public. (Before that time, pianists had presented only part of a concert program, the rest of it being devoted to other kinds of music.) Instead of sitting with his back to the audience or facing it, as had been the custom hitherto, he sat with his profile to the public, which was a much more effective arrangement. He toured Europe again and again, and was received everywhere with rapturous enthusiasm.

However, he realized more and more that the life of a traveling virtuoso did not give him the peace of mind he needed in order to compose. Finally he reached a decision. At the height of his fame he retired from the concert stage and became director of music at the court of the Grand Duke of Weimar (vý-mar), where he spent the next thirteen years. During this period he wrote his most important orchestral works.

The Weimar period saw Liszt's friendship with the woman who most strongly influenced his life, Princess Carolyne Sayn-Wittgenstein. She was the wife of a powerful noble at the court of the Tsar, who fell in love with Liszt during his last concert tour of Russia. Shortly thereafter she joined him in Weimar. For years she tried to obtain a divorce from her husband. When this was finally granted, she went to Rome to obtain a dispensation from the Pope. Everything was in readiness for the wedding when a courier arrived with the news that the Pope had turned down her request, and the marriage could not take place.

During his last years Liszt sought peace by entering the Church; he took minor orders and was known as Abbé Liszt. This was the period when he devoted himself to religious music. He divided his time between Rome, Weimar, and Budapest, the friend of princes and cardinals. At seventy-five he was received with enthusiasm in England. He went to visit his daughter Cosima, Richard Wagner's widow, in Bayreuth, and died there on July 31, 1886, at the age of seventy-five, admired all over the world as one of the foremost musicians of his time.

Liszt believed in "the renewal of music," as he called it, "through its inner connection with poetry." He created the symphonic poem, basing his compositions on *theme transformation*. By shifting a theme from soft to loud, from slow to fast, from low to high, from strings to woodwinds or brass (or the other way around), he was able to transform its character so that the same theme might suggest love in one section, a nature scene in another,

His Music

171

struggle in a third, and triumph in the last. He was a pioneer in regard to harmony, form, and orchestral color; and helped to create the modern piano technique. A great teacher, he raised a generation of famous concert pianists. And he influenced composers from Wagner and Berlioz to Ravel and George Gershwin.

Les Préludes

Les Préludes (lay pray-lóod, The Preludes) is the most popular of Liszt's symphonic poems. "What is our life," asks the program attached to the score, "but a series of preludes to that unknown song whose first solemn note is tolled by Death?" The soul dreams of immortality and searches for love, but the storms of life drive away happiness. Then man seeks refuge in the beauty of nature. Refreshed, he returns to the battle, to gain full knowledge of himself in the struggle with fate.

The music of *Les Préludes* illustrates Liszt's idea of theme transformation. The themes suggesting man's vision of immortality, his longing for love, his struggle with fate, his turning to nature, and his final victory are all derived from one basic idea, which is transformed from one mood to the next through changes in rhythm, meter, tempo, register, dynamics, and orchestration.

The basic motive of three notes is presented by the strings. The upward leap between the second and third note gives the motive the shape of a ques-

tion: What is life? A leap from B to E is an interval of a fourth (B-C-D-E; by an *interval* we mean the distance between two tones). This ascending interval is to be found in all the themes derived from the basic motive.

There follows a fortissimo section for full orchestra, Andante maestoso (at a going pace, majestic), the "prelude to that unknown song" which symbolizes the soul's striving for higher things. Notice that the upward leap of a fourth is present in both the melody and the accompaniment.

Next we hear two love themes. The first, espressivo cantando (expressively, singing), is played by string instruments. The basic motive (under bracket) is embedded in the melody.

The second love theme is played by muted violas and horns, espressivo ma tranquillo (expressive but tranquil). This melody seems to contrast with the preceding one. When we examine it closely, however, we see that it contains the three notes of the basic motive (notes marked *x*) in an expanded form:

espressivo ma tranquillo

The tempo quickens, tension mounts. The basic motive is heard against stormy chromatic scales. It is transformed into a theme of struggle, played fast and loud in high register by the brass.

Relaxation follows with the Allegretto pastorale, a peaceful nature scene. Again the basic theme is transformed. This time it is presented mezzo piano, at a flowing tempo, by woodwinds and horns:

The return to the fray is marked by an Allegro marziale animato (fast, martial, animated). The two love themes, transformed into battle calls, are played fortissimo by trumpets and trombones. Finally the "prelude to that unknown song" is heard again, and the symphonic poem ends on a note of triumph.

Hector Berlioz and the Program Symphony

The impulse toward program music grew so strong during the romantic period that it invaded even the stronghold of absolute music—the symphony. Thus developed the *program symphony*—a large piece for orchestra in several movements, in the form of a symphony, based on a literary or pictorial program. The most important work in this area was done by Hector Berlioz.

This great French composer was born in the province of Isère on December 11, 1803. His parents sent him to Paris to study medicine, but he soon abandoned his studies in order to devote himself to music. Paris at this time was the center of the new romanticism. Berlioz, along with Victor Hugo and the painter Delacroix, found himself in the forefront of the revolutionary movement in art. In 1830, when he was twenty-seven, he composed what has remained the most celebrated of all program symphonies, the *Symphonie fantastique* (sahm-fon-ée fan-tas-téek). In the following decades he produced a number of masterpieces, among them *The Damnation of Faust*, a large work for chorus and orchestra (from which we heard an excerpt, the *Hun-*

173

garian March); *Harold in Italy,* a program symphony inspired by the poem of Lord Byron; and *Romeo and Juliet,* a "dramatic symphony" with voices. He died in Paris, bitter because of the neglect of his countrymen, on March 8, 1869, in his sixty-sixth year. "Some day," wrote Richard Wagner, "a grateful France will raise a proud monument on his tomb." The prophecy has been fulfilled.

Berlioz's genius showed itself especially in the field of orchestration. He handled the instruments in such an original way that he opened up a new world of romantic sound. His discoveries influenced the composers who came after him. As a matter of fact, he has been called "the creator of the modern orchestra."

Symphonie fantastique

Berlioz's most famous work evokes the stormy emotions that accompanied his love for the Irish actress Harriet Smithson (whom he later married and of whom he soon grew tired). His program note for the symphony tells of a sensitive young musician who, hopelessly in love, "has poisoned himself with opium. The drug, too weak to kill, plunges him into a heavy sleep accompanied by strange visions. His sensations, feelings and memories are translated in his sick brain into musical images and ideas. The Beloved herself becomes for him a melody, a 'fixed idea' that haunts him everywhere."

This "fixed idea" becomes the basic theme of the symphony. It recurs throughout the five movements of the work with changes in rhythm, meter, tempo, register, dynamics, and orchestration, to suggest various moods. Thus the *Symphonie fantastique,* like *Les Préludes,* employs the technique of theme transformation.

Second Movement: *A Ball.* "Amid the tumult and excitement of a brilliant ball, he glimpses the loved one again." This movement of the symphony is marked Valse, Allegro non troppo (waltz, not too fast). The introduction presents arpeggios on the harp against a string tremolo—a combination that makes a lovely sound. The waltz itself begins "sweet and tender."

The movement is in A-B-A form. In the middle section the "fixed idea"—the theme of the Beloved—appears in waltz time, introduced by flute and oboe.

The climax at the end is built up through a crescendo, an accelerando, and a rise in pitch.

Fourth Movement: *March to the Scaffold.* "He dreams that he has killed his beloved, that he has been condemned to die and is being led to the scaffold. The procession moves to the sounds of a march now somber and wild, now brilliant and solemn. At the very end the 'fixed idea' reappears for an instant, like a last thought of love interrupted by the fall of the axe."

This march movement, an Allegretto in $\frac{4}{4}$ time, shows the nineteenth-century love of the fantastic. After a brief introduction, the lower string instruments play an energetic theme that moves downward along the scale. Then the diabolical march emerges in the woodwinds and brass.

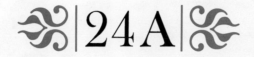

The theme of the Beloved appears at the very end, on the clarinet, and is cut off by a grim fortissimo chord ("like a last thought of love interrupted by the fall of the axe"). Composers today no longer try to make music depict an event so vividly. But when Berlioz wrote this he was opening up new areas of expression for his art.

Liszt and Berlioz are recognized today as major figures of the romantic period. Their music sums up the romantic love of drama, color, and picturesque atmosphere.

24A

Eighteenth-Century Classicism

The dictionary defines "classicism" in two ways: 1) pertaining to the highest order of excellence in art; 2) pertaining to the culture of ancient Greece and Rome. The eighteenth century admired the art of the ancient world because it was an orderly art, balanced and poised. The eighteenth century was the Age of Reason even as the nineteenth was an age of emotion.

Eighteenth-century art revolved around the palaces of kings and princes. Beneath the brilliant surface of this aristocratic society a storm was brewing. The American Revolution dealt a final blow to the doctrine of the divine right of kings. Before the century was over, Europe was thrown into

THE PARTHENON.
The qualities of order, stability, and poise associated with the classical style.

VIRGINIA STATE CAPITOL.
Thomas Jefferson introduced the style of classical architecture into the young republic.

turmoil by the French Revolution. The second half of the eighteenth century saw both the twilight of the old regime and the dawn of a new democratic society.

The old aristocracy based its wealth on ownership of the land. At this time it was losing its power to the new middle class, whose wealth was based on commerce and industry. The rise of the new society was made possible by the Industrial Revolution and its inventions. During the final decades of the century Watts invented the steam engine, Cartwright the power loom, and Eli Whitney the cotton gin. Science made important advances. Benjamin Franklin experimented with electricity in 1752, Priestley discovered oxygen in 1774, Jenner developed vaccination in 1796. During these years the political philosophers of the middle class, such as Voltaire and Jean Jacques Rousseau (zhon zhok roo-sów), wrote the books that prepared the way for the French Revolution.

In the second half of the eighteenth century aristocratic classicism and middle-class romanticism existed side by side. On the one hand we find a formal spirit in literature and painting. On the other hand we find a more emotional style in the poetry of Thomas Gray, Robert Burns, and their contemporaries. These poets, like Goethe in Germany, were the first voices of a dawning romanticism. Although they wrote in the final decades of the eighteenth century, they already foretold a new spirit in art.

The Artist Under Patronage

The eighteenth-century artist functioned under the system of aristocratic patronage. As a rule he was attached to a court and wrote his works for the entertainment of his princely masters. In other words, he created for a public that was high above him in social rank. This public was interested in his art rather than in him personally. Under such conditions he was not encouraged to become too personal. Indeed, it would have been almost impertinent for him to do so. Inevitably he took on the classical attitudes of objectivity and controlled emotion. (By *objectivity* we mean the artist's ability to remain outside the art work as well as inside it; his ability to view life and the world around him as they are, apart from himself, rather than in terms of his own personality and his own needs. The romantic artist, needless to say, approached art and life in a *subjective,* more emotional way.)

In comparing the artist under the patronage system with the "free" artist of the romantic period, it is well to remember that each had his advantages and disadvantages. The romantic artist was not only free to express himself but also, unfortunately, free to starve. The classical artist, on the other hand, had no financial worries if he found a generous patron. Each system was adapted to its time and its society. The important thing for us is that each in its own way produced great works of art.

Classicism in literature and painting reached its peak during the middle decades of the eighteenth century. In music the classic era came a little later, from around 1775 to 1825, and takes in the works of the four masters of the classic Viennese school—Haydn, Mozart, Beethoven, and Schubert.

It is clear at a glance that this period was not all of a piece. Part of it

JACQUES-LOUIS DAVID, *THE DEATH OF SOCRATES*.
Classicism in painting drew its inspiration from ancient Greece and Rome.

came before the French Revolution, part of it after. Certainly Beethoven and Schubert lived in a different world from that of Haydn and Mozart. What these four masters had in common, however, was that they all adhered to the classical ideal of *emotion controlled within a beautiful form*. Each felt himself to have inherited the tradition of those who came before him, to which he added the rich fantasy of his own genius.

Eighteenth-century classicism, then, mirrored that moment in history when an old world was dying and a new world was being born. From the meeting of these two forces sprang an art of noble simplicity that produced some of the supreme masterpieces of music.

Classicism and Romanticism: a Comparison

CLASSICISM	ROMANTICISM
1. About 1775–1825. Before and after the French Revolution.	1. About 1820–1900. An outgrowth of the French Revolution.
2. Artist works under the patronage of the aristocracy.	2. Artist works for a steadily increasing public based on the middle class.
3. International in spirit. Its two main forms—Italian opera and Viennese symphony—stood above national frontiers.	3. Rise of musical nationalism.
4. Turned for inspiration to the culture of ancient Greece and Rome.	4. Found inspiration in the Middle Ages.
5. Center of musical life is the palace.	5. Center of musical life is the public concert hall.
6. Art strives to be objective and stresses universal values.	6. Art is intensely subjective and personal. Emphasis on self-expression.

CLASSICISM	ROMANTICISM
7. The emotion, no matter how deeply felt, is *controlled within a form*.	7. The emotion tends to overpower and loosen the form.
8. Composers looked upon music as an independent, self-contained art. Emphasis on *absolute music*.	8. Composers tried to bring music closer to literature and painting. Emphasis on *program music*.
9. The symphonies of Haydn and Mozart were conceived in terms of the aristocratic salon. Orchestra consists of 35 to 40 players.	9. Symphonies and concertos were conceived in relation to a large concert hall. Orchestra steadily increases in size.
10. Essentially aristocratic in nature (even though the Viennese masters frequently drew inspiration from popular song and dance).	10. Increasing emphasis on folklore, fairy tales, folk song and dance. A democratic art.
11. Classic music did not lay great emphasis on nature.	11. Romantic music glorified nature in numerous landscapes and sea scenes.
12. The classic composer concentrated on the development of abstract musical ideas. Subordinated all details to the logic and clarity of the overall form.	12. Romantic art emphasized exotic atmosphere and picturesque details.
13. The classic masters perfected the large instrumental forms—symphony, concerto, string quartet, solo sonata.	13. Emphasis on short lyric forms: songs and piano pieces of Schubert, Schumann, Chopin. Expanded the symphony and concerto. Created the symphonic poem. Emphasized the concert overture.
14. Music essentially optimistic, cheerful, an adornment of gracious living.	14. Music increasingly dramatic, tragic, allied with romantic ideas —man against Fate, struggle for freedom, nature, God, country.

Joseph Haydn

Joseph Haydn was born in Rohrau, a village in lower Austria, on March 31, 1732. He was the son of a wheelwright. Even at the age of three he showed great interest in music. At village festivals he would imitate the fiddlers, rubbing two sticks together in perfect time with the singing and dancing. His

His Life

father wanted Joseph to have a better opportunity in the world than he had had, and sent the boy to live with a cousin who was a schoolmaster in the neighboring town of Hainburg. There Joseph learned to play the violin and other instruments. On Sundays he sang in the church choir; his beautiful soprano voice aroused great admiration.

One Sunday morning an important visitor arrived in the church. This was the choirmaster of St. Stephen's Cathedral in Vienna, who was looking for a boy soprano for his choir. When he heard Joseph he knew at once that he had found the right one, and wrote to the boy's parents for their permission. A week later Joseph, at the age of eight, set out for the capital of the Austrian empire.

At St. Stephen's, where he remained for eight years, Joseph received a sound musical education. When he was sixteen his voice broke, and he left the school to take up the career of a professional musician. In those days there was much music in the streets of Vienna. Groups of players wandered through the city, stopping at a street corner or beneath the windows of a house to perform a piece or two. Joseph joined these roving bands and was able to earn his living. He accompanied singers, gave lessons, and played the organ at church. After long hours of work he would climb up the six flights of stairs to his attic and sit far into the night studying the works of great composers. Only one thing mattered to him: to master every branch of his art and to become as fine a composer as he could.

During the next years Haydn was engaged to play and conduct his compositions at the homes of various Austrian noblemen. In 1761, when he was twenty-nine, he found his great opportunity. He entered the service of Prince Esterházy, a fabulously wealthy Hungarian nobleman who was famous for his patronage of the arts. He remained with the Esterházy family

THE ESTERHÁZY PALACE, one of the most splendid in Europe.

for almost thirty years—that is, for the greater part of his creative career.

The Esterházy palace was one of the most splendid in Europe. The various princes of the family entertained lavishly; music played an important part in their festivities. Haydn had under his direction an orchestra, an opera company, a marionette theater, and the chapel choir, for all of which he supplied the music. His career is an example of the patronage system at its best. "My Prince was always satisfied with my works," he wrote. "I not only had the encouragement of constant approval but, as conductor of an orchestra, I could make experiments, observe what produced an effect and what weakened it, and was thus in a position to improve, alter, make additions or omissions, and be as bold as I pleased. I was cut off from the world, there was no one to confuse or torment me, and I was forced to become *original.*"

After Prince Nicholas Esterházy's death Haydn made two visits to England, where he conducted his works with remarkable success. He returned to his homeland laden with honors and financially well off. He died in Vienna on May 31, 1809, at the age of seventy-seven, revered by his countrymen and acknowledged throughout Europe as the foremost musician of his time.

His Music

Haydn lived at a time when musicians were developing a new language for the instruments. He experimented with new forms and idioms, and moved forward steadily in the course of his career. He played a leading role in developing the classic orchestral style, the symphony and the string quartet. His genius leaned towards instrumental music; he showed endless imagination in developing his themes. He wrote more than 100 symphonies and 83 string quartets; also much church music, and a wide variety of instrumental and vocal works.

Haydn's was the optimism of a man who found life—even in its darker moments—supremely worth living. He had a clear vision of his goal. "Often when I was struggling against obstacles of all kinds, often when strength of mind and body failed me and it was difficult to persevere in the course on which I had set out, an inner voice whispered to me, 'There are so few happy and contented people here below. Everywhere men are burdened with sorrow. Perhaps your work may be a source of relief and joy for those oppressed by care.' Here was a powerful reason for going on!"

Andante and Minuet from the Surprise *Symphony*

The best known of Haydn's symphonies, the *Surprise,* is one of a set of six that he wrote for his first visit to London in 1791. The second movement of this symphony, the celebrated Andante, is a theme and variations. The theme, announced by the violins, staccato, has the simplicity of a folk song.

This eight-measure phrase is repeated very softly and ends in an abrupt fortissimo crash—the "surprise" that gives the symphony its name. "There,"

Haydn remarked to a friend, "all the ladies will scream." Behind the wish to make the ladies scream lay a deeper motive: the desire of a master musician to explore the possibilities of the orchestra. The dramatic contrast between soft and loud was one of the exciting effects of the new symphonic style.

Variation 1. The theme is combined with a descending figure in the first violins.

Variation 2. The third note of the melody, E, is lowered to E-flat. This, as we shall see in the next chapter, involves a shift from major to minor. The theme is played fortissimo.

Variation 3 returns to the major. The theme is heard in a new rhythm.

In the second half of this variation the theme is combined with a melody played by solo flute and oboe.

Variation 4. The theme is heard with changes in dynamics, register, and orchestration; also with a new accompaniment in triplets. The second half of this variation introduces a new version of the melody.

This striking variation ends on a sustained chord that leads into the coda. Now the theme appears above new harmonies. The final measures of the movement are like a gentle summing up. They have a wonderful sound.

We have mentioned the fact that in the late eighteenth century aristocratic and democratic elements existed side by side. This is well reflected in the third movement of the Surprise Symphony. The form is that of the aristocratic minuet; but the spirit is that of a jolly peasant dance. Marked Allegro molto (very fast), the movement is full of an earthy good humor much closer to the village green than to the palace.

Allegro molto

The middle section, or Trio, is quieter. It combines bassoon and string tone. Then the first section is repeated da capo (from the beginning), giving a clear-cut A-B-A form.

The last movement of the Trumpet Concerto is a perfect example of the lively rondo with which Haydn liked to end a work. The secret of such an Allegro is its dance-like gayety and lightness.

 The movement is based on two lively themes, which are presented in the orchestra before being taken over by the solo instrument. These two melodies are repeated over and over. Haydn added, varied, and created new patterns with each repetition. As a result, this rondo not only repeats the basic themes but also develops them.

Concerto for Trumpet and Orchestra— Third Movement

The Creation, for soloists, chorus, and orchestra, is based on Milton's *Paradise Lost* and the Book of Genesis, which tells how God created the earth. In this work the earth and its beauties are described with that feeling of wonder which only children and artists know.

 The Heavens Are Telling, which ends the first part, is a splendid example of Haydn's choral style. This is a sturdy Allegro in $\frac{4}{4}$; the sections for chorus are set off by passages sung by a trio of angels (soprano, tenor, and bass). Haydn skillfully contrasts the massive sonority of the chorus with the gentler sound of the trio.

The Heavens Are Telling *from* The Creation

CHORUS

Die Himmel erzählen die Ehre Gottes, und seiner Hände Werk zeigt an das Firmament.

The heavens are telling the glory of God, And the firmament shows the wonder of his work.

TRIO

Dem kommenden Tage sagt es der Tag; die Nacht, die verschwand, der folgenden Nacht.

Each day reveals it to the following day, Each night that passes, to the following night.

CHORUS

Die Himmel erzählen die Ehre Gottes, und seiner Hände Werk zeigt an das Firmament.

The heavens are telling the glory of God, And the firmament shows the wonder of his work.

TRIO

In alle Welt ergeht das Wort, jedem Ohre klingend, keiner Zunge fremd.

The word spreads throughout the world, Resounding in every ear, known to every tongue.

CHORUS (*as before*)

183

Notice that certain phrases and lines of the text are repeated over and over. This is a typical feature of choral writing. The masters realized that music takes longer to establish a mood than words do. For example, it takes only a second to say "happy," but it takes music considerably longer to establish a happy mood. For this reason they used a few lines of text to establish the mood of a choral number, and repeated the same words again and again while the music interpreted the words.

The final passage is sung by the *tutti* (all). Here Haydn directs that the movement be taken faster, which provides a fitting climax for this majestic chorus.

Chamber Music

By *chamber music* we mean music for from two to eight or nine players. There is a basic distinction between chamber and orchestral music. We found that in orchestral music a number of instruments play a single part—eighteen first violins, sixteen second violins, twelve violas, and so on. In chamber music, on the other hand, there is only one player to each part. The sound, in consequence, is much lighter and more transparent than that of the orchestra.

The characteristic trait of chamber music is its *intimacy and refinement.* Its natural setting is the home, just as the natural setting for orchestral music is the concert hall. In chamber music the various instruments are part of a group, and strive above all for perfect teamwork. Each player asserts himself not as an individual but through the group.

JACK LEVINE, *STRING QUARTET.*
The central position in classic chamber music was held by the string quartet.

The classic era saw the golden age of chamber music. Haydn and Mozart, Beethoven and Schubert established the true chamber-music style, which is like a friendly conversation among equals. Theirs is a noble art, marked by clear thinking and freshness of feeling.

The central position in classical chamber music was held by the string quartet. Consisting of first and second violins, viola, and cello, this group came to represent the ideal type of happy comradeship among instruments. Other favorite combinations were the duo sonata—piano and violin or piano and cello; the trio—piano, violin, and cello; and the quintet, usually consisting of a string quartet and a solo instrument such as piano or clarinet. The classical masters also produced memorable examples of chamber music for the larger groups—sextet, septet, and octet.

Haydn was in his early twenties when he wrote his first string quartet. He was past seventy when he began his last. His 83 string quartets bear witness to a half century of artistic growth.

The six quartets of Opus 3 were written some time after 1760, during his first years in the service of the Esterházys. (*Opus,* abbreviated Op., is the Latin word for "work." Followed by a number, it is used to show the position of a particular piece in a composer's total output. For example, "Opus 3" indicates the third work that the composer wrote or published. Sometimes an opus may contain several works, in which case we speak of Opus 3, No. 1; Opus 3, No. 2; and so on.) The fifth of the set contains an Andante cantabile (fairly slow, songful) which is a favorite with the public. It is known as the "Serenade." The first violin, muted, carries a lovely melody against a pizzicato accompaniment in the other strings.

One has only to hear it to realize how strongly the master was influenced by Austrian popular song.

Haydn's music is as fresh and delightful today as when it was written. Behind it stands a great creative spirit who love life, and who projected that love into his art.

How Musical Sounds
Are Organized

What Is A Key?

When you listen to a musical program, you will notice that the pieces are identified as Symphony in A major, Melody in F, Minuet in G, Waltz in C-sharp minor, according to the key in which they are written—that is, according to the group of tones on which each piece is based.

The group is held together by a central tone to which all the others gravitate. Try singing the series *do-re-mi-fa-sol-la-ti*. When you stop on *ti* you are left suspended, and feel an almost physical urge to continue on to *do*—that is, to *resolve* the *ti* to *do*. This *do* is the central tone or *keynote* of the group. The term has come to be used outside of music, as when we speak of the keynote of the President's speech, meaning the central point. By a *key*, then, we mean a family of related tones with a common center to which they all resolve. The keynote is also known as the *tonic*.

The keynote gives its name to the group. When we speak of a Symphony in A we mean a symphony based on the members of the key of A major, that resolve to the central tone or keynote, A. This tone is heard at the end of the melody, and the chord based on this tone is the *tonic chord* that gives you a feeling of conclusion at the end of the piece.

This loyalty to a central tone or tonic is known as *tonality*. All music written in the eighteenth and nineteenth centuries—which means the greater part of the music you will hear—is based on the principle of tonality. When, at the end of a long movement, the orchestra repeats the final chord over and over again, it is telling you that the conclusion has been reached. The tension within the piece has been resolved, the action has been completed.

The Major Scale

If you look at the piano keyboard, you will notice that between one C and the next there are seven white and five black keys. Each of these is a half-tone distance from its neighbor. This means that the octave, in our music, is divided into twelve half-tones or semitones. These are duplicated in the different octaves. As the composer Paul Hindemith used to tell his pupils, "There are only twelve tones. You must treat them carefully."

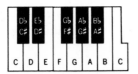

Note: As we learned in Chapter 7B, the black keys are named in relation to their white neighbors. When the black key between C and D is thought of as a semitone higher than C, it is known as C♯. When it is regarded as a semitone lower than D, the same key is called D♭. Which of these names is used depends upon the scale in which a particular sharp or flat appears.

Out of these twelve tones, seven are picked in order to form a key. Since the first tone—or keynote—is repeated at the end of the series, the group consists of eight tones. If you play the eight white tones from C to C you will hear the familiar *do-re-mi-fa-sol-la-ti-do* pattern. These eight tones, beginning on C, form the group or key of C major.

Look closely at the keyboard, and you will notice that these eight tones are not all equally distant from each other. Where the two white keys have a black key between them they are two semitones or a whole tone apart. At two places on the keyboard the white keys have no black key between them: E-F (steps 3-4) and B-C (steps 7-8). These tones therefore are only a semitone apart. When we sing the *do-re-mi-fa-sol-la-ti-do* pattern we are marking off a series of whole tones except between *mi-fa* (steps 3-4) and *ti-do* (steps 7-8).

A *scale* presents the tones of the key in consecutive order, ascending or descending. The *do-re-mi* series—the one we have just examined—is the *major scale,* which consists of eight tones that are a whole tone apart, except steps 3-4 and 7-8, which are a half tone apart. This was the basic scale of the classic and romantic periods.

The major scale may be built from any one of the twelve tones of the octave. In other words, you can measure off the *do-re-mi-fa-sol-la-ti-do* pattern from any one of these twelve tones. Whichever is used as starting-point, that tone at once takes on the role of tonic or key center. It becomes the point of departure *and return.* With each starting-point we will get a different group of seven out of twelve. As the musician says it, each key will have a different number of sharps or flats, and a different keynote. C major is the only key that has no sharps or flats. All the others have.

Suppose you build the major scale from G. You will need an F♯ in order to make the tones fit the pattern of whole and half steps:

G-A-B-C-D-E-F♯-G
1-2-3-4-5-6-7-8

If you play *America* beginning on G—in the key of G major—you will have to play an F♯ in the course of the melody. Should you play F♮ it would be a wrong note, since there is no F♮ in this group. If you build the major scale from D you will need two sharps—F♯ and C♯—to fit the pattern:

D-E-F♯-G-A-B-C♯-D
1-2-3-4-5-6-7-8

*The Minor
Scale*

When we say that a piece is in D major, we mean it is based on the eight tones of the group that has two sharps and gravitates to the keynote D.

The minor scale differs from the major mainly in that its third step is lowered. In the most popular version of this scale the sixth step is lowered as well, so that the C minor scale reads: C-D-E♭-F-G-A♭-B-C. *Minor,* the Latin word for "smaller," refers to the fact that the interval C-E♭ is smaller than the corresponding interval C-E in the major (larger) scale.

Like the major, the minor scale may be built from each of the twelve tones of the octave. In each case there will be a different group of seven tones out of twelve—that is, each minor scale will have a different number of sharps or flats. Thus every tone in the octave may serve as a starting point or keynote for either a major or minor scale; which gives us twelve major keys and twelve minor keys. In identifying a piece, the minor is always specified, the major may or may not be: Melody in F, Minuet in G, Symphony in A major, Grieg's Piano Concerto in A minor, Mendelssohn's Violin Concerto in E minor.

The minor scale has a certain exotic ring to Western ears and is popularly associated with oriental and east European music. The folk songs of eastern Europe—Russia, Poland, Hungary, and the Balkans—favor the minor, just as the folk music of the United States and western Europe—France, England, Germany—leans towards the major. However, there are many exceptions to this rule.

Is the minor "sadder" than the major? Composers of the nineteenth century seem to have thought so. The funeral marches of Beethoven, Mendelssohn, Chopin, and Wagner are in the minor, while the triumphal finales of a number of symphonies and overtures of the same period are in the major. Shifting a melody from minor to major brightens it. We heard an example of this in Smetana's *The Moldau.* The chief melody of this work appears first in E minor. Towards the end of the piece, when the music is moving towards a mood of triumph, the same tune reappears with the third and sixth scale steps raised—that is, shifted to E major. There can be no question that this shift brightens the color.

When a piece is in a key requiring sharps or flats, they are written at the beginning of each line of music and are known as the *key signature.* You will find a table of the twelve major and twelve minor key signatures and scales in Appendix B, on page 341.

Our major-minor system may be compared to a two-story structure that has twelve rooms on the first floor and twelve on the second. The rooms on the lower floor give the impression of being larger and brighter than the twelve on the second floor.

Any one who lived in such a house would certainly not spend his life in one room only. He would use the corridors and doorways leading from one room into the next. So, too, composers as a rule do not write a piece in a single key. They establish one key as the home area; in the course of the piece they will shift to another key, then return to the one from which they set out. Or they may wander farther afield, through several foreign keys, before the inevitable return home.

The act of going from one key to another is known as *modulation*. It is an expressive effect in music, for it "lifts" the listener from one key to another. As one of the leading composers of the twentieth century, Arnold Schoenberg, put it, "Modulation is like a change of scenery." As a result of modulation, a musical movement really moves.

This is especially true of sonata-allegro form, which is based on a conflict between the home key and a contrasting key. Needless to say, the home key is the victor. The first theme establishes the home key, the second theme represents the contrasting key. The Exposition, consequently, starts out from the home key and modulates to the contrasting key. In the Development the composer heightens our excitement by leading us from key to key, building up tension against the inevitable return home. With the Recapitulation we return to the home key; we hear the first theme as we heard it at the beginning of the movement. The second theme is usually shifted into the home key, and the coda affirms the final victory of the home key. On page 147 we presented an outline of sonata-allegro form in regard to the themes that make up the movement. We may now expand this outline to include the key structure:

EXPOSITION	DEVELOPMENT	RECAPITULATION
First theme—home key	Modulates from key to key, but avoids home key	First theme—home key
Bridge—modulates to contrasting key		Bridge
	Increase in tension	
Second theme—contrasting key		Second theme—shifted to home key
	At the end of this section, a transition leads back to home key	
Codetta—contrasting key		Coda—reaffirms the home key

Modulation is not limited to this form. In almost every piece of any length there is apt to be a departure from and return to the home key. By taking advantage of the power of modulation to "change the scenery," the composer introduces action and direction into the music. Once the home key is established the music flows into other territories, and then brings us back safely to the home base.

189

❧|25B|❧

Wolfgang Amadeus Mozart

Of all the wonder children in the history of music, Wolfgang Amadeus Mozart (vólf-gahng a-ma-dáy-us móh-tsart) was the most extraordinary. He grew up to be one of the greatest artists that ever lived.

He was born in the Austrian city of Salzburg (sáhlz-boorg) on January 27, 1756, the son of an esteemed composer-violinist at the court of the Prince-Archbishop. His father trained him carefully from his earliest childhood. The boy began to compose before he was five, and his fame soon spread throughout Salzburg. When he was six he played before the Empress Maria Theresa, who was enchanted with his talent. His father took him on two extended tours, in the course of which he visited various European countries. The lad played before the French king, Louis XV, at Versailles (ver-sígh). Then he went to London, where he played before George III. His genius and his charm impressed all who heard him. By the time he was thirteen he had written concertos, symphonies, sonatas, chamber music, religious works, and operas.

Wolfgang reached manhood having attained a mastery of all forms of his art. The speed and sureness of his creative power were unmatched by any other composer. "Though a composition be long," he wrote, "it is complete and finished in my mind. For this reason I can put it on paper quickly enough, since everything is already finished, and it rarely differs on paper from what it was in my imagination."

Wolfgang's patron, the Prince-Archbishop of Salzburg, was a true lover of music who fully appreciated the young man's genius. He was succeeded by Count von Colloredo, who treated his court musicians as little better than servants. Wolfgang was a high-spirited youth who rebelled against the social restrictions of the patronage system. "The two valets sit at the head of the table," he informed his father. "I at least have the honor of sitting above the cooks." Finally he could bear his position no longer. He quarreled with the Archbishop and was dismissed. He did not regret the break. At last he was free to leave Salzburg and seek his fortune in Vienna, the capital of the Empire.

He was twenty-five when he established himself in Vienna. Only ten more years remained to him. These were spent in a tragic struggle to achieve financial security and to find again the lost happiness of his childhood. Success depended on the favor of the court; but the Emperor Joseph II—Maria Theresa's son—passed him by in favor of lesser men. When Mozart was finally taken into the Emperor's service he was assigned to tasks unworthy of his genius, such as composing dances for the balls at court. Upon receiving his pay he remarked with bitterness, "It's too much for what I do, too little for what I could do."

He fell in love with a pretty young singer named Constanze Weber. His father opposed the match, because Constanze had no money. But Mozart did what his heart told him, and married her. Unfortunately Constanze had neither the strength of character nor the resources to help her husband in his struggle. Not till many years after his death did she realize, from the admiration of the world, the greatness of the man whose life she had shared.

In Vienna Mozart became friendly with the court poet Lorenzo da Ponte. They both loved fun and laughter, and decided to collaborate on a comic opera. Thus came into being *The Marriage of Figaro,* written in 1786 on da Ponte's libretto. This work marked the peak of Mozart's career as far as worldly success was concerned. *Figaro* made a sensation in Vienna and Prague.

He was commissioned to do another work for the following year. With da Ponte again as librettist he produced *Don Giovanni.* The opera baffled the Viennese. We today look upon his music as being so clear and graceful; yet the public of his time found him hard to understand. One publisher advised him to write in a more popular style. "In that case," he answered, "I can make no more by my pen. I had better starve and die at once."

The last years of his life were spent in growing want; more and more often he was forced to turn to his friends for aid. His letters reflect his helplessness and despair. He describes himself as "always hovering between hope and anxiety." He asks for a loan so that he may work "with a mind *more free* from care and *with a lighter heart* and thus earn more. . . . If I only had at least 600 gulden I should be able to compose with a fairly easy mind. Ah! I must have peace of mind." As the disappointments piled up, his former gayety and love of life began to desert him. Again and again he set out on a journey that promised to solve all his difficulties—only to return empty-handed. A note of defeat crept into his letters to Constanze. "I cannot describe what I have been feeling. A kind of emptiness that hurts me dreadfully —a kind of longing that is never satisfied, that never ceases, that persists— no, rather increases daily."

Music had flowed from his brain since his childhood. Now came a time when he was too discouraged to compose. Then, in the last year of his life, he nerved himself to the final effort. A man named Emanuel Schikaneder, who owned a little theater on the outskirts of Vienna, asked him to write an opera in popular style, so that the common people could enjoy it. Mozart agreed, and based his opera on Schikaneder's libretto. Instead of using Italian, the language of operas at court, they wrote their opera in German so that the audience would understand the action. In this manner was born the first great German opera, *The Magic Flute.*

With a flurry of hope Mozart set off for Prague, for the coronation of Leopold II as King of Bohemia. The opera he composed for this event was overshadowed by the ceremonies of the coronation. He returned to Vienna broken in body and spirit. With a kind of feverish desperation he plunged into his last work, the Requiem, which had been ordered from him by a Count who loved music. As Mozart wrote this work he became convinced that this Mass for the Dead was intended for himself, and that he would not live to finish it. A hopeless race with time began as he forged ahead with this masterpiece.

His last days were cheered by the growing popularity of *The Magic Flute*. Watch in hand, he would follow the performance in his mind. "Now the first act is over. . . . Now comes the aria of the Queen of Night. . . ." His forebodings concerning the Requiem came true; he failed rapidly while in the midst of the work. His favorite pupil completed the Mass from the master's sketches, with additions of his own.

Mozart died shortly before his thirty-sixth birthday. Because of his debts he was given "the poorest class of funeral." The weather was bad, and his friends turned back at the city gates. Thus, with no one to do him honor, this prince of music was cast into a pauper's grave, without even a tombstone to mark his resting place. But his monument is more enduring than marble.

His Music

Mozart occupies a unique position in the history of his art. He was as great in opera as in symphony and concerto, in religious music as in chamber music. It has been said that he taught the instruments how to sing. In truth he filled his beautiful instrumental forms with a songful lyricism drawn from the great vocal art of the past. In Mozart's works the restlessness and the longing are transformed by the serene loveliness of classical art. He is the voice of pure beauty in music, and probably the most completely musical composer that ever lived.

The Marriage of Figaro— Overture and Two Arias

The Overture to *The Marriage of Figaro* is a gay, busy theater piece that puts the audience in the proper frame of mind for a comedy. The themes and the material that connects them are in one mood, so that the forward drive of the music never slackens.

The opening melody, in the home key of D, glides along as lightly and rapidly as possible:

192

The contrasting theme, in the key of A, sustains the mood even though it is not quite so active a melody; this idea expands into a vigorous section. There follows a third theme in A, a saucy little tune that is truly Mozartian in its high spirits.

A brief codetta rounds off the Exposition. There is no Development; in other words, the Recapitulation begins almost immediately, and follows the course of the Exposition. All three themes are now heard in the home key of D major. The coda begins pianissimo and builds up in an exciting crescendo to the gay ending.

The action of the opera revolves around Figaro, the steward of the Spanish Count Almaviva, who is engaged to the Countess' pretty maid Susanna. Unfortunately the Count is attracted to the girl, which complicates matters for everybody. In the end Figaro with the help of Susanna and the Countess outwits his master, and the lovers are united. As for the unfaithful Count, he begs—and obtains—his wife's forgiveness.

Cherubino, the Count's page, is a lively boy whom everyone loves. With the best will in the world he is continually getting himself—and others—into hot water. At one point the Count decides to send him away, and appoints him captain in a regiment stationed in Seville. Figaro sings the famous aria *Non più andrai* (non pyoo an-drý) : "From now on," he tells the lad, "you'll be a soldier and have no more time for romantic adventures."

Non più andrai, farfallone amoroso,	No more flitting about at your leisure,
notte e giorno d'intorno girando,	Days and nights of carousing and pleasure,
delle belle turbando il riposo,	While you dance and you flirt with the ladies,
Narcisetto, Adoncino d'amor.	And disturb them with sweet words of love!
Delle belle turbando il riposo,	While you dance and romance all the ladies,
Narcisetto, Adoncino d'amor.	And disturb them with sweet words of love!
Non più avrai questi bei pennacchini,	No more will you wear those handsome plumes,
quel cappello leggiero e galante,	That elegant cap at a rakish angle,
quella chioma, quell'aria brillante,	Curly hair, dashing air,
quel vermiglio donnesco color,	That pink, almost girlish complexion,
quel vermiglio donnesco color.	That pink, almost girlish complexion!
Non più avrai quei pennacchini,	No more will you wear those plumes,
quel cappello, quella chioma,	That cap, curly hair,
quell'aria brillante.	And that dashing air.
Non più andrai farfallone amoroso,	No more flitting about at your leisure,
notte e giorno d'intorno girando,	Days and nights of carousing and pleasure,
delle belle turbando il riposo,	While you dance and you flirt with the ladies,

Narcisetto, Adoncino d'amor.
Delle belle turbando il riposo,

Narcisetto, Adoncino d'amor.

And disturb them with sweet words of love!
While you dance and romance all the ladies,
And disturb them with sweet words of love!

Fra guerrieri, poffar Bacco!
Gran mustacchi, stretto sacco,
schioppo in spalla, sciabola al fianco,
collo dritto, muso franco;

Among warriors, by Jove!
Thick mustache, tight jacket,
A gun at your shoulder, a sword at your side,
Standing at attention with a bold expression;

un gran casco, o un gran turbante,
molto onor, poco contante!
Ed invece del fandango
una marcia per il fango.
Per montagne, per valloni,
colle nevi, e i sollioni,
al concerto di tromboni,
di bombarde, e di cannoni,
che le palle in tutti i tuoni,
all'orecchio fan fischiar.

A big helmet, or a big turban,
Much honor, but little money!
And instead of a gay dance,
Marching through the mud,
Over hill and dale,
In snow or scorching sun,
To the sound of trombones,
Of guns and cannon,
With cannon-balls thundering
And whistling in your ears.

Non più avrai quei pennacchini,
non più avrai quel cappello,
non più avrai quella chioma,
non più avrai quell'aria brillante.

No more plumes,
No more cap,
No more curly hair,
No more that dashing air!

Non più andrai, farfallone amoroso,
notte e giorno d'intorno girando,
delle belle turbando il riposo,

No more flitting about at your leisure,
Days and nights of carousing and pleasure,
While you dance and you flirt with the ladies,

Narcisetto, Adoncino d'amor.
Delle belle turbando il riposo,

Narcisetto, Adoncino d'amor.

And disturb them with sweet words of love!
While you dance and romance all the ladies,
And disturb them with sweet words of love!

Cherubino, alla vittoria,
Alla gloria militar!

Cherubino, march to victory
And the glory of war!

[repeated]

Notice how vividly the music traces the change from the life of a carefree young fellow to the rigors of army life. This of course involves trumpets and drums in the final measures of the aria.

Cherubino, who is very much attached to the Countess, writes a song in which he expresses his love for his noble mistress. Susanna makes him sing it to the Countess, which he does while Susanna accompanies him on the guitar. The strings play a pizzicato accompaniment to suggest that instrument. As is the case in many operas of the eighteenth century, the part of the young boy is sung by a soprano. This little aria, *Voi che sapete* (voy kay sa-páy-teh), an Allegretto in $\frac{2}{4}$, is one of Mozart's most enchanting melodies.

CHERUBINO SINGS *VOI CHE SAPETE* TO SUSANNA AND THE COUNTESS.

Voi, che sapete che cosa è amor,	Ladies so gracious, tell me, I beg,
donne vedete, s'io l'ho nel cor,	What is this feeling, can it be love?
donne vedete s'io l'ho nel cor.	Tell me quite frankly, am I in love?
Quello ch'io provo vi ridirò,	What I experience, I tell you,
è per me nuovo, capir nol so.	Is something new for me, that I cannot understand.
Sento un affetto pien di desir,	I feel an emotion full of desire,
ch'ora è diletto, ch'ora e martir.	Which now delights me, now tortures me.
Gelo, e poi sento l'alma avvampar,	I freeze, then I feel my soul aflame,
e in un momento torno a gelar.	And in a moment I turn to ice.
Ricerco un bene fuori di me,	I seek a happiness outside myself,
non so ch'il tiene, non so cos'è.	I know not who has it or what it is.
Sospiro e gemo senza voler,	I sigh and grieve without wanting to,
palpito e tremo senza saper.	I shiver and tremble without knowing why.
Non trovo pace notte nè dì,	I find no peace, night or day,
ma pur mi piace languir così.	And yet I love my misery . . .
Voi che sapete che cosa è amor,	Tell me quite frankly, am I in love?
donne vedete, s'io l'ho nel cor.	Ladies so gracious, tell me, I beg.

Andante con moto

mf

Voi, che sa - pe - te che co - sa è a - mor,
La - dies so gra - cious, tell me, I beg,

don - ne, ve - de - te, s'io l'ho nel cor!
What is this feel - ing, can it be love?

don - ne, ve - de - te, s'io l'ho nel cor!
Tell me quite frank - ly, am I in love?

Eine kleine Nachtmusik— *First Movement*

The elegance and lightness of touch that we associate with Mozart are embodied in this celebrated "serenade for strings," whose German title (pronounced éye-nuh kléye-nuh náhkt-moo-seek), means "A Little Night Music." The piece was composed, or at any rate written down, in a single day. The score calls for first and second violin, viola, cello, and double bass. When the work was performed there were probably several players to each part, so that this Serenade stands between chamber and orchestral music. It is in four movements, graceful, intimate, and beautifully proportioned. We heard the last two movements—the Minuet and Rondo—in connection with Chapter 5.

The first movement is a sonata-allegro form in $\frac{4}{4}$ time. The three themes of which the movement is fashioned—the first in the home key of G major, the other two in D—contrast in mood. The first is an assertive theme in the character of a march, as if the musicians were arriving for their cheerful task:

Allegro

f

The second and third themes are light and graceful. Their development is brief. In the Recapitulation all three themes are heard in G, thereby reaffirming the home key.

This is typical eighteenth-century music that conjures up a world of crystal chandeliers, powdered wigs, and lace ruffles. Therein lies its charm.

Symphony No. 40 in G minor— *First Movement*

In the summer of 1788, during the darkest period of his life, Mozart—in the space of a little over six weeks—composed his three last and greatest symphonies: No. 39 in E-flat, No. 40 in G minor, and No. 41 in C (*Jupiter*). In the G-minor Symphony he looked beyond the classic period towards the dawn of a new era. The impassioned note of this work heralds the romantic age.

The first movement is in sonata-allegro form. The Exposition opens with an intense theme played by the violins, which establishes the home key of G minor. It flowers out of a three-note motive that is capable of growth and development.

A vigorous bridge passage leads into the key of B-flat major. The second theme, shared by woodwinds and strings, provides an area of relaxation in the impetuous drive of the movement.

The codetta echoes the three-note motive of the opening. As was the custom of the classic era, the Exposition is repeated.

The Development is brief and packed with action. Mozart searches out the possibilities of the first theme, concentrating on the three-note motive. The music modulates from key to key. The principal theme is heard in sequence —that is, now higher, now lower—with an occasional change in the pattern of the melody. The music builds up tension against the inevitable return home. With the reappearance of the first theme we are back in the home key.

The Recapitulation follows the course of the first section, except that the second theme is shifted to G minor. The coda confirms the home key, bringing to a close one of the most beautiful movements in the symphonic literature.

The final movement of Mozart's Piano Sonata in A has always been a favorite with the public. The exotic or "Turkish" character of the piece is underlined by the main theme in A minor that reappears throughout the rondo, softly:

Turkish Rondo

This is followed by a loud and lively theme in A major:

The contrast between the two themes is most effective. Notice how bright the major sounds when it follows directly on the minor. This music has all the charm of the eighteenth-century style. It has, besides, that inner grace which we associate with the art of Wolfgang Amadeus Mozart.

26

Ludwig van Beethoven

Ludwig van Beethoven (lúd-vig van báy-toh-ven) belonged to the first generation that came to maturity under the influence of the French Revolution. His motto was "Freedom above all!"

His Life

He was born in Bonn, in the Rhineland, on December 16, 1770. His father and grandfather were singers at the Prince's court. The boy grew up in an unhappy home; his father was a weak-willed man who drank heavily and bullied his family. He was very strict with Ludwig and made him practice the piano for hours every day, since he wanted him to become a famous pianist as young Mozart had been. The time came when Ludwig's father was no longer capable of working. The boy had to take over the support of his mother and two younger brothers. At the age of twelve he played the piano and organ in the Prince's palace. The following year he was put in charge of orchestra rehearsals in the court theater. The men in the orchestra were astonished when a boy came out to lead them; but they were so impressed with his talent that they soon accepted him as their conductor.

He was a silent, moody lad; his responsibilities made him serious beyond his years. Fortunately, at the palace he came in contact with musicians who taught him much about the art of composition. When he was twenty-two he realized that there was nothing further for him to learn at Bonn. The Prince arranged for him to study in Vienna with Haydn. With high hopes he left his native city, never to return.

The youth did not get on too well with his teacher. The aging Haydn was shocked by the young man's stormy temperament, his independence of spirit, and his outspoken sympathy with the French Revolution. Beethoven soon went to other teachers, one of whom stated that "he has learned nothing and will never do anything in decent style."

Meanwhile his powers as a pianist made a deep impression on the aristocracy of Vienna. Archduke Rudolph, a brother of the Emperor, became his pupil and friend. To this "princely rabble," as he called them, the young genius came—in an era of revolution—as a passionate rebel, forcing them to receive him as an equal. "It is good to move among the aristocracy," he observed, "but it is first necessary to make them respect you." The day had passed when the artist in livery waited in the antechamber to receive his instructions. One evening, when a nobleman persisted in talking while Beethoven was playing the piano, he broke off, jumped up, and cried, "For such pigs I do not play!" On another occasion one of his patrons, Prince Lichnowsky, insisted that he play when he was not in a mood to do so. Beethoven stormed out of the palace in a rage, smashed a bust of Lichnowsky that he owned, and wrote to his exalted friend: "Prince! what you are, you are through the accident of birth. What I am, I am through my own efforts. There have been many princes and there will be thousands more. But there is only one Beethoven!" Never before had any one dared to affirm that an artist was as important as a prince. Such was the force of Beethoven's personality that he was able to make the aristocrats around him accept him on his own terms.

Beethoven functioned under a modified form of the patronage system. He was not attached to the court of a prince, as Haydn had been. Instead, the Viennese princes helped him in various ways—by paying him handsomely for lessons, or through gifts. He was also helped by the growth of the middle-class public, which resulted in many more concerts and greater activity in music publishing. At the age of thirty-one he was able to say, "I have six or seven publishers for each of my works and could have more if I chose. No more bargaining. I name my terms and they pay."

Then, just as the young eagle was spreading his wings, Fate struck him in a vulnerable spot: he began to lose his hearing. This affliction dealt a shattering blow to his pride. "Ah, how could I possibly admit an illness in the one sense that should have been more perfect in me than in others. A sense I once possessed in the highest perfection. Oh I cannot do it!" As his deafness closed in on him—the first symptoms appeared during his late twenties—he became ever more aware of how lonely he was, how apart from other men. His malady became the symbol of all the defiance, insecurity, and hunger for love that had seethed in him from as far back as he could remember. "Forgive me," he wrote in a moving letter to his brothers, "when you see me draw back when I would gladly mingle with you. My misfortune is doubly painful because it must lead to my being misunderstood. For me there can be no recreation in the society of my fellows. I must live like an exile!"

His doctors advised him that he ought to spare his hearing by being alone as much as possible. Accordingly, in the summer of 1802 Beethoven retired to a village outside Vienna. A terrible struggle shook him, between the destructive forces in his soul and his desire to live and create. He went through one of those inner crises that either break a man or leave him stronger. "But little more and I would have put an end to my life. It was only art that held me back. Ah, it seemed impossible to leave the world until I had produced all that I felt called upon to produce, and so I endured this wretched existence."

Slowly he realized that art alone could give him the happiness which life denied him. Only through creation would he win the victory of which Fate had threatened to rob him. The will to struggle asserted itself within him; he fought his way back to health. "I am determined to rise superior to every obstacle! With whom need I be afraid of measuring my strength? If possible I will bid defiance to my fate, although there will be moments in life when I will be the unhappiest of God's creatures. . . . I will take Fate by the throat; it shall not overcome me! Oh how beautiful it is to be alive—would that I could live a thousand times!"

Having conquered the chaos within himself, he came to believe that man could conquer chaos. This became the heroic theme of his music—from conflict to serenity, from serenity to joy, and from joy to triumph. Out of his own suffering he forged a message of hope, a vision of man as master of his fate. "Whoever truly understands my music," he said, "is thereby freed from the miseries that others carry about in them."

Portraits of Beethoven have made us familiar with the squat sturdy figure—he was only five feet four, the same as Napoleon—as he walked through the suburbs of Vienna. His brow furrowed in thought, he would stop every so often to jot down an idea in his sketchbook—an idea which, because he was forever deprived of its actual sound, he imagined all the more vividly in his mind. A ride in an open carriage in bad weather brought on an illness that proved fatal. He died in Vienna on March 26, 1827, in his fifty-seventh year, famous and revered throughout the musical world.

His Music

Beethoven is the supreme architect in music. He inherited the symphony from Haydn and Mozart, and put upon it the stamp of his own personality. He expanded the first movement, especially the coda. The slow movement became, in his hands, a hymn-like adagio. The third movement, which had been a minuet, he transformed into a scherzo bursting with energy. He also enlarged the fourth movement so that it became equal in importance to the first, and ended the symphony—as the new age required—on a note of triumph. His nine symphonies are orchestral dramas of universal appeal. They are conceived on a scale too grand for the aristocratic drawing room. In these works Beethoven addresses the world.

His Third Symphony, the *Eroica*, Beethoven originally dedicated to Napoleon Bonaparte, First Consul of the Republic, whom he saw as a symbol of the revolution and the freedom of man. When the news reached him that Napoleon had proclaimed himself Emperor, Beethoven was disillusioned. "He too is just like any other! Now he will trample on the rights of man and serve nothing but his own ambition." The embittered composer tore up the dedication and renamed the work "Heroic Symphony to celebrate the memory of a great man." A conqueror himself—did he not once declare, "I too am a king"?—he understood Bonaparte. "It is a great pity I do not comprehend the art of war as well as I do the art of music. I would conquer him!"

Among his many instrumental works the thirty-two piano sonatas are of major importance, as are the five piano concertos, the violin concerto, and sixteen string quartets. He enriched the literature of vocal music with the opera *Fidelio,* the Missa Solemnis (Solemn Mass), and the choral finale of the Ninth Symphony. In addition, he wrote a number of beautiful songs.

Beethoven's life fell in almost equal parts in the eighteenth and nineteenth centuries. His career bridged the transition from the old society to the new. Because of his impassioned style, many people thought of him as a romantic. But we today see him as one who brought the great classical forms to their final development. Throughout his works he succeeded in controlling emotion, imposing upon it the logic and discipline of classical form. That is why, despite the powerful feeling in his music, we regard him as one of the great masters of the classical style.

The most popular of all symphonies, Beethoven's Fifth, is in the key of C minor. It begins with an Allegro con brio (fast, with vigor). The movement springs out of the rhythmic idea of "three shorts and a long" that dominates the whole symphony.

Out of it flowers the first theme which repeats the "three shorts and a long" at different levels of the scale, sometimes with different intervals.

The movement surges forward with relentless drive. We reach an area of relaxation with the lyric second theme in E-flat major. Yet even here the movement does not slacken in its course. Underneath the caressing melody, the "three shorts and a long" persist in the bass, uttered by the cellos and double basses.

Basic rhythm

FIRST PAGE OF BEETHOVEN'S MANUSCRIPT FOR HIS FIFTH SYMPHONY.

The Development is woven out of the basic rhythm. Characteristic of Beethoven are the violent contrasts between soft and loud, and the crescendos that grow with irresistible power. We reach the home key when the whole orchestra proclaims the basic rhythm, fortissimo. The Recapitulation is interrupted by an oboe solo that introduces a note of gentleness. The second theme is shifted into C major. And the home key emerges triumphant in the extended coda.

The second movement is a theme and variations marked Andante con moto (at a going pace, with movement). There are two melodic ideas. First is a serene theme sung by violas and cellos.

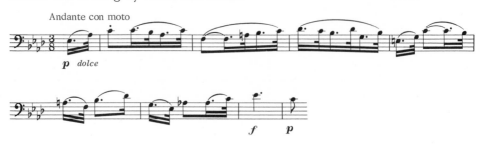

202

This melody returns twice, embellished first in sixteenth notes, then in thirty-second notes. It alternates with a broad melody that moves upward with a hymn-like power, echoing the "three shorts and a long" of the opening movement.

In the course of the movement this theme is varied in orchestration, dynamics, register, and type of accompaniment. The coda, marked Più mosso (faster), creates excitement through the use of syncopated rhythm.

The third movement, a Scherzo in $\frac{3}{4}$, returns to the somber C minor that is the home key of the work. A mysterious theme rises from the depths of the bass register, introduced by cellos and double basses:

Now the "three shorts and a long" reappear fortissimo in the horns, reminding the listener of the basic rhythm. The movement steadily gathers force. The middle section, the Trio, is based on a playful motive of running eighth notes, which is imitated in ever higher register by the strings. This boisterous mood contrasts with the mysterious atmosphere of the first section.

The Scherzo returns. But instead of bringing the movement to an end, Beethoven leads directly into the fourth movement. This unusual transition unfolds while the kettledrum taps out the basic rhythm. There is a growth of tension until the orchestra, in a blaze of light, surges into the triumphal Allegro in C major.

In this large finale three instruments make their appearance for the first time in the symphonies of the classical Viennese school: piccolo, double bassoon, and trombone. Beethoven here was leading the way towards the larger orchestra of the nineteenth century. This sonata-allegro form is based on three ideas. The first, in C major, presents a chord-and-scale pattern. It is announced by full orchestra:

203

The second theme serves as a bridge from C to G major:

Third is a vigorous theme based on triplet rhythm, that represents the contrasting key:

The Development is dynamic and stormy. Then—an amazing stroke!—Beethoven brings back the "three shorts and a long" from the preceding movement, so as to build up to the Recapitulation. The coda grows faster and faster, sweeping all before it until the end, when the tonic chord is hurled forth by the orchestra again and again.

This is music of tremendous power. Behind it stands the Olympian figure of an artist who imposed his will and his imagination on the world.

27

The Classic Era

(CONCLUDED)

*Beethoven:
Overture to
Coriolan*

Sonata-allegro form had one important feature in common with the drama. The classical tragedy centered around the conflict in the hero's heart between two opposing forces such as love and duty. Classical sonata-allegro form centered around a conflict between two opposing themes representing a home key and a contrasting key. Sooner or later composers were bound to adjust the musical drama to the literary one.

It was Beethoven who made this adjustment. In his Overture to *Coriolan*, a drama by a Viennese playwright named Collin, he represented the basic conflict of the drama by two themes, one rhythmic and aggressive, the other lyrical and tender. The hero of Collin's tragedy, as of Shakespeare's, is the Roman noble Coriolanus. He opposes the tribunes who represent the people, with the result that he is exiled from the city. He goes over to the Volscians, a tribe hostile to Rome. Gathering a huge army he marches on his native city, determined to lay it waste. A deputation of his countrymen pleads with him to spare Rome, but he turns a deaf ear. As a last resort his mother, wife, and little son are dispatched to his camp. Their entreaties finally move him to spare the city. In Plutarch's account, as in Shakespeare's, Coriolanus is murdered by the angry Volscians. In Collin's play the remorseful general commits suicide.

The Overture to *Coriolan* projects the essence of the tragedy. After a brief introduction we hear a fateful motive that establishes the home key of C minor. This theme suggests Coriolanus's somber state of mind as he decides to march against his countrymen.

This rhythmic idea is opposed to a tender melody in E-flat, which represents the entreaties of his wife and mother.

There is also a third theme that rounds off the Exposition.

Its full importance is not revealed at first, but only when it becomes the basis for the Development. This is a powerful and dramatic section. The Recapitulation presents the material in shortened form. There is a stirring coda.

Beethoven, we know, was concerned with the hero as the highest type of man. *Coriolan* is one of several works—the Third Symphony (the *Eroica*) and the Fifth are among the others—in which he was inspired by this idea.

Schubert: Unfinished Symphony— First Movement

Franz Schubert gave expression, in his songs and piano pieces, to an awakening romanticism. But in his symphonies he was the heir of the Viennese classical tradition. His most famous symphony includes traits of both the classic and romantic styles.

His Symphony No. 8 in B minor is known as the *Unfinished*. This title is misleading, for it implies that the composer was snatched away by death before he could complete the work. Actually he wrote it when he was twenty-

five years old. A musical society in the town of Graz had made him a
member. In return he promised to present the society with one of his compositions. He wrote down two movements of a symphony and sent the score
to Graz. He also sketched the opening measures of a scherzo, but never went
ahead with it. In the case of a composer who wrote as quickly as Schubert,
we can conclude that if he did not continue the symphony it was because he
had said all he had to say in the first two movements. Also, it is unlikely
that he would have sent to the society in Graz a work he considered incomplete.

In any case, this glorious score was never performed during Schubert's
lifetime. It lay on a shelf in Graz, gathering dust, until thirty-five years after
Schubert's death, when it was finally given to the world.

The *Unfinished Symphony* shows Schubert's radiant orchestral sound,
above all his wondrous gift of melody. The first movement is a sonata-allegro
form based on three ideas. The first, in the nature of an introductory theme,
establishes the home key of B minor. It emerges out of the lower register in
a mysterious pianissimo, played by cellos and double basses.

The second theme is a broadly curved melody in the home key. Given out by
an oboe and clarinet over the restless accompaniment of the strings, it has
that quality of gentle longing so characteristic of Schubert.

Third is the great lyric theme in G major, sung by cellos against syncopated
chords in the clarinets and violas. This stands among the immortal melodies.

The Development is remarkable for its dramatic intensity and drive. Schubert picks what seems to be the least promising of his themes—the first—and
shows what it is capable of in the way of development and growth. The violent contrasts between loud and soft, between high and low intensify the
drama. Tension builds steadily to the inevitable return to the home key.

The Recapitulation restates the material of the first section. And the coda
brings back the opening idea, so that the movement ends with the germ
theme out of which it flowered.

In the summer of 1819, when he was twenty-two, Schubert and a friend visited the picturesque town of Steyr, where they were entertained by a music lover who was an amateur cellist. Probably with him in mind, the young composer decided to write a chamber-music work with a prominent part for the cello. He also conceived the happy idea of presenting, in the fourth movement, a set of variations on his lovely song *The Trout*. Written for piano and four strings, the *Trout Quintet* became one of the most popular of Schubert's works.

If he had picked the usual instruments of the string quartet—first and second violin, viola, and cello—his cellist friend would have had to carry the bass part. But Schubert wanted the cello part to be free to soar and to be as lyrical as possible. He therefore selected, for his four strings, a violin, a viola, cello, and double bass. This combination presents a natural contrast between the piano sound and the sound of the strings. Each instrument contributes its special color to the ensemble, so that this light-hearted quintet is in the truest sense a "conversation among equals."

In the song, the melody is accompanied by a rippling figure on the piano that suggests the trout flashing through the water. In stating his theme, Schubert presented only the melody:

Variation 1: The piano takes over the melody an octave higher, embellishing it with trills. The violin follows with trills in high register. Variation 2: The viola carries the tune, combined with a countermelody in steady triplets on the first violin. Variation 3: Cello and double bass present the melody against an onrushing accompaniment of thirty-second notes on the piano. Variation 4: The melody is shifted from major to minor, fortissimo, in a rather dramatic way. Then Schubert suddenly changes the key and the mood. Variation 5: The cello carries the melody, which takes on the serene beauty of a folk song. Here Schubert is at his grandest. Variation 6: In the final variation he returns to the lighthearted mood—and the rippling piano accompaniment—of the original song.

The creator of this inspired music passed his uneventful life in the city of Beethoven. Too shy to approach the great man, he worshipped from afar. He never suspected that, of all the composers of his time, his name alone would be linked to that of his idol. They who far surpassed him in wordly success have long been forgotten. Today we speak of the four masters of the classical Viennese school: Haydn, Mozart, Beethoven—and Schubert.

28 A

The Baroque

Characteristics
of the
Baroque

The Baroque period extended over an exciting century and a half of European history. It began about the year 1600 and came to a close around the time of Bach's death in 1750. This was the period when the New World was being colonized. The struggles among the European powers during these years influenced the early history of our country.

The word *baroque* (ba-róke) was probably derived from the Portuguese *barroco,* a pearl of irregular shape much used in the jewelry of the time. This term denotes a style of pomp and grandeur, massive and dramatic,

BERNINI, *FOUNTAIN OF THE RIVERS,* IN ROME. The Baroque is a style of pomp and grandeur.

marked by energy and emotion. The Baroque was an era of absolute monarchy. Princes throughout Europe tried to imitate the splendor of Versailles. They maintained opera companies, chapel choirs, orchestras, and chamber groups. Their way of life was summed up by Louis XIV's famous

PETER PAUL RUBENS,
*MARIE DE MEDICI FLEEING
FROM THE CHATEAU
DE BLOIS.*
The painting of Rubens captured
the sweep and splendor of
Baroque art.

remark, "I am the State." It was a time when art and culture served to glorify the king and his nobles.

In the growing cities, bankers and rich merchants created a culture of their own. These new patrons of art vied with the court in their love for splendor. They responded to the richness of baroque art, to the beauty of brocade and velvet, marble and jewels and precious metals. This side of the Baroque found expression in the art of the Flemish painter Peter Paul Rubens (1577–1640). His canvases captured the sweep and splendor of baroque art. They show a driving energy and joy in life typical of the period.

The Baroque was an extremely devout period. It was a time of fierce religious wars between the Protestant countries—England, Scandinavia, Holland, and North Germany—and the Catholic camp, led by Spain, Austria, and France. Religious passion found an outlet in art, in both Catholic and Protestant lands. Literature, music, painting, sculpture, and architecture all served to express man's search for God. They also served the church. The Baroque, indeed, was the last period of great religious artists such as John Milton (1608–1674), author of *Paradise Lost;* John Bunyan (1628–1688), who wrote *Pilgrim's Progress;* the mystical Spanish painter El Greco (1548–1614); the Italian sculptor Gianlorenzo Bernini (1598–1680); and the composers Bach and Handel.

The artist played a variety of roles in baroque society. He could be a friend of princes, as was Rubens; or a political figure, as was Oliver Cromwell's secretary John Milton; or a priest. In social standing he ran the gamut

209

THE COUNCIL CHAMBER IN THE PALACE OF VERSAILLES SHOWS THE
SUMPTUOUS BEAUTY OF THE BAROQUE.

from favorite at court to something just above a valet or cook. But he was
first and foremost an artist. To the wealthy patrons whom he served he not
only offered elegant entertainment but also, for those who truly understood
him, brought inspired visions that opened up new worlds.

*The Texture
of Music:
Homophonic
and
Polyphonic*

When we speak of the *texture* of a piece of music we mean almost the same
as when we speak of the texture of a piece of cloth—the way the threads are
woven together. Melody unfolding over chords is like a horizontal line over
vertical columns of sound. The horizontal threads, the melodies, are held
together by the vertical threads, the harmonies. Out of their interaction
comes a weave that may be light or heavy, coarse or fine.

In the music of the classic and romantic eras there is a principal melody
that is heard against a background of harmony. This single-melody-with-
chords is known as *homophonic* texture. It is what we hear when the pianist
plays a melody with his right hand while the left sounds the chords.

When two or more melodic lines are combined we have a *polyphonic*
(many-voiced) texture. This kind of texture is based on *counterpoint,* a
term that comes from the Latin *punctus contra punctum,* "dot against dot"
or "note against note"—that is, one line or voice part against another.
Counterpoint is the art and science of combining several lines or voices
into a single musical fabric. In contrapuntal texture each part has a melodic
and rhythmic life of its own. The music derives its power and its interest
from the interplay of the different lines. The Baroque was a period of great
polyphonic music. Its leading composers produced masterpieces of contrapuntal art.

The different kinds of texture require different kinds of listening. Homophonic music poses no special problem. We are able to distinguish the melody from its accompaniment and can follow the way they are combined. We are helped in this by the fact that most of the music we hear consists of melody and chords.

The case is different with polyphonic music. Here we must be aware of the independent lines as they flow alongside each other. Polyphonic music demands greater concentration from the listener. It does not yield its secrets as readily as do the less complex kinds of music. Only through repeated hearings do we learn to follow the individual voices and to separate each within the contrapuntal web. And with every re-hearing we seem to discover something new.

Johann Sebastian Bach

Historians divide the century and a half of Baroque art into three periods: early Baroque (from around 1600 to 1650); middle Baroque (around 1650–1700); and late Baroque (around 1700–50). Foremost among the great masters of the late Baroque stands Johann Sebastian Bach.

His Life

He was born in the town of Eisenach, in central Germany, on March 21, 1685. The Bachs were a very large family and had been musicians for generations. Johann Sebastian's earliest memories were associated with music. He was ten years old when he lost his mother; his father died within the year. Johann Sebastian left the scene of his happy childhood and went to live with his oldest brother Johann Christoph in the town of Ohrdruf. Johann Christoph taught him the organ and other instruments, as well as the art of composition. He was a severe taskmaster, but the boy profited greatly from his teaching.

When he was fifteen, Johann Sebastian felt he had learned all he could from his brother. The time had come for him to make his way in the world. His thoughts turned to St. Michael's church in the town of Lüneburg, where there was a choir school that offered scholarships to ambitious young musicians. Lüneburg was two hundred miles away, and Johann Sebastian had no money for the stagecoach. Nothing daunted, he set out and walked most of the way.

He soon made a place for himself at St. Michael's. He sang in the church choir, played violin and viola in the orchestra, and spent many happy hours in the library studying all the music he could lay hands on. By the time he was eighteen Johann Sebastian was known as the most gifted organist in that part of the country. Despite his youth he was appointed organist and choirmaster in the church at Arnstadt. The members of the congregation were proud of their young organist. On Sundays people came from all over to hear him play.

In spite of his success the young man had his problems. When he played the chorales in church he let his imagination carry him away and added all kinds of harmonies to the melody. The church elders reproved him "for having made many curious variations in the chorale and mingled many strange tones in it, and for the fact that the Congregation had been confused by it." Shortly thereafter the church authorities were inquiring "by what right he recently caused a strange maiden to be invited into the choir loft and let her make music there." The maiden apparently was his cousin Maria Barbara, whom he married. He now needed to earn more, and found a post with a larger church in the town of Mühlhausen.

After a year at Mühlhausen Bach, at the age of twenty-three, received his first important position: he was appointed organist and chamber musician at the court of the Duke of Weimar, where he remained until he was thirty-two. These nine years passed pleasantly at Weimar. Bach and Maria Barbara were absorbed in the joys and cares of raising a family. His fame as organist and composer grew steadily. The Duke was especially fond of organ music. This period, accordingly, saw the composition of Bach's great works for his favorite instrument.

Although the Duke admired Bach's music, he was a tyrannical man who treated everyone around him in a most haughty manner. When the position of court conductor fell vacant, instead of promoting Bach he gave the job to an inferior musician. Bach, deeply disappointed, decided to accept an offer from the Prince of Anhalt-Cöthen. But he needed his master's permission before he could take another post, and this the angry Duke refused to give. The musician stood up for his rights. Whereupon, as the court chronicle relates, "on November 6 the former Concertmaster and court organist Bach was placed under arrest in the County Jail for too stubbornly forcing the issue of his dismissal, and finally on December 2 he was freed from arrest with notice of his unfavorable discharge."

At Cöthen Bach served a prince who was fond of chamber music. In his five years there he produced suites, concertos, and sonatas for various instruments. The Cöthen period was saddened by the death of Maria Barbara in 1720. The composer subsequently married Anna Magdalena, a young singer in whom he found a loyal and understanding wife. Of his twenty children— seven by the first marriage and thirteen by the second—half did not survive infancy. Four of his sons became leading composers of the next generation: Wilhelm Friedemann and Karl Philipp Emanuel, sons of Maria Barbara; and Anna Magdalena's sons Johann Christoph and Johann Christian.

THE ST. THOMAS
CHURCH AND SCHOOL
IN LEIPZIG.
Here Bach worked for the
last twenty-seven years of
his life.

Now that his sons were growing up, Bach wanted to live in a city with a university so that he could supervise their education. He was thirty-eight when he applied for one of the most important posts in Germany, that of Cantor of St. Thomas's in Leipzig. The Cantor taught at the school that trained the choirs of the city's principal churches. He also served as music director, composer, choirmaster, and organist of St. Thomas's. Several candidates were considered before him, among them composers who at that time were much more famous (and have since been forgotten). They were not available for the position and so—as a member of the town council put it—"since the best men could not be obtained, lesser ones would have to be accepted." It was in this spirit that Leipzig received the greatest of her cantors.

Bach's twenty-seven years in Leipzig saw the production of stupendous works. Outwardly his life was uneventful, his days were divided between the cares of a large family and his professional duties. There were also endless quarrels with a host of officials of town, school, and church who never suspected that they had in their employ one of the supreme artists of all time—quarrels that irritated Bach exceedingly, and took up time and energy that might have gone into better things.

The routine of his life was broken by frequent journeys to nearby towns, when he was asked to test new organs. His last and most interesting journey was to the court of Frederick the Great at Potsdam, where his son Karl Philipp Emanuel served as accompanist to the flute-playing King. On that memorable evening Frederick announced to his courtiers with some excitement, "Gentlemen, old Bach has arrived." He led the composer through the palace, showing him the new pianos that were beginning to replace the harpsichord. Bach asked the King to give him a theme, on which

AN EIGHTEENTH-
CENTURY HARPSI-
CHORD, SUCH AS
USED BY BACH.

he improvised. After his return to Leipzig he further elaborated on the
royal theme, added a sonata for flute, violin, and clavier, and dispatched
The Musical Offering to "a Monarch whose greatness and power, as in
all the sciences of war and peace, so especially in music everyone must
admire and revere."

At last the labors of a lifetime took their toll; his eyesight failed. He
was stricken blind after a stroke, but persisted in his final task, which was
to revise eighteen organ preludes based on chorales. The dying master
dictated to his son-in-law the last of these, *When in the Hour of Deepest
Need.* He died on July 28, 1750, at the age of sixty-five.

His Music

Bach brought to perfection all the forms that he inherited from the past.
His mastery of the technique of composition has never been equaled. With
this went the utmost depth of thought and feeling. He was the last of the
great religious artists. "The aim and final reason of all music," he declared,
"should be nothing else but the Glory of God and the refreshment of the
spirit."

Bach's contemporaries knew and admired his work, even if they did not
fully realize his greatness. It was the following generations that neglected
him. For fifty years after his death no single work of his was considered
worthy of being published. To the musical public of the 1760s the name
Bach meant his four sons, whose success as composers was far greater than
his. Even they considered his music old-fashioned.

Then the revival began, slowly at first but with ever-increasing force.
The romantic era felt akin to his richly emotional style. In 1829 Mendelssohn, then twenty years old, revived the *St. Matthew Passion,* which had

been forgotten for more than three-quarters of a century. Chopin practiced Bach before his concerts, Liszt arranged his organ works for the piano; Schumann helped to found the Bach Society, which brought out a complete edition of the master's works. At last the Cantor of Leipzig came into his own.

We see him today not only as a great artist who brought to perfection every form he touched, but as one of the giants of Western culture.

A *chorale,* we saw, is a hymn tune, especially one associated with the Lutheran church. In Germany the chorales were handed down from generation to generation since the time of Martin Luther. They nourished several centuries of German music, and came to full flower in the art of Johann Sebastian Bach.

A *cantata* (from the Italian *cantare,* "to sing"—that is, a piece to be sung) is a composition for solo singers, chorus, and instrumentalists, in several movements such as recitatives and arias, duets, and choruses. It is based on a poetic text, either religious or secular. In Germany the cantata developed into the most important type of Lutheran church music. Bach was the great master of this form. Many of his cantatas are based on a chorale, which runs through the several movements like a unifying thread.

As an exercise in listening contrapuntally, let us take a simple example, the chorale *Wachet auf, ruft uns die Stimme* (Awake, a Voice Is Calling) from Bach's cantata of that name. The tenors sing the melody in the middle register, mostly in quarter notes. Above them the violins and violas play a lively counterpoint.

Below them the cellos and double basses—along with the harpsichord—carry the bass line, mostly in quarter and eighth notes. Thus the three lines are made clear to the ear by differences not only in register but also in rhythm and color. Listen to the piece several times, concentrating first on the chorale itself, then on the two upper voices, finally on all three voices together. You will become aware of the fascinating patterns that are created when several lines unfold simultaneously.

The chorus sings of Zion who hears the watchmen, her heart leaping for joy. "She awakes and quickly arises. Her friend comes from heaven, resplendent, strong in grace, powerful in truth; her light shines bright, her star rises . . ." The "leaping for joy" is reflected in the strongly rhythmic, vigorous countermelody of the violins and violas. (When the principal melody is combined with another, the latter is called a *countermelody*—that is, a melody "against" the main melody—or a *countertheme*.)

"Little" Fugue in G minor for Organ

From the art and science of counterpoint came one of the most exciting types of baroque music, the fugue (fyoog). The name is derived from *fuga*, the Latin for "flight," indicating the flight of the theme from one voice part to the other—or a flight of fancy. (The various contrapuntal lines are called "voices" even when played by instruments.)

A *fugue* is a contrapuntal composition, generally in three or four voices, in which a theme or subject dominates the entire piece, entering now in one voice, now in another, against counterpoint in the other voices. The subject is often rather short and of strongly marked character. It unifies the piece.

A fugue may be written for a group of instruments; for a solo instrument such as organ, piano, or even violin; for several solo voices, or for chorus. The *subject* or theme is stated alone at the beginning of the fugue in one of the voices—soprano, alto, tenor, or bass. It is then imitated in another voice—this is the *answer*—while the first continues with a *countersubject* or countertheme. The subject will then appear in a third voice and be answered in the fourth (if there is a fourth), while the first two weave a counterpoint against them. The fugue, therefore, is based first of all on the principle of *imitation:* the theme, presented in one voice, is immediately imitated by the other voices. When the theme has appeared in each voice once, the first section of the fugue, the Exposition, is at an end. From there on the fugue alternates between expositions and passages known as *episodes,* which serve as areas of relaxation.

The baroque fugue was also based on the principle of contrast between a home key and other keys. The subject of the fugue is stated in the home key. The answer is given in a contrasting key. There is also modulation to foreign keys in the course of the fugue, which builds up tension against the return home.

As the fugue unfolds the composer reveals new facets of the theme. He may present it in longer or shorter note values, turned upside down, backwards, or even upside down and backwards. He may combine it with new subjects; he may bring it back now softly, now vigorously, now in low register, now in high. At the very end the theme appears in a triumphal mood: the mission has been accomplished, the tension has been released.

Johann Sebastian Bach was a master of fugal writing. His fugues combine immense contrapuntal skill with all the resources of a great artist's imagination and feeling. The Fugue in G minor for his favorite instrument—the organ—is a splendid example of his style. It is known as "the Little" to distinguish it from a longer fugue in the same key called "the Great," and is one of his most popular works in this form.

The subject is announced in the soprano. It is then answered in the alto while the soprano continues with a countersubject. Next it enters in the tenor and is answered in the bass. These four entries alternate between the home key (G minor) and the contrasting key (D minor). The subject is a sturdy melody.

The Exposition completed, an episode appears in which a motive is heard in imitation between alto and soprano. This motive takes on increasing importance as the fugue unfolds.

The subject is presently shifted to B-flat major. The material is expanded and moves to a climax. The theme makes its final appearance, fortissimo, in the home key. The fugue closes with a triumphal major chord.

The *concerto grosso* of the Baroque was based on the contrast or opposition between two different masses of sound. (The Latin verb *concertare* means "to contend with," "to vie with.") A small group of instruments—the *concertino*—was pitted against the large group, the concerto grosso. The contrast was one of dynamics as well as color: an even level of soft sound produced by the solo group contrasted with an even level of louder sound produced by the accompanying group. This alternation between two even levels or terraces of sound is known as *terraced dynamics,* and is as typical of the Baroque as the crescendo-diminuendo is typical of the classic and romantic eras. Thus, if a composer of the late eighteenth or nineteenth century desired a bigger tone, he instructed the musicians to play louder. If a composer of the Baroque desired a bigger tone, he wrote for a larger group of players. The contrasting areas of soft and loud may be compared to the areas of light and shade in baroque painting.

Bach was one of the masters of the concerto grosso. His finest works in this form are the six concerti grossi known as the Brandenburg Concertos,

A PAGE FROM THE MANUSCRIPT OF BACH'S BRANDENBURG
CONCERTO NO. 2.

after a German prince, the Margrave Christian Ludwig of Brandenburg,
to whom they were dedicated. It is not known whether the Margrave ever
looked at the works that made his name immortal. After his death Bach's
manuscripts were sold in a lot for the equivalent of about ten cents each.

The second of the set, in F major, has always been a favorite. The solo
group consists of trumpet, flute, oboe, and violin, all of them instruments in
high register. The accompanying group includes a full string section supported by a harpsichord that fills in the harmonies.

The third movement of this concerto is a bright, vigorous Allegro. Trumpet, oboe, violin, and flute enter in turn with the subject of a four-voiced
fugue:

The movement reaches its destination when the trumpet, at the very end,
jubilantly sets forth the opening motive.

This Finale illustrates five important characteristics of baroque music:

1. The texture is polyphonic, with the instruments imitating each other
within the contrapuntal web.

2. The melody of the classic period, we found, unfolded in symmetrical
phrases—generally four measures long, each rounded off by a cadence.

This resulted in a balanced structure that was immediately apparent to the ear. Baroque melody, on the other hand, pushes forward steadily, flowering into new patterns and never stopping until it reaches the final cadence. What we hear in this movement, consequently, may be described as *continuous melody,* as distinguished from the phrase-and-cadence structure of Haydn's and Mozart's melody.

3. The movement maintains two even levels of dynamics, the soft level of the four solo instruments and the louder level of the accompanying group. We have here the *terraced dynamics* characteristic of baroque music.

4. The music is driven forward by a beat that never lets up. This *unflagging rhythm* is a prime characteristic of the Baroque.

5. In the classic era a movement was generally based on two contrasting themes—one forceful and rhythmic, the other lyric. This established two moods that had to be reconciled within a single movement. In baroque music, on the other hand, a movement was based on a single "affection." (This is the eighteenth-century word for an emotion or mood.) The basic "affection" is established by the opening motive, and is maintained without letting up until the end of the movement.

The Finale of the Brandenburg Concerto No. 2 is a gay and tuneful movement. The trumpet part requires a player who is very agile on his instrument. This movement has all the drive and energy that we associate with the Baroque, and is an excellent example of the concerto-grosso style.

Shortly after he came to Leipzig Bach wrote the Magnificat, a hymn of praise for the Feast of the Visitation. In its richness of fantasy and inspiration, this work stands among his greatest.

Opening Chorus from the Magnificat

The opening number is a festive chorus marked by all the pomp and splendor of the Baroque. The basic "affection" of this chorus is established by a joyous orchestral introduction. Notice the prominence of the trumpets and drums, baroque symbols of praise and glory.

In *The Heavens Are Telling* from Haydn's *The Creation*, we noticed that single lines and phrases of text are frequently repeated in choral music. This trait is especially prominent in the music of the Baroque. Not only are single words repeated again and again, but a single syllable may be extended over many notes, as if the music had overflowed and dissolved the words. The repetition is very much in evidence in the opening chorus of the Magnificat. The text consists of a single line—*Magnificat anima mea Dominum* (My soul magnifies the Lord). When the voices take over the melody from the instruments, the first syllable is extended over groups of notes. Nor is there need for more text, since the music expands upon the idea of joy contained in the word *Magnificat* (magnifies).

The chorus is rather short. Here is an inspired expression of faith by a deeply religious man who was also a supreme artist.

❧ 28C ❧

George Frideric Handel

If Bach represents the religious mysticism of the late Baroque, Handel reveals its worldly pomp and splendor. Although they were born in the same year, the two greatest composers of the late Baroque never met. The Cantor of Leipzig spent his life in the secluded atmosphere of church and choir school. Handel, on the other hand, was made for an international career. He was lured by the glamor of the opera house; he felt at home amid the excitement and intrigue of royal courts. And he dominated the musical life of England, his adopted country, for a century after his death.

His Life

He was born in Halle (há-leh) in Saxony on February 23, 1685. His father, a prosperous barber-surgeon, disapproved of the boy's passion for music and wanted him to become a lawyer. But George, after a year at the University of Halle, left in order to devote himself to the career on which he had set his heart. His first operas were produced when he was in his early twenties. There followed a three-year stay in Italy, where several of his operas were performed with enormous success. At the age of twenty-five Handel was appointed conductor to the Elector of Hanover. He received the equivalent of fifteen hundred dollars a year at a time when Bach, at Weimar, was paid eighty.

A visit to London in the autumn of 1710 brought him for the first time to the city that was to be his home for almost fifty turbulent years. The opera *Rinaldo,* written in two weeks' time, enchanted the English public with its melodies. A year later Handel obtained another leave and returned to London. With the *Birthday Ode for Queen Anne* and the Te Deum (Hymn for Thanksgiving) for the Peace of Utrecht, he entered upon the writing of large works for great public occasions. The Queen rewarded him with a pension, whereupon nothing would make him return to his master in Hanover. He overstayed his leave.

By an unexpected turn of events his master came to him. Anne died, and the Elector of Hanover ascended the throne of England as George I. The

220

A VIEW OF LONDON IN HANDEL'S TIME.
Painting by Canaletto.

monarch was annoyed at his truant composer; but his love of music was greater than his annoyance, and he soon restored him to favor.

Handel staked his career on the success of Italian opera in London. As director of the Royal Academy of Music and its successor, the New Royal Academy, he wrote forty operas in thirty years. Despite occasional successes, these ventures finally collapsed and left Handel owing thousand of pounds. For a time he was in danger of going to prison for his debts.

At this lowest point in his fortunes he found his way from opera in Italian to oratorio in English, from ruin to immortality. An *oratorio*—the name comes from the Italian word for a place of prayer—is a large musical work for solo voices, chorus, and orchestra, set to a libretto of sacred or serious character. It is longer than a cantata and is not part of a religious service, although it is frequently based on a Biblical story. The action unfolds in a series of recitatives and arias, ensemble numbers and choruses. Handel soon realized the advantages of presenting a type of entertainment that did not need expensive Italian singers and lavish scenery. The oratorio, with its Biblical heroes and stirring choruses, was much more suited to the taste of the English middle class than was Italian opera. Handel still had many dark moments before him, but his ultimate success was assured. In 1739, when he was fifty-four, he produced two of his greatest oratorios, *Saul* and *Israel in Egypt,* both composed in a little over three months. There followed a group of six oratorios that included *Messiah* and *Judas Maccabaeus.* The final oratorios were presented when he was in his sixties. With these the master brought his work to a close.

He still had to face the final enemy—blindness. Yet even this blow did not cause him to fall idle. Like Milton and Bach, he dictated his last works, which were mainly revisions of earlier ones. He continued to appear in public, conducting his oratorios and exhibiting his powers on the organ. One re-

221

port tells how, when *Samson* was performed, at Milton's famous lines on the blinded hero—"Total eclipse—no sun, no moon; All dark amid the blaze of noon"—"the view of the blind Composer then sitting by the Organ affected the audience so forcibly that many persons present were moved to tears."

Shortly after his seventy-fourth birthday he began his usual oratorio season, conducting ten major works in little over a month to packed houses. *Messiah* closed the series. He collapsed in the theater at the end of the performance and died some days later, on April 14, 1759. The nation he had served for half a century accorded him its highest honor. "Last night about Eight O'clock the remains of the late great Mr. Handel were deposited at the foot of the Duke of Argyll's Monument in Westminster Abbey. There was almost the greatest Concourse of People of all Ranks ever seen upon such, or indeed upon any other Occasion."

His Music

Like Bach, Handel believed in the spiritual power of music. When a nobleman complimented him on his ability to entertain the public, he replied, "Milord, I should be sorry if I only entertained them. I wished to make them better." The oratorios of Handel are choral dramas of enormous vitality and grandeur. He made the chorus—the people—the center of the drama. One must hear one of his choruses to realize what a simple $\frac{4}{4}$ time can achieve in the way of power. (We heard the celebrated Hallelujah Chorus from *Messiah* in connection with Chapter 1.) Of his big choral pieces to celebrate occasions of national rejoicing, the most famous are the *Coronation Anthems* he wrote when George II mounted the throne. One of these has helped to crown every subsequent ruler of England. Of his instrumental works, the most popular are the *Water Music, Royal Fireworks Music,* the concertos for organ and orchestra, and the twelve Concerti Grossi, Opus 6.

See, the
Conquering
Hero Comes!
from Judas
Maccabaeus

The heroic tone of Handel's oratorios is evident in *Judas Maccabaeus.* The work is based on the account, in the Old Testament, of how the Jews rose in arms against the Syrian tyrant who threatened to enslave them and desecrate their temple. They were led to victory by the fearless Judas Maccabaeus.

One of the high points of the work comes when the people welcome the victorious hero. This famous number begins pianissimo, sung by a children's chorus. The opening phrase is followed by a soft passage played by the trumpets, making a beautiful effect. Then the maidens of Israel welcome the hero, and the people acclaim him.

> CHILDREN
> See, the conquering hero comes,
> Sound the trumpets, beat the drums;
> Sports prepare, the laurel bring,
> Songs of triumph to him sing.
> [*Last 2 lines repeated.*]

MAIDENS

See the godlike youth advance,
Breathe the flutes and lead the dance;
Myrtle wreaths and roses twine
To deck the hero's brow divine.
[*Last 2 lines repeated.*]

THE PEOPLE

See, the conquering hero comes,
Sound the trumpets, beat the drums;
Sports prepare, the laurel bring,
Sports prepare, the laurel bring.
[*First 2 lines repeated.*]

With its broad outlines and noble simplicity, this chorus could almost be a national anthem. In majestic effects such as these Handel was without a peer.

Baroque opera has not survived in the present-day repertory (although several of Handel's operas have been revived, with success, in recent years). It came out of a theater that was completely different from our own; and its elaborate plots, which permit little or no development of living characters on the stage, cannot appeal to modern audiences in the way that *Carmen, Aïda,* or *Madame Butterfly* can. Nonetheless, Handel poured a wealth of great music into his operas, and certain arias from them have maintained their popularity throughout the years. Such a one is the famous melody known as "Handel's Largo." It is really an aria from his opera *Serse* (Xerxes), which came towards the end of his operatic career; he wrote only one more opera after it. The work centers around Xerxes, the celebrated king of ancient Persia. (In Italian his name is Serse.) The opening scene of the opera shows Xerxes in a splendid garden, resting in the shade of his favorite plane tree. He sings an aria in praise of the tree, thanking it for the peace it has brought him.

*Ombra mai fù
from* Serse

RECITATIVE

Frondi tenere e belle	O fair and tender leaves
del mio platano amato;	Of my beloved plane tree,
per voi risplende il fato.	May Fate shine brightly on you.
Tuoni, lampi e procelle	May thunder, lightning, and storms
non voltraggino mai la cara pace,	Never disturb your sweet peace,
ne giunga a profanarvi austro	Nor the greedy south wind profane you!
rapace!	

ARIA

Ombra mai fù	Shadow so sweet,
di vegetabile,	shield and protect me,
cara ed amabile,	Never was tree so fair,
soave più.	so fair as you.

Notice the difference in style between the speech-like character of the recitative and the graceful melodic curve of the aria. The words of the aria are repeated three times. This serenely flowing melody is characteristic of the master's noble style.

223

MUSIC IN
HISTORY:
STYLES AND
PERIODS

La
Réjouissance
from Music
for the Royal
Fireworks

The *suite* was an important type of baroque instrumental music, consisting of a series of fairly short movements in the same key. These were modeled after dance forms drawn from French, German, Italian, Spanish, and English sources. Some of the dances were slow and stately, others in moderate tempo, still others gay and lively. Between these might be inserted a song-like movement. There was also an elaborate piece at the beginning that served as an overture.

The *Music for the Royal Fireworks,* consisting of an Overture and five short pieces, was written for a public celebration held in London on April 27, 1749 to mark the peace of Aix-la-Chapelle. Handel's orchestra, in this festive suite, included 56 wind instruments—9 trumpets, 9 horns, 24 oboes, 12 bassoons, 1 or more contrabassoons, side drums, and 3 pairs of kettle-drums. George II had expressed a desire that only instruments of a military character should be used on this occasion. According to one courtier, the King "said he hoped there would be no fiddles." Handel objected at first, but in the end gave in to his royal master.

Everything went wrong on the great day. The fireworks refused to light up. A pavilion caught fire and burned down. "Very little mischief was done," wrote Horace Walpole, "and but two persons killed." An allegorical statue of "George giving Peace to Britannia dropped, with his head aflame, into a cauldron of fire." And to top it all, the designer of the fireworks went out of his mind. There was only one successful aspect of the show—Handel's music. It pleased then, and has continued to please in the more than two centuries since.

Handel later rewrote the work for a normal orchestra of wind and string instruments. However, you will hear a special recording that uses his original orchestration, which gives the music a bright outdoor sound. *La Réjouissance* (ray-jwee-sáhns—the rejoicing), the fourth number of the suite, is a colorful Allegro in Handel's most melodious style. The martial melody makes a gallant effect. Notice that measure 3 repeats the pattern of measure 2 a tone higher; that is, in sequence:

The piece is a two-part (A-B) form. The first part modulates from D major to A; the second starts out in D and stays there. It contains another example of Handel's fondness for sequence: the same pattern is repeated in the melody four times, each time a step lower.

Each part is played twice; first loud, with emphasis on horns, trumpets and drums; then soft, with emphasis on oboes and bassoons. The terraced dynamics are typical of baroque music. Then the piece is played again by the full ensemble, with all the pomp and vigor of the Baroque.

The creator of this grand sound was a mighty figure in his own time, and has remained so for those who came after. It was Beethoven who said of him, "He was the greatest of us all."

Music of Earlier Times

Until about a thousand years ago music consisted of single-line melody. Then the West parted company from the East. The music of the Orient remained with single-line melody to this day. In Africa and Asia, when instrumentalists accompany a singer they may ornament the melody, but the music basically consists of a single line. European musicians, on the other hand, developed the art of combining several melodies at the same time. Thus were born the arts of counterpoint and harmony.

This development took place at about the same time that European painting developed the science of perspective. The painters of the East, on the other hand, clung to the flat canvas in which figures and objects are

Gregorian Chant

GIOTTO, *MEETING OF ST. JOACHIM AND ST. ANNA AT JERUSALEM* (AROUND 1300). European painting developed the science of perspective.

seen in a single dimension. Consequently, hearing in depth and seeing in depth are the special achievements of Western art. It should be added that the artists of the Orient made up for this lack by developing subtle effects that are unknown to us.

JAPANESE SCREEN PAINTING (AROUND 1600).
The painters of the East clung to the flat surface.

The great monument of single-line melody in the West consists of the chants of the early Christians, which developed into the musical service of the Catholic Church. Descended from the religious melodies of the ancient Hebrews and Greeks, *Gregorian chant* takes its name from Pope Gregory the Great, who reigned from 590 to 604 and played an important part in assembling the sacred melodies. Also known as *plainchant* or *plainsong,* Gregorian chant presents pure melody without the "third dimension" of harmony or counterpoint. It is not bound by metrical patterns such as two-four or three-four time. As a result, it bears the same relation to metrical music as the rhythm of prose bears to poetry.

Gregorian chant avoids the excitement of wide leaps and dramatic contrasts. It embodies the ideal of pure religious expression. "Everything in this music combines to give peace." The sacred text is set phrase by phrase; occasionally words are repeated. The music is subordinate to the text, which is clearly heard throughout. As Thomas Merton, the famous author who is a member of the Trappist Monks, explains it, "Pure Gregorian chant never leaves the hearer with the impression that the composer has been striving for musical effects. Everything is directed to God and to His praise." (Merton's voice is heard on the record, translating the Latin text.)

Vox in Rama and Dirigatur

The Mass that mourns the slaughter of the children by Herod contains a particularly lovely antiphon. (The term *antiphon* denotes a certain type of Gregorian chant, usually based on a short text from Scriptures.) The

226

melody of this antiphon evokes a mood of tenderness and sorrow suitable to the text:

Vox in Rama audita est,	A voice was heard in Rama . . .
ploratus et ululatus:	Lamentation and great mourning.
Rachel plorans filios suos,	Rachel, bewailing her children,
noluit consolari,	Would not be comforted
quia non sunt.	Because they are not.

Dirigatur is a gradual from a Sunday Mass. (A *gradual* is a chant sung at High Mass.) The melody embodies the spirit of serene prayer so typical of Gregorian chant.

Dirigatur oratio mea	Let my prayer be directed
sicut incensum in conspectu tuo, Domine.	As incense in Thy sight, O Lord.
Elevatio manuum mearum	The lifting up of my hands
sacrificium vespertinum.	As evening sacrifice.

The prayers that make up the Mass form the central creed of the Catholic faith. Throughout the centuries, composers devoted their genius to making musical settings of this most important rite of the Church.

Palestrina: Sanctus from the Mass for Pope Marcellus

However, as the art of counterpoint advanced, the music of the Mass grew more and more complex. The words of the sacred text began to be drowned out by the music. In addition, singers—eager to show off their voices—added all kinds of ornaments of their own, thereby corrupting the ancient Gregorian melodies. These and similar abuses confronted the authorities with a serious problem. At the Council of Trent, which met in the middle of the sixteenth century to discuss various reforms in the Church, certain cardinals went so far as to argue that counterpoint should be abolished altogether in the Catholic service, and that religious music should return to the pure Gregorian chant. Fortunately for music, the committee of cardinals assigned to deal with this problem did not take so drastic a step. Instead they issued general instructions for a more dignified service that would allow the sacred texts to be heard, that would avoid vocal display, and that would encourage religious feeling in the listener.

Of the composers who attempted to carry out these instructions, the most famous was Palestrina (pah-less-trée-nah, around 1525–1594). The problem, as he saw it, was to reconcile the needs of music with the needs of religion. He solved this so successfully that for later generations he has remained *the* Catholic composer. Palestrina served as organist and choirmaster at various churches, including that of St. Peter's in Rome, where he spent the last twenty-three years of his life. The mystical beauty of his music does not exclude intense emotion, but this emotion is directed towards God.

Palestrina was a master of the *a cappella* style. This term denotes a vocal work that is not accompanied by instruments. A cappella music represents the purest type of choral music, and reached its golden age in the sixteenth century—the age of Palestrina. In his most celebrated work, the *Mass for Pope Marcellus,* he reveals himself as a true Italian in his eloquent writing for the voice. The work is for six voices—soprano, alto, two tenors, and two basses. Chracteristic is the fourth movement, the Sanctus. The music unfolds in a sweet, gentle flow of lines that crisscross like threads in a melodious pattern. Each voice enters in turn, often imitating—that is, repeating— what the preceding voice has sung.

San - - - - - ctus

The harmonies are *modal;* that is, they are based on the old modes (the scales that were used before the major-minor system). So as to give the music time to establish the mood, the word *Sanctus* (holy) is repeated over and over again. Occasionally the first syllable extends over a series of notes, as if the word were dissolved in music. There is similar repetition on the next phrase of text, *Dominus Deus Sabaoth* (Lord God of Hosts).

The final phrase, *Pleni sunt coeli et terra gloria tua* (Heaven and earth are full of Thy glory), evokes the glory of God. The movement ends, in simply beauty, with a cadence on a C major chord. Listening to it, one can understand why, to Palestrina's countrymen, his music suggested a heavenly choir.

Claudio Monteverdi: Incenerite spoglie

Under the influence of the Renaissance, art turned more and more from religious to secular—that is, non-religious—subjects. And music began to reflect the eternal themes of man's emotional life, especially the joys and sorrows of love. The composer who tried above all to make his music express the emotions of life was Claudio Monteverdi, who was born in 1567—three years after Shakespeare—and died in 1643. This great master spent the first part of his career at the court of the Duke of Mantua and his later years at St. Mark's Cathedral in Venice. "The modern composer," he declared, "builds upon the foundation of truth." By truth he meant dramatic truth. His aim, he explained, was to express "the principal emotions of mankind."

Monteverdi was a master of the madrigal, one of the principal forms inherited from the Renaissance. The *madrigal* was an aristocratic form of poetry-and-music that developed at the small Italian courts. Its text was a short lyric poem marked by refined feeling and elegant language.

Monteverdi's handling of a poetic text is well illustrated by his madrigal *Incenerite spoglie* (in-chéh-neh-ree-teh spóh-lyeh). This is the first of a set of six madrigals called *Tears of a Lover at the Tomb of his Beloved.* The text is complicated, in the manner of the court poetry of that time; but the music comes straight from the heart. The pure sound of the voices, without instruments, seems somehow to heighten the mood.

Incenerite spoglie, avara tomba	Beloved ashes, the greedy tomb is now made Heaven,
Fatta del mio bel Sol terreno Cielo.	Holding what was my beautiful Sun on earth.
Ahi lasso! I'vengo ad inchinarvi in terra!	Alas, I grieve! I come to bury you in the earth!
Con voi chius' e il mio cor' a marmi in seno	My heart is buried with you, turned to stone.
E notte e giorno vive in pianto, in foco,	Night and day, in tears, in fire,
In. duol' in ira il tormentato Glauco.	Tormented Glaucus lives in sorrow and in rage.

Notice how the voices enter in turn, each imitating the one before. How dramatic are the repeated notes in the opening phrase. How expressive are the modal harmonies, and how beautiful the interweaving of the five voices—two sopranos, alto, tenor, and bass. Notice too how important words and lines are repeated, in order to give the music time to establish the mood: *Ahi lasso!* (Alas, I grieve!) in line 3, and the final line that sums up the grief in the lover's heart.

England took over the madrigal from Italy and transformed it into a native art form. (The same was true, in poetry, of the sonnet.) A brilliant school of madrigalists flourished during the reign of Queen Elizabeth and on into the time of James I.

Thomas Morley: Sing We and Chant It

Thomas Morley (1557–c. 1603) was one of the most individual among these composers. He cultivated a type of madrigal known as the *ballett*—a light choral piece which, as its name implies, was in the style of a dance-song. The fa-la refrain was a typical feature of this English type of song. (A *refrain*, we learned, is a line or two of poetry that is repeated at the end of each stanza. It also refers to the music to which such a line is set.)

A delightful example of Morley's art is the famous *Sing We and Chant It* which, like so much light verse of that period, urges the listener to seize the moment and enjoy life's pleasures:

> Sing we and chant it, while love doth grant it,
> Fa-la-la-la-la-la, fa-la-la-la.
> Not long youth lasteth, and old age hasteth;
> Now is best leisure to take our pleasure.
> Fa-la fa-la la-la-la, fa-la fa-la la-la-la.
>
> All things invite us, now to delight us,
> Fa-la-la-la-la-la, fa-la-la-la.
> Hence, care, be packing! No mirth be lacking!
> Let spare no treasure to live in pleasure!
> Fa-la fa-la la-la-la, fa-la fa-la la-la-la.

229

This is a ballett for five voices, in lively triple meter. The same music is used for both stanzas; hence the song is in strophic form. The voices move in simple chords. With its simple charm and gay rhythms, this piece is in the finest tradition of English lyricism.

29 B

Baroque Masters

Henry Purcell: Did's Lament *from* Dido and Aeneas

Henry Purcell (1659–95) occupies a special place in the affection of his countrymen. He was the last great English composer until the rise of the modern English school almost two hundred years later. His brief career unfolded at the court of Charles II, extending through the turbulent reign of James II into the period of William and Mary. He held various posts under these monarchs as singer, organist, and composer. Purcell's works cover a wide range, from the massive choruses of his religious anthems to popular tunes and patriotic songs.

His opera *Dido and Aeneas* is regarded as the finest that England has produced. Based on the love story in Virgil's epic poem *The Aeneid,* the action concerns the queen of Carthage who takes pity on the shipwrecked Aeneas, falls in love with him, and kills herself when the Trojan hero sails away to fulfill his destiny and found Rome.

The high point of the opera is Dido's lament after Aeneas's departure, in which she makes clear her intention to commit suicide:

RECITATIVE
Thy hand, Belinda, darkness shades me;
On thy bosom let me rest.
More I would, but death invades me.
Death is now a welcome guest.

ARIA

When I am laid in earth,
May my wrongs create
No trouble in thy breast. Remember me—
But ah, forget my fate!

This moving aria unfolds over a *ground bass*—a phrase in the bass repeated over and over again while the melody soars above it. Purcell's ground bass descends along the chromatic scale. To the composers of the Baroque, this pattern symbolized deep grief:

The aria builds steadily until it rises to its heartbreaking climax on the words "Remember me"—one of those strokes of genius which, once heard, is never forgotten.

Despite his early death at the age of thirty-six, Purcell ranks as one of the masters of the middle Baroque. His position as national artist was well summed up in the next century: "Purcell is as much the boast of England in music as Shakespeare in the drama, Milton in epic poetry, Locke in metaphysics, or Sir Isaac Newton in mathematics."

For many years the public was so greatly interested in Bach and Handel that the other masters of the late Baroque were neglected. None suffered more from this than Antonio Vivaldi (c. 1675–1741), who has been rediscovered by the twentieth century. This highly original musician composed quantities of concertos and sonatas, operas and choral pieces, many of them still unknown. He was born in Venice, the son of a violinist, and became a priest in his early twenties. During the greater part of his musical career he was connected with the schools of his native city.

Vivaldi's music marks one of the high points of the Italian violin school. He also played a leading part in the development of the concerto grosso.

Antonio Vivaldi: Concerto in D minor for Two Violins and Orchestra— Third Movement

231

He was a true Venetian in his love of brilliant color. His powerful rhythms illustrate the forward drive of the Baroque. Above all, he brought into his instrumental works all the drama of operatic music.

Characteristic of his writing is the gay finale of his Concerto in D minor for Two Violins and Orchestra. The supporting ensemble consists of strings and harpsichord. The movement, an Allegro molto (very fast) in $\frac{2}{4}$, opens with a vigorous tutti (all)—that is, an extended passage for the entire group. Notice the echo effects, where two loud measures are answered by two soft ones. A staccato theme establishes the basic mood at the outset: an energetic forward drive that never loses its power.

The usual baroque traits are all present in this lively movement: contrapuntal texture, terraced dynamics, rhythm marked by a steady beat, continuous melody, and a single "affection." Vivaldi gets the movement under way, keeps it moving, and brings it to a close without wasting a note.

His art flowered from a noble tradition, while his dynamic style pointed the way to the future. We see him today as one of the great figures of the Baroque.

Harpsichord Music of the French Rococo: Couperin and Rameau

The age of Louis XIV, with its love of pomp and grandeur, came to an end. It was followed by the pleasure-loving era of Louis XV. Now the grand style of the Baroque gave way to the playfulness of the Rococo, whose elegant prettiness is familiar to us from the gilt mirrors, crystal chandeliers, and graceful curves of the Louis XV style.

In music, painting, sculpture, architecture, and interior decoration, the Rococo created a "gallant style" that came to flower in France at the beginning of the eighteenth century and spread all over Europe from around 1725 to 1775. Baroque and Rococo, consequently, overlapped. Elements of both are to be found in the works of the two leading composers of the French Rococo—François Couperin (1668–1733) and Jean Philippe Rameau (1683–1764).

During both the Baroque and the Rococo, the *harpsichord* was a favorite keyboard instrument. The harpsichord differs from the piano in two important ways. First, its strings are not struck by hammers but plucked by quills; this produces a bright silvery tone. Second, whether you press hard or lightly on the keys, the tone is the same. In other words, the harpsichord cannot produce the crescendo and diminuendo of the piano. But it is very well suited for contrapuntal music, since it brings out the separate voices in the clearest fashion. It has two keyboards, which enable it to achieve an even level of soft and loud—that is, the terraced dynamics of baroque music. The harpsichord was extremely popular until the end of the eighteenth century, when it was replaced by the piano.

François Couperin (frán-swah có-pran) spent the major part of his

THE SALON OF MARIE
ANTOINETTE IN THE
PALACE OF
FONTAINEBLEAU
illustrates the grace and elegance
of the Rococo.

career at the court of Louis XIV. Like Bach, he was a member of a family
of distinguished musicians; he became the greatest of the French school of
harpsichord composers. His art mirrors the graceful world of the French
Rococo. He gave titles to his little harpsichord pieces—*The Prude, Two
Harvesters, Tender Nanette,* and the like. Many of these elegant miniatures
are in two-part form (A-B). The first part goes from the home key to a
contrasting key, and the second part returns.

Le Moucheron (le moosh-rón—The Little Fly) is characteristic of Couperin's style. The melody shows the fondness for trills and ornaments
typical of rococo music. Couperin takes advantage of the silvery sound of
the harpsichord to suggest the buzzing and darting about of the little fly.
He does this by repeating a motive over and over again in the opening
phrase. (The trills are indicated by a little sign above the note.)

Jean Philippe Rameau (zhahn fi-léep ra-mó) did not win fame until the
era of Louis XV. He was admired during his lifetime as a composer of operas,
ballets, and books on musical theory. Today he is remembered chiefly for
his instrumental works. Extremely popular is his *Tambourin* (tahm-boo-
ráhn); the title denotes an eighteenth-century dance of rustic origin. In
Rameau's piece a catchy little tune is heard a number of times, alternating
with other melodies, so that the composition is really in the form of a

rondo (A-B-A-C-A-D-A). The droning bass suggests a folk instrument such as a bagpipe. With its simple country atmosphere, a little gem such as this must have appealed strongly to an age when the ladies at court liked to masquerade as shepherdesses.

Listening to these pieces, one understands why the greatest composer of modern France, Claude Debussy, said: "French music aims first of all to give pleasure. Couperin, Rameau—these are true Frenchmen!"

Domenico
Scarlatti:
Sonata in F

Domenico Scarlatti (1685–1757) was one of the most original artists in the history of music. He left Italy in his middle thirties to take a post at the court of Portugal. When his pupil, the Infanta (Princess) of Portugal, married the heir to the Spanish throne, the composer followed her to Madrid, where he spent the last twenty-eight years of his life.

Scarlatti's genius was as delicately attuned to the harpsichord as was the genius of Chopin, a century later, to the piano. His absorbed all the charm and grace of the Rococo. Scarlatti's fame rests on the over five hundred sonatas that he wrote for his favorite instrument. Only thirty were published by the composer himself, under the modest title of *Exercises for Harpsichord*. The sonata of Scarlatti is a one-movement form in two parts: the first modulates from the home key to a contrasting key; the second returns.

The lively Sonata in F is a playful Allegro in $\frac{3}{4}$.

Characteristic of the master's style are the graceful rhythms and appealing melody; brilliant runs, rapid scales, trills and arpeggios; contrasts of low and high register, and quick crossing of hands. All of these require the utmost precision. The first part modulates from F to C major, with a brief excursion into minor on the way. The second part makes its way back to the home key, F. This is aristocratic music, the work of an artist of boundless imagination.

In recent years there has been an upsurge of interest in the music of the Baroque and earlier times. More and more the public is discovering a wealth of beauty in this older music that richly rewards those who seek it out.

UNIT VII

THE
TWENTIETH
CENTURY

30

The Post-Romantic Era

By the end of the nineteenth century, romanticism had run its course. During the post-romantic era, which extended from around 1890 to 1915, composers either expanded the romantic tradition or broke away from it. In so doing they prepared the way for the New Music of the twentieth century.

Jan Sibelius

Finland's famous composer was born on December 8, 1865. His career began at a time that was crucial for his country: Finland was under the rule of Tsarist Russia and was struggling to win its independence. Sibelius' works reflected this struggle and brought Finnish culture to the attention of the world. His music mirrored the brooding forests and lakes of his native land, and the soul of his people. "I love the mysterious sounds of the fields and forests, water and mountains. It pleases me greatly," he wrote, "to be called a poet of nature, for nature has truly been the book of books for me." After a productive life this truly national artist died, at the age of ninety-two, on September 20, 1957.

Finlandia

Finlandia, written in 1899, gave expression to the revolutionary spirit which at that time swept the Finnish people. The piece opens on a note of defiance, with snarling chords of the brass in low register, Andante sostenuto (fairly slow and sustained). There follows an organ-like passage in the woodwinds that is solemnly answered by the strings. This prayerful mood leads to an Allegro moderato based on a rhythmic pattern that is repeated over and over again (ostinato). Stirring trumpet calls resound like a summons to action. Then appears the famous melody of *Finlandia,* like a prayer. It has became a national anthem in the composer's homeland.

237

An exciting interlude follows. Then the melody returns fortissimo, like a jubilant chorale, as if the composer were promising his countrymen that their cause will win. Thus, like *Overture 1812, Finlandia* moves from a mood of struggle to one of triumph.

Gustav Mahler

Gustav Mahler was born in Bohemia on July 7, 1860. In his youth he was influenced by Wagner. He made a reputation as a conductor and for ten years was director of the Vienna Opera. He came to New York to conduct at the Metropolitan Opera House, and in 1909 became conductor of the New York Philharmonic Orchestra. Two years later, at the height of his career, he died in Vienna at the age of fifty-one.

Mahler was intensely emotional by nature. "I am thrice homeless," he remarked. "As a Bohemian born in Austria. As an Austrian among Germans. And as a Jew throughout the world." In associating music with personal feelings he was truly a romantic. "The act of creation in me is so closely bound up with all my experience that when my mind and spirit are at rest I can compose nothing." Music for him was "a mysterious language from beyond."

Mahler's melodies have their roots in Austrian popular song. In his nine symphonies he combined the grand form of the past with song lyricism So, too, in his songs for voice and orchestra, the orchestra not only accompanies the voice but also comments on the text in extended interludes, and develops themes as in a symphony.

Mahler's music did not achieve its full measure of fame until after his death. In recent years his popularity has grown steadily in this country. When his contemporaries failed to appreciate his music he would say, "My time will come!" It did.

Revelge

Early in his career Mahler found inspiration in a collection of German folk poetry known as *The Youth's Magic Horn,* and set a number of its poems to music. In his last years he returned to *The Youth's Magic Horn* and found there the text of one of his greatest songs, *Revelge* (reh-vél-geh). The German word, like the French *reveille,* signifies the trumpet call that awakes soldiers in the barracks. It is used here in an ironic sense, for the soldiers in the poem are dead. Like *The Two Grenadiers,* this song begins as a dialogue between two soldiers. But the mood is different. Schumann's song evokes the glory of war; Mahler's suggests the suffering and the sorrow.

The supernatural atmosphere of the poem, with its procession of dead soldiers, appealed to the romantic in him. The refrain, *trallali, trallaley, trallalera*—which is often used in folk songs to express gayety and high spirits—takes on a heartbreaking quality in this somber setting. As in many folk songs, there is no transition between one stanza and the next. In the first stanza the soldier is taking leave of his girl; in the next he is on the battlefield, wounded. The folk poet summons up an eerie vision that is matched by Mahler's powerful music: the dead soldiers arise to the beating of the drum, they drive back the foe, then they fall in for roll call, row upon row of ghosts. And the drummer leads the procession as they march past his sweetheart's house! Here is a dramatic ballad, rich in pity and wonder, in the great romantic tradition. It is a masterpiece.

Des Morgens zwischen drei'n und vieren,	Between three and four in the morning,
da müssen wir Soldaten marschieren	We soldiers must keep marching
das Gässlein auf und ab,	Up and down the little street,
trallali, trallaley, trallalera,	Trallali, trallaley, trallalera,
mein Schätzel sieht herab!	Where my sweetheart can look down and see me!
Ach Bruder, jetzt bin ich geschossen,	Oh brother, now I am wounded,
die Kugel hat mich schwere, schwer getroffen,	A bullet has wounded me badly, badly.
trag' mich in mein Quartier!	Carry me to the camp!
Trallali, trallaley, trallalera,	Trallali, trallaley, trallalera,
es ist nicht weit von hier!	It is not far from here!
Ach, Bruder, ach, Bruder, ich kann dich nicht tragen,	Ah brother, my brother, I cannot carry you,
die Feinde haben uns geschlagen!	The foe has beaten us!
Helf' dir der liebe Gott,	May the dear Lord help you,
helf' dir der liebe Gott!	May the dear Lord help you!
Trallali, trallaley, trallalera,	Trallali, trallaley, trallalera,
ich muss, ich muss marschieren bis in Tod!	I must march onward, onward until death!
Ach Brüder, ach Brüder, ihr geht ja mir vorüber,	Ah comrades, my comrades, you pass me by,
als wär's mit mir vorbei,	As if I were cold and dead
als wär's mit mir vorbei!	As if I were cold and dead!
Trallali, trallaley, trallalera,	Trallali, trallaley, trallalera,
ihr tretet mir zu nah,	You hurt me deeply,
ihr tretet mir zu nah!	You hurt me deeply!
Ich muss wohl meine Trommel rühren,	I'll rise and beat the drum,
ich muss meine Trommel wohl rühren,	I'll rise and beat the drum,
trallali, trallaley, trallali trallaley,	Trallali, trallaley, trallali trallaley,
sonst werd' ich mich verlieren,	Or else I shall be lost,
trallali, trallaley, trallala!	Trallali, trallaley, trallala!
Die Brüder, dick gesät,	The dead lie in heaps,
die Brüder, dick gesät,	The dead lie in heaps,
sie liegen wie gemäht.	As if they had been mowed down.
Er schlägt die Trommel auf und nieder,	He beats the drum with might and main,
er wekket seine stillen Brüder.	He awakens his dead comrades.
Trallali, trallaley, trallali trallaley,	Trallali, trallaley, trallali trallaley,
sie schlagen und sie schlagen ihren Feind, Feind, Feind,	They beat, they beat the foe, foe, foe,
trallali, trallaley, trallalerallala,	Trallali, trallaley, trallalerallala,
ein Schrecken schlägt den Feind,	Terror strikes the foe,
ein Schrecken schlägt den Feind!	Terror strikes the foe!
Er schlägt die Trommel auf und nieder,	He beats the drum with might and main,
da sind sie vor dem Nachtquartier schon wieder,	And now they're all back in camp,
trallali, trallaley, trallali trallaley!	Trallali, trallaley, trallali trallaley!

Ins Gässlein hell hinaus, hell hinaus,	In the little street it's light outside, light outside,
sie zieh'n vor Schätzleins Haus,	They pass his sweetheart's house,
trallali, trallaley, trallalera,	Trallali, trallaley, trallalera,
sie ziehen vor Schätzeleins Haus.	They pass his sweetheart's house.
Trallali!	Trallali!
Des Morgens stehen da die Gebeine	In the dawn the ghosts stand
in Reih' und Glied, sie stehen wie Leichensteine	In rank and file, they stand like gravestones
in Reih', in Reih' und Glied,	In rank and file,
die Trommel steht voran,	The drummer heads the line,
die Trommel steht voran,	The drummer heads the line,
dass sie ihn sehen kann,	That she may see him,
trallali, trallaley, trallalera,	Trallali, trallaley, trallalera,
dass sie ihn sehen kann!	That she may see him.

The opening measures establish a march-like dotted rhythm which, repeated over and over, takes on hypnotic power. Over this the opening phrase of the melody unfolds in a broad curve.

The use of the minor imparts a brooding character to the speech of the first soldier (Stanzas 1 and 2). The speech of the second soldier is ushered in by a change to major. Mahler shifts from minor to major and back, which adds to the haunting atmosphere of the song. The dotted rhythm returns as an introduction to Stanza 4. Then the orchestra takes over with an interlude of trumpet calls and the tramp-tramp of marching feet. Suddenly an endless legion seems to be on the march, and the song is no longer concerned with one or two soldiers but with the fate of all who have marched to battle.

As the poem moves from the realm of the living to that of the dead, trills on the flutes and clarinets cast a ghostly spell over the music. In the next interlude Mahler directs the violinists to tap the strings with the sticks of their bows: *col legno* (coal lén-yo)—"with the wood," which creates an eerie effect. He wanted the final phrase to be sung *mit Verzweiflung*—in despair!

His songs and symphonies speak to the heart in a most poignant way. For his admirers (and their number increases with every year!), Gustav Mahler's music occupies a very special place.

Leoš Janáček

Leoš Janáček (yá-na-shek) is the chief composer of the modern Czech school. He was born in the northernmost part of Bohemia (now Czechoslovakia) on July 3, 1854, and died in Prague on August 12, 1928 at the age of seventy-four. He spent most of his life in the town of Brno as organist, conductor, and teacher. Fame came slowly to Janáček. He was past sixty when his opera *Jenufa* was presented in Prague and created a sensation. Suddenly its composer was transformed from an obscure teacher in a small town into a musician with a European reputation. Janáček followed in the footsteps of Smetana and Dvořák. Like them he was strongly influenced by the folk music and the legends of his native land. His operas, choral music, and instrumental works are widely admired in Europe, but it is only in recent years that he has acquired an audience in America. Now that his principal compositions have been made available on records, music lovers in this country are discovering a highly individual artist whose music bears the stamp of a powerful imagination.

Sinfonietta— Fourth Movement

Characteristic is the fourth movement of his Sinfonietta. (This term is used to indicate a "little symphony.") Marked Allegretto, this movement is an example of Janáček's great fondness for the theme-and-variations form. The theme is a short tune in the style of a Czech folk song. The melody shows several characteristics associated with folk music: movement by step or narrow leap within a narrow range, and much repetition. For example, the opening note is heard four times. So, too, the first three measures are immediately repeated. These traits impart to the melody a simple, even primitive quality.

Various instruments take turns in presenting the melody; fascinating countermelodies are added to the tune. Changes in register (high-low), dynamics (soft-loud), tempo (Adagio-Presto), and harmony underline the changes in orchestration. At times the melody is presented in a new key. A few measures of Prestissimo, marked *ff* and spiced with dissonances, bring these variations to an exciting conclusion.

Sergei Rachmaninov

Sergei Rachmaninov (ser-gáy rakh-máh-ni-noff) was one of the best known Russian composers of the post-romantic generation. He was born on April 1, 1873 in the province of Novgorod. Rachmaninov achieved fame as a composer and pianist fairly early in life. He was out of sympathy with the Bolshevik Revolution and left his homeland in 1917, never to return. During the rest of his life he traveled widely and gave concerts in all the musical centers of Europe and America. He spent much time in the United States and was extremely popular in this country both as composer and pianist. He died in Beverly Hills, California, on March 28, 1943, at the age of seventy.

Rachmaninov was a traditional composer who followed in the footsteps of Tchaikovsky. He was also influenced by the German romantics such as Schumann and Brahms. His melodies have an immediate appeal. For this reason a number of his themes—especially those of his most popular work,

241

the Second Piano Concerto—have been transformed into popular songs. Rachmaninov favored the short lyric forms and wrote a number of effective piano pieces and songs.

Prelude in G minor

Rachmaninov's piano style is well shown by the popular Prelude in G minor, which begins as a march-like piece of great rhythmic energy. It is based on a fairly simple melody with chords above it:

The piece is in A-B-A form, with a decided contrast between the first section and the middle part. Since the opening section is martial and dramatic, the middle part is legato and lyrical; it presents an oriental-sounding melody. A transition leads back to the mood of the first section. The coda begins fortissimo but traces a steady diminuendo to the final measures. The piece ends with an ascending run that ripples along the keyboard and dies away.

Floods of Spring

Floods of Spring, one of Rachmaninov's best-known songs, shows his lyricism at its best. Marked Allegro vivace, the melody suggests the expectancy that mankind feels when winter snows begin to melt and the promise of spring fills the air. You will hear the song sung in the original Russian.

Yestcho v'palach belayet snyeg,	The snow enfolds the fields in white,
A vodi oosh vesnyoi shoomyat.	But floods of spring are stirring now.
Begoot ee boodyat soni bryeg,	They run to wake the sleeping banks,
Begoot ee blestchoot ee glasat,	They rush and gleam and roar with joy,
Anee glasat voh vsyeh kantzi,	They shout to all the earth
Vesna eedot! Vesna eedot!	That Spring is here, that Spring is here!
Me maladoi vesnee gontsi,	"We are the heralds of the Spring,
Ana nas veeslala v'perod,	Her joyful coming we proclaim!
Vesna eedot! Vesna eedot!	Now Spring is here! Now Spring is here!
Ee teekheeekh tyoplich	And soon the warm quiet days of May
maiskeek dneh,	
Rumyanee svyetlee kharavod,	Will come in radiant array,
Talpeetsa veseloh za nyai!	Following her in a joyful train!"

The impetuous piano accompaniment, which is equal in importance to the voice part, sets the mood with surging arpeggios. The broad curve of the melody gives an impression of strength and hope:

The entire song is in the nature of a proclamation. The mood is sustained by rushing arpeggios and chords in the piano part, which carry on an impassioned dialogue with the voice until the joyous ending.

31

Impressionists: Debussy and Ravel

In 1863 the French painter Claude Monet (mo-náy) exhibited a picture called *Impression: Sun Rising*. Before long *impressionism* came into use as a term that made fun of the hazy paintings of this artist and his school. Among Monet's associates in the new styles were Edouard Manet (mah-náy), Edgar Degas (day-gáh), and Auguste Renoir (ren-wár).

French Impressionism

They tried to take painting out of the studio into the open air, to record their impressions of the world around them. What fascinated them was the change in the appearance of things as the light shifted. Instead of mixing their paints on the palette, they put brush-strokes of pure color on the

CLAUDE MONET, *BANKS OF THE SEINE, VÉTHEUIL.*
The shimmering light and veiled outlines are characteristic of impressionist painting.

243

canvas, leaving it to the eye of the beholder to do the mixing. At first people laughed. Whoever saw grass that was pink and yellow and blue? But the impressionists persisted, and taught the world to see nature in a new way.

There was bound to appear a composer who would translate the dreamy outlines of impressionist painting into his music. His name was Claude Debussy (deh-buh-sée).

Claude Debussy

The foremost French composer of the early twentieth century was born in the town of St.-Germaine-en-Laye (san zher-mán ahn lay), near Paris, on August 22, 1862. He died in Paris on March 25, 1918, during the German bombardment of the city in the First World War.

Debussy was against tradition. From the beginning of his career he looked for new ways of expressing himself. "I love music passionately," he wrote, "and because I love it I try to free it from the barren traditions that stifle it. It is a free art, an open-air art, boundless as the wind, the sky, the sea! It must never be shut in and become an academic art!"

Debussy above all was a Frenchman. He felt that his countrymen had fallen too much under the influence of German music; he tried to lead them away from the symphony of Beethoven and the music drama of Wagner, towards an art that would be completely French. His delicate mood-pieces evoke the favorite images of the impressionist painters: gardens in the rain, sunlight through the leaves, clouds, moonlight, sea, mist.

Debussy was fascinated by the scales of the Far East. Especially he was attracted to the whole-tone scale—a scale, that is, consisting entirely of whole tones, as in the sequence, C, D, E, F♯, G♯, A♯, C. This was particularly well suited to the misty effects he sought to achieve. In his desire to find a fresh sound he went back to the scales of the Middle Ages—the modes that had been used for centuries before the major-minor scales became popular. For this reason many of his harmonies may be described as modal. (This was the term, you may recall, that we applied to the harmonies of Palestrina and Monteverdi.) He obtained many magical effects by leaving dissonant chords unresolved. Often, at the end of a piece by Debussy, there is no definite cadence as in the works of the classic and romantic periods. The music seems to fade away into silence.

No less subtle is his manner of orchestration. He avoided the grand climaxes of the romantic orchestra; his orchestration is delicate and full of atmosphere. We saw that the impressionist painters placed specks of pure color on the canvas instead of mixing them on their palette. Similarly Debussy did not mix his colors. He wrote in such a way that individual instruments stood out clearly against the orchestral mass.

Debussy worked slowly; his fame rests on a comparatively small number of works. A sensitive tone poet who transformed his impressions of nature into sounds of haunting loveliness, he became the first major composer of our era.

OPENING PAGE OF THE MANUSCRIPT OF THE *PRELUDE TO THE AFTERNOON OF A FAUN.* ⟶

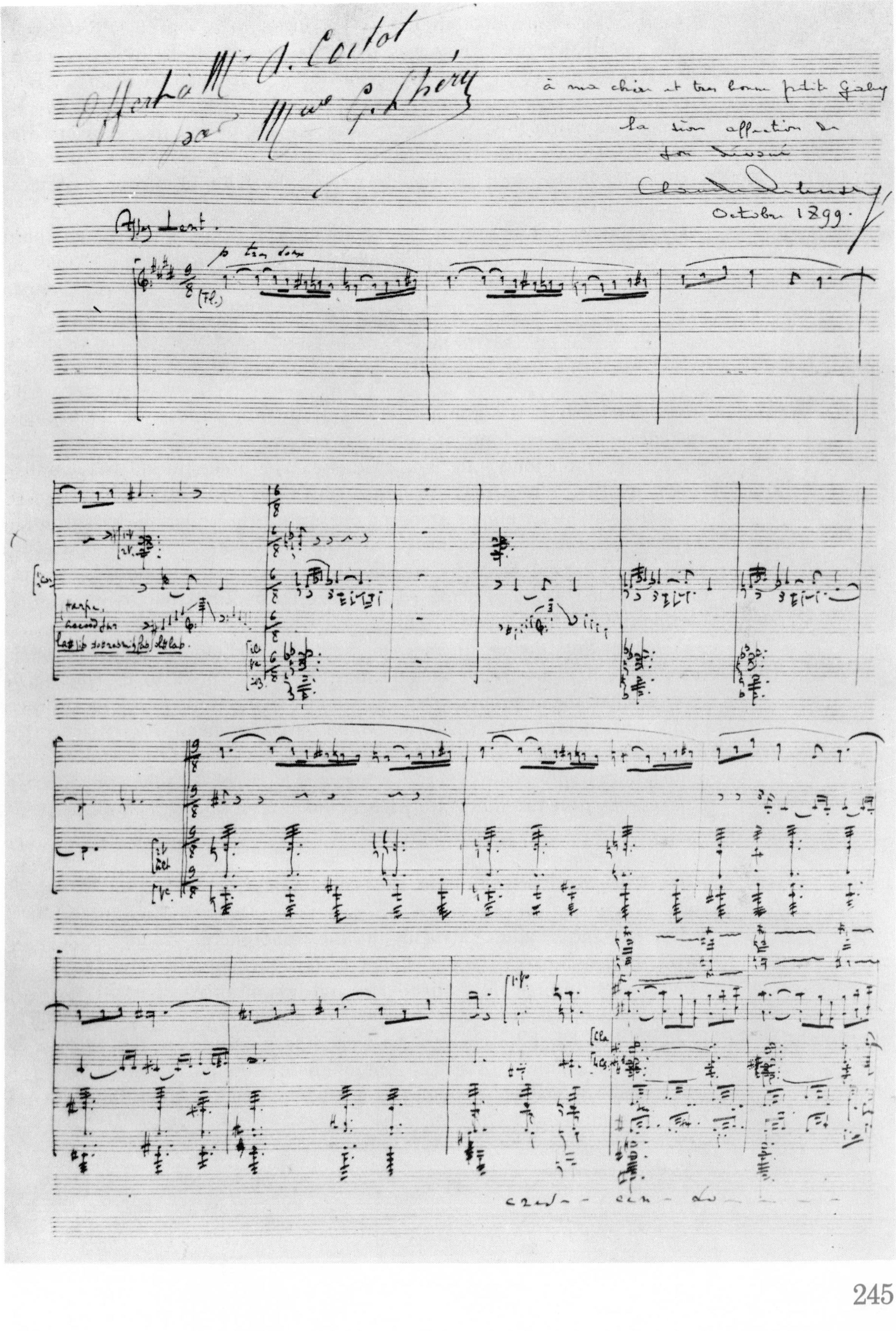

Octobre 1899.
Assez Lent.

Prelude to The Afternoon of a Faun

Debussy's best-known orchestral work was inspired by a poem of Stéphane Mallarmé (mal-ar-máy) that evoked the landscape of pagan Greece. (A faun is a mythological creature of the forest, half man, half goat.) The faun awakes in the woods and tries to remember: Did he see three lovely nymphs pass by on their way to the nearby pond, or was this a dream? He will never know. "The music of this prelude," Debussy wrote, "projects a changing background for the dreams of the faun in the heat of that summer afternoon."

It opens with a flute solo in the velvety lower register. The melody glides gently along the chromatic scale, narrow in range, dream-like.

This music avoids the grand climaxes of the romantic style. Pianissimo and mezzo-piano predominate; there is only one fortissimo in the entire piece. The whole-tone scale is in evidence. The orchestration has a transparent quality. The strings are muted; flute and oboe, clarinet and horns are used as solo instruments, standing out against the orchestral background. Typical is the rhythm that flows across the barline in a continuous stream, without a clear-cut beat. By weakening and even wiping out the accent on the "One," Debussy achieved a dream-like motion that is one of the leading traits of impressionist music.

A contrasting theme emerges, marked "In the same tempo and very sustained." It is an ardent melody that carries the piece to its emotional climax. Then the first melody returns, slightly changed. At the close, antique cymbals are heard, *ppp*. (*Antique cymbals* are tiny metal discs attached to thumb and forefinger and struck together.) Mysterious chords sound on the muted horns and violins, very far away. The work dissolves in silence. It takes only nine minutes; rarely has so much been said with so little.

Fêtes

Fêtes (feht, which may be translated as *Holidays* or *Festivities*) is one of three *Nocturnes for Orchestra*. In this piece Debussy tried to capture movement and rhythm "dancing in the atmosphere," as he explained, "with sudden bursts of light. There is also the episode of a procession which passes through the festive scene and becomes part of it."

The piece opens fortissimo, in a blaze of light. A basic rhythm in triplets is established by the orchestra. An ascending glissando on the harp gives the effect of a shower of sparks—one of those "sudden bursts of light" of which Debussy spoke. A melody emerges, holding the attention with its tense rhythm:

This idea is expanded into an exciting section. There is a sudden pianissimo; the procession sets forth, shadowy and far off. The music seems to come ever closer as the sound increases in volume. A climax is reached; merry-makers seem to have arrived at where we are standing. The procession passes us by and begins to move off in the distance. This effect is achieved through a gradual decrescendo, which leads to a mysterious ending. A cymbal is brushed ever so lightly with a drumstick, and the music floats off into silence.

The piano, with its floating sounds and its capacity for creating a mood, was a favorite instrument of the impressionists. Debussy was extremely fond of the instrument.

His most famous piano piece, *Clair de lune* (Moonlight), evokes the soft radiance of a moonlit night. The melody, marked Andante and *très espressif* (very expressive), glides in a gently descending curve, moving by step and narrow leap in a flowing rhythm. The first section has a dream-like quality. In the second, haunting chords move in parallel motion over a sustained tone in the bass.

The third section takes on more movement, although it remains within the pianissimo range. A transitional passage leads back to the opening melody. A brief coda brings this lovely mood-piece to its quiet ending.

Clair de lune

Ravel was born on March 7, 1875, near Saint-Jean-de-Luz (san zhahn de luz) in the southwestern corner of France. He died in Paris on December 28, 1937, at the age of sixty-two. He stands in the same relation to Debussy as the painter Cézanne does to Monet: he was a post-impressionist. Like Cézanne he feared that impressionism, with its emphasis on dream-like atmosphere, might destroy musical form. He had a need for clarity and organization. It was this that made him turn back—even as did Cézanne—to the classical conception of form and order.

Like Debussy, Ravel was attracted to the scales of medieval music as well as those of the Far East. Both men were attracted by the same aspects of nature: the play of water and light, clouds and fountains; the magic of daybreak and twilight; the wind in the trees. And both loved exotic dance rhythms.

Maurice Ravel

A number of French composers found inspiration in the colorful music of Spain. We have heard two works that showed this trend: Bizet's *Carmen* and Chabrier's *España*. Ravel too was fascinated by the Iberian Peninsula to the south of his homeland. In his *Spanish Rhapsody* he used his mastery of the orchestra to achieve some stunning effects. The last movement, *Feria* (The Fair), is gay and full of excitement.

Piccolos and flutes launch the movement. Then Ravel lays down a dark curtain of sound. Out of this rises an impetuous Spanish rhythm. It introduces a suave melody that is similar in mood to some of the tunes in *España* (although Ravel uses it in his own way):

Rapsodie espagnole—Feria

PAUL CÉZANNE, *MONT SAINTE VICTOIRE*.
Cézanne, like Ravel, was a post-impressionist in his desire to restore the principles
of classical form.

The movement is in A-B-A form, with the greatest possible contrast in
mood between the first and second sections. The tempo changes from an
Allegro to an Andante. Ravel uses the English horn to introduce a melody
in the style of flamenco song. (*Flamenco* is the passionate style of the
Spanish Gypsies, as shown in their folk songs and dances.) A brief transition
leads to the return of the first section.

We have noticed that nineteenth-century composers used three devices to build a climax: crescendo, accelerando, and a rise from low register to the more brilliant high. To these Ravel was able to add a fourth: the dissonant harmony of the twentieth century. In the final measures of this movement the music not only grows faster and louder and higher; in addition, the harmony becomes more dissonant and builds up increasing tension. Tambourine and castanets, triangle and xylophone, celesta and great glissandos on the harp make a luminous sound. And the piece ends with crashing dissonances, in a blaze of light.

❧ | 32 | ❧

Away From Impressionism

Impressionist music achieved enormous popularity in the first quarter of our century. A whole generation of musicians, both in Europe and America, fell under its spell. Sooner or later, however, a reaction was bound to set in against the twilight moods and vague outlines of the impressionist style. This reaction began where the movement itself had taken shape: in France.

Erik Satie
and Les Six

Erik Satie (1866–1925) is a composer who, although his works have never been played very much, exerted a major influence on the course of twentieth-century music. He was the spokesman for a new spirit in music that aimed at "emotional simplicity and directness of speech." His clean modest orchestration was as different as could be from the gently poetic style of Debussy or the gorgeous coloring of Ravel. The famous writer Jean Cocteau (coc-tóh), who was Satie's friend, expressed the new creed: "Enough of clouds, waves, aquariums, nymphs and perfumes of the night. We need a music that is down to earth—an everyday music." In the titles Satie gave to some of his pieces he made fun of the poetic titles of the impressionists: *Disagreeable Perceptions, Cold Pieces, Three Flabby Preludes, Three Pieces in the Shape of a Pear.* In the same spirit he scattered humorous directions throughout his works, such as "To be played in the most profound silence," or "Like a nightingale with a toothache."

Satie gathered around him a number of disciples, some of whom were

destined to become more famous than himself. Chief among them was a group of six young composers who achieved great prominence in the 1920s. They reacted not only against impressionism but against the entire romantic tradition of the nineteenth century. They found inspiration in the songs of the Parisian music halls and in American jazz. They glorified the city and the machine, rather than the nature scenes that had inspired the romantic and impressionist composers. They wanted music to be clever and entertaining; they were interested in motion rather than in emotion.

As with the Russian "Five," *Les Six* (lay see) were not equal in talent. Three were soon forgotten. But the other three—Darius Milhaud, Arthur Honegger and Francis Poulenc, whose works we shall study in this chapter—became the leaders of the next generation of French composers.

Satie: Le Chapelier

Typical of Satie's love of musical humor is his setting of *Le Chapelier* (le sha-pel-yáy), a French poem about the Mad Hatter of *Alice in Wonderland*.

Le chapelier s'étonne de constater	The Hatter was astonished to find
que sa montre retarde de trois jours,	That his watch was three weeks behind,
bien qu'il ait eu soin de la graisser toujours	Even though he was careful always to grease it
avec du beurre de première qualité.	With butter of the finest quality.
Mais il a laissé tomber des miettes de pain	But he had let bread-crumbs drop
dans les rouages,	Into the little wheels,
et il a beau plonger sa montre dans le thé.	And he even dipped the watch into his tea.
Ça ne la fera pas avancer davantage.	That would hardly make it go much longer.

The song is marked Allegretto. The accompaniment begins with chords in the right hand and a fragment of the melody in the left. The piece flows along in a simple and direct manner. The second stanza does not repeat the music of the first; hence the song is through-composed in form. The climax comes on the next-to-last line, which tells how the Mad Hatter plunged his watch into his tea. Here the melody line reaches its highest point and takes on additional weight by slowing up. The final comment is made gently and leads to the pianissimo ending. It is all very charming, very French, and very Satie.

Je te veux

For many years Satie earned a living by playing the piano in a cabaret in Paris. This brought him into contact with the songs of the music halls. He came to love these popular tunes, and found in them an inspiration for his art. This aspect of Satie's music is beautifully illustrated by *Je te veux* (zhuh tuh vuh—I want you) a waltz song in the style of the Parisian music hall. The music is lightly sentimental, with a melody that achieves Satie's goal of simple and direct expression. The words are appropriate to the mood. The lady informs her sweetheart that she understands his yearning because she shares it. She goes on to confide to him that she has only one desire—to spend the rest of her life with him.

This song is not only French, but Parisian. In its lilting measures Satie captured the atmosphere of the city he adored.

A more serious side of Satie's art is summed up in a number of short piano pieces to which he gave unusual titles. *Gnossienne* (nos-yén) is a word he made up that had a Greek flavor to it. In this way he suggested that his three *Gnossiennes* were inspired by classical antiquity. They are a set of dances that move with a stately simplicity. The third is the most beautiful.

He wrote it without any time signature or barlines—a daring procedure in 1890. The melody unfolds in short phrases over a simple chord accompaniment.

The modal harmony shows that Satie, no less than Debussy, was tired of the major-minor scales and gave his music a fresh feeling by turning back to the forgotten scales of the Middle Ages. For those who love Satie's music—and there are musicians who regard him as one of the most important composers of our century—this short piece sums up his style: a style simple and direct.

Darius Milhaud (mee-yó) was born in Provence on September 4, 1892, of a distinguished Jewish family that had lived in France for centuries. He has written a great deal of music in all forms: operas and ballets, symphonies and concertos, choral and chamber works, theater and film music, songs and piano pieces. His music is completely French in its elegance, charm, and sophistication.

During the Second World War Milhaud found a haven in the United States, where he was active as conductor and teacher. The *Suite française* (frahn-sáyz), a piece for band, was written during those years. "For a long time," Milhaud stated, "I have had the idea of writing a composition fit for high-school purposes, and this was the result. The five parts of this suite are named after French provinces, the very ones in which the American and Allied armies fought together with the French underground for the liberation of my country: Normandy, Brittany, Île-de-France (of which Paris is the center), Alsace-Lorraine, and Provence. I used some folk tunes of these provinces. I wanted young Americans to hear the popular melodies of those parts of France where their fathers and brothers fought to defeat the German invaders."

We hear the first and third movements of the suite. *Normandy* is bright and gay. The abrupt changes of key, mildly dissonant harmonies, and jaunty rhythms are characteristic of Milhaud; he uses the sound of the brass band to its best advantage. *Île-de-France* is based on a lively ostinato rhythm. Here too the sudden changes of key and pungent harmonies add zest to a movement that is extremely melodious and extremely French.

Scaramouche

In *Scaramouche* (sca-ra-móosh) Milhaud turned to a medium that has attracted a number of modern composers: music for two pianos. This suite is named for a figure out of classical French comedy. The finale, *Brazileira* (in Brazilian style), is a *samba*—that is, a lively dance in $\frac{2}{4}$ time. Milhaud conjures up happy memories of the time he spent as a young man in Brazil. This movement is a fine example of twentieth-century exoticism. Milhaud here joins the long line of French composers who have found inspiration in the songs and dances of foreign lands.

Arthur Honegger

Arthur Honegger was born in Le Havre on March 10, 1892, in the same year as his friend Milhaud. His parents were Swiss. He died in Paris in 1955 at the age of sixty-three.

Honegger won fame in 1921 with his dramatic oratorio *Le Roi David* (King David). Equally successful, three years later, was *Pacific 231,* a symphonic poem glorifying the locomotive. Like Milhaud, Honegger wrote much. His list of compositions includes more than a dozen operas and stage works, twelve ballets, about thirty film scores, large choral pieces with orchestra, five symphonies, compositions for solo instrument and orchestra, chamber music, piano pieces, and songs.

Pacific 231

The popularity of *Pacific 231* was due, in part, to the novelty of its subject. Certainly no one before had had the idea of writing a musical composition about a locomotive. Honegger explained his choice of subject in the following way: "I have always had a passion for locomotives. In *Pacific 231* I did not try to imitate the noise of the engine, but rather to express in music a visual impression and a physical joy. The piece begins with an impression of the quiet breathing of the engine at rest, the strain of starting, then the gradual working up of speed, finally the lyricism and grandeur of a locomotive of 300 tons rushing through the stillness of the night at a mile a minute."

We hear a few measures of introduction. Then the darker instruments—bassoons and contrabassoons, horns, tuba, bass drum, cellos, and double basses—establish the mood. In a piece of this kind rhythm and harmony play a more important part than melody. The "gradual working up of speed" is suggested by the use of ever shorter notes in the opening section—halves, quarters, eighth notes, triplets, sixteenths.

As the train gets under way, there is a steady build-up through crescendo and faster motion. The composer has captured the "lyricism and grandeur" of his poetic symbol as it plunges through the night. The music slows up at the end to suggest that the train has reached its destination. The sound is dark and rough, supported by great blocks of dissonant harmony that give an impression of vast tension and strength. Here Honegger is the modern man celebrating the power of the machine.

Francis Poulenc was a Parisian to the core. He was born in Paris on January 7, 1899, and died in his country home at Noizay on January 30, 1963. His music has the wit, the clarity, and the elegance that we associate with French art. These characteristics are prominent in his chamber music, his piano pieces, and orchestral works. They represent, however, only one side of his musical nature—the side that was closest to the doctrines of Erik Satie. His songs, religious choral music, and operas reveal a poetic musician. His works are cherished by an ever growing circle of admirers on both sides of the Atlantic.

Francis Poulenc

Concerto for Two Pianos and Orchestra— Finale

In the brilliant Finale of his Concerto for Two Pianos and Orchestra, Poulenc used the piano as an instrument capable not only of singing melody but also of percussion-like rhythm and dissonant harmony. We hear march-like tunes full of driving rhythms, alternating with tender melodies. The movement, marked Allegro molto, is in the form of a rondo (in which, you will remember, a principal theme returns again and again in alternation with other melodies). There is a brief introduction based on rapid triplets that require the most nimble fingers. The main theme is in the manner of a striking march, rhythmically tense and impulsive. It is presented as a dialogue between the two pianos, while the orchestra adds vigorous comments.

This theme alternates with three lyric melodies that provide areas of relaxation in the forward drive of the movement. The final section begins in an agitated manner, but calms down with the appearance of one of Poulenc's loveliest tunes. A series of dissonant chords brings this exciting movement to an end.

National Composers:
Villa-Lobos, Vaughan Williams,
Walton, Britten

*The New
Nationalism*

Musical nationalism, which had been a powerful force in the nineteenth century, remained so in the twentieth. Nations with established musical cultures continued to be active along national lines. In addition, several nations that had not been musically creative in the nineteenth century—such as Spain, England, Finland, and the United States—developed national schools of composition in the twentieth. In previous chapters we have studied the works of a number of modern composers who either worked within a national tradition or tried to create one. Among them were Debussy and Ravel; Richard Strauss and Mahler; Stravinsky, Glière, and Khatchaturian; Janáček and Weinberger; Respighi, Falla, Elgar, Kodály, Sibelius, and Ginastera; Roy Harris, George Gershwin, Virgil Thomson, Douglas Moore, Aaron Copland, and Morton Gould.

In one important respect twentieth-century nationalists differed from their forebears. The romantic composers listened to folk music with nineteenth-century ears. If a folk song departed from either the major or minor scale they "corrected" the tune to make it fit. Similarly, if a folk song departed from the standard meters ($\frac{2}{4}$, $\frac{3}{4}$, $\frac{4}{4}$, or $\frac{6}{8}$) they adjusted the rhythm to fit the metrical patterns to which they were accustomed. But many folk songs originated centuries ago, long before the major-minor scales, and were modal in character. Many were in irregular rhythmic patterns that were used long before the standard meters. By correcting what they took to be mistakes, the nineteenth-century composers often changed the character of the song.

Twentieth-century composers approached folk music in a more scientific frame of mind. They went into the villages with recording equipment, so as to take down the ancient tunes exactly as the peasants sang them. Since they were eager to get away from the major-minor scales and the standard meters, they appreciated the irregularities of folk music instead of treating them as "mistakes." Through their efforts nationalism remained as important a force in the music of the twentieth century as it had been in the music of the nineteenth.

The foremost composer of Latin America, Heitor Villa-Lobos, was born in Rio de Janeiro, Brazil, on March 5, 1887. He died there on November 18, 1959, at the age of seventy-two. Villa-Lobos was an eloquent advocate of musical nationalism. "I compose in the folk style," he declared. "An artist must select and transmit the material given him by his people."

Villa-Lobos was an amazingly productive composer; he composed well over 1,500 pieces. A number of these were lost because, once he wrote down the music, he was not always careful to save the manuscript. He left behind him more than a dozen symphonic poems, twelve symphonies, fifteen string quartets, operas, ballets, choral music, piano pieces, and songs, as well as music for all kinds of instrumental and vocal combinations.

Heitor
Villa-Lobos

Throughout his life Villa-Lobos tried to combine the melodies of his homeland with the traditions of Western music. He had a great admiration for Bach, whom he considered a universal composer, "a mediator among all races." He therefore decided to write a series of suites based on the folk music of Brazil but conceived "in homage to the great genius of Bach." He called them *Bachianas Brasileiras*—that is, Brazilian Bach-pieces. The Aria from the fifth of these, for soprano accompanied by cellos, became one of his best-loved works.

The Aria, an Adagio, opens with the pizzicato of the cellos, which suggests the sound of guitars. This, like the staccato accompaniment in Schubert's *Serenade*, immediately creates a romantic atmosphere. The soprano

Aria from
Bachianas
Brasileiras
No. 5

sings no words in the opening section; she intones the notes on the syllable "ah." This type of wordless singing is known as *vocalise* (vo-cah-léez). Since there is no text, the meaning of the melody rests purely in itself. The voice, in such a case, is used as if it were an instrument.

The middle section of the Aria is a setting of a Brazilian poem that evokes the quiet hour of early evening when the heart is filled with longing. It is sung in Portuguese, the language of Brazil.

Tarde, uma nuvem rósea lenta e transparente,	At night a pink transparent cloud moves slowly
sobre o espaço sonhadora e bela!	Across the beauteous space of heaven!
Surge no infinito a lua docemente,	From infinite distance the moon arises gently,
enfeitando a tarde, qual meiga donzela	Enhancing the night like a lovely maiden
que se apresta e alinda sonhadoramente,	Who hurries to adorn herself,

em anseios d'alma para ficar bela, grita so céo e a terra, toda a Natureza!	Anxious at heart to reveal her beauty, Hailed by heaven and earth and by all Nature!
Cala a passarada aos seus tristes queixumes, e reflete o mar toda a sua riqueza	To the passers-by she calls her plaintive cry, And is reflected in the sea in all her richness.
suave a luz da lua desperta agora, a cruel saudade que ri e chora!	Gentle moonlight fills the soul, forcing it To a cruel longing that laughs and weeps!
Tarde, uma nuvem rósea lenta e transparente, sobre o espaço sonhadora e bela!	At night a pink transparent cloud moves slowly Across the beauteous space of heaven!

The middle section reflects the mood of the words. Then the first section is repeated, so that the piece is in A-B-A form. This time, however, the melody is not sung but hummed; which gives the voice a veiled quality that is extremely effective against the dark color of the cellos. You will hear the Aria sung in a beautiful performance by the Brazilian soprano Bidú Sayão, who for many years was a leading singer at the Metropolitan Opera House. It is conducted by the composer.

The Little Train of the Caipira

Villa-Lobos made many trips to the central provinces of Brazil in order to hear and to collect the songs of the peasants. On one of these he rode a train that carried berry-pickers from their homes to their work in the fields. Villa-Lobos remembered the gay songs of the berry-pickers as the train chugged and puffed its way along the mountain road. He recreated the scene in the charming piece he named *The Little Train of the Caipira*. (A *caipira* is a Brazilian peasant.)

He described this composition as a Toccata. A *toccata*, in the Baroque era, was a virtuoso piece for a keyboard instrument. (The name was derived from the Italian *toccare*, "to touch," referring to the keys.) In the twentieth century the toccata became a brilliant piece for either piano or orchestra based on a driving rhythm. In Villa-Lobos's toccata a steady rhythm conjures up the movement of the train. Soon the violins begin to sing a melody in the style of a Brazilian folk song that unfolds over the ostinato rhythm of the wheels.

The music reaches a climax. The melody is repeated. There is a gradual ritardando as the train slows down and grinds to a halt with dissonant harmonies. A bell rings, a whistle blows. The berry-pickers—and the piece —have arrived at their destination.

The English

For almost two hundred years after Purcell's death England produced no major composer. Various reasons have been given for this long silence on the part of a nation that had been musically creative for centuries. Perhaps it was because German musicians—from Handel to Mendelssohn—became so popular in England that they ended by dominating the musical life of the country. In any case, when a school of native composers arose towards the end of the nineteenth century it filled a long-felt need. Now England was able to resume her rightful place in the concert of nations.

Ralph Vaughan Williams was the foremost figure among the English nationalists of his generation. "The art of music," he stated, "above all other arts is the expression of the soul of a nation. The composer must love the tunes of his country and they must become an integral part of him."

Vaughan Williams was born in Down Ampney, in Gloucestershire, on October 12, 1872. He died in London on August 26, 1958, at the age of eighty-six. Of his nine symphonies the best known are the *London,* the *Pastoral,* and the dramatic Symphony in F minor, the Fourth. He wrote many instrumental and choral works, songs and operas, and religious compositions. His music came from a manly personality and a warm heart.

The Fantasia on *Greensleeves* was adapted from Vaughan Williams's opera *Sir John in Love.* (Sir John is Falstaff, and the opera is based on Shakespeare's *Merry Wives of Windsor.*) *A fantasia* is an imaginative piece that follows no set form. The Fantasia on *Greensleeves* presents one of the most beautiful of old English love songs:

> Alas! my love, you do me wrong
> 　　To cast me off discourteously;
> And I have lovéd you so long,
> 　　Delighting in your company.
>
> Greensleeves was all my joy,
> Greensleeves was my delight,
> Greensleeves was my heart of gold,
> 　　And who but my Lady Greensleeves.

The piece opens with a brief introduction: a flute solo heard against arpeggios on the harp. The melody is marked Lento moderato (moderately slow) and is in $\frac{6}{8}$ time. The celebrated tune is sung by second violins and violas against a background of arpeggios on the harp, while the first violins play a countermelody above it.

Greensleeves dates from the sixteenth century. It is therefore a modal melody; that is, it is based on the old modes. Notes that would be flats according to the major scale are, in *Greensleeves,* natural. This imparts to the tune a far-away quality that is one of its principal charms.

The Fantasia is in A-B-A form. The middle section, an Allegretto, shifts to $\frac{4}{4}$ time and is based on the folk song *Lovely Joan.* This too evokes the atmosphere of Old England. Then *Greensleeves* is repeated.

"The greatest artist," Vaughan Williams declared, "belongs inevitably to his country as much as the humblest singer in a remote village." This conviction shaped his music. As a result he became, as one of his countrymen called him, "the most English of English composers."

William Walton: Scene from Belshazzar's Feast

William Walton is one of England's leading composers. He was born in Oldham on March 29, 1902. Among his well-known works are a violin concerto, a viola concerto, and the oratorio *Belshazzar's Feast,* and also his film scores for Sir Laurence Olivier's *Henry V* and *Hamlet.*

Belshazzar's Feast comes out of the tradition of choral singing that has flourished in England for centuries. The text, drawn from the Psalms and the Book of Daniel, tells how the Jews were driven into exile and how they wept by the waters of Babylon. Then Belshazzar, the King of Babylon, made a great feast, in the course of which he saw the handwriting on the wall. And that night he was slain, and his kingdom was divided.

The scene of the royal banquet is, of course, one of the high points of the score. The sacred vessels are filled with wine; the King and his court worship their idols:

> And then spake the King:
> "Praise ye the god of gold,
> Praise ye the god of silver,
> Praise ye the god of iron,
> Praise ye the god of wood,
> Praise ye the god of stone,
> Praise ye the god of brass,
> Praise ye the gods!"

The orchestra announces an imperious motive. The chorus sings the opening line fortissimo, and is followed by a baritone solo. He is answered by the chorus:

The music at this point is ablaze with color and movement. Fiercely dissonant harmonies and syncopated rhythms add to the excitement. An energetic march conjures up a scene of barbaric splendor. Glockenspiel and triangle join in praise of the god of silver, gong and anvil are used to praise the god of iron. Xylophone and woodblock pay homage to the god of wood, cymbals hail the god of stone, and two extra brass bands help praise the god of brass.

Notice how Walton follows the tradition of baroque choral music by repeating words; the entire final section of the chorus is an expansion of two words—*Praise ye!* He also follows tradition in expanding a single syllable so that it extends over a series of notes, on the word *Praise.* The orchestration is imaginative in the highest degree; and the number ends with the same imperious motive with which it began.

The creator of this exciting choral drama is now known as Sir William Walton. The title goes well with a style that is fresh, manly, and British to the core.

Benjamin Britten, the most important English composer of his generation, was born in Lowestoft, in Suffolk, on November 22, 1913. He is one of the few present-day composers who have achieved success in the realm of opera. Among his best-known operas are *Peter Grimes; The Turn of the Screw,* based on a story by the American novelist Henry James; *A Midsummer Night's Dream,* on Shakespeare's immortal comedy; and *Billy Budd,* a deeply moving work based on a story by the American writer Herman Melville. Britten has also written a wide variety of instrumental and vocal works.

Benjamin Britten: Fugue from The Young Person's Guide to the Orchestra

In 1945 the British Ministry of Education produced a film whose purpose it was to explain to young listeners how the orchestra functions. Britten was asked to write music for the film that would show off the various instruments, their natures and capacities. The result was one of his most popular works, *The Young Person's Guide to the Orchestra,* its subtitle being *Variations and Fugue on a Theme of Purcell.* In this fashion the most gifted composer of England today paid homage to her greatest composer of the past.

The piece consists of thirteen variations on Purcell's theme, which show how the strings, woodwinds, brass, and percussion instruments are used in the orchestra. The variations are followed by a brilliant fugue marked Allegro molto (very fast). You will remember, from our discussion of the music of the Baroque, that the fugue was one of the great forms of the seventeenth and early eighteenth centuries. Britten here returned to what was one of the main types of music in Purcell's time.

The theme of the fugue is a lively tune that is strongly rhythmic in character:

It is introduced by the piccolo and taken over in turn by flutes, oboes, clarinets, and bassoons. During this section the music moves from a soft beginning to a fortissimo. Now it is the turn of the strings. The first violins present the tune, followed almost immediately by the second violins, violas, cellos, and double basses, against interesting counterpoint in the rest of the orchestra. In this section too, the music moves from a quiet beginning to a fortissimo. Next the theme is presented by the harp, the brass, and the percussion. At the climax of the fugue Britten combines his melody with Purcell's.

This makes a stunning effect and brings the piece to an exciting close.

National Composers: Bloch, Orff, Prokofiev, Shostakovich

Ernest Bloch

Ernest Bloch was born in Geneva on July 24, 1880. He came to the United States in 1916. He died in Portland, Oregon, on July 16, 1959, at the age of seventy-nine.

Bloch differed from other composers of Jewish origin such as Meyerbeer and Offenbach, who became part of the French school of their time; or Mendelssohn and Mahler, who took over the traditions of the German school. He found his way as a composer by identifying himself with his Jewish heritage. "I am a Jew. I aspire to write Jewish music because it is the only way I can produce music of vitality—if I can do such a thing at all."

Bloch's "Jewish Cycle" includes *Schelomo* (Solomon), a Hebrew Rhapsody for cello and orchestra; the *Israel Symphony; Three Jewish Poems;* Psalms 114 and 137, for soprano and orchestra; *Baal Shem Suite,* for violin and piano or orchestra; and a Sacred Service. He also wrote a number of works that lie outside the sphere of nationalism, such as the Concerto Grosso No. 1 for strings and piano, and the Quintet for piano and strings.

The *Baal Shem Suite* for violin and piano consists of "Three Pictures of Hassidic Life." Baal Shem, "Master of the Sacred Name," was a wonderworking Rabbi of the Hassidim, a mystical sect that flourished among the Jews of Eastern Europe. The most popular number of the Suite is the second, *Nigun.* (This is the Hebrew word for *melody.)*

The violin unfolds an intensely emotional song that is free in rhythm. The melody has an oriental cast, underlined by wide leaps, the use of the minor scale, and flowery cadenzas that suggest a mood of exaltation.

Nigun from
Baal Shem
Suite

The *Nigun* is in A-B-A form. The middle part is in a more measured rhythm, after which the rhapsodic style of the opening section returns. In music such as this Bloch not only expressed his own personality but also captured the spirit of his people.

Carl Orff was born in Munich on July 10, 1895. He has spent most of his life in his native city. There is a strong nationalist element in Orff's music. He has been greatly influenced by the clear-cut melodies and vigorous rhythms of Bavarian folk song and dance.

Carl Orff

His best-known work is *Carmina Burana,* a "dramatic cantata" for solo singers, chorus, and orchestra. The text was drawn from a famous thirteenth-century collection of songs and poems that were discovered in the Bavarian monastery of Benediktbeuren; hence the Latin name *Carmina Burana* (Songs of Beuren). These songs were written in a mixture of medieval Latin, German, and French by wandering students, minstrels, vagabond poets, and runaway monks—the rascals, artists, dreamers, and bohemians who stood outside the circle of respectable society. Their poems are in praise of nature, love, the joys of the tavern, and the free life; yet they contain also an undercurrent of protest against the cruel fate of those who

Two Numbers
from Carmina
Burana

261

do not fit in.

The first section, entitled *Fortune, Empress of the World,* opens with a passionate outcry against the unknown force that governs the destinies of men:

O Fortuna, velut luna
  statu variabilis,
semper crescis aut decrescis;
  vita detestabilis
nunc obdurat et tunc curat
  ludo mentis aciem,
egestatem, potestatem
  dissolvit ut glaciem.
	O Fortune, you are
	  as changeable as the moon,
	Always growing either greater or smaller.
	  Detestable life
	First resists us, and then capriciously
	  heeds our desires,
	Dissolving both poverty and power
	  as the sun dissolves the ice.

Sors immanis et inanis,
  rotatu volubilis,
status malus, vana salus
  semper dissolubilis,
obumbrata et velata
  michi quoque niteris;
nunc per ludum dorsum nudum
  fero tui sceleris.
	Cruel and empty fate,
	  you are a spinning wheel,
	An evil thing, taking from me
	  my hope of salvation.
	Although you are hidden and veiled,
	  you shine for me too.
	Now, because of your wicked games,
	  I have lost everything.

Sors salutis et virtutis
  michi nunc contraria
est affectus et defectus
  semper in angaria.
Hac in hora sine mora
  corde pulsum tangite;
quod per sortem sternit fortem,
  mecum omnes plangite!
	All my hopes of salvation
	  are being defeated,
	My feelings and my weakness
	  are in constant torment.
	Now, without further delay,
	  let us pluck the strings!
	Since fate crushes the brave,
	  weep, all of you, with me!

The chorus comes in with a mighty shout. Then the melody unfolds, over an ostinato rhythm in triple meter:

This number illustrates Orff's masterly handling of the choral medium. It also gives a good idea of his music: his appealing melodies; his driving rhythms, spiced with syncopation, repeated over and over again; his traditional harmonies, much less dissonant than those of most twentieth-century composers; and his dramatic contrasts between soft and loud.

The second part of the work, entitled *In the Tavern,* opens with a baritone solo in which a vagabond poet laments his shortcomings. This is a man's song; the rousing melody conjures up a vision of the open road. Dotted rhythms heighten the excitement.

Estuans interius ira vehementi in amaritudine loquor mee menti: factus de materia, cinis elementi similis sum folio, de quo ludunt venti.	In rage and bitterness I talk to myself. Made of matter, ash of the elements, I am like a leaf that the wind plays with.

Cum sit enim proprium viro sapienti	If it is proper for a man who is wise
supra petram ponere sedem fundamenti,	To build his house firmly upon a rock,
stultus ego comparor fluvio labenti,	I, fool that I am, resemble a gliding river
sub eodem tramite nunquam permanenti.	That never follows the same course.
Feror ego veluti sine nauta navis,	I am swept onward like a ship without a pilot,
ut per vias aeris vaga fertur avis;	Like a bird swept onward by the wind.
non me tenent vincula, non me tenet clavis,	No chains, no locks can ever hold me;
quero mihi similes, et adiungor pravis.	I seek those like me, and join the lawless ones.
Mihi cordis gravitas res videtur gravis;	A serious life weighs heavily upon me;
iocus est amabilis dulciorque favis;	Fun and jesting are sweeter to me than sweets;
quicquid Venus imperat, labor est suavis,	What Venus commands is a labor of love
que nunquam in cordibus habitat ignavis.	That never dwelt in an ignoble heart.
Via lata gradior more iuventutis,	On the broad road I move along as youth loves to do.
implicor et vitiis immemor virtutis,	I am entangled in evil and unmindful of virtue,
voluptatis avidus magis quam salutis,	More greedy for pleasure than for salvation,
mortuus in anima curam gero cutis.	With death in my soul I live only for pleasure!

The first two stanzas are set to an introductory melody. Then the main tune appears, and a rousing one it is. It is repeated three times, once for each of the last three stanzas.

Orff is like a painter who paints with great sweeps of the brush. The overall effect of his music is one of immense excitement. For this reason he has become one of the most popular among the composers of our time.

Serge Prokofiev

Serge Prokofiev (proh-kóh-fyef), the foremost Russian composer of his generation, was born in a village near Ekaterinoslav on April 23, 1891, and died in Moscow on March 5, 1953, in his sixty-first year.

Prokofiev's music is characterized by bold thrusting melodies and march-like rhythms. It has wit, energy, imagination. A great number of his works have established themselves as modern classics, among them *Lieutenant Kijé,* which we will study; *Peter and the Wolf,* a "symphonic fairy-tale for young and old"; the cantata *Alexander Nevsky,* the ballets *Romeo and Juliet* and *Cinderella,* the *Classical Symphony,* and the Piano Concerto No. 3.

Suite from Lieutenant Kijé

From the music he wrote for the film *Lieutenant Kijé* (kee-zháy), Prokofiev fashioned a concert suite that has become popular all over the world. The film, a satire on Imperial Russia, concerns a lieutenant who existed on paper only. He came into being when the Tsar misread a

263

telegram from the front, putting together the last syllable of one word and the first of another. He thought that this was the name of an officer who had distinguished himself in action, and his courtiers were too frightened of the Tsar to point out his error. When His Majesty questioned them about the lieutenant, they invented one episode after another about his life. Finally, when it became too difficult to keep up the lie, they informed the Tsar, with sad faces, of the gallant death of his favorite officer.

The Birth of Kijé. A cornet in the distance announces that the fictional lieutenant has come into existence. The movement itself is an Allegro in $\frac{4}{4}$. Two themes come to our notice. One is a saucy little tune on the flute, accompanied by a piccolo and snare drum. And a wide-ranging melody it is.

Notice how Prokofiev varies the tune in the second phrase. The other is a more thoughtful melody introduced by the oboe.

Can it be that these are supposed to represent both sides of the gallant lieutenant's character? The movement ends, as it began, with a fanfare on the cornet, now muted.

Kijé's Wedding. The wind instruments make a festive sound at the beginning of this Allegro in $\frac{2}{2}$. Prokofiev directed that this should be played "pompously." The movement goes at a lively tempo with the cornet playing one of Prokofiev's most charming melodies. This alternates with the "Birth of Kijé" theme played by the tenor saxophone. The pompous opening passage returns at the end.

Troika. A troika is a three-horse sleigh much used in Russia. Sleighbells jingle merrily, conjuring up visions of a winter in St. Petersburg in the early nineteenth century. A brief introduction leads into an Allegro con brio (fast, with vigor) in $\frac{4}{4}$. Tenor saxophone and bassoon carry the melody against a shimmering curtain of sound. This music is typical of Prokofiev. His brilliant gifts won him a place among the masters of our time.

*Dmitri
Shostakovich*

The outstanding composer of the present-day Russian school is Dmitri Shostakovich (shuh-stah-kóh-vich). His music, like Prokofiev's, has been played very much in the United States.

He was born in what was then St. Petersburg on September 25, 1906, and was eleven years old when the Tsar was overthrown. Dmitri made his way to school through streets crowded with soldiers. "I met the October Revolution on the street." he later remarked. Among the lad's first efforts at composition were a *Hymn to Liberty* and a *Funeral March for the Victims of the Revolution.*

Shostakovich is essentially a symphonist. He has a natural fondness for the large forms of absolute music. The central place in his list of works is occupied by his thirteen symphonies, two piano concertos, the Cello Concerto, the Piano Quintet, and six string quartets. He has also written sonatas for various instruments, much film and ballet music, piano pieces, choral music, and songs.

Shostakovich wrote his First Symphony when he was nineteen years old. It was his graduation piece from the Leningrad Conservatory. The work quickly established itself as a favorite with the public because of its fresh melodies and vigorous rhythms.

The Scherzo is an Allegro full of wit and fancy. After a brief introduction the first violins introduce a playful little tune at an extremely rapid tempo.

This is taken over by the piano and repeated by the bassoon in low register, where it takes on a humorous character. The second theme, by contrast, is a plaintive melody in the style of a Russian folk song.

The first theme returns, pianissimo at first but gathering force as it proceeds. When the second theme comes back, marked *fff,* Shostakovich cleverly combines it with the first theme, which gives the movement a stunning climax.

35A

The New Music

Music has changed from one generation to the next throughout the centuries. Nor is it difficult to see why. Art reflects life and since life is continually changing, art has to change with it. Besides, when the composers of one generation have said a certain thing, those who come after cannot go on imitating them but have to find their own means of expression.

PABLO PICASSO, *THREE MUSICIANS*.
Art has changed from one generation to the next throughout the centuries.

The first task of the New Music was to free itself from everything the nineteenth century had stood for. As a result, modern music for a time struck out in the direction of anti-romanticism. Composers began to cultivate humor and satire in their music. They turned for inspiration to the machine and factory, and wrote pieces about locomotives and turbines instead of waterfalls and twilight. They felt that European art had become too refined. So they turned to the vigor of primitive music, even as the fine arts found inspiration in African sculpture. This tendency towards *primitivism* went hand in hand with an attempt to put new life into the rhythm of European music.

JOAN MIRÓ, *DUTCH INTERIOR*.
Twentieth-century artists began to cultivate humor and satire in their works.

**AN EXAMPLE OF PRIMITIVE
SCULPTURE FROM THE MALI
REPUBLIC, AFRICA.**
European art found inspiration in African
sculpture.

*New
Conceptions
of Rhythm*

The New Music developed rhythms more complex than any known before.
These differed from the rhythms of the past in three ways. 1. Composers
turned away from the standard patterns of two, three, four, or six beats to a
measure. They used metrical patterns that were not symmetrical, based on
odd numbers—five, seven, nine, eleven beats to the measure. 2. In nineteenth-century music a single meter usually prevailed throughout an entire movement or section. Twentieth-century music is more flexible. The
meter may shift constantly, sometimes even with each measure, as in the
following excerpt from Stravinsky's *The Rite of Spring*.

3. In the classic and romantic periods music usually presented to the ear
one rhythmic pattern at a time. Now composers turned to *polyrhythm*—the
use of several rhythmic patterns simultaneously.

Through these innovations, the composers of our time revealed to the
world new rhythmic patterns of enormous force and tension.

Contemporary melody has abandoned the symmetrical structure of four- or eight-measure phrases set off by evenly spaced cadences. Composers today do not repeat as much as they once did. They say a thing once rather than two or three times; they expect the listener to be alert. The result is a concentrated melody from which every unnecessary note has been cut away.

Nineteenth-century melody was conceived in relation to the voice. Composers tried above all to make the instruments "sing." Twentieth-century melody is not conceived in relation to what the voice can do. It is basically instrumental in character. Melody today abounds in wide leaps and dissonant intervals. The following example—the second theme from the opening movement of Shostakovich's First Symphony—shows how twentieth-century melody is instrumental rather than vocal:

As a result of these and similar developments, twentieth-century composers have greatly expanded our conception of what is a melody.

The chords of traditional harmony—the triads—were formed by combining three tones on alternate degrees of the scale; for example, 1-3-5 or *do-mi-sol* (in the C-major scale, C-E-G); 2-4-6 or *re-fa-la* (D-F-A), and so on. Such chords are based on intervals of a third. (The distance from step 1 to step 3 of the scale is known as an interval of a *third*.) Twentieth-century composers constructed more complex combinations of six and seven tones by combining two or even three triads, one on top of the other. In other words, simple triads that had formerly been heard in succession were now presented to the ear together in complex "skyscraper" chords:

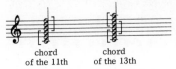

chord   chord
of the 11th   of the 13th

Formerly composers had combined two or more lines of melody. Now they began to combine two or more streams of harmony. In a famous example from Stravinsky's *Petrushka* the two harmonic streams clash, producing the bright hard sound that is typical of the new music:

Composers also began to build chords out of intervals other than a third. The following example shows chords built in fourths. (An interval of a *fourth* is found between steps 1–4 of the scale or *do-fa*—in the C-major scale, C-F; steps 2–5 or *re-sol*—in the C-major scale, D-G, and so on.) Such chords, widely used by contemporary composers, produce a sound that is very much of the twentieth century.

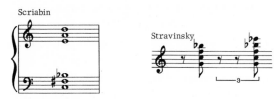

Thus modern composers have greatly expanded the resources of harmony, and have taught our ears to accept tone-combinations that in former times would have sounded strange and bewildering.

*New
Conceptions
of Tonality*

In its conception of key the twentieth century differs from the nineteenth in two ways:

1. In the major-minor system seven tones were chosen out of twelve to form a key. This "seven out of twelve" way of hearing music has been expanded in the twentieth century to a "twelve out of twelve"—that is, the use of all twelve tones around a central tone or keynote.

This does away with the difference between major and minor. Composers formerly presented major and minor in succession. Today both are presented at the same time. A piece will be, let us say, in F major-minor, using all the twelve tones around the center F instead of dividing them into major and minor, as was done in the past.

2. Tonality is based on a single key and a single tone center. The next step was to present two or more keys at the same time. *Polytonality* has opened up new possibilities, as in the following excerpt from Prokofiev's *Sarcasms,* a piano piece in which right and left hand play in different keys:

*The New
Classicism*

Many modern artists tried to get away from romanticism. This led to the New Classicism, or neo-classicism, as it was commonly called. ("Neo-" means new or modern.) Composers turned their backs on such romantic forms as the symphonic poem and Wagnerian music drama. They went back to the classical forms of the age of Haydn and Mozart—symphony, concerto, sonata, and the various types of chamber music. In consequence, they turned away from program music to absolute. They also found inspiration in the masters of the Baroque—Bach, Handel, Scarlatti, Vivaldi, and the great composers who had come before those. There was a movement "back to Bach"—that is, a revival of interest in polyphonic texture and counterpoint, and a revival of such baroque forms as the fugue, concerto grosso, toccata, and suite.

Thus, after music had gone as far as possible along the romantic path, the New Classicism pointed the way to a style that exalted the classical virtues of order, objectivity, balance, and proportion.

GIORGIO DE CHIRICO, *THE DELIGHTS OF THE POET*.
The New Classicism exalted the classical virtues of order, balance, and proportion.

The emphasis on contrapuntal texture brought a new style in orchestration. Whereas the romantic orchestrator made his colors swim together in a brilliant cloud of sound, the twentieth-century classicists used sober colors to bring out the lines of the counterpoint. Some turned away from the huge orchestra of Richard Strauss, Mahler, and Ravel, preferring an orchestra of modest size, such as the orchestra of Beethoven or Mendelssohn. Just as in painting there was a turning away from the shimmering colors of the impressionists to more sober colors, orchestral sound in the twentieth century became leaner, lighter, more transparent.

Texture and Orchestration in the Twentieth Century

The changes we have described in this chapter had far-reaching effects on the language of music. Out of the combined efforts of all the composers of the modern era came a new sound: the music of our time.

❧ | 35 B | ❧

Igor Stravinsky

The foremost composer of our time is Igor Stravinsky, who was born in Russia, near St. Petersburg, on June 17, 1882. He studied for three years with Rimsky-Korsakov. Fame came early to Stravinsky. He wrote three works for the Russian ballet in Paris—*The Firebird, Petrushka,* and *The Rite of Spring*—that made history. In 1939 Stravinsky came to the United States. He settled in California, outside Los Angeles, and in 1945 became an American citizen. The widespread celebration of his eightieth birthday in June 1962 showed that he is revered not only in his adopted country but throughout the world.

The three ballets we mentioned date from Stravinsky's early—that is, nationalist—period, when he made wide use of Russian folk material. In these we find the polytonal harmonies and dynamic rhythms that became associated with his style. After the First World War he became the chief spokesman for the New Classicism. He turned back to the eighteenth century, found inspiration in the music of Bach and other masters, and revived the use of counterpoint. Among the works of this neo-classical period (1920–50) are the "opera-oratorio" *Oedipus Rex,* the *Symphony of Psalms,* and an opera—*The Rake's Progress.*

Russian Dance *from* Petrushka

Petrushka is one of the most widely enjoyed ballets of the twentieth century. The setting is a street fair during carnival week in St. Petersburg, in the 1830s. The opening scene shows the crowds milling about the booths and stalls of the fair ground. The Magician summons them to his marionette theater with a roll on the drum. The curtain rises, disclosing three puppets: Petrushka, the Ballerina, and the Moor. The Magician touches each of the dolls with his flute, whereupon, to the delight of the crowd, they spring to life and perform a Russian dance.

In the following scenes Petrushka falls madly in love with the Ballerina, who of course prefers the handsome, stupid Moor. Petrushka suffers all the tortures of jealousy and is finally killed by his rival. The crowd is horrified at this; but the Magician picks up and shakes the little body, to show them that it is only a doll stuffed with sawdust. He begins to drag the puppet

272

THE MOOR, THE BALLERINA, AND PETRUSHKA.

away when, above the little theater, he catches sight of Petrushka's ghost: he had not foreseen that his creation, through suffering, would become human and achieve a soul. Stricken with fear, the Magician drops the doll and steals away.

The *Russian Dance* is an Allegro giusto (jóo-sto, in strict time) in $\frac{2}{4}$. The chief theme is an energetic tune that shows the characteristics we have found in several melodies in folk-song style: movement by step or narrow skip within a narrow range, symmetrical four-measure phrases, and much repetition. This melody moves entirely by step:

The *Russian Dance* is in the form of a rondo. The main theme is heard three times in alternation with subordinate melodies (A-B-A-C-A). These too show the traits of folksong. The main theme is always heard fortissimo, while the two subordinate themes are played more softly. Like all good ballet music, the *Russian Dance* suggests physical movement and gesture. One can almost see the three puppets whirling about in their furious dance.

Tarantella and Toccata from Pulcinella

Shortly after the First World War Stravinsky was asked to write a ballet based on the music of Giovanni Battista Pergolesi, an eighteenth-century Italian composer who died at the age of twenty-six. At this time Stravinsky already was turning towards the neo-classical point of view, and was most sympathetic to the eighteenth-century style. In *Pulcinella* (pool-chee-nél-lah), which is scored for a small orchestra, he paid homage to the spirit of classicism and the Baroque, both of which mingle in Pergolesi's music. As for the title, Pulcinella is a clown in the old Italian comedy.

The Tarantella is in B-flat major. A *tarantella* is a popular Italian dance in quick $\frac{6}{8}$ time. (At this rapid tempo the ear hears not six beats in a measure but two groups of three.) After a few measures of introduction, the Tarantella begins with a staccato melody played by the violins:

Stravinsky here combines the elegance of the eighteenth century with the harmonies of the twentieth.

The Toccata follows without a pause. It is an Allegro in $\frac{2}{4}$ time. The melody is presented by a solo trumpet. Notice that the emphasis is on the wind instruments rather than on the strings. This makes the sound less personal. The music shows several baroque traits: light orchestral texture, contrapuntal imitation between different instruments, a single theme and a single mood, and continuous melody that leads without pause to the vigorous ending.

Scene from The Rake's Progress

Under the influence of the New Classicism, Stravinsky was eager to lead opera back to the ideals of the eighteenth century. In 1950 he wrote *The Rake's Progress,* on a libretto by two poets, W. H. Auden and Chester Kallman. They based the opera on a series of engravings by the celebrated English painter William Hogarth (1697–1764), whose works vividly mirrored the life of his time. In *The Rake's Progress* Hogarth shows how a young man from the country comes to London, lured by the pleasures of the city, and falls in with evil companions who lead him to his ruin. The setting in 18th-century London gave Stravinsky and his librettists an ideal subject for an opera in the Mozartian style, with recitatives and arias, duets and ensemble numbers. As Stravinsky expressed it, "I will lace each aria with a tight corset."

In the opening scene Tom Rakewell sets out for London, determined to seek his fortune. He takes tender leave of his sweetheart, Anne Truelove,

AN ENGRAVING FROM HOGARTH'S SERIES *THE RAKE'S PROGRESS*
showing the young man being arrested for debt.

and promises to bring her to London as soon as he has established himself
there. Although he forgets his promise, Anne remains faithful to him. We
hear the scene in which she decides to follow him to London. It is a summer
night; a full moon shines down on the garden. Anne enters in traveling
clothes. She expresses her love for Tom and her fears. Her father calls her
from the house. Anne wavers in her resolve—but only for a moment. She
realizes that Tom may need her more than her father does, and decides to
proceed with her plan in spite of all obstacles.

SONG

Quietly, night, O find him and caress,
　And may thou quiet find
His heart, although it be unkind,
　Nor may its beat confess,
Although I weep, it knows of loneliness.

Guide me, O moon, chastely when I depart,
　And warmly be the same
He watches without grief or shame;
　It can not be thou art
A colder moon upon a colder heart.

(*Her father calls, "Anne, Anne."*)

275

RECITATIVE

My father! Can I desert him and his devotion for a love who has deserted me? *(She starts walking back to the house. Then she stops suddenly.)* No, my father has strength of purpose, while Tom is weak, and needs the comfort of a helping hand. *(She kneels.)*

O God, protect dear Tom, support my father, and strengthen my resolve.

*(**She bows her head, then rises and comes forward with great decision.**)*

ARIA

I go to him.
Love can not falter,
Can not desert;
Though it be shunned
Or be forgotten,
Though it be hurt,
If love be love
It will not alter.

[repeated]

O should I see
My love in need
It shall not matter
What he may be.

I go to him.
Love can not falter,
Can not desert;
Time cannot alter
A loving heart,
An ever-loving heart.

The lovely song to the moon opens with a melody that glides upward along the scale and then leaps down:

There are two stanzas, so that the song is in strophic form even though the second stanza presents the material with some changes. Words and phrases are repeated, such as *Although I weep* in the first stanza and *It cannot be* in the second. Such repetition gives the music time to establish the mood of the text, and also makes it easier for the listener to catch the words.

There is a marked difference in style between the song and the recitative that follows it. This recitative leads into a brilliant coloratura aria. (*Coloratura,* you may recall, refers to a high soprano voice that has great agility in executing rapid trills, scales, and arpeggios.) In this aria, too, important lines and phrases are repeated. The accompaniment moves in rapid sixteenth notes, which adds excitement. This beautiful aria is the final number of the first act.

The composer of this music has had an international career stretching over more than half a century. He has exerted enormous influence upon the music of our time.

Béla Bartók

The great Hungarian composer Béla Bartók was born in the province of Transylvania on March 25, 1881. Fame came to him slowly; but by the 1930s he was recognized as one of the foremost musicians of his generation. He taught at the Academy of Music in Budapest. Despite his official position, Bartók expressed his opposition to government policy at the time when Hungary drew steadily closer to Hitler's Germany. His friends, fearing for his safety, persuaded him to leave before the Nazis struck back at him.

Bartók and his wife came to this country in 1940 and settled in New York City. For a time they gave two-piano concerts. But with our entry into the Second World War, the time was not ripe for an advanced composer like Bartók to make a career here. In addition, he fell ill of leukemia and could no longer play in public. He died in poverty, on September 26, 1945. Almost immediately there was an upsurge of interest in his music that took on the proportions of a boom. As though to make up for their neglect of his works while he was still alive, everybody—conductors, performers, record companies, radio stations, and even his publishers—rushed to pay him the homage that might have brought him comfort had it come a little sooner.

Bartók was one of the leading nationalists of the twentieth century. As a young man he went into the Hungarian villages, together with his friend Zoltán Kodály, to record the ancient folk tunes exactly as the peasants sang them. He also did valuable research in the folk music of Slovakia, Rumania, Bulgaria, Yugoslavia, and Turkey. Bartók, along with Stravinsky, was a leader in bringing a new vitality into our century's music. His pounding rhythms have a primitive force and tension. Bartók's orchestration ranges from brilliant mixtures to threads of pure color. It brings out the interweaving of the contrapuntal lines, and shows his wonderful sense of sound.

The town where Bartók was born is now a part of Rumania. Consequently, the idiom of Rumanian folk music was as close to him as that of the Hungarian peasants. He captured the full flavor of that idiom in his *Rumanian Folk Dances,* a suite of six little pieces for piano that became one of his most popular works. (He later arranged them for orchestra.) These melodies show the traits that we have come to associate with folk song; they move mostly by step or narrow leap within a narrow range, with much repetition. They unfold over dissonant harmonies that give the music a special tang.

First is a *Dance With Sticks,* an energetic piece marked Allegro moderato that derives its gaiety from syncopated rhythm.

Notice that the F♯ in measure 2 becomes an F♮ in the next measure, while C, which is natural throughout the two phrases, becomes C♯ in the last chord. As a result of these changes the music hovers between major and minor, between minor and modal, and takes on an exotic quality that is very pleasant to the ear.

The fourth number of the suite is a *Hornpipe Dance.* It has a haunting melody that sounds almost oriental. The music moves in a graceful triple meter, in the manner of a round dance.

No. 5 is a lively *Rumanian Polka* which is, of course, an Allegro. Its active melody, ornamented with grace notes, outlines a broken chord (arpeggio). Unlike the two Czech polkas that we heard, this one is in changing meters: two measures of $\frac{3}{4}$ followed by one of $\frac{2}{4}$.

The droning bass that accompanies the melody is typical of folk instruments of the bagpipe family. We associate bagpipers with the Scottish highlands, but these instruments—in one form or another—were used by the peasants of many lands.

Last is a *Quick Dance.* This piece too has a drone bass, over which we hear a gay and active tune. The second section of this dance is taken at a faster tempo, and bring Bartók's suite to a jolly conclusion.

In the summer of 1943 Bartók, already incurably ill, was confined in a hospital in New York. One day he received a visit from Serge Koussevitzky, the conductor of the Boston Symphony Orchestra, who offered him a

thousand dollars for any piece he cared to write. Bartók at first refused the
offer, for he did not think he would be well enough to undertake a major
composition. But he was immensely cheered by the thought that at last an
American orchestra was waiting to perform his music. He was able to leave
the hospital and went to Asheville, North Carolina, where he set to work.
The Concerto for Orchestra was completed in 1944, the year before he died.
It is a masterpiece.

The title Concerto for Orchestra indicates that this is a concerto for a
virtuoso—but the virtuoso is the entire orchestra. The fourth movement is
the *Interrupted Intermezzo.* (*Intermezzo* is the Italian word for interlude.)
A plaintive tune in folk-song style is introduced by the oboe and continued
by the flute.

The rhythm, which alternates ¾ and ⅝ time, is derived from Bulgarian folk
music and gives the movement its charm. Presently the strings introduce a
legato theme that is one of the great tunes of the twentieth century:

The first theme returns. But the mood of the Intermezzo is interrupted by
a lively melody in the style of a cabaret song. The interruption is brief; the
lyric theme returns on the muted strings with poetic effect. At the end we
hear a tender remembrance of the opening theme.

The final movement opens with a theme for the horns:

Then, against a pizzicato accompaniment, the violins take off on a whirlwind
Presto in ²₄. This type of movement, which never pauses for breath, is
known as a *perpetuum mobile* (perpetual motion; the second word is
pronounced mó-bi-leh). Behind this music stand generations of Hungarian
village fiddlers whose passionate playing is here transferred to the realm
of art.

A PAGE FROM THE MANUSCRIPT OF BARTÓK'S CONCERTO FOR ORCHESTRA.

The movement relaxes for a moment with a melody in the style of a folk song. Then the *perpetuum mobile* becomes a background for a tense melody on the trumpet, the theme of an exciting fugue.

A horn answers, but instead of imitating the trumpet it plays the theme in *inversion*—that is, upside down. Where the melody line moved up the first time, it now moves down, and vice versa:

The fugue unfolds with all the devices of counterpoint. Bartók keeps the listener fascinated with wonderful contrasts between the string instruments and the woodwinds, the woodwinds and the brass. He plays around with the theme, expanding it here, contracting it there. The perpetuum mobile returns, so that the movement resembles a rondo. At the very end the trumpets pronounce the fugue theme in a triumphant fortissimo.

"What is the best way," wrote Bartók, "for a composer to reap the full benefits of his studies in peasant music? It is to assimilate the idiom of peasant music so completely that he is able to forget all about it and use it as his musical mother tongue." Because he based his art on the enduring elements of his national heritage, Bartók ended by speaking to all men. He was one of the supreme artists of our time.

From Germany: Kurt Weill and Paul Hindemith

Kurt Weill

Kurt Weill was one of the most original composers in Germany after the First World War. He was born in Dessau March 2, 1900; his career unfolded in Berlin. His great success came in 1928 with *The Three-penny Opera.* Weill left Germany when Hitler came to power. After his arrival in the United States he made a place for himself in the Broadway musical theater. He wrote the music for a number of successful plays, among them Moss Hart's *Lady in the Dark,* Elmer Rice's *Street Scene,* and Maxwell Anderson's *Lost in the Stars.* He was making plans to collaborate with Anderson on an opera based on Mark Twain's *Huckleberry Finn* when he died in New York of a heart attack, on April 3, 1950.

Pirate Jenny
from The
Three-penny
Opera

Weill based his most famous work on *The Beggar's Opera* of John Gay, which had been a tremendous success on the London stage two hundred years before. Kurt Weill and his librettist, the poet Bert Brecht, transformed Gay's rollicking play of the underworld into a biting satire of their own time. Theirs was a tragic time. Germany in the 1920s was in the throes of inflation and unemployment. Butter cost a hundred thousand marks a pound; Hitler's Brown Shirts were on the march. It was this moment in history that Weill and Brecht captured in their biting satire. Launched in 1928, *The Three-penny Opera* became an international success. It achieved more than two thousand performances in Germany, was translated into eleven languages, and was presented all over Europe. In 1954 it was revived in New York City in English, with Weill's widow Lotte Lenya singing the role she had created twenty-six years before. It ran for seven years.

Weill said that when he heard his melodies in his head, he heard them in Lotte Lenya's voice. You will hear her sing one of the haunting numbers of the score, the ballad of *Pirate Jenny.* This is about a little chambermaid who is ordered around by the guests of the hotel. Out of her humiliation and bitterness she fashions a daydream of revenge. How eloquently Weill's music has captured the spirit of Brecht's powerful verse!

Meine Herren, heute sehen Sie
mich Gläser abwaschen
Und ich mache das Bett für jeden.
Und Sie geben mir einen Penny
und ich bedanke mich schnell
Und Sie sehen meine Lumpen und
dies lumpige Hotel
Und Sie wissen nicht, mit wem Sie
reden,
Und Sie wissen nicht, mit wem Sie
reden.

Aber eines Tags wird ein Geschrei
sein am Hafen
Und man fragt: "Was ist das für
ein Geschrei?"
Und man wird mich lächeln sehn
bei meinen Gläsern,
Und man fragt: "Was lächelt die
dabei?"
  Und ein Schiff mit acht Segeln
  Und mit fünfzig Kanonen
  Wird liegen am Kai

Man sagt: "Geh, wisch deine
Gläser, mein kind,"
Und man reicht mir den Penny hin,
Und der Penny wird genommen
Und das Bett wird gemacht.
Es wird keiner mehr drin Schlafen
in dieser Nacht,
Und die wissen immer noch nicht,
wer ich bin,
Und die wissen immer noch nicht
wer ich bin.

Und in dieser Nacht wird ein Getös
sein am Hafen
Und man fragt: "Was ist das fur
ein Getös?"

Und man wird mich stehen sehen
hinterm Fenster,
Und man fragt: "Was lächelt die so
bös?"
  Und ein Schiff mit acht Segeln
  Und mit fünfzig Kanonen
  Wird beschiessen die Stadt.

Meine Herren, da wird wohl ihr
Lachen aufhören
Den die Mauern werden fallen hin
Und am drittten Tage ist die Stadt
dem Erdboden gleich,
Nur ein lumpiges Hotel wird
verschont von jedem Streich,
Und man fragt: "Wer wohnt
Besonderer darin?"

Gentlemen, now you see me washing the
glasses
And I make up all the beds.
And you tip me a penny and I thank you
very kindly,
And you see my rags and this crummy hotel,

And you don't know whom you're talking
to,
You just don't know whom you're talking
to.

But one day there'll be a shout in the
harbor,
And people will ask: "What's all the
shouting about?
And they will see me smiling over my
glasses,
And they'll ask: "What's she smiling
about?"
  And a ship with eight sails
  And fifty cannon
  Will approach the dock.

They'll say: "Go wipe your glasses, girl,"

And they'll hand me that penny.
And I'll take the penny
And make up the beds,
But there'll be no sleeping that night,

For they still don't know who I am,

They still still don't know who I am!

But that night there'll be a shot in the
harbor,
And people will ask: "What's all the
shooting about?"

And they'll see me standing at my window,

And they'll ask, "What's that evil sneer on
her face?"
  And a ship with eight sails
  And fifty cannon
  Will start bombarding the town.

Gentlemen, you'll stop laughing soon
enough,
For the walls will cave in
And the third day the town will be flattened
to the ground,
Only a crummy hotel will be spared and
left undamaged.
And they'll ask: "What important person
lives there?"

Und in dieser Nacht wird ein Geschrei um das Hotel sein,	And on that night they'll be crying all around the hotel.
Und man fragt: "Warum wird das Hotel verschont?"	And they'll ask: "Why was this hotel spared?"
Und man sieht mich treten aus der Tür gegen morgen,	And they'll see me coming out the door towards morning.
Und man sagt: "Die hat darin gewohnt?"	And they'll say: "Did *she* live there?"
Und das Schiff mit acht Segeln	And the ship with eight sails
Und mit fünfzig Kanonen	And fifty cannons
Wird beflaggen den Mast.	Will run a flag up her mast.
Und es werden kommen Hundert gen Mittag an Land	And a hundred armed men will land at noon
Und werden in den Schatten treten	And search out every spot,
Und fangen einen jegliche aus jeglicher Tür	They'll capture everyone everywhere
Und legen ihn in Ketten und bringen ihn mir	And put them in chains and bring them to me,
Und mich fragen: "Welchen sollen wir töten?"	And they'll ask me: "Whom shall we kill?"
Und mich fragen: "Welchen sollen wir töten?"	They'll ask me: "Whom shall we kill?"
Und an diesem Mittag wird es still sein am Hafen,	That day it'll be very quiet in the harbor,
Wenn man fragt: "Wer wohl sterben muss."	When they ask me: "Who must die?"
Und da werden Sie mich sagen hören: "Alle!"	Then you will hear me say: "All!"
Und wenn dann der Kopf fällt, sag ich "Hoppla!"	And when their heads begin to roll, I'll say, "Hoop-la!"
Und das Schiff mit acht Segeln	And the ship with eight sails
Und mit fünfzig Kanonen	And fifty cannon
Wird entschwinden mit mir.	Will take me away—and disappear.

This terrible fantasy draws its power from the fact that it seems so strangely unreal. Alas, within a few years history was to prove that it wasn't so unreal after all.

Paul Hindemith

Paul Hindemith, the leading German composer of his time, was born in Hanau, near the city of Frankfurt, on November 16, 1895. He came to the United States shortly before the outbreak of the Second World War and joined the faculty of Yale University, where many young Americans came under his influence. He died in Zurich, Switzerland, on December 28, 1963, at the age of sixty-eight.

Hindemith wrote a huge quantity of music. His list of works includes solo sonatas, chamber music, concertos, and symphonies. He produced a number of choral pieces, among them a beautiful setting of Walt Whitman's *When Lilacs Last in the Dooryard Bloom'd.* Among his major works are two ballets—*Nobilissima Visione* and *The Four Temperaments*—and the opera *Mathis der Maler* (Matthias the Painter).

FROM
GERMANY

Symphonic
Metamorphosis
on Themes of
Carl Maria
von Weber—
Scherzo

In his *Symphonic Metamorphosis on Themes of Weber,* Hindemith turned to the classical theme-and-variation form. The use of the word *metamorphosis* in the title indicates that he did not hesitate to change or transform the original melodies whenever it suited his purpose. The word *symphonic* as used here means that these variations were conceived in terms of the orchestra. Carl Maria von Weber (váy-ber) was a younger contemporary of Beethoven. Like Franz Schubert he belongs to the period of early romanticism—that is, he bridged the transition from the classic to the romantic era. Since both classic and romantic elements intermingle in Hindemith's music, we can see why he felt drawn to Weber.

The second movement of the *Symphonic Metamorphosis,* the Scherzo, is particularly colorful. It is based on a melody that Weber used in his music for a play about a Chinese princess named Turandot. Weber's melody— whether Chinese or not—sounds quite exotic to Western ears. Hindemith gives the tune a brilliant treatment. The melody is repeated over and over again, variety being supplied by changes in the other elements—the harmony,

rhythm and meter, tempo and dynamics, register, type of accompaniment, and countermelodies; above all, in the orchestration. The movement follows a simple but extremely effective plan. From a pianissimo beginning the music grows steadily to a great fortissimo climax. This half of the Scherzo consists of a melody with harmonic background. The second half of the movement is contrapuntal in texture. Here the tune is treated as a *fugato*— that is, in the style of a fugue without quite being one. In this section too the music works up to a climax, then subsides, so that the movement ends—as it began—with a pianissimo. When you hear this picturesque movement you will realize why it has become a modern classic.

36 B

From Vienna: Arnold Schoenberg and His School

Expressionism

If Paris was the center of impressionism and the New Classicism, Vienna remained the stronghold of romanticism. Here appeared the movement known as *expressionism,* which was the German answer to French impressionism. Where the Latin genius delighted in delicate impressions of the outside world, the German temperament preferred to dig down into the shadowy regions of the mind. Expressionism tried to release the primitive impulses that lie hidden in human nature. As in the case of impressionism, the impulse for the movement came from painting. Vassily Kandinsky and Paul Klee (clay) were among the painters who influenced the expressionist composers, even as Manet and Renoir influenced Debussy.

Expressionism inherited the romantic love of intense emotion, of all that is strange and demonic. The movement won its major triumphs within the circle of German culture, and reached its peak under the Weimar Re-

PAUL KLEE,
THE MOCKER, MOCKED.
The distorted images of the expressionists defied all conventional notions of beauty in order to achieve the most powerful expression of the artist's inner self.

286

public—that is, in the 1920s. It is familiar to Americans through the paintings of Kandinsky and Klee, the writings of Franz Kafka, the dancing of Martha Graham. Expressionism is apparent in the passions that assert themselves in Strauss's operas *Salome* and *Elektra*. It came to full tide in the dramatic works of Arnold Schoenberg and his disciple Alban Berg.

Atonality

We have seen that the concept of tonality was greatly expanded in the twentieth century. Sooner or later there had to appear a composer who would feel that the major-minor system of keys had outlived its day; in other words, who would reject the principle of tonality altogether. This was Arnold Schoenberg, the exponent of *atonality*—that is, the absence of any key. Schoenberg uses the twelve tones of the chromatic scale for his music. But whereas composers in the past regarded one of the twelve tones as being of greater importance than the rest, he considers them as being of *equal* importance. As a result, there is no keynote or tonic to which they all resolve. Schoenberg's *twelve-tone scale,* therefore, differs from the chromatic scale of the past in this very important respect.

Schoenberg also did away with the distinction between consonance and dissonance. He rejected consonance because, according to him, it had become too familiar to be able to express anything new. In his music dissonance is the norm. His music moves from one level of dissonance to another, marked by tremendous emotional tension. As we just saw, German expressionism dealt with moods of great emotional intensity; and so, inevitably, atonal music became the musical language of expressionism.

For centuries the principle of tonality has been as basic to Western music as the principle of gravity is to physics. To depart from the system of major-minor keys was a revolutionary move of tremendous importance. Music lovers had been accustomed all their lives to works based on the concept of key, and were utterly bewildered when faced with a harmonic language that had no key center (tonic). It is not surprising that when Schoenberg's music was first presented to the public it was met with laughter and hisses.

He persevered in his path despite all opposition, and ended by opening up a new world of sound to his followers. In time he organized atonal music according to a complicated set of rules which he named "the method of composing with twelve tones." This system of composition has gained enthusiastic adherents everywhere. Today, *twelve-tone music* represents one of the most important schools of thought on the contemporary scene.

Arnold Schoenberg was born in Vienna on September 13, 1874. He was mostly self-taught. When he was twenty-five he wrote *Verklärte Nacht* (Transfigured Night), a romantic work that showed the influence of Wagner. The following year several of his songs were performed in Vienna and created a scandal. "And ever since then," he later remarked with a smile, "the scandal has never ceased."

Schoenberg left Germany when Hitler came to power in 1933. He became professor of composition at the University of California in Los Ange-

*Arnold
Schoenberg*

les, where he taught until his retirement. He died in Los Angeles on July 13, 1951, in his seventy-seventh year. During his stay in this country he produced some of his best-known works, such as the brilliant Piano Concerto and *Ode to Napoleon* (1944), a setting of Byron's poem.

Piece for Orchestra, Opus 16, No. 1

The Five Pieces for Orchestra, Op. 16, may be regarded as one of the most important among Schoenberg's atonal works. The first piece is called *Vorgefühle* (Premonitions). Its basic theme is an ascending motive announced at the outset by muted cellos. This theme reappears throughout

the piece in a variety of disguises, with changes in rhythm and in the size of its intervals. There is a sense of mounting tension. The climax comes with the climb to the final note. Schoenberg exploits striking instrumental effects, such as the frightening rasp of muted horns and trombone, and flutter-tonguing on the muted trumpet. (*Flutter-tonguing*, a quick rolling movement of the tongue, is used in playing the wind instruments to produce a rapid succession of tones with maximum clarity.)

This music illustrates several characteristics of Schoenberg's style. 1. The absence of a key center, which imparts a restless, unresolved quality to the music. 2. This effect is reinforced by the absence of consonance. The music moves from one level of dissonance to another. 3. Orchestral writing in which each instrument stands out against the ensemble. 4. Continual variation of the thematic material. Once a motive is presented, we never hear it again in exactly the same way. This creates a feeling of continuous growth. 5. An intricate contrapuntal texture. 6. Fluid rhythms freed from the traditional meters. 7. The thinning-out of the sound, due to the fact that only a few instruments play at a time.

Schoenberg's art opened up a new chapter in the history of music. He was one of the major figures of our era.

Alban Berg

Of the disciples who gathered around Schoenberg in Vienna, two became important composers in their own right: Alban Berg and Anton von Webern. They worked closely with their teacher and helped shape the language of atonal music. Schoenberg, Berg, and Webern are the three masters of the modern Viennese school.

Berg was born in Vienna on February 5, 1885. He met Schoenberg when he was nineteen and studied with him for six years, during which he acquired the mastery of technique that marks his later work. Berg produced only a handful of works; but each was an important contribution to his art. He also wrote about music, mostly about the aims of Schoenberg and his school. An infection caused by an insect bite proved fatal; he died in Vienna on December 24, 1935, at the age of fifty, when he was at the height of his powers.

A PAGE FROM THE MANUSCRIPT OF SCHOENBERG'S OPUS 16.

To the world at large Berg is best known for his powerful opera *Wozzeck* (vúh-tsek). The hero of the opera, a stolid infantryman, becomes a symbol for all the underdogs of the world. He is bullied by the hysterical Captain and the calculating Doctor. He is alone in the world save for his girl, Marie. When she proves unfaithful to him he kills her. He returns to the pond where the murder has taken place, in order to retrieve his knife. Crazed with grief and guilt, he drowns. In the final scene children are playing in front of Marie's house. The little son of Wozzeck and Marie is riding a hobbyhorse. His playmates cry that there's been a murder, and run off. He does not understand and continues to ride and sing. Then, noticing that he has been left alone, he rides off after the others.

Wozzeck, then, uses a theme similar to that of Bizet's *Carmen.* But it does so in twentieth-century terms, and with all the dissonance-tension of which modern music is capable. What both works have in common is that they are both ablaze with genius.

The Interlude is played between the scene of Wozzeck's death and the final scene. The music begins slowly, on a note of muted sorrow. This orchestral lament is a meditation on the life and death of a man. It begins gently; we hear the sweet tones of a solo violin. Then the tension mounts. The music builds to a mighty outcry of grief and anger at the senselessness of Wozzeck's life and his death. The brass instruments thrust to the fore, and it is they who intone the melody of mourning, its power heightened by fierce dissonant harmonies.

There is a tremendous concentration of emotion in this brief interlude. Its pages are among the most exciting in the music of the twentieth century.

Anton Webern

Anton von Webern (váy-bern) was born in Vienna on December 3, 1883. (In later life he dropped the "von," which in his country is a title of the nobility.) The turning point in his artistic development was his meeting with Arnold Schoenberg, which took place when he was twenty-one. Together with Alban Berg he became—and remained—a staunch disciple of the master. He died in 1945, accidentally shot by a soldier of the American occupation forces.

Throughout his career Webern cultivated a style of the utmost economy; he cut out every repetition and expansion of an idea, in order to say what he had to say in the shortest possible time. As a result, his pieces are exceedingly short; some of them last less than a minute. His scores call for the most unusual combinations of instruments. The instruments are used in extremely high or low register; they often play one at a time and very little. Hence the texture of his music is extremely thin. It is woven out of short motives and flashes of color. There are passages where each tone in a melodic line is played by a different instrument. Sometimes his music hardly rises above a whisper; yet the tones are chosen with the utmost precision and logic.

Webern's Six Pieces for Orchestra, Opus 6, is a fairly early work (1909) in which for the last time he used the large orchestra of the post-romantic period. The set is dedicated to "Arnold Schoenberg, my teacher and friend, in deepest affection." The first piece, marked *Langsam* (slow), lasts fifty seconds. It opens with an ascending-descending motive on the flute, followed

by a melody played very softly by clarinet. Short motives trace delicate patterns in the air. A brief crescendo leads to the climax. The music quickly subsides, and ends with a single note on the harp, *ppp*.

The second number of the set is a little over a minute long. Like Schoenberg's Opus 16, No. 1, this piece could very well accompany a scene of terror and suspense. It is marked *Bewegt,* the German word for "with movement," and opens with a brief motive traced by the bass clarinet. Tremolos on the muted strings create an atmosphere of mystery. The music builds up to a fortissimo climax. Forced tones on the muted brass make an ominous sound. Once heard, these are not soon forgotten.

The Five Pieces for Orchestra, Opus 10, were written in the years 1911–13. These pieces are even more concentrated than the earlier set; all five take only four and a half minutes to play. Clearly Webern was functioning in another dimension of time, which bore no relation to the time sense of other composers. The work is scored for a chamber orchestra in which each instrument is a soloist.

Webern was a true son of Austria in his love for the mountains of his native land and their bell sounds. The third piece of Opus 10 is a study in bell sonorities. The piece is eleven and a half measures long, in $\frac{6}{4}$ time, and takes a little over a minute and a half to play. It is marked "very slow and extremely calm." Included in the score are mandolin and guitar, two instruments favored by the modern Viennese school because of their bright pointed sound; also harmonium (a small organ-like instrument), celesta, harp, drums, glockenspiel, and cowbells. They play trills and tremolos that suggest distant bells heard through the clear open spaces of a mountain landscape. Characteristic is Webern's direction for the cowbells, "barely audible," and his parting instruction: "dying away."

This music comes from one of the most extraordinary imaginations in the history of music. And one of the most influential. For most young composers today—and many of their elders—this is the Age of Webern.

UNIT VIII

MUSIC
IN
AMERICA

✻| 37 |✻

The American Scene (I)

Our forefathers were too busy with the task of conquering a continent to be able to devote themselves wholeheartedly to music. All the same, the art flourished in our country from its earliest days. The first book to be printed in the New World was an almanac; the second was the Bay Psalm Book, published in Massachusetts in 1640. This collection indicates what was the chief function of music in early New England: the singing of psalms and hymns.

Virginia, on the other hand, developed a society that cultivated the social graces of England. Here, as in the aristocratic circles of Europe, music served for elegant entertainment. Thomas Jefferson was an amateur violinist. (At the beginning of this book, we quoted his description of music as "the favorite passion of my soul.") He played string quartets at the weekly musicales of Governor Fauquier, and invented a violin stand that, when folded, did duty as an end table.

Music in colonial America lacked an aristocracy to act as patrons of the art. It had to find other outlets, one of which was the public concert. The first of which we have any record took place in Boston in 1731. Operettas were given in Charleston as early as 1735. Boston soon passed a law against these, on the ground that they discouraged industry, frugality, and piety (in that order). To get around the law, musical shows were billed as "moral lectures" and "readings." By the end of the century, the Bostonians had allowed themselves to be tempted by several dozen "ballad operas" (a type of entertainment with song and dance that appealed to the eighteenth century in much the same way that the Broadway musical appeals to the public today).

The first American-born composer was an aristocratic amateur: Francis Hopkinson (1737–1791), who belonged to the same level of society in Phila-

The
Beginnings

295

delphia as did his friend Jefferson in Virginia. Composing was but one of the many interests of this lawyer, writer, statesman, signer of the Declaration of Independence, and framer of the Constitution. His collection of songs "in an easy, familiar style, intended for young practitioners on the harpsichord or forte piano," for which he also wrote the words, appeared in Philadelphia in 1788. The volume was dedicated to George Washington, to whom Hopkinson wrote, "However small the Reputation may be that I shall derive from this work, I cannot be refused the Credit of being the first Native of the United States who has produced a Musical Composition." To which Washington replied, "I can neither sing one of the songs, nor raise a single note on any instrument to convince the unbelieving. But I have, however, one argument which will prevail with persons of true estate (at least in America)—I can tell them that *it is the production of Mr. Hopkinson.*"

A more important figure was William Billings (1746–1800), a tanner by trade. He taught himself what little he knew. Billings wrote pieces in which he treated psalms and hymn tunes contrapuntally. This fugal writing, based on a simple kind of imitation, produced music that was, he claimed, "twenty times as powerful as the old slow tunes. Each part striving for mastery and victory. The audience entertained and delighted." Billings' psalms, anthems, humorous pieces, and patriotic songs were very popular in the late eighteenth century. He was rewarded for his efforts with a pauper's grave near Boston Common. His memory lived on, however, to inspire some of our modern composers (as we shall find when we study William Schuman's Overture for Band, *Chester*).

The Nineteenth Century

The young republic attracted musicians from England, Germany, and France. They brought with them a knowledge of music that raised the level of the art in the New World. In addition, famous European artists—pianists, violinists, singers—began to come to the United States to give concerts. Towards the middle of the century, America produced its own virtuoso pianist in Louis Moreau Gottschalk (1829–1869), who was born in New Orleans, the son of an English Jew and a Creole. A handsome and magnetic figure, Gottschalk became one of the adored pianists of the romantic era. Two of his piano pieces—*The Last Hope* and *The Dying Poet*—were extremely popular at one time. More important were pieces such as *Bamboula, The Banjo, Le Bananier,* in which he captured the atmosphere of New Orleans. These pointed the way to an awakening American nationalism.

The revolutions of 1848 caused thousands of liberals to emigrate from Europe. German musicians came over in large numbers, forming the backbone of the symphony orchestras, singing societies, and chamber music groups that were springing up all over the country. Through their efforts, the traditions of Leipzig and Weimar, Munich and Vienna were established in the New World.

But the great American composer of the pre-Civil War period did not come out of the tradition of Haydn and Mozart. He came out of the humbler realm of the minstrel show. Stephen Foster (1828–1864) was born in Lawrenceville, Pennsylvania. He grew up in a comfortable, middle-class world in which music was not even considered to be a proper career for a man. His parents noticed his talent but did nothing to train it. Foster's lyrical gift found its outlet in popular song.

He was, as one of his biographers described him, "a dreamer, thoroughly impractical and never businessman enough to realize the commercial value of his best songs." Foster's path led him from a few early successes to the failure of his marriage, and from there—with tragic inevitableness—to a bedroom on the Bowery and the lonely death of an alcoholic at the age of thirty-eight. In that time he managed to write some two hundred songs, a number of which have become part of our national heritage. This lovable weakling was the despair of his parents, his wife, and his brothers. He remains in history as one of our great artists, and stands among the very few who have created the songs of a nation.

In the decades after the Civil War, musical life expanded throughout the country. During these years our composers went to Europe, and especially to Germany, to study; when they came back they wrote in the style of Schumann and Mendelssohn, or of Wagner and Liszt. Yet slowly a new spirit was making itself felt in their music—a growing awareness of their own country as a source of inspiration for their art.

Out of this generation came the first American composer whose music won fame in Europe; the first, too, whose works still live as part of the repertory.

Edward MacDowell

Edward MacDowell was born in New York City on December 18, 1861, of Scotch-Irish parentage. He studied in France and Germany, and after his return to this country played a leading part in musical life, first in Boston, then in New York. He was the first professor of music at Columbia University, but resigned his post with bitterness because the university did not give music the importance he felt it deserved. He died in New York City on January 23, 1908, at the age of forty-seven. After his death his wife founded the MacDowell Colony on their property at Peterborough, New Hampshire, where musicians, painters, and writers are given an opportunity to do their work undisturbed by the cares of daily living. It is a fitting memorial to America's first important composer.

MacDowell's songs and piano pieces show his gift for appealing melody and the charm of his imagination. He also wrote big works. His two piano concertos and four piano sonatas reveal a romantic tone poet.

Indian Suite—
*First
Movement:*
Legend

"The thematic material of this work," MacDowell wrote, "has been suggested for the most part by melodies of the North American Indians." In basing his music on this native material, MacDowell was doing for his country what the nationalist composers of Europe had done for theirs.

The first movement, *Legend,* sets the scene for a tale of olden times. MacDowell did not specify whether he had in mind the tale of Hiawatha, Pocahontas, or some other figure out of the Indian past. Rather he tried to capture the spirit of all legends: an epic mood suggesting the deeds of

WINSLOW HOMER, *THE GULF STREAM*.
Homer, like MacDowell, was an American post-romantic.

heroes. In an earlier chapter we established two categories—absolute and program music. *Legend* does not have a definite program attached to it, but it does give the listener the feeling that the music is based on a poetic story. It can best be described as *programmatic*.

A brief introduction marked "Not fast, with much dignity and character," presents a commanding idea played by the horns. The movement itself goes "Twice as fast, with decision." The main theme is based on a ceremonial song of the Iroquois tribe. It consists of two eight-measure phrases. Notice, in the middle of the second phrase, the syncopation that results when a shorter note is tied to a longer one across the barline:

His second theme is a flowing melody derived from the first. The Development section is brief and agitated. It is based on the main theme, but also brings back the commanding idea heard in the opening measures. In the Recapitulation, both themes are presented in a shortened version, with changes of key; and the coda brings the piece to an exciting close, *ffff*.

In this composition Edward MacDowell showed how an American composer could base his music on native materials. His works gave notice to the world that music in America had come of age.

The first generation of modern American composers—men born in the 1870s and 1880s—faced a double handicap. In the first place their music was modern, and was regarded with indifference by most music lovers who worshipped Beethoven and Brahms. In the second place, their music lacked the made-in-Europe label that carries so much weight with the American public. The career of Charles Ives illustrates only too clearly that the American composer at that time was a stepchild in his own country.

Ives was born in Danbury, Connecticut, on October 20, 1874. He was active in music throughout his four years at Yale University, but realized that he would never make a living by composing. He entered the business world and ultimately became head of the largest insurance agency in the country. He composed at night, on weekends, and during vacations, working by himself, concerned only to write down the sounds he heard in his head. But the sounds he heard were so far ahead of his time that those whom he tried to interest in his works called them impossible to play. A few even suspected that the man was mad.

Ives's double life as a business executive by day and composer by night finally took its toll. In 1918, when he was forty-four, he suffered a physical breakdown that left his health damaged. The years of discouragement had taken more out of him than he suspected. Although he lived almost forty years longer, he produced nothing further of importance.

Charles Ives

GRANT WOOD, *AMERICAN GOTHIC.* Like Ives, the painter Grant Wood found inspiration in the American scene.

299

The tide turned when the American pianist John Kirkpatrick played the *Concord Sonata* at a recital in New York in January, 1939. Ives was then sixty-five. The piece was repeated several weeks later and scored a triumph. The next morning one of the leading critics called it "the greatest music composed by an American."

Ives was now "discovered" by the general public and hailed as the grand old man of American music. In 1947 his Third Symphony was finally performed, and won a Pulitzer Prize. This story of recognition-at-last was carried by newspapers throughout the nation. Ives awoke at seventy-three to find himself famous. In 1951 the Second Symphony was given its first performance by Leonard Bernstein and the New York Philharmonic, exactly half a century after it had been written. The composer died in New York City three years later, on May 19, 1954, at the age of eighty.

His Music

Ives found inspiration in his New England heritage. His keen ear caught the sound of untrained voices singing a hymn together, some in their eagerness straining and sharping the pitch, others just missing it and going flat; so that instead of the single tone there was a cluster of tones that made a dissonant chord. Some were a trifle ahead of the beat, others lagged behind, so that the rhythms sagged and turned into a pattern of polyrhythms. He heard the clash of dissonance when two bands in a parade, each playing a different tune in a different key, came close enough to overlap. All these, he realized, were the heart and soul of American musical speech; and he wrote them down exactly as he heard them.

Thus he found his way to such conceptions as polytonality, atonality, unresolved dissonances, polyrhythms, and changing meters. All this in the last years of the nineteenth century, when Schoenberg was still writing in a post-Wagner idiom, when neither Stravinsky nor Bartók had yet begun their careers, when Hindemith had just been born. All the more honor, then, to this extraordinary musician who foretold the path that modern music would follow.

His four symphonies occupy the central place in his output, together with the *114 Songs*. Among his other orchestral works are *Three Places in New England* and *Three Outdoor Scenes—Hallowe'en, The Pond*, and *Central Park in the Dark*.

Three Places In New England— *Second Movement*

Three Places in New England is a set of three orchestral pieces written between 1903 and 1911. The second of these tone poems is about a Fourth of July picnic in a small Connecticut town. A little boy wanders off to the spot where General Putnam's soldiers had their quarters in the winter of 1778–79. The long rows of camp fireplaces stir his imagination. "As he rests on the hillside of laurel and hickories," Ives wrote, "the tunes of the band and the songs of the children grow fainter and fainter." He falls asleep and dreams of the tales he has heard so often, how during that cruel winter long ago the soldiers lost heart. In his dream "he sees a tall woman standing. She reminds him of a picture he has of the Goddess of Liberty,—

but the face is sorrowful—she is pleading with the soldiers not to forget their 'cause' and the great sacrifices they have made for it. But they march out of camp with fife and drum to a popular tune of the day. Suddenly a new national note is heard. Putnam is coming over the hills from the center,—the soldiers turn back and cheer. The little boy awakes, he hears the children's songs and runs down past the monument to 'listen to the band' and join in the games and dances."

The opening section, an Allegro marked "In Quick-Step Time," suggests the gaiety of the picnickers, the shouting and the horseplay, the two bands in the parade whose sounds overlap and clash, the drummer who comes in just a little too late for the beat, and the trumpet slightly off key. The opening measures may sound harsh to you at first; but if you listen to the piece three or four times, you will be astonished at how quickly you will grow accustomed to these twentieth-century sounds.

The main theme of this section is a marching song of the kind often heard in parades:

The music is woven out of scraps of popular American songs. In some cases Ives quotes only a few notes: the melody passes by so quickly that the listener barely has time to recognize it, as when he presents the first four notes of *Yankee Doodle* and suddenly gives the tune another twist.

A mysterious chord, *ppp,* ushers in the middle section—the little boy's dream. A lively tune suggests how Putnam's soldiers "marched out of camp with fife and drum."

This section builds up to a climax marked *fff.*

We hear again the main theme of the opening section. The movement consequently is in A-B-A form, except that the picnic music is now even more rowdy than before. Especially vivid is the impression of two bands overlapping, each playing its own tune. The final pages of the score are extremely complicated in terms of countermelodies and polyrhythms. Excitement rises steadily until the piece ends on a whopping dissonance.

A deep love for all things American lies at the heart of this music. Like Emerson and Thoreau, the two writers whom he admired most, Charles Ives has become an American classic.

Charles Tomlinson Griffes

Charles Tomlinson Griffes was one of the most imaginative composers this country has produced. Like Ives, he appeared upon our musical scene before the public was ready to understand his art.

He was born on September 17, 1884, in Elmira, New York. After four years of study in Berlin, he returned to the United States and took a teaching

position at the Hackley School in Tarrytown, New York. Griffes was expected to give piano lessons to the boys and to take charge of all musical activities at the school. These duties would not have been too heavy for someone who wanted only to teach. For a creative artist they were a terrible burden. He continued to compose, nonetheless: at night, during weekends and holidays, and in the all-too-short summer vacations.

After years of discouragement, he finally saw the fruits of his efforts. His orchestral works were accepted for performance in Boston, New York, and Philadelphia. Since he could not afford to engage copyists to prepare the orchestral parts, Griffes did much of the copying himself, working late every night after the long day at school. He had a real triumph when the Boston Symphony Orchestra presented *The Pleasure-Dome of Kubla Khan* in New York. He sat in a box at Carnegie Hall and received the applause of the crowd.

A few days later, the years of overwork took their toll at last. He collapsed. The doctors diagnosed his illness as pleurisy and pneumonia. The deeper cause was exhaustion of the physical and nervous system. He lingered for a few months and died in the New York Hospital on April 8, 1920, at the age of thirty-six.

Griffes found his way to a dream-like art that reveals him as the most

CHILDE HASSAM, *BAILEY'S BEACH.*
Hassam, like Griffes, was an American impressionist.

gifted of our impressionists. His imagination was stimulated by far-away places and far-off times. He was not a nationalist; his music borrowed nothing from American folk songs. He found inspiration in the exotic scales of Oriental music—the music of India, China, Japan, Java, and Bali—and in the modal scales that existed before the major-minor. His songs, piano pieces, and orchestral works are among the most beautiful that this country has produced.

The White Peacock was written in 1916 as a piano piece. Three years later Griffes arranged it for orchestra. The score carries a quotation from a poem by the Scottish poet William Sharp. The following lines are typical:

> Here where the sunlight floodeth the garden,
> Where the pomegranate reareth its glory of gorgeous
>   blossoms . . .
> Pale, pale as the breath of blue smoke in far woodlands,
> Here, as the breath, as the soul of this beauty,
> Moves the White Peacock.

The piece is marked Largamente (broadly). It begins with a haunting little motive played by a solo oboe. A flute answers with the dream-like theme that symbolizes the White Peacock. This is a languid melody that glides along the chromatic scale in dotted rhythm:

A second theme is introduced by a clarinet. Then another melody appears, played by the flutes con passione (pah-syó-neh, with passion). These are accompanied by impressionistic harmonies that caress the ear. There is a great upsurge of sound at the climax, as if the magic bird were spreading its feathers in the sunlight. At the very end we hear again the little motive on the oboe with which the piece began.

The creator of this haunting music captured a vision of beauty that was of great importance to the composers who came after. Charles Tomlinson Griffes remains one of the most appealing figures in the history of American music.

As American composers became more sure of themselves, they tried more and more to give expression to the life around them. They became aware of a wealth of native material that was waiting to be used: the songs of the southern mountaineers, which preserved the melodies brought over from England three hundred years ago; the hymns and religious tunes that meant so much to Americans everywhere; spirituals, Negro and white; the patriotic songs of the Revolution and the Civil War, many of which had become folk songs; and the tunes of the minstrel shows, which had reached their high point in the songs of Stephen Foster. There were the work

THOMAS HART BENTON, *THE COTTON PICKERS.*
As American composers became more sure of themselves, they tried more and more
to give expression to the life around them.

songs from various parts of the country—songs of sharecroppers, lumber-
jacks, miners, and river men; songs of prairie and railroad, chain gang
and frontier; and the songs of the city dwellers—popular ballads, musical
comedy, and jazz. In addition, there were songs of the various national
and racial groups that had come to America to form our melting-pot civilization. Out of all these came the music of the modern American school—a
music that has all the vitality and freshness of youth.

The second generation of modern American composers—born between
1890 and 1900—had an easier time than those who came before them.
The gradual victory of modern music in Europe made the American public
a little more friendly to twentieth-century works. As a result, the lot of the
American composer became considerably brighter in the second quarter of
the century.

We have, in previous chapters, studied works by five members of this
generation. You may wish to know a little more about them.

Douglas
Moore

Douglas Moore, whose folk opera *The Devil and Daniel Webster* we discussed in Chapter 17, was born on August 10, 1893, at Cutchogue on Long
Island. He was professor of music at Columbia University. Throughout his

career Moore advocated a wholesome Americanism in music. "The particular ideal which I have been striving to attain," he has stated, "is to write music that will reflect the exciting quality of life, traditions, and country which I feel all about me." At the same time Moore is a modern romantic who believes that the romantic approach is closest to the American character.

Moore has found his greatest success as an opera composer. His operas are rich in appealing melodies, dramatic feeling, and atmosphere. Among them are *The Ballad Of Baby Doe* and *Carrie Nation*. These, like *The Devil and Daniel Webster,* are American to the core.

Walter Piston

Walter Piston, whose ballet *The Incredible Flutist* we studied in Chapter 7, was born in Rockland, Maine, on January 20, 1894, of Italian-American parentage. (The family name originally was Pistone.) He became professor of music at Harvard University, where he spent the major part of his career. Piston's talent found its natural expression in the large forms of absolute music: symphonies, concertos, sonatas, string quartets, and the like. His seven symphonies reveal him as a neo-classicist devoted to beauty of form and elegance of manner. Because of this point of view Piston differs in a fundamental way from composers like Charles Ives and Douglas Moore, who tried to create a distinctly American music. He is a leading figure among those of our composers who advocate an international out-

CHARLES SHEELER, *AMERICAN LANDSCAPE.*
An American example of the New Classicism.

look. "The plain fact is," he maintains, "that American music is music written by Americans. Ours is a big country and we are a people possessing a multitude of different origins." Therefore, Piston feels, the American composer should not limit himself to American material but should strive for values that will have meaning to the whole world.

Virgil
Thomson

We listened to Virgil Thomson's music for the documentary film *The River* in connection with Chapter 17. He was born in Kansas City on November 25, 1896. The years he spent in Paris gave him a deep understanding of European culture as well as a finer appreciation of his American heritage. He won fame not only as a composer but also as a critic. His reviews in the *New York Herald Tribune* and other publications contained some of the most brilliant musical criticism of our time.

Thomson is a romantic at heart. His music is rooted in the hymns and folk tunes, the Civil War melodies and popular waltzes with which he grew up. His simple melodies, supported by clear-cut harmonies, are altogether American in character. He felt that modern music was becoming too involved, too intellectual. So he moved towards a new romanticism which, as he explains, aims "to express sincere personal sentiments" as simply and directly as possible.

Thomson won fame in 1928 with the opera *Four Saints in Three Acts*,

JOHN KOCH, *THREE MUSICIANS*.
Like Moore and Thomson, John Koch is an American romantic.

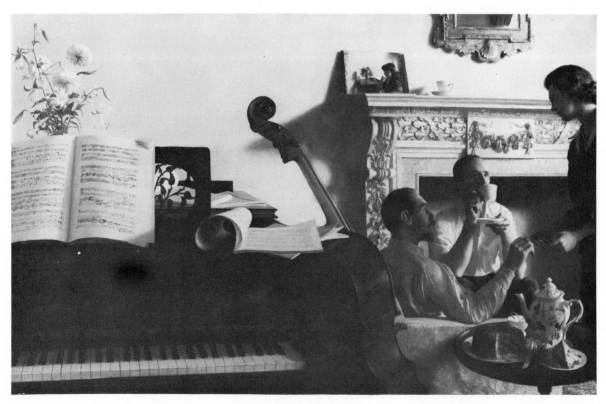

on a libretto by Gertrude Stein. In 1947 he wrote a second opera with Miss Stein, *The Mother of Us All.* His list of works shows his activity in all branches of his art: symphonies, tone poems, film music, chamber and choral music, organ and piano pieces, and songs.

We discussed *Johnny Comes Marching Home,* the finale of Roy Harris's *Folksong Symphony,* in Chapter 2. Harris was born on Lincoln's Birthday, 1898, in Lincoln County, Oklahoma. It was not until he was twenty-four, after he had tried all sorts of occupations, that he decided to become a composer. Recognition came to him quickly. In the 1930s he burst upon our musical scene as a homespun young man from the West who boldly upheld his American heritage.

Roy Harris

Harris's music is American in its optimism and drive. His nine symphonies place him squarely in the camp of the New Classicism, whose goal it was to revive the great forms of absolute music. He has also written chamber music, choral works, and piano pieces.

In Chapter 2, we heard an excerpt from *Porgy and Bess,* by George Gershwin, who has become something of a legend among us. He is the most widely played among modern American composers. Not even his most enthusiastic admirers could have foreseen that, a quarter century after his death, he would become a world figure.

George Gershwin

Gershwin was born in Brooklyn, New York, on September 28, 1898, the son of Russian-Jewish immigrants. He was twenty-one when he produced his first song hit, *Swanee.* During the Twenties and early Thirties, with his brother Ira as lyricist, he wrote many of the tunes that have become classics of our popular-song literature. The list includes *Somebody Loves Me, Lady Be Good, Fascinating Rhythm, The Man I Love, That Certain Feeling, Someone to Watch Over Me, 'S Wonderful, Liza, Embraceable You,* and *I Got Rhythm.* In the Twenties, too, he wrote the three symphonic works that carried his name around the world: *Rhapsody in Blue* (1924), Concerto in F, and *An American in Paris.* These were followed in 1935 by his masterpiece, the romantic "folk opera," *Porgy and Bess.*

Gershwin spent the last year and a half of his life in Hollywood, writing music for motion pictures. He missed New York, but never returned. After a brief illness he was found to have a brain tumor, and died during the operation, on July 11, 1937, at the age of thirty-nine. Many people are inclined to think of him solely in relation to the Broadway theater. It is well to remember that so severe a judge as Arnold Schoenberg said at the time of his death, "I grieve over the deplorable loss to music, for there is no doubt that he was a great composer."

Aaron Copland was born in Brooklyn—"on a street that can only be described as drab," he recalls—on November 14, 1900. Like Gershwin, he was the son of a Russian-Jewish immigrant who had come to the United

States in search of a better life. By the time he was sixteen he had decided that he was going to be a composer. From then on he pursued his goal with the perseverence of those who are destined to reach it.

When he returned from three years of study in Paris, he wrote complex works in the new neo-classical style. Before long a disturbing question presented itself to him: Whom was he trying to reach with his music? "During these years I began to feel an increasing dissatisfaction with the relations of the music-loving public and the living composer. It seemed to me that we composers were in danger of working in a vacuum." A new public for contemporary music, he felt, was being created by the radio, phonograph, and film score. "It made no sense to ignore them and to continue writing as if they did not exist. I felt that it was worth the effort to see if I couldn't say what I had to say in the simplest possible terms."

Once he had taken this decision, he produced a series of works that spread his fame all over the world and established him as the leading figure of the modern American school. Among these were three American ballets—*Billy the Kid, Rodeo, Appalachian Spring*—and *El Salón México*. Also two works designed for high-school students—*Second Hurricane*, a "play-opera," and *Outdoor Overture*. Among his highly successful motion-picture scores are *Quiet City, Of Mice and Men, Our Town*, and *The Red Pony*. His later works include *A Lincoln Portrait* for speaker, chorus, and orchestra, based on the Great Emancipator's speeches; the Third Symphony; and an opera, *The Tender Land*. He also wrote a number of large instrumental works that show his leaning towards neo-classic ways of thought.

Billy the Kid— *Excerpts*

Billy the Kid—the Brooklyn-born William Bonney—had a brief but intense career as a desperado and lover; he became one of the legends of the Southwest. The ballet, for which Copland wrote one of his most appealing scores, touches on the chief episodes of Billy's life.

First we hear *The Open Prairie*. This music, which serves as a prologue to the ballet, is marked Lento maestoso (slow and majestic). Oboes and clarinets introduce a haunting melody that evokes a vast landscape, calm and remote.

Throughout this prologue the wind instruments make a lovely outdoor sound. The music works up to a fortissimo climax, with the entire orchestra proclaiming the prairie theme.

"The first scene," Copland explained, "is a street in a frontier town. Familiar figures amble by. Cowboys saunter into town, some on horseback, others with their lassoes." A jaunty little tune is introduced by the piccolo, staccato.

Various instruments join in presenting this melody. The home key of A-flat persists while Copland introduces a typical cowboy tune in the key of F. The polytonal effect is startling. It is as if the second melody had been thrust head-on against the first.

This music suggests physical movement, as good ballet music should.

For the celebration after Billy's capture Copland wrote one of the most attractive episodes of the ballet. The melody here is a devil-may-care tune in cowboy style.

A SCENE FROM THE BALLET *BILLY THE KID*.

309

Allegro

mp

The theme of the prairie returns as an epilogue. It rounds off the piece and sums up the action. Men may come and men may go, but the prairie remains forever.

It is in music such as this that Aaron Copland shows himself to be—as he has often been described—the most American of our composers.

38

The American Scene (II)

*The Third
Generation*

The third generation of the modern American school—men born between 1905 and 1925—profited from the efforts of those who had come before them. The battle for American music had been won, and the public was much more responsive to modern works during the Forties and Fifties than it had been in the Twenties and Thirties. By this time our composers had mastered the techniques of contemporary musical speech; their scores compared well with the best of Europe's. In the decade before the Second World War the United States became the musical center of the world. The most important composers of Europe were living in this country—Stravinsky, Schoenberg, Bartók, Hindemith, Milhaud, and a number of others. This had a great effect on our musical life. Many of our young musicians studied with these masters and came under their influence.

During these years, publishing houses and recording companies began to take a friendlier attitude towards contemporary American music. Important too was the emergence of the opera workshop in colleges and other institutions, which encouraged the writing of American operas. The government came to the assistance of deserving musicians through the Fulbright grants, and the large foundations began to contribute to our musical life. As a result, the third generation of the American school found a much more favorable climate for its work than did its predecessors.

We have studied the music of one member of this generation—Morton Gould, who was born in New York City on December 10, 1913 (*Guaracha* from *Latin-American Symphonette,* Chapter 18). Gould is a prolific composer who is known for his brilliant orchestration. He has developed a style that appeals to a wide public through his combination of American material with modern harmonies and rhythms. Among his works are *Chorale and Fugue in Jazz, A Foster Gallery, Spirituals for Orchestra, Cowboy Rhapsody, Latin-American Symphonette,* and the ballet *Fall River Legend.*

Marc Blitzstein

Marc Blitzstein was born in Philadelphia on March 2, 1905. He graduated from the University of Pennsylvania and received his musical training at the Curtis Institute. He also studied for a time with Arnold Schoenberg in Berlin. Blitzstein was strongly influenced by the social-political satires of Kurt Weill and Bert Brecht. *The Cradle Will Rock* (1936) was one of the memorable documents of the Depression. While serving with the Air Force during the Second World War Blitzstein composed *The Airborne,* a symphony for soloists, chorus, and orchestra that was commissioned by and dedicated to the 8th Army Air Force.

Blitzstein had considerable literary ability. He wrote all his own texts; thus he was able to achieve complete unity between words and music. "I am a musician addicted to the theater," he said, "not a playwright. If I write plays, it is in order to put music to them." His librettos capture the rhythms of everyday American speech. They reveal him, in spite of his love of satire, as a romantic at heart.

Blitzstein died in Martinique on January 22, 1964, at the age of fifty-nine.

Rain Quartet *from* Regina

Blitzstein's most ambitious work, the opera *Regina,* was based on Lillian Hellman's famous play *The Little Foxes.* Regina and her brothers—the Hubbards—are the little foxes, cruel, cunning, and ready to stop at nothing in their quest for wealth and power. The "good people" in the play are their victims: Regina's husband Horace, who is dying of a heart condition; their daughter Alexandra (Zan); Oscar Hubbard's wife Birdie, who has taken to drink to escape his brutality; and the family servant, Addie. It is they who sing the *Rain Quartet* at the beginning of Act III.

This number shows Blitzstein's ability to create character, mood, and atmosphere through music—an ability that marks the true musical dramatist. Notice how beautifully our language sings when handled by a composer who knows how to unlock the music hidden in its simplest words and phrases.

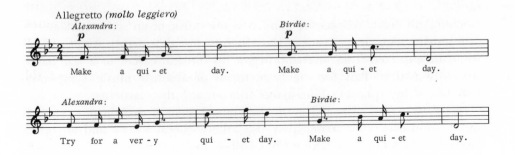

Alexandra, Birdie, Horace, and Addie are together in the living room. Their quartet is in A-B-A form. The opening section is an Allegretto. The text suggests the quiet joy they find in each other's company as they sit listening to the rain. Simple phrases are bandied about among the four: "Make a quiet day. Try for a very quiet day. Let's keep it steady and low, shall we? Let's don't bang or bellow, shall we? . . . Listen to the sound of rain. And keep it low, very low."

Notice the syncopation in measures, 1, 3, 5, and 7, when a shorter note (a sixteenth) is followed by a longer (an eighth). This repeated rhythm gives such words as *quiet* and *very* a special quality. At one point the four sing notes without words, on the syllable *la*. You may recall a similar effect, known as a *vocalise*, in the Aria from *Bachianas Brasileiras No. 5* by Villa-Lobos. This passage gives the composer an opportunity to imitate the patter of the "nice quiet rain."

The middle section, an Andante, opens with a solo by Horace: "Consider the rain. The falling of friendly rain that serves the earth, then moves on again. Some people eat all the earth. Some stand around and watch while they eat, while they eat the earth . . ." The others repeat his words, until Alexandra cries, "Papa, we're so solemn!" At once they return to the mood and the words of the opening. As so frequently happens in twentieth-century music, the first section is repeated in a shortened version.

Their singing is interrupted briefly when Jabez, another servant, and his Angel Band sing a chorus backstage in the style of a spiritual: "Have you got good religion? Certainly, Lord. Have you been baptized? Certainly, Lord. Have you been to the well? Certainly, Lord."

The quartet resumes and ends with "Listen to the sound of rain. And keep it low, very low . . ."

In *Regina* Marc Blitzstein brought American opera a long step forward. He well deserved Virgil Thomson's description of him as one who could "draw laughter and tears as few living composers can."

William Schuman

William Schuman was born in New York City on August 4, 1910. He did not decide to become a composer until he was twenty; then he worked furiously to make up for lost time. For several years he taught at Sarah Lawrence College, a progressive school for young women in Bronxville, New York. In 1945 he became head of the Juilliard School of Music, and in 1961 he was appointed president of one of the most ambitious artistic projects of our time—Lincoln Center for the Performing Arts in New York City.

Schuman's music reflects the man. It is the music of an active personality —optimistic, vigorous, assertive. His rhythms are thoroughly American, as might be expected from one who began his musical career in a jazz band. He has a natural flair for the large forms of absolute music—symphony, concerto, string quartet. This places him among the classicists.

His eight symphonies make up the central item in his output. He has also written concertos, string quartets, ballets, choral works, and an opera inspired by a famous poem about baseball—*Casey at the Bat.*

In *Chester* Schuman pays homage to one of our earliest composers. *Chester* was a popular hymn by William Billings, whom we spoke about in Chapter 37. During the American Revolution it became a marching song for the Continental Army. "Let tyrants shake their iron rods," the words and the music proclaimed, "We'll fear them not, we trust in God!"

In his Overture for Brass Band, Schuman uses the historic melody as the basis for a set of variations. The piece opens with a statement of the theme by the woodwinds in G major, in a mood of quiet faith. The music is marked Religioso. Notice that the melody consists of four regular phrases, each rounded off by a cadence:

*Chester—
Overture for
Band*

Now the brass instruments present the melody in a majestic fortissimo that reveals its dignity and strength. From then on Schuman uses all his craftsmanship and imagination to vary the tune and present it in an ever fresh garb. The tempo changes to Allegro vivo (fast and lively); the theme appears as a marching song in high register, suggesting a fife and drum and conjuring up the Spirit of '76. Here is how the melody looks in notes of half the value:

Certain notes drop out, so that the tune appears only in outline—in a skeleton version, as it were. The melody keeps returning with changes in harmony, rhythm, dynamics, color, and register, or brightly arrayed in jazz-like syncopation. One part of the tune hurries by in shorter notes while another holds back in longer notes. Presently we hear the melody sung in stately fashion by the trumpets. Throughout all these changes the hymn tune retains its sturdy outlines, its hope and faith and strength, until the rousing climax in which Schuman exploits to the full the powerful sound of the massed brass.

In basing his piece on so historic a tune, William Schuman follows the example set by the ardent European nationalists of the past. He does so with all the assurance that characterizes the modern American school.

Samuel Barber was born on March 9, 1910, in West Chester, Pennsylvania, a little town not far from Philadelphia. He showed great talent at an early age and received a thorough grounding in music at the Curtis Institute in Philadelphia. Fame came early to Barber. When he was only twenty-three

*Samuel
Barber*

the Philadelphia Orchestra performed his *Overture to "The School for Scandal."* The following year the New York Philharmonic presented his *Music for a Scene from Shelley.* Then the celebrated conductor Arturo Toscanini conducted two of the young man's works: *Adagio for Strings* and *Essay for Orchestra.* Before long Barber was one of the most frequently performed of all American composers.

Barber's art is rooted in the romantic tradition. He is at his best in works marked by poetic lyricism. He is one of the few composers who was trained as a singer, which may help to explain the lyric quality of his music. (Most composers are instrumentalists.) Although he is completely American in his background—he is a descendant of Robert Fulton—he does not share the interest in native song of composers such as Douglas Moore, Roy Harris, or Aaron Copland. On the contrary, he has lived abroad and has responded to the European tradition. As a result, he is one of the internationally minded members of the American school.

A SCENE FROM *VANESSA*.
The Baroness is on the extreme left.

Intermezzo from Vanessa

Barber's first opera, *Vanessa,* was presented at the Metropolitan Opera House in 1958. The action takes place in a European country in a villa in the mountains, around 1905. The heroine is a beautiful baroness named Vanessa who had an ardent love affair in her youth and has waited for twenty years for her lover to come back to her. On the night when he is finally supposed to return, it is his handsome son who appears instead. The young man informs her that his father is dead. Vanessa gradually transfers her affection to him. In doing so she breaks the heart of her niece Erika who —encouraged by the dashing stranger—has also fallen in love with him.

The Intermezzo, which is played between the two scenes of the fourth act, is an eloquent tone poem that sums up the romantic mood of the opera. Perhaps it suggests that Erika will now know the same longing, the same years of futile waiting that her aunt endured. A haunting melody is presented by the oboe against arpeggios on the harp.

The melody takes on an ardent lyricism when repeated by the strings in unison and octaves. The piece builds up to a passionate climax. This music sings of love, its bittersweet sorrow, its illusions, and its longings. When it is over we marvel that Barber was able to say so much in so short a space.

He is a romantic composer who has reached a wide public. Which shows that the need for romantic lyricism lives on in our time.

Of the composers who came into prominence in the 1940s, none is more widely admired by musicians than Elliott Carter. His works are not the kind that achieve easy popularity with the public. They are marked by profound thought, and illustrate Carter's belief that music should express "the more important aspects of life."

Elliott Carter was born in New York City on December 11, 1908. He studied at Harvard University, then spent three years in Paris. He taught at St. John's College in Annapolis, Maryland, until 1942, when he resigned from his post. Since then he has taught occasionally, but most of his time has been devoted to composing.

Carter uses the language of atonality in a very personal way, and is one of a number of American composers who have adopted the ideals of European expressionism. Of his earlier works the best-known is the ballet *Pocahontas*. The later ones include serious instrumental compositions such as the Sonata for Cello and Piano; two very important string quartets; the Variations for Orchestra; and the Double Concerto for Harpsichord and Piano with Two Chamber Orchestras.

Elliott Carter

The *Eight Etudes and a Fantasy* came into being as a result of Carter's activity as a teacher. He had asked his students to bring in examples illustrating the use of the different woodwind instruments, and had invited four woodwind players to the class to perform them. Disappointed in

From Eight Etudes and a Fantasy

315

what the class had written, he sketched some passages on the blackboard for the woodwind players to try. These he later reworked into *Eight Etudes and a Fantasy* for woodwind quartet—flute, oboe, clarinet, and bassoon. (An *etude,* you may remember from the chapter on Chopin, is a study piece that centers around a technical problem.)

Etude No. 2: *Quietly.* The flute announces a rippling motive. Sharps and flats are used in abundance. As a result, the very appearance of this music shows that it is atonal.

This motive passes from one to another of the four instruments. In this way Carter is able to contrast the sound of the motive in the flute with the way it sounds on the clarinet, oboe, or bassoon. At the end of the piece the motive enters in close succession in each of the four instruments, in ascending order—bassoon, clarinet, oboe, flute. The piece ends on a sustained chord marked *mf.*

Etude No. 3: *Adagio possibile* (as slow as possible). In this little piece Carter studies the ability of the woodwinds to sustain tone. The Etude is fashioned out of the three tones of the D-major triad: D-F#-A. This chord continually changes its color. But we are not aware of the exact moment of change because of "sneak entrances": one instrument quietly slips in and continues where the other left off.

Etude No. 4: *Vivace.* This study is woven out of a motive consisting of two tones followed by a rest. Out of this tiny kernel grows a complete composition—melody and harmony, rhythm and color, counterpoint and dynamics. Here we can see the artist's imagination at work. For the essence of art is creation, and creation means the ability to make much out of little.

George Perle:
Monody I for
Solo Flute

George Perle was born in Bayonne, New Jersey, on May 6, 1915. He has been strongly influenced by the modern Viennese school. Perle has developed a harmonic language that combines the doctrines of Schoenberg with certain features of the traditional major-minor system.

Perle is one of several American composers who have written works in monophonic texture—that is, consisting of single-line melody. We studied this texture in connection with Gregorian chant. Perle has produced a number of pieces for unaccompanied flute, clarinet, bassoon, violin, double bass, and other instruments. Monophonic texture differs in one important respect from the single line of melody that is heard, let us say, when we whistle a tune. In doing so, we are aware that the chords are missing. But a piece in monophonic texture presents its entire content through the melody alone, which is conceived as a thing in itself, without any harmonic background or accompaniment.

Perle's *Monody I for Solo Flute* illustrates his interest in music for unaccompanied instruments. *Monody* comes from the same stem as *monophonic* and, when used by modern composers, refers to a melody without accompaniment. Perle's piece is written in the style of an improvision, as if the flutist were making it up on the spur of the moment. The melody moves freely through a series of tone centers. Certain intervals return again and again, and become the cells out of which the melody flowers. The music is not based on phrases of fixed length. Instead the beat varies from one phrase to the next, which gives the piece an extremely flexible rhythm. Indeed, it seems at moments as if the music were being propelled by the player's breath. This changeable pulse adds to the impression that the piece springs directly out of the player's fantasy, instead of having been written down in notes. Perle's *Monody,* therefore, tries to recapture the rapturous quality of oriental song, the melodic and rhythmic freedom of Gregorian chant. It combines monophonic texture with twentieth-century ways of thinking, and represents a fascinating experiment in the output of the modern American school.

39

The American Scene (III)

Gian Carlo Menotti does not belong, strictly speaking, to the American school. Out of loyalty to his native land he has never renounced his Italian citizenship. Yet there are good reasons for regarding him as one of us. In the first place, he received his musical training in this country and has spent most of his life here. In the second, he writes his own librettos in English. Most important of all, it is in the United States that he has won his greatest success.

He was born on July 7, 1911, in a little town in northern Italy named Cadegliano. He wrote a song when he was four, and at the age of six decided to become a composer. After studying at the Conservatory of Milan, he came to the United States when he was seventeen and continued at the Curtis Institute of Philadelphia. His first successful opera, *Amelia Goes to the Ball,* was produced at the Curtis Institute when he was twenty-six. The following season it was presented at the Metropolitan Opera House, and launched its composer on an international career.

Gian Carlo Menotti

Menotti is the most widely performed opera composer of our time. Among the works that have endeared him to the public are *Amelia Goes to the Ball, The Old Maid and the Thief, The Medium, The Telephone, The Consul, Amahl and the Night Visitors,* and *The Saint of Bleecker Street.* His stage works are effective because he is able to see life in terms of dramatic conflict, suspense, surprise. His art is based on strong simple emotions and on a romantic approach to life. "First, last, and always," he maintains, "the appeal of any stage piece must be to the heart."

The Medium— *Act Two, Opening Scene*

The Medium shows Menotti's ability to communicate emotion, his command of theatrical effect, and his rich imagination. The action concerns Madame Flora, a fake medium who gives seances at which she makes her clients believe that they are communicating with the children they have lost. She is aided by her daughter Monica, who imitates the voices of the dead; and by Toby, a Gypsy boy whom she has adopted, who is a mute. Madame Flora—or Baba, as she is called by her daughter—both fears and hates the strange dreamy boy who can speak only with his eyes. She beats him when she is drunk or angry, which happens quite often.

One night, during a seance, Baba feels a hand around her throat. Crazed with fear, she dismisses her clients and tries to force Toby to tell her the truth. Was it he who touched her, in order to frighten her? Or could it have been one of the spirits in whom she does not believe? She tries to wheedle the truth out of Toby. When she can get nothing out of him she beats him mercilessly. In vain she seeks to escape the torment that eats at her soul.

In the course of the second act Baba tries to drive away her clients, telling them that she is a fraud. But they have come to depend so much on her seances that they refuse to believe her. They are not able to surrender the lie which for them has become truth. Baba, in her terror, sends Toby away too. When Monica tries to follow him, Baba locks the girl in her room. Alone, Baba drinks herself into a stupor. She falls into a troubled sleep from which she is awakened by footsteps. Is this the ghost finally coming to take revenge? It is only Toby who has stolen back to see his adored Monica. In his fear of Baba, Toby hides behind a curtain. Flora draws a revolver out of a drawer and cries hysterically, "Speak out or I'll shoot!" But Toby cannot speak, and is too frightened by Baba to reveal his presence. Baba, driven mad by her delusions, shoots. As Toby dies she bends over him muttering insanely, "Was it you? Was it you?"

The opening of the second act is one of the finest scenes of the play. The Prelude repeats the menacing chords that opened the opera; they will return again at the very end when Toby dies. Now the music establishes a mood of lyric tenderness. The curtain rises to reveal Monica seated in front of a little puppet theater, watching a performance put on by Toby. We hear a brief Allegro, with the woodwinds chirping staccato in high register. The performance ends with the puppets falling in a heap. Toby comes out to acknowledge Monica's applause.

MONICA

Bravo! And after the theater, supper and dance.
Music! Um-pa-pa, um-pa-pa . . .

> *(She sings a waltz song to which Toby, bare-
> footed, dances about the stage.)*

Up in the sky someone is playing a trombone and a guitar.
Red is your tie, and in your velvetine coat you hide a star.
Monica, Monica, dance the waltz, Monica, Monica, dance the waltz.
Follow me, moon and sun, keep time with me, one two three one.

If you're not shy, pin up my hair with your star and buckle my shoe.
And when you fly, please hold on tight to my waist, I'm flying with you.
Oh, Monica, Monica, dance the waltz, Monica, Monica, dance the waltz.
> Follow me, moon and sun, follow me, follow me . . .

> *(Toby seizes Monica abruptly by the arm.)*

What is the matter, Toby? What is it you want to tell me?

> *(He looks at her in desperation, and gently
> touches her face. Monica begins to understand.)*

Kneel down before me, and now, tell me . . .

> *(Toby kneels. She kneels behind him, as if the
> words were coming from him, and makes Toby
> look up as if she were still standing in front of
> him. There follows a strange love scene in which
> Monica speaks the words that Toby would have
> spoken if he could.)*

Monica, Monica, can't you see that my heart is bleeding, bleeding for you?
I loved you, Monica, all my life, with all my breath, with all my blood.
You haunt the mirror of my sleep, you are my night.
You are my light and the jailer of my day.

> *(Quickly she gets up and stands before him.)*

How dare you, scoundrel, talk to me like that! Don't you know who I am?
I'm the Queen of Aroundel! I shall have you put in chains.

> *(She kneels behind him again. Toby, falling in
> with the game, mimics her words with gestures.)*

You are my princess, you are my queen, and I'm only Toby, one of your
  slaves.
And still I love you, and always loved you with all my breath, with all my
  blood.
I love your laughter, I love your hair, I love your deep and nocturnal eyes.
I love your soft hands, so white and winged, I love the slender branch of
  your throat.

> *(She stands up before him.)*

Toby, don't speak to me like that! You make my head swim.

> *(She runs behind Toby.)*

Monica, Monica, fold me in your satin gown.
Monica, Monica, give me your mouth, Monica, Monica, fall in my arms.

> *(Toby suddenly hides his face in his arms.
> Monica, bewildered:)*

Why, Toby! You're not crying, are you?

> *(She caresses his head. Then, lifting his tear-
> stained face, she looks into his eyes and says with
> great tenderness:)*

Toby, I want you to know that you have the most beautiful voice in the
  world!

How moving is this scene, how rich in fantasy and tenderness. Its creator is one of the best-loved figures in the music of our time. Gian Carlo Menotti occupies a special place in the world of art. He has created a popular operatic theater all his own.

Norman Dello Joio

Norman Dello Joio comes of a line of Italian musicians who were organists in a little town near Naples. He was born in New York City on January 24, 1913. Dello Joio stands among those composers who have sought to give contemporary music a popular appeal. He is a twentieth-century romantic. His melodies are supple and expressive. An important element of his style drives from his interest in jazz; lively jazz rhythms give his music its lightness and thrust. Dello Joio feels that art should be emotional rather than intellectual, so as to reach the broad mass of listeners. His works include *New York Profiles* for orchestra; the ballet *On Stage!*; a group of choral works on texts by Walt Whitman—*Vigil Strange, Mystic Trumpeter,* and *Jubilant Song;* three sonatas and a number of short pieces for piano; and *The Trial at Rouen,* an opera about Joan of Arc.

Air Power— *Excerpts*

In November, 1958, the Columbia Broadcasting System presented a series of documentary films on television, tracing the development of air power from its earliest beginnings to the age of the jet. Dello Joio was asked to compose the music for this ambitious project. He subsequently arranged the material into a symphonic suite for orchestra called *Air Power,* from which we hear three excerpts. (The term *symphonic suite* implies full use of the resources of the orchestra.)

1. Introduction. A spacious melody is presented by the first violins and continued by the brass. This is a romantic theme that sings of vast open spaces, of mountain tops and the boundless sea, of brave men poised for adventure.

2. *Skylarking* is one of three numbers depicting the "Frolics of the Early Days." It is a lively little piece in $\frac{6}{8}$ time, marked Leggiero (lightly) and with much staccato in both the wind instruments and the strings. The woodwinds and brass suggest an outdoor atmosphere. The main melody has a lighthearted, devil-may-care quality.

Leggiero

Notice how the octave leaps and grace notes in the second phrase underline the sense of physical activity conveyed by this music.

3. The Sport Meet: Polka. This piece conjures up the hair-raising scenes from the early days of aviation when daredevil flyers came together and performed all sorts of stunts, such as standing on the wings of their planes or flying upside down. The melody, marked Con molto spirito (with much spirit), is cast in the form of a lively polka that unfolds over an ostinato rhythm in the bass.

This music displays the composer's personal lyricism and spirited rhythms, his colorful orchestration and adroit handling of the small forms. Among the composers of his generation Norman Dello Joio is a staunch representative of the New Romanticism.

Hugo Weisgall

A number of American composers have been strongly influenced by the traditions of German expressionism and by the atonal idiom that came out of Vienna through the works of Schoenberg and Berg. These composers inevitably lean towards the chromatic language associated with the Viennese school.

Hugo Weisgall is one of them. He was born in Czechoslovakia on October 13, 1912. His family came to this country while he was a child and settled in Baltimore. Weisgall studied at the Peabody Conservatory and the Curtis Institute. Most of his operas are based on dramas by European writers: *The Stronger,* on a play by August Strindberg; *Six Characters in Search of an Author,* on the famous play by Pirandello; *The Tenor,* on a play by the German writer Frank Wedekind (váy-duh-kind), two of whose dramas furnished the libretto for Alban Berg's last work, the opera *Lulu.*

*The Tenor—
Gerardo's
Arietta*

The Tenor centers around a theme very popular in European literature: the conflict between reality and make-believe in the life of an artist. The hero is Gerardo, a famous tenor who plays romantic roles in the opera house with great success, but who runs into difficulty when he plays the romantic lover in real life.

In the opening scene of the opera he has just finished an engagement and is preparing to leave the city. The action takes place in his hotel suite; his valet is packing his things. Gerardo, watching, is not satisfied with the valet's efforts. He lifts a pair of tails from the suitcase and, in a charming *arietta* (little aria), proceeds to show the valet how it should be done:

> Packing clothes is quite an art.
> First the coat, the really vital part.
> Fold back the collar, notch to notch exactly.
> Lay one lapel upon the other. Thus!
> Press arm-hole into arm-hole, thus. Thus!
> And then . . . and then you smooth the tails
> And fold them over, thus.
> Is that so hard?

Although the text occupies itself with nothing more important than the folding of a pair of tails, the music is highly expressive. As a result, there is a marked contrast between the simple content of the words and the emotional content of the music. This ironic contrast is part of the expressionist point of view, which holds that art must always be as intense as possible. The melody has wide leaps that extend over a wide range, and builds up steadily to the high B on the final word. Weisgall's idiom is close to the language of Mahler and Berg. His opera captures the spirit of the European expressionist theater.

We have divided American composers into two categories, nationalists and internationalists. The latter can be further subdivided into those who were influenced by the neo-classicism of Paris and those who found inspiration in the expressionism of Vienna. The second group numbers one of its foremost representatives in Hugo Weisgall.

Our National Minorities and American Music

The United States differs from European countries in one important respect; our people do not come from a single stock. On the contrary, ours is a melting-pot culture in which many nations are represented. To the English stock of Colonial times were added a variety of elements: Spanish and French, Negro, Scottish and Irish, Scandinavian, German, Italian, Russian, Polish, Jewish, Hungarian, Czech, and others. It goes without saying that this variety is reflected in our country's music. American composers come from various origins. For example, Walter Piston, Gian Carlo Menotti, Norman Dello Joio, and Peter Mennin are of Italian background. A number of composers are Jewish, among them George Gershwin, Aaron Copland, Morton Gould, and Leonard Bernstein. Otto Luening is of German ancestry, Edgard Varèse of French-Italian; Ulysses Kay is a Negro.

The Negro's strong musical gift showed itself at first mainly in the field of popular music, spirituals, and the minstrel show. Jazz is the Negro's specific contribution to the music of America, just as it is America's specific contribution to the music of the world. It developed in New Orleans just before 1900. In its early years it was known as "ragtime," and took over elements from the "blues" and the Negro spirituals, especially syncopated rhythm and "blue" notes—the flatted third and seventh of the scale.

While definitions of jazz differ, they all agree on two things: first, this music cannot be written down but is improvised on the spur of the moment; second, what is improvised has a highly emotional quality. As the great jazz trumpeter Louis Armstrong puts it, "Anything played with beat and soul is jazz." Similarly the composer Duke Ellington, one of the most creative figures in the history of jazz, says, "No notes represent swing. You can't write swing because swing is the emotional element in the audience and there is no swing until you hear the note. Swing is liquid and though the same group of musicians may play the same tune fourteen times, they may not *swing* until the fifteenth time."

The jazz idiom became popular in the years after the First World War. This music seemed to reflect the hectic pace of modern life, the restlessness and hunger for excitement of a war-weary world. Besides, the chamber-music character of the jazz band appealed to many listeners. A jazz band of the 1920s was an ensemble of soloists in which the "reeds" (saxo-phones and clarinets) and the "brasses" (trumpets, cornets, trombones) carried the melody over the steady throb of the "rhythm" (piano, string bass, banjo, or guitar, bolstered by drums and other instruments of per-cussion). The jazz idiom was refined by several generations of singers and players, among whom Negroes played a prominent role, from W. C. Handy, "the Father of the Blues," to such famous performers as Bessie Smith, Bil-lie Holliday, Ella Fitzgerald, Maxine Sullivan, Louis Armstrong, Duke El-lington, the clarinetist Sidney Bechet and the remarkable blind pianist Art Tatum, to mention but a few.

The Negro in America has also mastered the techniques of so-called "ser-ious" music. Among the Negro composers of the modern American school may be mentioned William Grant Still, Ulysses Kay, Howard Swanson, and Julia Perry. Paul Robeson and Marian Anderson were among the great singers of their generation, as is Leontyne Price today. Among the younger generation of gifted Negro artists are the baritone William War-field, the pianist André Watts, the mezzo-sopranos Shirley Verrett and Grace Bumbry; Camilla Williams and Lawrence Winters, whom you heard sing the love duet from *Porgy and Bess;* and the conductor Dean Dixon, whom you heard in the *Legend* from MacDowell's *Indian Suite.*

After 1917, when a Negro jazz band scored a great success in Europe, jazz began to influence modern European composers. Among these were several whose music we have studied—Debussy, Ravel, Stravinsky, Hinde-mith, Milhaud, and Honegger. At that time composers in this country were trying to find a musical language that would be truly American; yet most of them looked down on the popular idiom. The time was ripe for a composer who would break down the wall between "classical" and "popular" by combining the jazz idiom with the forms and techniques of serious music. That composer was George Gershwin. "I regard jazz," Gershwin declared, "as an American folk music, a very powerful one which is probably in the blood of the American people more than any other style of folk music. Jazz is the result of the energy stored in America. I believe it can be made the basis of serious symphonic works of lasting value." Other composers followed in his footsteps. As a result of these efforts, jazz became a vital part of our serious music.

It becomes clear that the music of the present-day American school does not follow any single path. It has been enriched by many influences, both native and foreign. It has absorbed the musical heritage of the differ-ent national groups within our borders. In addition, it reflects all the tendencies that have emanated from Europe in our century—Debussy's im-pressionism, Stravinsky's neo-classicism, Schoenberg's expressionism, the art of Mahler, Hindemith, Satie, Poulenc, Prokofiev, and many others. For this reason many of our composers feel that American music is simply any kind of music written by an American. Given the special character of the American scene, probably no other definition is possible.

Ulysses Kay

What's in a
Name?

Ulysses Kay, one of the outstanding Negro composers of his generation, was born in Tucson, Arizona, on January 7, 1917. He studied at the Eastman School of Music and with Paul Hindemith at Yale University; during the Second World War he served in the Navy.

Kay unites neo-classic and romantic elements in his music. He has been strongly influenced by the polyphonic style of the sixteenth and seventeenth centuries. He leans towards the large forms of absolute music, which he handles with great adroitness; he has also written an impressive array of vocal works. His list includes the *Suite for Orchestra, Concerto for Orchestra,* and *Song of Ahab* for baritone and ten instruments. He has written a number of film scores; the best known is his music for *The Quiet One.*

What's in a Name? is a "modern American madrigal" for mixed chorus. The text concerns William Dawes, who on the eve of the Battle of Lexington was dispatched together with Paul Revere on a midnight ride that made history. Revere became immortal because Longfellow wrote a poem about him; Dawes was forgotten. In the following lines by Helen More, the ghost of Dawes laments his fate. His name was not as poetic as Revere's; therefore, the poet picked Revere to write about—and the world never heard about William Dawes.

> I am a wand'ring, bitter shade;
>   Never of me was hero made.
> Poets have never sung my praise,
>   Nobody crown'd my brow with bays;
> And if you ask me the fatal cause,
>   I answer only, "My name was Dawes."
>
> 'Tis all very well for the children to hear
>   Of the midnight ride of Paul Revere,
> But why should my name be quite forgot,
>   Who rode as boldly and well, God wot?
> Why, should I ask? The reason is clear,
>   My name was Dawes and his Revere.
>
> When the lights in the Old North Church flashed out,
>   Paul Revere was waiting about,
> But I was already on my way.
>   The shadows of night fell cold and gray
> As I rode with never a break or pause.
>   But what was the use, when my name was Dawes?
>
> History rings with his silv'ry name;
>   Closed to me are the portals of fame.
> Had he been Dawes and I Revere,
>   No one had heard of him, I fear.
> No one has heard of me because
>   He was Revere and I was Dawes.

In this charming piece Kay looks back to the madrigal of the Renaissance, and to the pure a cappella style based on voices without instruments.

His harmonies, needless to say, are of the twentieth century. As in the old madrigals, each voice enters in turn with the same line of poetry, one voice imitating the other and interweaving in contrapuntal patterns. Consequently, lines and phrases are repeated over and over. The music has great rhythmic flexibility, as is clear from the frequent changes of meter:

The piece is written in two tempos—Andantino for Stanzas 1 and 3, Allegro for Stanzas 2 and 4. Notice the shuddering effect on the key word—*Dawes*—which leaves us in no doubt as to the cause of William's woe.

David Diamond is an impressive figure on the contemporary scene. He has written steadily through the years and has added a number of works to the present-day repertory. Diamond was born in Rochester, New York on July 9, 1915; he received his musical training at the Cleveland Institute of Music and the Eastman School. His large instrumental pieces show his leanings towards neo-classicism; the list includes eight symphonies and ten string quartets. Into these classical forms he has poured an intensely personal music that marks him as a romantic.

David Diamond

Diamond's lyricism has found an outlet in his vocal music, especially his songs. These show his gift for melody of a simple, heartfelt nature. Typical is *This World Is Not My Home,* based on a moving text by an anonymous poet:

This World Is Not My Home

> This world is not my home,
>   I'm only passing through.
> My treasures and my hopes
>   Are all beyond the sky.
>
> I've many friends and dear ones
>   That's gone along before,
> So I can't feel at home
>   In this world any more.

The song is marked Andante sostenuto (fairly slow and sustained). The melody suits the folk-like simplicity of the poem. Beneath it, however, dissonant harmonies create an emotional tension that heightens the power of the music. The meter alternates between three-four and four-four, giving this song a pleasing freedom of movement. Short and to the point, this song bears the mark of a true lyric poet.

Gail Kubik was born in South Coffeeville, Oklahoma, on September 5, 1914; he is of Czech and English-Irish ancestry. He attended the Eastman School, worked with Walter Piston at Harvard, and continued his studies

Gail Kubik

The Puppet
Show *from
Divertimento
No. II*

in Paris. In addition to his serious works, such as his three symphonies, Kubik has written a number of works in a light, witty style. These bring into American music something of the love of humor associated with Erik Satie and *Les Six.* Kubik has written a considerable amount of film music. His score for the animated cartoon *Gerald McBoing-Boing,* which won an Academy Award, shows his vivid imagination. His choral arrangements of American folk songs have been performed by high-school and college groups throughout the country.

Kubik holds to the neo-classic point of view. He favors bright orchestral colors, neat clear-cut forms, and lively rhythms; his music is simple and direct in expression. These qualities are apparent in his Divertimento No. II for eight instruments—flute, oboe, clarinet, bassoon, trumpet, trombone, viola, and piano. The *divertimento,* a suite in several short movements, was a popular form of Viennese music in the late eighteenth century. As its name implies, it was a "diversion"—that is, a form of light social music. Kubik is one of a number of modern composers who adapted this charming classical form to twentieth-century ways of thinking. In his Divertimento No. II he explores the color contrasts possible for a small group of instruments, each of which is treated as a soloist. This piece, therefore, represents a modern type of chamber music.

We hear the third movement, *The Puppet Show.* The opening melody is played by the instruments in unison. It is, as Kubik describes it, "fast and furious." Oboe, clarinet, and trumpet are pitted against the trombone and piano; their mocking chatter contrasts with an impudent sliding sound (glissando) on the trombone. The music suggests that, as the composer says, "Punch and Judy are busily exchanging blows, to the delight of both infants and adults." The piece reaches a furious—but always slightly mocking—climax and quickly subsides to a quiet ending. As the composer explains, "The fun is over, Punch and Judy are put away for another day."

This Scherzino (little scherzo) evokes a lively scene in a most imaginative way. It reveals a composer who has a rare eye for the lighter side of life.

Peter Mennin

Peter Mennin was born in Erie, Pennsylvania, on May 17, 1923. He studied at Oberlin Conservatory and, by the time he was nineteen, had finished his First Symphony, a string quartet, and a number of songs. During the Second World War he served in the Air Force, and after his discharge attended the Eastman School of Music, where he worked with Howard Hanson. He taught for eleven years at the Juillard School, then was appointed director of the Peabody Institute in Baltimore. During these years he established his reputation as one of the outstanding talents of his generation. In 1962 he succeeded William Schuman as head of the Juilliard School.

Mennin's music is characterized by high spirits and energy. His mind leans naturally towards contrapuntal thinking. His seven symphonies show how easily he handles the large forms of absolute music. These and other large instrumental works place him firmly in the camp of the classicists.

Mennin was only twenty-three years old when he wrote his Third Symphony. The work reveals his vigorous rhythms, his bright orchestral sound, and his ability to shape long singing melodies.

The first movement, an Allegro robusto (fast and vigorous), represents a modern version of sonata-allegro form: that is to say, the classical structure is handled freely. The movement is based on three ideas. First is a strongly rhythmic theme announced by strings and bassoon. This idea returns throughout the movement as a unifying thread:

Second is a striking theme introduced by the horns and expanded by the woodwinds. The third idea is a flowing melody that rises to a peak and subsides. A codetta rounds off the Exposition.

In the Development, Mennin combines his themes in contrapuntal patterns. He builds up tension until the Recapitulation, when the orchestra bursts into full song with the return of the second theme. We hear again the third idea, and a brief coda brings the movement to a quiet ending.

Mennin belongs to a generation of composers that arrived on the scene after the battle for American music had been won. He does not regard Americanism in music as something the composer has to strive for. "I cannot see," he states, "how the musical language of the young American composer can fail to have an American flavor, unless he leads a shut-in existence, or the past is too much with him." He himself lives in the present and has forcefully captured the rhythm of our time.

40

The American Scene (IV)

Leonard Bernstein

Leonard Bernstein is known to millions of Americans as conductor, composer, pianist, educator, and television personality. He is one of the most spectacular figures in the musical world.

He was born in Lawrence, Massachusetts, on August 25, 1918. His father emigrated from Russia and, after years of poverty and hard work, built up a successful business. He resolutely opposed a musical career for his son. This was only the first obstacle in the young man's way. When Bernstein finally decided to devote his life to music, he met with one discouragement after another. But he persevered in the path he had chosen. Finally, at the age of twenty-five, he was appointed assistant conductor of the New York Philharmonic. Several weeks later Bruno Walter, the conductor who was to have led the Sunday afternoon performance, fell ill. Bernstein took his place without a rehearsal, turned in a magnificent performance, and awoke next morning to find himself famous.

Bernstein's music is exuberant, warm, overflowing with movement and rhythmic vitality. He is a romantic at heart. His orchestration is colorful and sumptuous. His works include *Jeremiah Symphony;* the ballets *Fancy Free* and *On the Town;* his Second Symphony, *The Age of Anxiety;* and the *Kaddish Symphony.* In *Wonderful Town* Bernstein succeeded in creating a type of musical play more sophisticated than what is usually seen on Broadway. *West Side Story* transplanted the immortal tale of Romeo and Juliet to the slums of New York, and did so with a poignance that no one who saw either the play or the motion picture is likely to forget.

Overture to Candide

Candide is a comic operetta based on the famous satire by Voltaire. Bernstein's gay and melodious Overture establishes the mood of the play. Its impetuous rhythm and vivid orchestration show Bernstein's style at its best. Marked Allegro molto con brio (very fast, with energy), the Overture leaps off the ground with the opening measure and never loses its drive. The first theme, played by flutes and violins *ff* and *brillante,* is an upward-leaping melody that is extremely active. The second idea is a romantic melody consisting of two six-measure phrases. Notice the change from duple meter to triple:

Several subordinate themes help to round out the form. The material is restated with increasing tension, leading to a climax through crescendo, accelerando, and a rise to the upper register.

This music is thoroughly American in its nervous energy and its directness of feeling. Leonard Bernstein expresses the American point of view in a fresh, breezy way all his own.

Serial Music

Once Schoenberg passed beyond the borders of tonality, he needed a new principle by which to organize his music. He found this in his Method of Composing with Twelve Tones (which is the basis of what is popularly known as *twelve-tone music*). According to this method, every piece is supposed to be based on a *tone row*—that is, a particular series of all the twelve tones of the chromatic scale. This series or row is the idea that unifies that particular composition. The series of twelve tones is repeated over and over throughout the piece, always in the same order. No tone can appear twice in the same row, so that it will not take on the importance of a tonic. The tone row may be played forwards, backwards, upside down, or upside down and backwards. This gives four possible versions of the tone row on each of the twelve tones of the scale. Out of these different versions come all the melodies, harmonies, and countermelodies of the piece. In other words, a piece of twelve-tone music is held together by the tone row in the same way that a piece of tonal music is held together by the key.

Schoenberg's disciples, Alban Berg and Anton Webern, developed their master's method; their followers carried it even farther. Where Schoenberg had used only a series of pitches, the new generation of twelve-tone composers began to use also series of durations, dynamics, tone colors, tempos, rests, and other elements. Thus came into being the concept of *serial music*—that is, music based on series that are repeated over and over in the course of a composition and hold it together. Serial music has given rise to a new way of composing. Serial music is a dynamic art that is in the process of developing as composers discover new ways of combining sounds.

In all the musical capitals of the world there are small groups of composers creating—and small audiences listening to—a "far-out" kind of music from which all the old landmarks have disappeared, a music whose like was never heard before.

ROBERT MOTHERWELL, *THE VOYAGE*.
The composers of serial music resemble the new school of abstract or
non-objective painters.

Lukas Foss

Lukas Foss was born in Berlin on August 15, 1922. His parents left
Germany in 1933 when Hitler came to power. They arrived in the United
States when the future composer was fifteen. He studied at the Curtis
Institute, and became known as one of the strongest talents of his generation.
He has been professor of composition at the University of California, and
is now conductor of the Buffalo Symphony Orchestra.

Foss's personal growth reflects some of the major developments of our
time. From his European background he inherited the tradition of German
romanticism and came under the influence of Gustav Mahler. Arriving
here as a boy he quickly assimilated the thinking and feeling of his new
home. He began to admire Copland's music and produced a splendid
example of American nationalism in his cantata *The Prairie,* a large-scale
work based on a poem by Carl Sandburg. From Stravinsky he took over
the influence of neo-classicism. He then became interested in Schoenberg
and Webern, and was drawn to their techniques. Now he is one of the leaders
of the *avant-garde*—the "advance guard," that is, which experiments with
new ways of organizing sounds.

Echoi I

Echoi, a work for clarinet, cello, percussion, and piano, was completed in
1963. The title (ék-wee) refers to ancient Arabian scales. It also suggests
the many echo sounds that occur throughout the piece, with one instrument
imitating the other. We will hear the first movement.

This music creates the impression that it is being made up on the spur of

330

the moment. Partly this is due to the rhythmic freedom given to the players, who are required to be together at certain points but have a certain amount of leeway in between. They are able to stay together not by counting but only by listening to each other. The percussion consists of vibraphone and a variety of drums, big and little.

This piece comes out of the serial method of composing, although Foss adapted the method to his own purpose. He used series of pitches, rhythms, colors, dynamics, and other elements to obtain the raw material, as he calls it, of his piece. "In composing in this manner," he writes, "the composer, after having obtained an abundance of serial material, composes not by adding but by deleting, erasing, arranging, choosing."

Foss's purpose is to explore combinations of sounds rather than to arouse emotions. The composers of serial music resemble the new school of abstract or non-objective painters, who do not try to represent the world around us but create instead a world derived purely from color and line, that has no relation to the "real" world.

The music proceeds in spurts and surges of sound, based on contrasts between high and low, slow and fast, staccato and legato, soft and loud, harsh and gentle, single lines and counterpoint. The piece may strike you as disconnected; yet if you hear it a number of times you will be astonished at how quickly you will adjust to it. Like a good deal of contemporary poetry and painting, this music is not for everyone. But if you are one of those who do respond to it, you will derive from it a musical sensation such as you have never known before.

Sounds so different from the traditional ones must also look different on the page, as is evident from the illustration on page 332.

The World of New Sounds

We have seen that a number of twentieth-century composers tried to establish new ways of combining the old sounds. At the same time other composers were looking for new ways of producing sounds. At first their efforts were timid and did not seem to make much of an impression. But their experiments steadily gained in scope until, in our own time, a world of new sounds has been brought into being, completely different from any that man has known till now.

We can trace this search through five stages of development.

1. New Ways of Using Conventional Instruments

In the 1920s, the American composer Henry Cowell attracted much attention by his novel way of playing the piano. By pressing down the keys with his palms, fists, and forearms, he created "tone clusters"—striking combinations of sounds with an atmosphere all their own. Nor did he limit himself to the keyboard. He got up from the piano bench and put his hands inside the piano. By scratching, plucking, slapping, and sweeping the strings, he drew sounds from the instrument that no one had ever thought it was capable of producing.

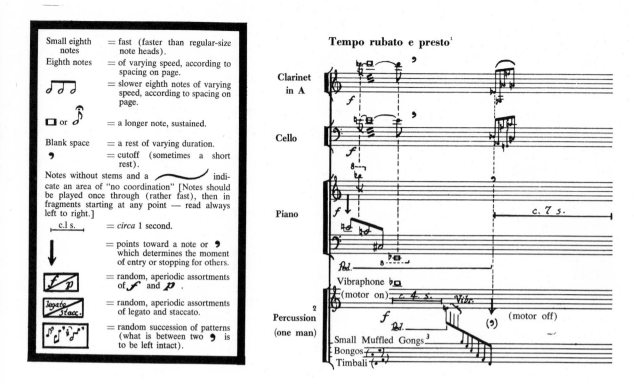

Tempo rubato e presto[1]

Small eighth notes	= fast (faster than regular-size note heads).
Eighth notes	= of varying speed, according to spacing on page.
♪♪♪	= slower eighth notes of varying speed, according to spacing on page.
▭ or ♪	= a longer note, sustained.
Blank space	= a rest of varying duration.
❜	= cutoff (sometimes a short rest).

Notes without stems and a 〜 indicate an area of "no coordination" [Notes should be played once through (rather fast), then in fragments starting at any point — read always left to right.]

c.1 s. = *circa* 1 second.

↓ = points toward a note or ❜ which determines the moment of entry or stopping for others.

f p = random, aperiodic assortments of *f* and *p* .

legato stacc. = random, aperiodic assortments of legato and staccato.

♪♩♪♩ = random succession of patterns (what is between two ❜ is to be left intact).

Henry Cowell was born in Menlo Park, California, on March 11, 1897, and died in Shady, New York, on December 10, 1965. He was an extremely prolific composer and wrote more than a thousand works, including an opera and fourteen symphonies.

The Banshee is Cowell's most popular piano composition. A Banshee, in Irish and Scottish folklore, is a female spirit whose wailing outside a house warns a family that one of them is about to die. In this piece Cowell creates an eerie atmosphere out of which come strange murmurings and a wailing that is almost human.

The Banshee is played on the open strings of the piano; the player stands in the bend of the instrument while someone else sits at the keyboard and holds down the *damper pedal* (that is, the pedal on the right, which raises the dampers and allows the strings to continue to vibrate). Here is what the music looks like, with an explanation of some of the symbols:

Henry Cowell:
The Banshee

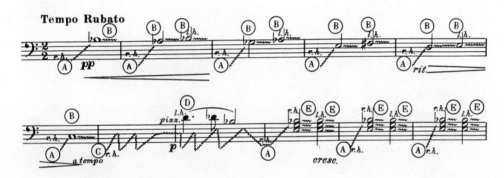

Explanation of Symbols

"The Banshee" is played on the open strings of the piano, the player standing at the crook. Another person must sit at the keyboard and hold down the damper pedal throughout the composition. The whole work should be played an octave lower than written.

R. H. stands for "right hand." L. H. stands for "left hand." Different ways of playing the strings are indicated by a letter over each tone, as follows:

(A) indicates a sweep with the flesh of the finger from the lowest string up to the note given.

(B) sweep lengthwise along the string of the note given with flesh of finger.

(C) sweep up and back from lowest A to highest B-flat given in this composition.

(D) pluck string with flesh of finger, where written, instead of octave lower.

(E) sweep along three notes together, in the same manner as (B).

This little tone poem manages to conjure up the atmosphere of a ghost story. Through his original handling of the piano, Cowell succeeded in transforming its usual sound into something quite new.

2. *Transforming the Character of Conventional Instruments*

The second step was to change the character of conventional instruments. The American composer John Cage, a pupil of Cowell, was a leader in this field. In his efforts to carry Cowell's theories to a further stage of development he invented the "prepared piano." The preparation consists of attaching to the strings a variety of rubber, felt, or wood objects, as well as screws, nuts, and bolts. These may also be inserted between the strings. All this changes the pitch and timbre of the piano. In Cage's hands the traditional instrument of Chopin and Liszt has become an instrument of rhythm and percussion, with delicate tone colors that suggest the sound of the *gamelan*—the orchestra of gongs and drums popular in the Far East.

A BALINESE *GAMELAN* ORCHESTRA.

John Cage:
Dance

John Cage belongs to the ultramodern group among his generation. He was born in Los Angeles on September 5, 1912. Among his teachers in composition, besides Cowell, was Arnold Schoenberg; he has been strongly influenced by the techniques of twelve-tone music. Cage's interest is neither in melody nor harmony; he concentrates on rhythm and timbre.

Cage's *Dance,* written in 1944, is played on a "prepared" piano whose sound bears no resemblance to what we know as piano tone. Flexible rhythms are repeated over and over again in ostinato patterns. They sound as if they were beaten out by little wooden mallets. The music begins mezzo forte and gradually fades away to a pianissimo.

Cage's interest in pure sound has led him into various fields of experimental music. Throughout his career he has been a persistent seeker after new paths.

3. Instrumental Sound Treated Electronically

The third step came in the 1940s with the development of music for tape recorder. This was based on the electronic treatment of tones produced by the human voice or musical instruments, or of the sounds of nature. Magnetic tape made it possible to split a tone, change its overtones, and combine its elements into new tones. As a result, it was possible to hear piano sound two octaves below the lowest A, or to transfer the sound of the tuba to the upper flute range. Also, several tapes could be combined by playing them at the same time, with fascinating results.

Among the pioneers in this field was Otto Luening, who carried on important experiments with his younger colleague at Columbia University, Vladimir Ussachevsky. Their *Rhapsodic Variations for Tape Recorder and Orchestra* and *A Poem of Cycles and Bells*—both works have been recorded—show their imaginative use of the new medium. Luening was born in Milwaukee on June 15, 1900. Since he is one of the directors of the Electronic Music Center at Columbia University, he stands in the center of recent developments in this field. Luening has also written a variety of works for conventional instruments. Among his orchestral pieces are *Two Symphonic Fantasias, Two Symphonic Interludes,* and *Prelude on a Hymn Tune by William Billings.* His list includes three string quartets, the opera *Evangeline,* choral music, pieces for various instruments, songs, and piano music. As professor of composition at Columbia University, he has had a wide influence on the younger generation of American composers.

Otto Luening:
Moon Flight

In *Moon Flight* he has created a piece that shows both the agility of the flute and the resources of the tape recorder. *Moon Flight* evokes the world of outer space. It is, the composer explains, "the musical description of an astronautical adventure. The complications of flight, the mystery, the strange sounds in and out of the ship, the azure sky and the feeling of weightlessness are suggested in sound."

This little piece shows how the pure tones of the flute can be changed by electronic treatment. Through re-recording, the composer is able to obtain both his melody and harmonies from the sound of a single flute. The various elements of the piece are produced separately, but they are re-recorded and mixed on the tape recorder, producing vague echo effects and flickering sounds that seem to be floating high above the earth.

335

A melody in the style of a folk song celebrates the lonely landing and brings the composition to an end. It is played in the normal tone of the flute, against shadowy echoes in the background.

It is clear that the tape recorder represents an important step forward into the new world of sound. By treating tones electronically, the composer was able to create sonorities such as had never been heard before.

4. *Industrial Sounds and Noises Treated Electronically*

Music for tape recorder used tones produced by the human voice or musical instruments, or the sounds of nature. The next step came when composers began to include, in their experiments with sound, the noises of the city and of industry; the grinding of train wheels; the whirring of machines, motors, propellers; the shrieking of sirens and auto horns. These elements, when treated electronically, brought about a further breakthrough into the new world of sound.

*Edgard
Varèse*

Edgard Varèse, one of the most original spirits in the music of our time, was born in Paris on December 22, 1883, of French-Italian parentage. He came to the United States when he was thirty years old, and lost no time in making a place for himself in the musical life of his adopted land. His revolutionary works, such as *Hyperprism, Ionisation,* and *Intégrales,* were written during the 1920s and early '30s. Varèse found a champion in the conductor Leopold Stokowski, who performed his scores despite the booing and hissing of conservative audiences. But the lack of a public ultimately affected Varèse as it did his contemporary Charles Ives. He fell silent when he should have been at the height of his powers. During the next twenty years he followed closely the new scientific developments in the field of electronic instruments. He began to compose again in 1952.

By that time the scene had changed; there existed a public that was willing to listen to "far-out" music. Presently the younger generation of European composers, who were experimenting with tape-recorded sound, discovered Varèse as their most important forerunner. The long-neglected master finally came into his own; he was hailed and admired throughout the musical world. He died in New York City on November 6, 1965, at the age of eighty-one.

Varèse's music evokes a machine civilization. His interest in rhythm—rather than in melody or harmony—led him to a most imaginative handling of the percussion instruments. The abstract images that brood over Varèse's music are derived from the life of the big city: the rumble of motors, the clang of hammers, the shriek and hiss of factory whistles, turbines, steam drills.

"I have been waiting a long time," Varèse wrote, "for electronics to free music from the limitations of musical instruments. Electronic instruments are the portentous first step toward the liberation of music." In the late 1940s music caught up with Varèse's prophetic vision.

With *Déserts* (day-zehr, the French word for deserts), Varèse entered the new world of electronic music. The work, composed in 1954, was for a group of instruments; but at three points tape-recorded sequences were inserted into the score. These sequences were derived not from musical tones but from industrial sounds, as Varèse put it, "of friction, percussion, hissing, grinding, puffing," which were processed—that is, filtered and mixed—electronically.

Electronic Sequence I conjures up a world of brooding visions. Tension is set up by opposing masses of sound that have a steely hardness to them, almost a cutting edge. We are confronted with a strange non-human music that has a power all its own, that seems to suggest some strange landscape from outer space. Thus, on the threshold of seventy, this bold explorer entered upon untrodden paths in order to reveal to his less adventurous fellows his vision of the new world of sound.

5. *Pure Electronic Sound*

The fifth and final step came in the 1950s with the emergence of *electronic music*. This was not derived from previously existing musical tones or noises, but produced by electric generators; in other words, a pure sound created artificially in the laboratory.

Of prime importance in this historic development was the perfecting of the RCA Electronic Synthesizer. This incredible "instrument," which costs a quarter of a million dollars, can generate any imaginable musical tone or combination of tones, in a variety of pitches, timbres, and complex rhythmic patterns that go far beyond what is possible for conventional instruments. In 1960 the Synthesizer was installed at Columbia University, and provided a great stimulus to further experiments in this field.

*Milton
Babbitt:
From*
Composition
for
Synthesizer

Milton Babbitt was born in Philadelphia on May 10, 1916. He studied with Roger Sessions privately and at Princeton University, where he is now professor of music. He is a trained mathematician and taught mathematics at Princeton during the war. Babbitt is an intellectual composer. His music is concentrated in thought and complex in texture. Among his works are *Composition for Twelve Instruments; All Set,* for seven jazz instrumentalists; and *Composition for Tenor and Six Instruments.*

Given his scientific turn of mind, it is only natural that Babbitt became very much interested in electronic music. He is one of the directors of the Electronic Music Center at Columbia University. His *Composition for Synthesizer,* from which we hear an excerpt, explores some of the possibilities offered by this new instrument.

The music ranges from bell-like tinklings in high register to shattering noises in low. Especially interesting are the flickering sounds that resemble trills and tremolos. This is strangely impersonal music, as free from a specific meaning as are the abstract patterns of non-objective painting.

THE RCA ELECTRONIC SOUND SYNTHESIZER.
This "instrument" can generate any imaginable musical tone.

Electronic music opens up to the composer the entire range of frequencies audible to the human ear, from about fifty vibrations per second to fifteen thousand. You have only to listen to it to realize that you are catching a glimpse of a new universe of sound, whose ultimate shape we cannot at this time even begin to foresee. The music of the future!

A Parting Word

It is to be hoped that the facts you learned in this book about the great composers and their works have enabled you to listen to music more intelligently and with greater appreciation. Getting to know music is the first step towards getting to love and enjoy it. And the best way to love and enjoy music is to be in constant touch with it: to listen when the great symphony orchestras play on the radio and television; to attend concerts; to hear operas; to collect records and to play your favorite selections over and over again until you really know them. When you do all these you will become one of the millions of people all over the world who find in music a wonderful pastime and a source of artistic and spiritual pleasure.

Should you become a true music lover, your days will be vastly enriched. Music will heighten your moments of happiness and offer you comfort in moments of sorrow. It will enhance everything that is worthwhile in your life. Listen, then, not casually or indifferently, but with devotion and passion. Listen not only with your ears, but with your mind and heart and soul. If you do, you will find yourself entering the magic world of one of the noblest arts of our civilization—a world where you will find endless beauty and joy.

APPENDICES

APPENDIX A
Comparative Range of Voices and Instruments

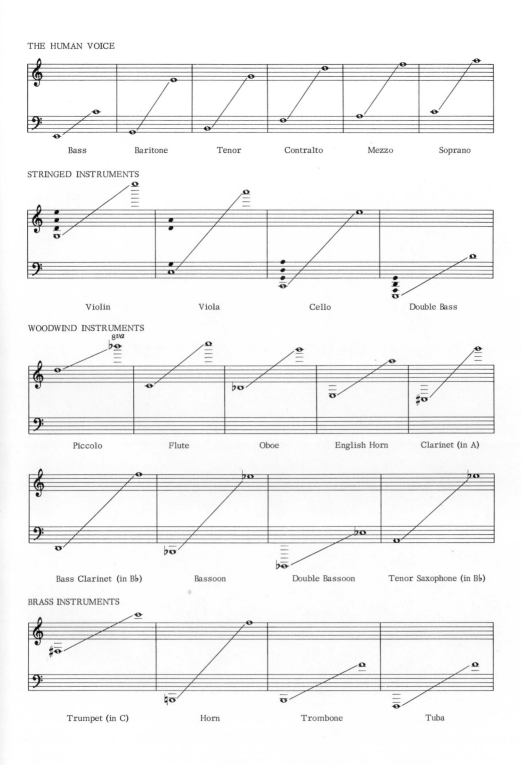

THE HUMAN VOICE

Bass   Baritone   Tenor   Contralto   Mezzo   Soprano

STRINGED INSTRUMENTS

Violin   Viola   Cello   Double Bass

WOODWIND INSTRUMENTS

Piccolo   Flute   Oboe   English Horn   Clarinet (in A)

Bass Clarinet (in B♭)   Bassoon   Double Bassoon   Tenor Saxophone (in B♭)

BRASS INSTRUMENTS

Trumpet (in C)   Horn   Trombone   Tuba

343

PERCUSSION INSTRUMENTS

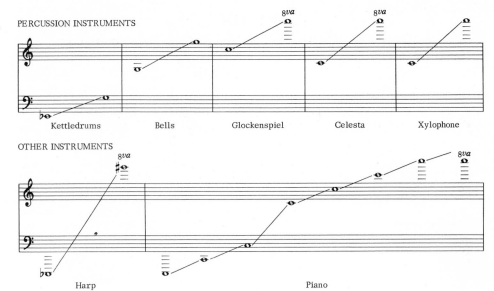

| Kettledrums | Bells | Glockenspiel | Celesta | Xylophone |

OTHER INSTRUMENTS

Harp   Piano

APPENDIX B
Complete List of Major and Minor Scales

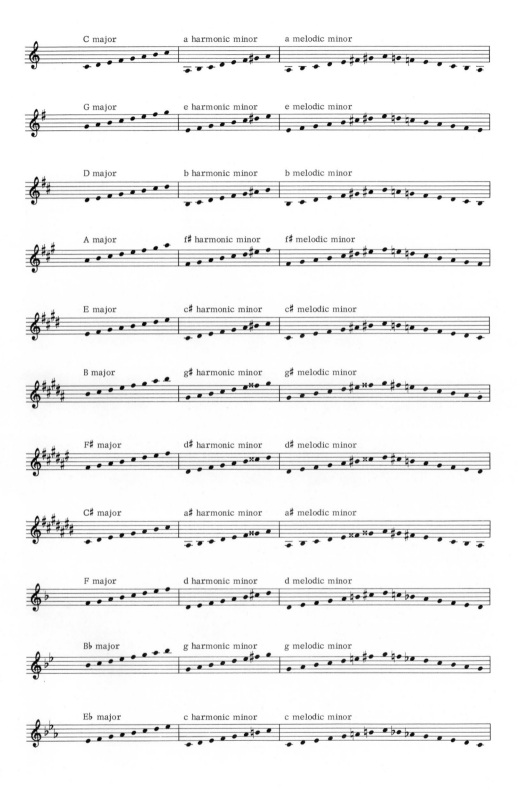

APPENDIX C
Glossary of Musical Terms

The following glossary contains definitions of the musical terms used in this book, plus a few other useful terms that you may wish to know about. Certain words in the definitions are printed in small capital letters. This means that each of those words has its own entry and definition in this glossary.

A-B. A basic pattern in music, made up of two sections that contrast with each other.

A-B-A. A basic pattern in music that involves the statement of a theme, departure to new material, and return to the theme. Also known as three-part or ternary form. Achieves both variety and unity through contrast and repetition.

Absolute music. Abstract tone patterns having no association with a specific story or scene, as opposed to PROGRAM MUSIC. Main forms: SONATA, SYMPHONY, CONCERTO, CHAMBER MUSIC.

A cappella. A vocal work not accompanied by INSTRUMENTS. The purest type of CHORAL music: Palestrina.

Accelerando (ah-cheh-leh-ráhn-do). Getting faster.

Accent. Emphasis or stress on a specific TONE or CHORD.

Accidentals. Signs such as a SHARP (#), a FLAT (♭), or a NATURAL (♮), used to change the PITCH of a NOTE.

Accompaniment. The background for the MELODY, as in a song with piano accompaniment.

Adagio (ah-dáh-jo). 1. Slow, leisurely. 2. A piece or movement in this tempo.

Air. A melody or tune.

Alla breve (¢). DUPLE METER, with a HALF NOTE receiving the BEAT instead of a QUARTER; 2/2 instead of 4/4. Implies a faster tempo than 4/4. Also known as cut time.

Allegretto. Fairly fast, not as lively as ALLEGRO.

Allegro. Fast, cheerful, lively.

Allegro giusto (joó-sto). In strict ALLEGRO time.

Allegro molto. Very fast.

Allegro non troppo. Not too fast.

Alto. 1. A woman's voice lower in RANGE than a SOPRANO; also called contralto. 2. The second highest PART in a four-part CHORUS. 3. An instrument in this range: alto saxophone.

Andante (ahn-dáhn-teh). Fairly slow, at a walking pace.

Andante con moto. At a walking pace, with movement.

Andantino (ahn-dahn-teé-no). A little ANDANTE, somewhat faster than andante.

Antiphon. A category of GREGORIAN CHANT, usually based on a short text from the Scriptures.

Antique cymbals. Tiny metal discs attached to the thumb and forefinger and struck together.

Aragonaise (ah-rah-go-néz). A Spanish dance from the province of Aragon, in lively 3/4 time.

Aria. A solo song with instrumental accompaniment in a larger work such as an OPERA or ORATORIO.

Arietta. A little ARIA.

Arpeggio (ahr-péh-jo). A broken CHORD, the tones played in succession rather than simultaneously.

Arrangement. Adaptation of a piece for instruments or voices different from those for which it was originally written; as an orchestral arrangement of a Bach organ FUGUE.

Art song. A composition for VOICE and INSTRUMENT, generally the piano.

A tempo. In time. A return to the original TEMPO.

Atonality. The absence of relationship to a KEY center, as in later works by Arnold Schoenberg.

Augmentation. The presentation of a theme in longer note values; for example, in half notes instead of quarter notes.

Ballad opera. A musical entertainment popular in eighteenth-century England and colonial America, consisting of a play enlivened by catchy songs and dances.

Ballet. A dance spectacle or the music that accompanies it. May be either part of an OPERA or an independent work.

Ballett. An English type of MADRIGAL in the style of a dance song, with a "fa-la" REFRAIN: Morley, *Sing We and Chant It.*

Band. An ENSEMBLE composed mainly of

wind instruments, such as a BRASS, jazz, or symphonic band.

Bar. 1. The BARLINE. 2. The NOTES and RESTS between two BARLINES; therefore, a MEASURE.

Baritone. 1. The male voice whose RANGE lies between TENOR and BASS. 2. An instrument in this range: baritone horn.

Barline. A vertical line placed before the first strong BEAT of a MEASURE to show where the ACCENT falls. Marks off the beginning of the measure.

Baroque (ba-róke). A style in music, painting, architecture, sculpture, interior decorating, etc., that flourished from about 1600 to 1750, marked by pomp and grandeur, massiveness, energy, and emotion. Main characteristics: 1. Rise of OPERA, perfection of ORATORIO, PASSION, CANTATA. 2. POLYPHONIC texture, perfection of COUNTERPOINT. FUGUE, CONCERTO GROSSO, SUITE, TOCCATA, and other CONTRAPUNTAL forms. 3. Differentiation between RECITATIVE and ARIA. 4. Continuous MELODY (instead of the PHRASE-and-CADENCE of the CLASSIC style). 5. Even levels of soft and loud: terraced DYNAMICS. 6. Unflagging RHYTHM. 7. A single "affection" or mood rather than two contrasting moods in a single MOVEMENT. 8. Much religious music. Composers: Monteverdi, Purcell, Vivaldi, Scarlatti, Bach, Handel. Painters: Tintoretto, Veronese, Rubens, El Greco. Writers: John Milton.

Bass. 1. The lowest male voice. 2. The lowest PART in a four-part CHORUS. 3. Usually the lowest member of a family of instruments: bass clarinet.

Beat. A single pulse within a MEASURE. May be either accented or unaccented.

Bel canto (Italian, "beautiful singing"). The great Italian vocal art of the eighteenth and early nineteenth centuries. A style made familiar through the operas of Mozart, Rossini, Donizetti, Bellini, etc.

Berceuse (behr-súz). A lullaby or cradle song.

Binary form. A-B form (two-part form).

Brass band. An ensemble largely used in outdoor concerts, parades, etc. Contains the BRASS INSTRUMENTS of the ORCHESTRA plus cornet, flügelhorn, baritone, and euphonium (tenor tubas), helicon or sousaphone (double-bass tuba), etc.

Brass instruments. Made of brass with cup- or funnel-shaped mouthpiece. Tone produced by column of air in the tube, made to vibrate by blowing through the tightly stretched lips of the player (which serve as reeds). Brass section of the orchestra usually consists of trumpets, French horns, trombones, and tuba.

Buffo (Italian, "clown"). A character in classic Italian OPERA. Hence, opera buffa, comic opera.

Cadence. A resting place in music. May be either incomplete, like a comma in punctuation, or complete, like a period at the end of a sentence.

Cadenza. A brilliant SOLO passage introduced into a musical work to show off the technique of the performer and the resources of the instrument.

Cantabile (can-táh-bee-leh). In a songful manner.

Cantata (from Italian *cantare*, "to sing"). A composition for SOLO singers, CHORUS, and instrumentalists; in several MOVEMENTS, such as RECITATIVES and ARIAS, DUETS, and CHORUSES; based on a poetic text, either religious or secular.

Chamber music. Music requiring from one to nine players, with one player to each PART.

Chamber orchestra. A small ORCHESTRA.

Choir. 1. A group of singers. 2. A group of instruments in the ORCHESTRA: *string* choir, woodwind choir.

Choral. Pertaining to CHOIR or CHORUS.

Chorale. A hymn, or a melody in the style of a hymn.

Chorale prelude. An organ piece based on a CHORALE: Bach.

Chord. Several tones that are played together and form a unit.

Chorus. 1. A large group of singers. 2. Music for such a group, usually in four PARTS: SOPRANO, ALTO, TENOR, BASS.

Chromatic. 1. Pertaining to the twelve SEMITONES of the CHROMATIC SCALE. 2. Movement by SEMITONES.

Chromatic scale. The twelve SEMITONES of the OCTAVE arranged in consecutive order. On the piano, the seven white and five black KEYS. Rapid chromatic scales are often associated, in nineteenth-century music, with effects of suspense, excitement, storm, etc.

Church modes. The scales used in medieval church music. They can be heard by playing the white keys on the piano between D and D, E-E, F-F, etc.

Classicism. A style in the arts marked by clarity, balance, and mastery of FORM; in music, refers especially to the style of the Viennese classic school, about 1775-1825: Haydn, Mozart, Beethoven, Schubert. 1. They perfected the SONATA, SYMPHONY, CONCERTO, and various types of CHAMBER MUSIC. 2. International in spirit; supremacy of Viennese SYMPHONY and Italian OPERA throughout Europe. 3. Artists worked under the patronage of an aristocracy. 4. Derived inspiration from the culture of ancient Greece and Rome. 5. Center of musical life was the palace. 6. Art strove to be objective and stressed universal values. 7. Emotion controlled within a form. 8. Music regarded as a self-contained art; emphasis on ABSOLUTE MUSIC. 9. The sound is conceived in terms of the aristocratic salon; orchestra of from 35 to 40 players. 10. The classic composer concentrated on the development of abstract musical ideas. 11. Music essentially optimistic, cheerful, an adornment of gracious living. Painters: Gainsborough, David. Writers: Goethe, Schiller, Dr. Johnson, Defoe, Swift, Gray, etc.

Clef. A sign written on the STAFF to indicate the PITCH of lines and spaces. 1. The G or TREBLE clef establishes the second line of the STAFF as the G above middle C. Used for instruments of high range, such as the violin or flute; in piano music, generally for the right-hand part. 2. The F or BASS clef establishes the fourth line of the STAFF as the F below middle C. Used for instruments of low range such as double bass and bassoon; in piano music, for the left-hand part. 3. The C clef is used in several positions—soprano, alto, tenor—for instruments and voices in the middle range.

Coda (Italian, "tail"). A section at the end of a piece that gives a sense of conclusion.

Codetta. A little CODA.

Col legno (Italian, "with the wood"). In violin playing, to tap the strings with the stick of the bow, producing a ghostly effect.

Coloratura soprano. A brilliant type of voice able to perform rapid SCALES, TRILLS, and wide skips in the highest REGISTER.

Common time (C). 4/4 time.

Concertante (kon-cher-táhn-teh). An orchestral style in which SOLO instruments are pitted against each other and against the larger group.

Concerto (con-tchér-to, from Latin concertare, "to contend with, to vie with"). A large work, often in several movements, for solo instrument and orchestra. Emphasizes VIRTUOSITY.

Concerto grosso. A Baroque form of instrumental music, based on the contrast or opposition between two different masses of sound. The small solo group, the "concertino," was pitted against the large accompanying group, the "concerto grosso." Bach, Brandenburg Concertos.

Concert overture. A composition for orchestra in one movement that suggests a specific story, scene, or mood. Differs from the SYMPHONIC POEM in that it has a definite musical FORM independent of its literary program.

Con passione (pah-syó-neh). With passion.

Consonance. A combination of two or more tones that gives the effect of completeness and rest.

Contralto. A woman's voice lower in RANGE than the MEZZO-SOPRANO. Sometimes called ALTO.

Countermelody. A melody "against" the main melody—that is, a melody combined with the main melody.

Counterpoint (Adjective, contrapuntal). The art and science of combining several melodic lines or VOICES into a single fabric.

Countersubject. A theme heard "against" the main theme of a FUGUE.

Countertheme. Same as COUNTERSUBJECT.

Crescendo (kreh-shén-do). Growing louder.

Cut time. See ALLA BREVE.

Cyclical form. Said of a composition in several movements when the THEMES of the earlier movements return in the later ones.

Da capo (Italian, "from the head"). Indicates that a piece or section is to be repeated from the beginning.

Damper pedal. On the piano, the pedal on the right. It raises the dampers, which allows the strings to continue to vibrate after the fingers have been raised from the KEYS.

Decrescendo (day-kreh-shén-do). Getting softer.

Development. 1. A technique of composition in which musical THEMES are enabled to change and grow by being broken into fragments, or MOTIVES, which are then combined into fresh patterns. 2. The middle section of SONATA-ALLEGRO FORM, marked by frequent MODULATION. May include changes in MELODY, HARMONY, RHYTHM, METER, TEMPO, DYNAMICS, REGISTER, TIMBRE; combination with new material in CONTRAPUNTAL texture, IMITATION, INVERSION; and presentation of the melody in longer or shorter notes.

Diatonic. Pertaining to the seven TONES of the MAJOR or MINOR SCALE and their related HARMONIES. Opposed to CHROMATIC, which pertains to all the twelve tones of the OCTAVE—the seven in the KEY and the five that are not.

Diminuendo (dih-min-yoo-én-do). Growing softer.

Diminution. The presentation of a theme in shorter note values; for example, in quarter notes instead of halves.

Dissonance. A combination of two or more TONES giving the effect of incompleteness, therefore requiring RESOLUTION to a CONSONANCE. Dissonance is the principle of activity and tension in music, while CONSONANCE represents completion and repose.

Divertimento. A popular type of Viennese music in the late eighteenth century, revived in the twentieth, intended as a "diversion": a light and entertaining work. For strings, winds, or mixed groups, usually with one or two players to a PART.

Do. The first (and last) tone of the *do-re-mi-fa-sol-la-ti-do* SCALE. The central tone, the KEYNOTE, or TONIC.

Dolce (dól-cheh). Sweetly, softly.

Dot. Prolongs a note or rest by half its value. A dotted HALF NOTE (d.) receives two BEATS plus one.

Dotted rhythm. A RHYTHM associated with dotted notes, as in the opening measures of *Battle Hymn of the Republic.*

Double flat (♭♭). A sign that lowers a note by two SEMITONES or a WHOLE TONE.

Double sharp (✗). A sign that raises a note by two SEMITONES or a WHOLE TONE.

Double stop. On STRING INSTRUMENTS, two or more tones sounded simultaneously.

Duet. A piece for two performers in which both parts are of equal importance.

Duo. 1. A DUET. 2. A team of two performers.

Duple meter. A pattern of two BEATS to a MEASURE, with the ACCENT on the first, as in 2/4 time.

Duration. Said of a tone in regard to the length of time it lasts.

Dynamics. The degree of loudness or softness at which the music is played.

Eighth note (♪). Receives half the time value of a quarter note. In 4/4 time, two eighths to a BEAT.

Electronic music. Music produced by electric generators: a pure sound derived not from previously existing musical tones or noises, but produced artificially in the laboratory. An electronic instrument such as the RCA Synthesizer opens up to the composer a world of PITCHES, RHYTHMS, and TIMBRES never available before.

Embouchure (ahm-buh-shóor). 1. The mouthpiece of a wind instrument. 2. The position of the player's tongue and lips.

Ensemble (ahn-sáhm-bul; French for "together"). 1. A group of vocal or instrumental performers who function as a unit. 2. In OPERA, a piece for more than two singers, or for soloists and CHORUS.

Entr'acte (áhn-tract). A piece played between the acts.

Episode. In a FUGUE, a section that serves as an area of relaxation between the appearances of the THEME.

Etude (áy-tood). A piece intended to develop technical mastery of an instrument.

Exoticism. A tendency, especially during nineteenth-century ROMANTICISM, to draw inspiration from the glamor of far-off lands. Bizet, *Carmen;* Rimsky-Korsakov, *Scheherazade.*

Exposition. 1. The first section of SONATA-ALLEGRO FORM. The first THEME is announced in the TONIC KEY; a bridge passage MODULATES to a contrasting key; the second theme and a CODETTA establish the contrasting KEY. May be preceded by a slow introduction. 2. The opening section of a FUGUE, during which the SUBJECT is introduced by each voice in turn.

Expressionism. A movement in twentieth-century art in Germany and Austria, aiming at the most powerful expression of the artist's inner self through distorted images that defied all conventional notions of beauty. Composers: Schoenberg, Berg, Webern. Painters: Klee, Kandinsky, Kokoschka. Writers: Kafka. Dancers: Martha Graham.

Fanfare. A short tune for trumpets, used as a signal in battle, hunting, or various ceremonies.

Fantasia. 1. An imaginative piece that follows no set FORM. 2. A piece based on melodies from an OPERA.

Farandole. A popular street dance of Provence in which couples hold hands, winding in and out as they follow the leader in a procession.

Fermata. A hold or pause in music.

Fifth. The INTERVAL from step 1 to step 5 of the scale (or step 2 to step 6, etc.), such as *do-sol* or C-G.

Finale (fih-náh-lee). The final number, section, or movement of a musical work.

First-movement form. See SONATA-ALLEGRO FORM.

Flamenco. The passionate style of the Spanish Gypsies, as shown in their folk songs and dances.

Flat (♭). The sign that lowers a note by a SEMITONE, as from B to B♭.

Fluttertonguing. In playing WOODWIND and BRASS INSTRUMENTS such as the trumpet or flute, a quick rolling movement of the tongue aimed at producing very rapidly repeated tones.

Form. The arrangement of material in such a way as to obtain the most artistic effect. Musical form seeks to achieve unity and variety through repetition and contrast.

Formalism. The emphasis of FORM over content.

Forte (*f*). Loud.

Fortissimo (*ff*). Very loud.

Four-four time. A pattern of four BEATS to a MEASURE, ACCENT on the first. May have a subordinate accent on the third beat: ONE-two-Three-four.

Fourth. The INTERVAL between step 1 and step 4 of the SCALE (or step 2 and step 5, etc.), such as *do-fa* or C-F.

Fugato. A piece or section that begins in the style of a FUGUE but does not adhere to the principles of a fugue.

Fugue (fyoog). A composition, generally in three or four VOICES, in which a THEME or SUBJECT pervades the entire piece, entering now in one voice, now in another, against COUNTERPOINT in the other voices.

Galop. A lively dance performed with light hopping movements.

Gamelan. The orchestra of gongs and drums popular in the Far East.

Gavotte. An old French dance in a moderate tempo, 4/4 time.

Glissando. A rapid SCALE effect achieved by sliding a finger across piano keys or along a violin string, which sounds all the PITCHES of the scale. Also possible on other instruments.

Grace note. A very short NOTE without time value of its own, attached as an ornament to the longer note that follows.

Gradual. A GREGORIAN CHANT sung at High MASS.

Gregorian chant. The chants used in the musical service of the Roman Catholic Church. Collected by Pope Gregory the Great (reigned 590-604). Also known as PLAINCHANT or PLAINSONG. The great monument of single-line (MONOPHONIC) MELODY that survives in the West.

Ground bass. In CONTRAPUNTAL music, a PHRASE in the BASS repeated over and over while the other PARTS weave fresh MELODIES and HARMONIES above it.

Guaracha (gwah-ráh-cha). A drinking song or dance popular in Latin America, marked by OSTINATO rhythms, stop-and-go effects, and SYNCOPATION.

Half note ($\,\bd\,$). Equivalent to two quarter notes. In 4/4 time, receives two BEATS.

Half tone. A SEMITONE, as from C to C♯ or B to B♭.

Harmonic. Pertaining to HARMONY.

Harmonics. 1. When a string or column of air vibrates, it does so not only as a whole but also in segments of 1/2, 1/3, 1/4, 1/5, etc. These segments produce harmonics—also known as OVERTONES—which are not heard distinctly, but merge with the fundamental tone. 2. High flute-like tones on STRING INSTRUMENTS, produced by touching the string lightly at certain spots instead of pressing it down, thus causing only a segment of the string to vibrate. 3. On WIND INSTRUMENTS, harmonics are produced by varying the pressure of the lips and breath, causing the air column in the tube to split into segments.

Harmonium. A small organ-like instrument.

Harmony. 1. The simultaneous sounding of two or more TONES. 2. The CHORDS that accompany and support the MELODY. 3. The study of chords, their movement, and relationships.

Harpsichord. A favorite keyboard instrument during the BAROQUE and ROCOCO. Differs from the piano: 1. Its strings are not struck by hammers but plucked by quills, producing a bright silvery tone. 2. The harpsichord is not capable of CRESCENDO and DIMINUENDO, since the volume of sound is not affected by the pressure of the fingers. Two keyboards make possible even levels of soft and loud (terraced dynamics) and enchanting echo effects. The clarity of sound is ideal for CONTRAPUNTAL music.

Homophonic texture. Denotes a single MELODY heard against a background of CHORDS.

Imitation. The principle on which a ROUND or FUGUE is based, according to which a theme presented in one voice is repeated or "imitated" in another.

Impressionism. A style in French painting and music, during the late nineteenth and early twentieth centuries. Reaction against German romanticism. Features of musical impressionism: use of WHOLE-TONE SCALE; MODAL HARMONY; exotic scales; vague outlines, flowing rhythms, shimmering orchestral colors, dreamlike moods. Composers: Debussy, Ravel, etc. Painters: Monet, Manet, Renoir, Degas.

Improvisation. The art of making up a composition, or embellishing a theme, as it is played, on the spur of the moment.

Incidental music. Background music for a play, performed between or during the scenes.

Instrument. A mechanism that sets up musical vibrations and launches them into the air.

Intermezzo (in-ter-méh-tso; Italian for "interlude"). 1. A composition that connects two scenes or acts in an opera. 2. A short lyric piece of romantic character.

Interval. 1. A pair of tones, named according to the distance between them: *do-re* or C-D, a second; *do-mi* or C-E, a third; *do-fa* or C-F, a fourth; *do-sol* or C-G, a fifth; *do-la* or C-A, a sixth; *do-ti* or C-B, a seventh; *do-do* or C-C, an OCTAVE. The tones may be sounded either together or in succession.

Inversion. The turning upside-down of a MELODY or THEME, each INTERVAL going up where it formerly went down, or vice-versa: C-E-G inverted is C-A-F.

Key. 1. A group of tones related to a common center (TONIC or KEYNOTE), on which a composition is based. 2. On KEYBOARD instruments, the part of the action pressed down by the finger in order to sound the required PITCH. 3. On WOOD-WIND INSTRUMENTS, a lever pressed down by the finger.

Keyboard. A set of keys on the piano, organ, HARPSICHORD, etc.

Keynote. The first tone of a SCALE. The central tone of a KEY, the DO or TONIC, which serves as a point of departure and return.

Key signature. The group of SHARPS or FLATS written at the beginning of a piece or section, indicating the KEY.

Largo. A very slow and broad tempo.

Legato. Smooth and connected.

Lento. Slow.

Libretto. The text of an opera.

Lied (German, "song"). An ART SONG with piano or orchestral ACCOMPANIMENT, set to a short lyric poem, rich in mood and feeling: Schubert, Schumann, Brahms, and others.

Madrigal. A sophisticated form of poetry-and-music that developed during the Renaissance at the Italian courts, based on a short lyric text marked by refined feeling and elegant language.

Maestoso (my-stó-so). Majestic.

Major (Latin, "larger"). Said of INTERVALS, CHORDS, SCALES, KEYS, in relation to MINOR. A major third is a HALF TONE larger than a MINOR THIRD.

Major-miner system. The twenty-four KEYS —twelve MAJOR and twelve MINOR—on which Western music was based from the seventeenth century to the twentieth.

Major mode. A collective name for all the twelve MAJOR SCALES and KEYS.

Major scale. The basic SCALE of Western music from the seventeenth century to the twentieth. *Do-re-mi-fa-sol-la-ti-do*: a succession of WHOLE TONES, except *mi-fa* (steps 3-4) and *ti-do* (7-8), which are SEMITONES. This pattern may be built beginning on any one of the twelve tones of the OCTAVE, giving 12 major scales. Each has a different KEYNOTE to which the tones resolve, and a different number of SHARPS or FLATS. C major is the only one that has no sharps or flats.

Malambo. A fast Argentinian folk dance.

Mass. The most important rite of the Catholic Church, often set to music for voices with or without ACCOMPANIMENT. Consists of five principal sections—Kyrie, Gloria, Credo, Sanctus, Agnus Dei—each of which may contain several MOVEMENTS.

Measure. A unit of TIME in a composition, containing one strong ACCENT. Sometimes called a BAR.

Melody. A series of TONES heard as a single musical thought.

Meno. Less.

Meno allegro. Less quickly.

Meter. The organization of musical TIME into MEASURES.

Mezza voce (méh-tsa vóh-tcheh). Italian for "half voice," that is, softly and gently.

Mezzo forte (*mf,* meh-tso-fór-teh). Moderately loud.

Mezzo piano (*mp,* méh-tso-pyáh-no). Moderately soft.

Mezzo-soprano (méh-tso). A female voice whose RANGE lies between that of SOPRANO and ALTO.

Middle C. The C in the middle of the piano KEYBOARD. The central NOTE between TREBLE and BASS STAFFS.

Minor (Latin, "smaller"). Said of INTERVALS, CHORDS, SCALES, KEYS, in relation to MAJOR. A minor third is a SEMITONE smaller than a major third.

Minor mode. A collective name for the twelve MINOR SCALES and KEYS.

Minor scale. Differs from the MAJOR SCALE in that certain tones are lowered a SEMITONE. In the most common version of this scale, the harmonic minor, the third and sixth steps are flatted. Each of the twelve major scales may be transformed into minor, giving twelve minor scales.

Minuet. 1. A stately dance, popular at the court of Louis XIV, in 3/4 time. 2. The third movement of the CLASSICAL SYMPHONY, in A-B-A form (minuet-TRIO-minuet).

Modal. Music based on the MODES—the medieval SCALES that were used before the MAJOR-MINOR SYSTEM.

Moderato. At a moderate pace.

Mode. 1. The pattern of whole and half steps in a SCALE or KEY. On any one of the twelve TONES we can build a scale according to the MAJOR, MINOR, WHOLE-TONE, or PENTATONIC mode, or according to one of the medieval CHURCH MODES.

In each of these modes, WHOLE and HALF TONES will be arranged in a different manner. 2. The collective name for all the scales that represent a certain mode. The twelve major scales and keys represent the MAJOR MODE. The twelve minor scales and keys represent the MINOR MODE.

Modulation. The act of going from one KEY to another.

Molto adagio. Very slow.

Molto allegro. Very fast.

Monophonic. Denotes single-line MELODY without HARMONY, either unaccompanied or with an ACCOMPANIMENT that duplicates the melody. Characteristic of the music of the ancient world and of the Orient today, as well as GREGORIAN CHANT.

Motet. A CHORAL composition, usually in CONTRAPUNTAL style, set to a sacred text.

Motive. A small unit within a THEME that may be taken out and treated in various ways in order to develop the theme.

Movement. A self-contained part in a larger work such as a SONATA, CONCERTO, SYMPHONY, etc.

Music drama. The name given by Wagner to his later operas, signifying the closest possible relationship between the music and the drama.

Mute. A small attachment that muffles and changes the sound quality of an INSTRUMENT.

Nationalism. A tendency in nineteenth- and twentieth-century music to emphasize national elements. 1. Use of folk songs and dances: Dvořák, *Slavonic Dances.* 2. Operas based on the life of the peasantry: Smetana, *The Bartered Bride.* 3. Operas based on national legends about gods and heroes: Wagner, *The Ring of the Nibelung.* 4. Pieces celebrating a national victory: Tchaikovsky, *Overture 1812.* 5. Pieces celebrating the beauty of the homeland: Smetana, *The Moldau.* 6. Music associated with a nation's poetry or drama: Schubert-Goethe, Schumann-Heine, Musorgsky-Pushkin, Grieg-Ibsen. National composers: Chopin (Poland); Liszt (Hungary); Smetana, Dvořák (Bohemia); Tchaikovosky, Musorgsky, Rimsky-Korsakov (Russia); Grieg (Norway); Sibelius (Finland); etc.

Natural (♮). The sign indicating that a note is neither sharped nor flatted, cancelling a previous SHARP or FLAT.

New Classicism (also Neo-classicism). A movement in twentieth-century music away from ROMANTICISM. Characteristics: 1. Influenced by the artistic goals of the seventeenth and eighteenth centuries. 2. A more objective approach towards art and life. 3. The forms of ABSOLUTE MUSIC—SYMPHONY, SONATA, DIVERTIMENTO, CHAMBER MUSIC. 4. Revival of COUNTERPOINT: CONCERTO GROSSO, FUGUE, SUITE, TOCCATA, etc. 5. Quieter, more sober colors in ORCHESTRATION; a lighter, more transparent TEXTURE.

Nocturne (French, "night piece"). A short lyric composition of a romantic nature, free in form. Perfected by Chopin.

Nonet. A piece for nine players or singers.

Note. The written symbol for a musical sound, showing its PITCH and DURATION.

Nuance (nóo-ahns). The subtle shadings in TEMPO and DYNAMICS, touch and PHRASING that add expressiveness to a performance.

Octave. The distance between a TONE and the tone of the same name above or below it, as from C to C in the series C-D-E-F-G-A-B-C. INSTRUMENTS are said to be playing "in octaves" when they play notes of the same name in different octaves.

Octet. A piece for eight players or singers.

Off-beat. The weak beat of the MEASURE, which ordinarily does not receive the ACCENT.

Opera. A play that is sung. Combines VOCAL and ORCHESTRAL music with BALLET, poetry, drama, acting, scenery, and costumes.

Operetta. A light opera in popular style with spoken dialogue.

Opus (abbreviated Op.). With a number following it, indicates the order of composition or publication of a composer's work: for example, Beethoven, Op. 31, No. 2.

Oratorio. A large musical work for solo voices, chorus, and orchestra, set to a libretto of sacred or serious character. Longer than a CANTATA; is not part of a religious service, although frequently based on a Biblical story.

Orchestra. A large group of instrumental players with a number of players to each PART. Organized in four sections or CHOIRS: STRINGS, WOODWINDS, BRASS, PERCUSSION.

Orchestral. Pertaining to the ORCHESTRA or its music.

Orchestration. The art of writing for ORCHESTRA or arranging a piece for orchestra.

Ornaments. Patterns used to embellish a MELODY, such as TRILLS, ARPEGGIOS, GRACE NOTES, etc. In earlier music, ornaments were IMPROVISED.

Ostinato (Italian, "obstinate"). A rhythmic or melodic pattern repeated over and over, especially in the BASS.

Overtones. See HARMONICS.

Overture. 1. An orchestral piece that serves to introduce an opera, drama, ballet, or similar long work. 2. A CONCERT OVERTURE.

Part. 1. The music performed by one VOICE or INSTRUMENT, alone or with others: cello part, tenor part. 2. A section of a piece, as in THREE-PART FORM.

Passion. A musical setting of the suffering and death of Christ. Bach, *Passion according to St. Matthew.*

Pastorale. A quiet lyrical movement in either 6/8 or 12/8.

Pavane (pah-váhn). A stately dance of the Spanish court, usually in slow DUPLE METER.

Pedal. 1. A mechanism operated by the feet, as on the harp in order to change the PITCH, or on the piano to change the color or DYNAMICS. 2. On the organ, the pedals form a KEYBOARD played with the feet.

Pentatonic scale. A five-note SCALE that is the basis of Chinese music: for example, C♯, D♯, F♯, G♯, A♯. Also prominent in Scottish folk songs, and often used in contemporary music.

Percussion instruments. The instruments that are made to sound by striking or shaking. Of definite pitch: timpani (kettledrums), glockenspiel, xylophone, celesta, chimes, marimba, vibraphone. Non-definite pitch: bass drum, side or snare drum, tambourine, castanets, triangle, cymbals, gong.

Perpetuum mobile (móh-bi-leh). Perpetual motion. Said of a type of movement that continues in a set rhythm without ever pausing for breath.

Phrase. A small unit of meaning within a larger musical structure.

Phrasing. Singing or playing in such a way as to bring out the phrase.

Pianissimo (*pp*). Soft.

Piano (*p*). Soft.

Pianoforte (Italian, "soft-loud"). Full name of the piano which suggests its wide range of DYNAMICS.

Pitch. That quality of a tone which enables us to call it "high" or "low." Depends on the rate of vibration, which depends on the length of the vibrating body (also its width, density, tension, etc.). The longer a string or column of air, the slower it vibrates and the lower the pitch; the shorter it is, the faster it vibrates and the higher the pitch.

Più (Italian, "more.") As in PIU ALLEGRO, faster.

Più allegro. Faster.

Più mosso. Faster.

Pizzicato (pih-tsih-cáh-toh; Italian, "plucked). In playing a STRING INSTRUMENT, involves plucking the string with the forefinger instead of using the bow.

Plainchant (*plainsong*). A chant of the early Christian Church. GREGORIAN CHANT.

Polka. A lively dance of Bohemia that became popular all over Europe.

Polonaise. 1. A stately dance that originated at the court of the Polish kings.

Polyphonic. A texture combining two or more MELODIC lines.

Polyrhythm. The use of two or more RHYTHMS at the same time.

Polytonality. The use of two or more KEYS at the same time.

Postlude. Opposite of PRELUDE. A section that comes at the end of a work, like an afterthought.

Post-romanticism. The style of the late nineteenth and early twentieth centuries (around 1890-1915). 1. German ROMANTICISM carried to farthest limits by disciples of Wagner. 2. Huge symphony ORCHESTRA. 3. In France, IMPRESSIONISM. 4. Transition to twentieth-century music. Composers: Strauss, Mahler, Debussy, Ravel, Puccini, Sibelius, Elgar, Delius, etc.

Prelude (préh-lyood). 1. A piece that introduces another piece: Prelude and FUGUE. 2. A lyrical mood piece that introduces an opera or an act of an opera. 3. A short poetic piano piece: Chopin, Debussy.

Prepared piano. A piano "prepared" by attaching to its strings a variety of rubber, felt, or wood objects as well as screws, nuts, and bolts, which changes the PITCH and tone color of the instrument.

Presto. Very, very fast.

Programmatic music. Stands midway between PROGRAM and ABSOLUTE music in that it gives the impression of being based on a poetic tale without actually having a definite program attached to it.

Program music. Music inspired by a "program"—that is, a poetic story, scene, or mood specified in the title or in a program note attached to the SCORE. Opposite of ABSOLUTE MUSIC. Main forms: SYMPHONIC POEM, CONCERT OVERTURE, INCIDENTAL MUSIC, PROGRAM SYMPHONY.

Program symphony. A large piece for ORCHESTRA in several MOVEMENTS, based on a literary or pictorial program.

Quadruple meter. A pattern of four BEATS to a MEASURE, ACCENT on the first, as in 4/4 time.

Quarter note (♩). Equivalent to two eighth-notes. In 4/4 time, receives one BEAT.

Quartet. 1. A piece for four players or singers. 2 .The group performing such a piece.

Quintet. 1. A piece for five players or singers. 2. The group performing such a piece.

Range. The distance from the lowest to the highest note of an instrument or voice.

Recapitulation. Also known as Restatement. The third section of SONATA-ALLEGRO FORM. The first THEME is heard, as at the beginning, in the TONIC KEY. A bridge leads to the second theme, which is now shifted into or close to the tonic key. The CODA reaffirms the victory of the tonic key and brings the movement to an emphatic close.

Recitative (reh-sih-tah-téev). In an opera, a kind of "talky" music that carries the plot and explains the action, imitating the RHYTHM of spoken dialogue. At lyrical moments, gives way to ARIA.

Refrain. One or two lines, easily recognized, repeated again and again in the course of a poem or song.

Register. 1. The general area where the music lies, whether low, middle, or high. 2. A part of the RANGE of an INSTRUMENT or VOICE, such as low, middle, or high.

Renaissance. The period between the Middle Ages and the Baroque, from about 1450 to 1600. Main characteristics: 1. Revival of CLASSICAL style: symmetrical form, clarity of thought, controlled emotion. 2. Sixteenth century—the great age of vocal POLYPHONY and A CAPPELLA style: MASS, MADRIGAL, MOTET. Composers: Josquin des Prèz, Roland de Lassus, Palestrina, Thomas Morley. Painters: Botticelli, Leonardo da Vinci, Michelangelo, Titian, Raphael. Writers: Shakespeare, Marlowe, Rabelais, Cervantes.

Requiem. A musical setting of the MASS for the Dead.

Resolution. 1. The movement of DISSONANCE to CONSONANCE, of tension to repose. An active TONE, INTERVAL, or CHORD resolves to one that is less active, or to one that is restful.

Rest. 1. An interval of silence in a composition. 2. The sign that indicates this pause.

Rhapsody. A fanciful composition that follows no set pattern and evokes a variety of moods.

Rhythm. The controlled movement of music in time.

Ritardando. Holding back, getting slow.

Rococo. The aftermath of the BAROQUE. A style in music and art of the mid-eighteenth century (around 1725-1775). A reaction against the grandeur of the Baroque: "gallant style." Main characteristics: 1. Daintiness, love of the miniature, aristocratic refinement. 2. Conception of life as enjoyment and art as elegant entertainment. Composers: Couperin, Rameau, Scarlatti. Painters: Watteau, Boucher, Fragonard.

Romanticism. A period in art marked by emphasis on emotion, personal expression, individualism, and revolt against accepted standards; in particular, the art of the nineteenth century (around 1820-1900), aftermath of the French Revolution. Main characteristics of musical romanticism: 1. Growth of middle-class public; music-making moved from the palace to the public concert hall. 2. Growth in size of the ORCHESTRA. 3. Emphasis on tone color and the art of OR-CHESTRATION. 4. Conservatories opened in the main cities of Europe. 5. Emphasis on VIRTUOSITY and the personality of the concert artist. 6. NATIONALISM. 7. EXOTI-CISM, emphasis on atmosphere and picturesque details. 8. An attempt to bring music closer to literature and painting through PROGRAM MUSIC, SYMPHONIC POEM, PROGRAM SYMPHONY. Nature scenes in music. 9. Short lyric forms: art song and piano piece with poetic title. 10. Emphasis on supernatural themes, "strangeness and wonder." 11. Expansion in size of classical SYMPHONY and of expressive HARMONY. 12. Music increases its power to express emotion: increasingly dramatic, tragic, allied with romantic ideas —man against Fate, struggle for freedom, nature, God, country, etc. Composers: Schubert, Berlioz, Mendelssohn, Schumann, Chopin, Liszt, Wagner, Verdi, Smetana, Brahms, Bizet, Tchaikovsky, Musorgsky, Rimsky-Korsakov, Dvořák, Grieg, etc. Painters: Delacroix, Turner, Corot, etc. Poets: Wordsworth, Coleridge, Byron, Shelley, Keats, Heine, Pushkin, Poe. Novelists: Scott, Balzac, Hugo, Dumas, Dickens, Thackeray.

Rondo. A lively MOVEMENT in which a THEME returns again and again in alternation with one or two contrasting ideas, in a pattern such as A-B-A-B-A, A-B-A-C-A, or A-B-A-C-A-B-A.

Round. A type of composition where each performer enters with the melody at a different time, so that various sections of the melody are combined CONTRAPUNTALLY.

Scale. 1. An arrangement of the TONES and SEMITONES in a KEY or MODE in consecutive (ascending or descending) order: MAJOR SCALE; MINOR SCALE; WHOLE-TONE SCALE; PENTATONIC SCALE.

Scherzo (skéhr-tso; Italian, "jest" or "joke"). 1. A movement in a SONATA, SYMPHONY, QUARTET, etc., often the third. Introduced by Haydn and Beethoven in place of the MINUET. Usually in rapid 3/4 time, strongly rhythmic and whimsical. Middle section is known as TRIO. 2. An independent piece of the same type.

Score. The arrangement on the printed page of all the parts of a work, one below the other on different staves (STAFF). Together they give a complete picture of what is going on in the music.

Second. The INTERVAL between two neighboring tones in a SCALE, such as *do-re* or C-D.

Seguidilla (say-guh-deé-ya). A graceful Spanish dance in triple meter.

Semitone. 1. The smallest INTERVAL in our musical system, as from C to C♯, or B to B♭. 2. Half of a WHOLE TONE; a half-step. Our OCTAVE consists of twelve semitones.

Septet. A piece for seven players or singers.

Sequence. A pattern within a melody that is repeated on a higher or lower scale step.

Serenade. An evening song, such as a lover would sing beneath the balcony of his beloved.

Serial music. Music that extends the "tone row" idea of Schoenberg to include not only series of PITCHES but also series of DURATIONS (time values), DYNAMICS, TONE COLORS, TEMPOS, and other elements.

Seventh. The INTERVAL between step 1 and step 7 (or step 2 and step 8, etc.) of the SCALE, such as *do-ti* or C-B.

Sextet. 1. A piece for six players or singers. 2. The group performing it.

Sextuple meter. A pattern of six BEATS to a MEASURE, the main ACCENT on the first beat, a lighter accent on the fourth; as in 6/4 or 6/8 time.

Sharp (♯). The sign that raises a note by a SEMITONE, as from C to C♯.

Sinfonietta. A little SYMPHONY.

Six-eight time. A pattern of six BEATS to a MEASURE, main ACCENT on the first beat, a lighter accent on the fourth: ONE-two-three-Four-five-six.

Sixteenth note (♪). Receives half the time value of an eighth note. In 4/4 time, four sixteenths to a BEAT.

Sixth. The INTERVAL between step 1 and step six (or step 2 and step 7, etc.) of the SCALE, such as *do-la* or C-A.

Solo (Italian, "alone"). Music for one player or singer.

Sonata (from Italian *suonare*, "to sound"). A composition for one or two instruments, in three or four movements that contrast in tempo and mood. A sonata for more than two players may be called a TRIO, QUARTET, QUINTET, SEXTET, SEPTET, OCTET, NONET; for SOLO performer and ORCHESTRA, a CONCERTO; for full orchestra, a SYMPHONY. The sonata therefore is the basic form of the greater part of ABSOLUTE MUSIC. The character of the movements: 1. Usually an impressive Allegro in SONATA-ALLEGRO FORM. 2. The slow movement, a lyrical Andante, Adagio, or Largo. It may be in A-B-A form or a THEME-AND-VARIATIONS. 3. A fairly lively dance: in the eighteenth century, a MINUET in A-B-A form (minuet and TRIO); in the nineteenth, the more impetuous SCHERZO in A-B-A form (scherzo and trio). 4. A large Allegro, Vivace, or Allegro molto that balances the first. It may be a RONDO, sonata-allegro form, or a theme and variations. The eighteenth-century symphony frequently ended with a gay rondo. In the nineteenth century, the symphony often ended on a note of triumph.

Sonata-allegro form. Also known as first-movement form or sonata form. A type of structure used for a single movement in a SONATA, CONCERTO, SYMPHONY, TRIO, QUARTET (etc.), or OVERTURE. Based on the contrast (opposition) between a first theme in the TONIC KEY and a second theme (or themes) in another key. Consists of three sections: 1. The EXPOSITION sets forth the first theme in the home key, followed by a bridge that MODULATES, the second theme in a contrasting key, and the codetta in the new key. 2. The DEVELOPMENT breaks the themes into their MOTIVES, treats those freely, modulates from key to key but avoids the home key. A transition leads back to the home key. 3. RECAPITULATION (Restatement): first theme in the home key; bridge; second theme shifted into or close to the home key. The coda reaffirms the triumph of the home key.

Sonatina. A small SONATA.

Song. A short piece for SOLO VOICE, generally with instrumental ACCOMPANIMENT.

Soprano. 1. The highest female voice. There are three main types: lyric, dramatic, COLORATURA. 2. The highest PART in a four-part CHORUS. 3. The highest in RANGE of any family of instruments: for example, soprano saxophone.

Staccato. Short and detached.

Staff. A series of five horizontal lines with four spaces between. Each line or space represents a degree of PITCH. NOTES are written on, above, and below the staff.

String instruments. Produce sound by means of taut strings either played with a bow or plucked. String section of the ORCHESTRA contains four bowed instruments: violin, viola, cello, double bass (also known as contrabass). Plucked-string instruments include harp, guitar, banjo, mandolin, lute, etc.

String quartet. The most important type of CHAMBER MUSIC, for first and second violins, viola, cello.

Strophic form. A song in which all stanzas of the poem are sung to the same tune.

Style. The characteristic way of presenting the material of art. 1. May refer to the function and type of music: SYMPHONIC or CHAMBER-MUSIC style, vocal or instrumental style, OPERATIC or ORATORIO style, ORCHESTRAL or CHORAL style. 2. May refer to an artist's personal manner: Beethoven's or Schubert's style. 3. May refer to a period: BAROQUE, CLASSICAL, or ROMANTIC style.

Subject. The THEME of a FUGUE.

Suite. 1. A work in several movements around a central idea. 2. A set of movements taken out of a longer work such as an OPERA or BALLET: Tchaikovsky, *Nutcracker Suite.* 3. A BAROQUE form of instrumental music consisting of a set of dance-like pieces in the same KEY.

Symphonic poem. Also known as TONE POEM. A composition for orchestra in one MOVEMENT, suggesting a specific story, scene, or mood. In a flexible form that follows the literary program on which it is based.

Symphony. A large work for ORCHESTRA in several movements (usually four) that contrast in TEMPO, character, and mood. For details of its structure, see SONATA.

Syncopation. The shifting of the ACCENT from the strong BEAT of the MEASURE to a weak beat (OFF-BEAT).

Tango. A dance of South-American origin.

Tape recorder music. Based on the electronic treatment of sounds produced by the human voice or musical instruments, or of natural sounds. The use of magnetic tape makes it possible to split a tone, change its overtones, and combine its elements into new tones, thus providing new sounds and new ways of using them.

Tempo. The rate of speed, the pace of the music.

Tempo giusto (joóh-sto). Strict time.

Tenor. The highest male voice; lyric or dramatic. 2. The second lowest voice in a four-part CHORUS. 3. An instrument in this RANGE: for example, tenor saxophone.

Ternary form. A-B-A (three-part) form.

Texture. The "weave" of the music, whether heavy or light, dense or transparent. A comparison with the warp and woof of a fabric, the horizontal "threads" being the MELODIES, the vertical ones being the CHORDS or HARMONIES. Three types: MONOPHONIC, HOMOPHONIC, POLYPHONIC.

Theme. A musical idea used in the construction of a larger work or MOVEMENT.

Theme and variations. A FORM in which a musical idea is presented in a number of transformations. Each variation explores a fresh aspect of the THEME. Various elements may be changed in the course of the variations—the MELODY, HARMONY, RHYTHM and METER, TEMPO, DYNAMICS, REGISTER, type of ACCOMPANIMENT, KEY, etc.

Theme transformation. A technique associated with Liszt, Berlioz, and others, based on the changes in mood of a theme due to changes in TEMPO, DYNAMICS, TIMBRE, REGISTER, etc. As a result, the same theme may be used to suggest love in one section, nature in another, struggle in a third, and triumph in a fourth.

Third. The INTERVAL between step 1 and step 3 (or step 2 and step 4) of the SCALE, such as *do-mi* or C-E.

Three-four time. A pattern of three BEATS to a MEASURE, ACCENT on the first.

Three-part form. See A-B-A.

Through-composed. A song whose music follows the course of the poem, changing with each stanza according to the text.

Tie. Connects two successive NOTES of the same PITCH, lengthening the first by the value of the second.

Timbre (tám-br). The tone color of the sound, which varies according to the INSTRUMENT that produces it.

Time. Refers to the DURATION of a NOTE, or to the METER and/or TEMPO of a piece.

Time signature. Placed at the beginning of a piece or during its course, to indicate the METER. Upper numeral shows the number of BEATS in a MEASURE; lower numeral indicates the kind of NOTE that receives one beat. Thus, 3/4 equals three beats in a measure, a quarter note receives one beat.

Toccata (from Italian *toccare*, "to touch," i.e., the keys). 1. A KEYBOARD piece that exploits all the technical resources of the instrument—CHORDS, ARPEGGIOS, SCALES, OCTAVES, etc. 2. In the twentieth century, an orchestral or piano piece based on a driving rhythm.

Tonality. Loyalty to a TONIC or KEYNOTE. All music written in the eighteenth and nineteenth centuries is based on this principle: the tones of the key find their final RESOLUTION in the TONIC CHORD with which the piece ends.

Tone. 1. A musical sound that has the properties of PITCH, DURATION, VOLUME, and TIMBRE. 2. An INTERVAL of two SEMITONES, as from C to D or *do* to *re;* a WHOLE TONE.

Tone row. In TWELVE-TONE MUSIC, a series of twelve tones on which a composition is based. The tone row includes all the twelve SEMITONES of the OCTAVE; each appears only once, so that it will not take on the importance of a KEYNOTE or TONIC. The row is repeated over and over throughout the piece, its tones always in the same order; it may be played forwards, backwards (retrograde), upside down (INVERSION), or upside down and backwards (retrograde inversion). These four possibilities may be begun on each of the twelve tones, giving forty-eight possibilities. From the row are derived all the melodies, harmonies, and counterpoint of the composition.

Tonic. The central tone of the KEY; the first and most important tone of the SCALE. The DO or KEYNOTE, point of departure and return.

Tonic chord. The TRIAD based on the TONIC or KEYNOTE, the chord to which all the other chords resolve. This chord of rest and completion generally brings the piece to an end.

Treble. 1. The upper register, as distinguished from the bass or lower part. 2. In piano music, the right-hand part. See CLEF.

Tremolo (Italian, "trembling"). 1. On STRING INSTRUMENTS, involves repeating a tone through a quick up-and-down movement of the bow. An effect often used in orchestral music for dramatic suspense and excitement. 2. On the piano, a rapid alternation of a TONE with its OCTAVE or other tones of the same CHORD. 3. In singing, a quavering tone.

Triad. 1. A CHORD of three tones formed by combining every other step of the major or minor scale: steps 1-3-5 or *do-mi-sol;* 2-4-6 or *re-fa-la;* 3-5-7 or *mi-sol-ti,* etc. Can be constructed on every step of the scale: in C major, C-E-G, D-F-A, E-G-B, etc.

Trill. A birdlike effect produced by rapidly alternating a TONE with the note above it.

Trio. 1. A piece for three players or singers. 2. The group performing such a piece. 3. The middle section of a MINUET or SCHERZO, at the end of which the first section is repeated.

Triple meter. A pattern of three BEATS to a MEASURE, ACCENT on the first, as in 3/4 time.

Triplet. Three NOTES that subdivide a BEAT.

Tutti (Italian, "all"). A section of a piece played by the orchestra as a whole.

Twelve-tone music. The "method of composing with twelve tones" devised by Schoenberg, based on the use of a TONE ROW from which are derived all of the melodies and harmonies of a composition.

Twelve-tone scale. A SCALE consisting of the twelve SEMITONES of the OCTAVE. Differs from the CHROMATIC SCALE in that these are considered to be of equal importance, therefore they are not thought of in relation to a central tone or KEYNOTE.

Twentieth-century music. "The New Music." Main characteristics: 1. A movement away from ROMANTICISM. Humor and satire; music inspired by the machine instead of by nature; primitivism. 2. More complex RHYTHMS, changing METERS, POLYRHYTHMS. 3. MELODY moves away from the four-measure PHRASE followed by a CADENCE. More concentrated, less repetition, instrumental rather than vocal. 4. HARMONY more dissonant and complex. Away from simple TRIADS based on a THIRD to chords based on other INTERVALS, such as the FOURTH. 5. POLYTONALITY. Expanded TONALITY: the "twelve-out-of-twelve" instead of "seven-out-of-twelve" way of hearing music. 6. The NEW CLASSICISM (neo-classicism). 7. ATONALITY and TWELVE-TONE MUSIC. Composers: Stravinsky, Schoenberg, Bartók, Hindemith, Berg, Webern, Milhaud, Honegger, Poulenc, Villa-Lobos, Vaughan Williams, Walton, Britten, Bloch, Orff, Prokofiev, Shostakovich, Griffes, Ives, Moore, Piston, Thomson, Harris, Gershwin, Copland, Blitzstein, Schuman, Menotti, Barber, etc. Painters: Picasso, Braque, Léger, Dérain. Writers: Hemingway, Steinbeck, Sartre, Camus.

Two-four time. A pattern of two BEATS to a MEASURE, ACCENT on the first.

Two-part form. See A-B (binary) form.

Unison. INSTRUMENTS are sounding in *unison* when they play the same NOTES.

Vibrato. The throbbing tone achieved when a string player, while pressing down on the string, keeps moving his finger away from and back to the required spot.

Virtuosity. The highest degree of technical perfection in an artist.

Virtuoso. A performer who has acquired technical mastery of his instrument.

Vivace (vee-váh-che). Vivacious, lively.

Vocal. Pertaining to music for the VOICE.

Vocalise (vo-cah-leéz). Singing without words, on a syllable such as *ah:* Villa-Lobos, *Aria* from *Bachianas Brasileiras No. 5.*

Voice. 1. The singing voice, most personal and expressive of all instruments. Female: SOPRANO, MEZZO-SOPRANO, CONTRALTO. Male: TENOR, BARITONE, BASS. 2. A vocal line; also a PART in CONTRAPUNTAL music, as when we speak of a FUGUE in four voices.

Volume. The amount of sound, said of a tone in reference to its being soft or loud.

Waltz. A popular dance in THREE-FOUR TIME.

Whole note (o). Equivalent to two HALF-NOTES. In 4/4 time, receives four BEATS.

Whole tone. An INTERVAL equal to two SEMITONES, such as *do-re* or C-D.

Whole-tone scale. A SCALE consisting only of WHOLE TONES, as in the sequence C-D-E-F♯-G♯-A♯-C.

Woodwind instruments. A group of instruments in which the tone is produced by a column of air vibrating inside a pipe with holes cut in the side. When one or another of these holes is opened, the length of the air column is changed, therefore the rate of vibration and the PITCH. The woodwind section in the orchestra consists of four principal instruments, each supplemented by one or more of the same family: 1. Flute (and piccolo). 2. Oboe (and English horn). 3. Clarinet (and bass clarinet). 4. Bassoon (and double bassoon or contrabassoon). Also, for some works, saxophones.

ACKNOWLEDGMENTS AND CREDITS

The following acknowledgments are made for permission to reprint music examples and related materials:

Samuel Barber, Intermezzo from *Vanessa*, © Copyright 1958 by G. Schirmer, Inc. Reprinted by permission.

Béla Bartók, Concerto for Orchestra, Copyright 1946 by Hawkes and Son (London) Ltd. Reprinted by permission of Boosey & Hawkes, Inc. Rumanian Folk Dances, Copyright 1918 by Universal Edition A. G. Renewed 1945. Copyright and Renewal assigned to Boosey & Hawkes, Inc., for U.S.A. Reprinted by permission of Boosey & Hawkes, Inc.

Alban Berg, *Wozzeck*, © Copyright 1926 by Universal Edition A. G., Vienna, renewed 1954 by Helene Berg. Reprinted by permission of Theodore Presser Company.

Leonard Bernstein, Overture to *Candide*, © Copyright 1955 by Leonard Bernstein. Reprinted by permission of G. Schirmer, Inc.

Marc Blitzstein, *Rain Quartet* from *Regina*, © Copyright by Marc Blitzstein. Used by permission of Chappell & Co., Inc.

Ernest Bloch, *Nigun* from *Baal Shem Suite*, Copyright MCMXXIV by Carl Fischer, Inc., New York. International Copyright Secured. Reprinted by permission.

Benjamin Britten, Fugue from *Young Person's Guide to the Orchestra*, Copyright 1947 by Hawkes & Son (London) Ltd. Reprinted by permission of Boosey & Hawkes, Inc.

Elliott Carter, Eight Etudes and a Fantasy, © Copyright 1955 by Associated Music Publishers, Inc. Used by permission.

Aaron Copland, *Billy the Kid*, Copyright 1941 by Aaron Copland. Reprinted by permission of Aaron Copland and Boosey & Hawkes, Inc., Sole Licensees.

Henry Cowell, *The Banshee*, © Copyright 1930 by Associated Music Publishers, Inc. Used by permission.

Norman Dello Joio, *Air Power*, © Copyright 1957 by Carl Fischer, Inc., New York. International Copyright Secured. Reprinted by Permission.

David Diamond, *This World Is Not My Home*, Permission for reprint granted by Elkan-Vogel Co., Inc., of Philadelphia, Pa., copyright owners.

Lukas Foss, *Echoi*, © Copyright 1964 by Carl Fischer, Inc., New York. International Copyright Secured. All rights reserved including public performance for profit. Reprinted by permission.

Alberto Ginastera, *Estancia*, Copyright 1953 by Barry & Cia. Reprinted by permission of Boosey & Hawkes, Inc.

Morton Gould, *Latin-American Symphonette*, © 1947 by Mills Music, Inc. Used by permission.

Charles Tomlinson Griffes, *The White Peacock*, Copyright 1917 by G. Schirmer, Inc. Reprinted by permission.

Paul Hindemith, *Symphonic Metamorphosis on Themes of Carl Maria von Weber*, Copyright 1945 by Schott & Co., Ltd. Used by permission.

Charles Ives, *Three Places in New England*, Copyright 1935 by Charles E. Ives. Used by permission of copyright owner, Harmony Twitchell Ives, and Mercury Music Corporation.

Leoš Janáček, *Sinfonietta*, © Copyright 1927 by Universal Edition A. G., Vienna. Reprinted by permission of Theodore Presser Company.

Ulysses Kay, *What's in a Name*, © Copyright 1956 by Duchess Music Corporation, New York, N.Y. Used by permission. All rights reserved.

Zoltán Kodály, *Háry János* Suite, Copyright 1927 by Universal Edition. Reprinted by permission.

Otto Luening, *Moon Flight*, Copyright 1967 by Otto Luening (BMI). Used by permission.

Peter Mennin, Symphony No. 3, Copyright 1948 by Hargail Music Press. Used by permission.

Gian Carlo Menotti, *The Medium*, © Copyright 1952 by G. Schirmer, Inc. Reprinted by permission.

Douglas Moore, *The Devil and Daniel Webster*, Copyright 1941 by Boosey & Hawkes, Inc. Reprinted by permission of Boosey & Hawkes, Inc.

Carl Orff, *Carmina burana*, Copyright 1937 by B. Schotts Söhne. Used by permission of the publisher and its agent for the United States, Associated Music Publishers, Inc.

Francis Poulenc, Concerto in D Minor (for Two Pianos and Orchestra) © 1934 by Editions Salabert, Paris. By permission.

Serge Prokofiev, *Cinderella*, Copyright 1949 by MCA Music, a division of MCA Inc., New York, N.Y. Used by permission. All rights reserved. *Suite* from *Lieutenant Kijé*. Copyright by Edition A. Gutheil. Copyright assigned 1946 to Boosey & Hawkes, Inc. Reprinted by permission of Boosey & Hawkes, Inc.

Giacomo Puccini, *Tosca—Recondita armonia*, English translation by Joseph Machlis, © 1956 by Franco Colombo, Inc., New York. By permission.

Sergei Rachmaninov, *Floods of Spring*, Used by permission of G. Schirmer, Inc.

INDEX

Italicized references indicate illustrations.

C